T0290617

Koen De Leus
Philippe Gijsels

The NEW WORLD ECONOMY

in 5 trends

Investing in times of
SUPERINFLATION,
HYPERINNOVATION
and CLIMATE TRANSITION

Lannoo

To Miriam & Kathleen

'Without whom life would be
like a broken pencil:
pointless.'

CONTENTS

WHY WE ARE
at a TIPPING POINT

We are on the cusp of a different world. Five defining waves will engulf the global economy. The first is the climate transition, a new trend. Then there are multiglobalisation and an innovation-driven productivity boom, both of which are shifting trends. The last two waves, ageing and rising debt, are existing trends that will go into overdrive in the coming decades.

To help you surf these waves, and not go under, we combine two different areas of expertise in this book: an in-depth economic analysis of the new world and a translation of it for the investor. Who are we? Koen De Leus, chief economist at BNP Paribas Fortis, provides the macro analysis, which starts with innovation and production from Chapter 3. What you can do with that macro knowledge as an investor is light-heartedly served up by Philippe Gijsels, chief strategist at the same bank. And we occasionally venture into some science fiction by making predictions about what 2050 will look like. That said, the ideas in this book should in no way be seen as investment advice. We are merely providing you with a few foundational concepts. So, be sure to do your own homework or ask a professional for advice before heading to the markets.

Spoiler alert! We will point out this book's most important insight in advance: we are leaving behind 40 years of ever-declining interest rates and inflation. The table on pages 402–403 shows the impact of these five waves – as we see them evolving – on economic growth, inflation and interest rates. Pluses and minuses largely cancel each other out in terms of growth, but with regard to inflation and nominal interest rates, the balance tilts towards higher levels. A world of higher inflation and interest rates awaits us.

Such a fundamentally new regime will have an enormous impact on any investment strategy. Interest rates are like gravity in our world. When they are low or even negative, all asset classes – including those of the heavy type like gold – take flight. When interest rates rise sharply, just about everything gets sucked down. Therefore, the megatrends we cover in this book cannot be separated from interest rate movements. At any given moment, we need to ask ourselves whether the money tap has been opened or closed.

You might also be thinking: what about China, or rising inequality and the associated populism? These are legitimate questions. First, we wanted to avoid the book going beyond its intended scope. Moreover, you will find that both China's role and rising inequality are covered extensively in the various chapters, as interrelated themes. Readers looking for insights on these topics will certainly not be disappointed.

Productivity and innovation is the first wave we will cover. Increasing productivity is the only source of future growth for ageing Western economies. It is therefore worrying that this source has become increasingly dry in recent decades. After the computer revolution, the digital revolution arrived a decade ago. To date, it has not brought a major acceleration in growth. Consumers do enjoy more wellbeing, more tools and apps that make their lives easy and, above all, more pleasant. But it has not had a concrete impact on our prosperity, on gross domestic product (GDP).

Artificial intelligence (AI) is fuelling hopes of accelerated productivity over time. The widespread diffusion of new technology takes time. Although we find it encouraging that a complex digital technology is being opened up to the general public so quickly.

From an investment perspective, you can consider AI as having as big of an impact as stealing fire from the gods, the invention of the wheel, agriculture or, more recently, the industrial revolution. That means there will be massive winners but also massive losers. This increases the danger that the winners will walk away with the lion's share.

ChatGPT is just one of many exponentially fast-evolving technologies coming our way. Others can be found in 3D printing, (green) energy, and biology. The unique thing about these technologies is that when their price drops, they pop up everywhere. And the more widespread, the faster the productivity growth. This is encouraging, although high productivity growth is not written in the stars. Major dangers include high energy prices following Russia's invasion of Ukraine, and deglobalisation.

Globalisation promoted the spread of ideas and capital investment. But the period of hyper-globalisation is well behind us. Outsourcing the manufacturing process to so-called low-wage countries has reached its limit. Companies want to reduce the complexity of the global supply chain, especially since the Covid-19 pandemic and the war in Ukraine exposed its vulnerabilities. In recent years, the slowdown in global goods trade over the past decade has translated into what is known as *reshoring*, or bringing supply chains closer.

The trade war between the US and China comes on top of this. The US feels that its hegemony is threatened. On technology issues, the US draws the line and works against China as much as possible. Goal: nip China's rise in the bud before it can compete with the US technologically. The US also drags other countries into its struggle. Separately, resentment is also growing in Europe over unfair Chinese trade practices. The symbiosis of past decades – Western technology in exchange for a huge Chinese market – is in jeopardy now that China is also entering the European market with its own products. The massive imports of Chinese electric cars into Europe will sooner or later lead to redundancies in the car industry, which is very important for Europe. That will be the moment when the European powers-that-be will implement countermeasures.

So, industrial policy is making a comeback. Protecting its own industry and rebuilding a less dependent supply chain are the goals of the moment. Dependence on China must be phased out. That promises to be a huge challenge, especially for everything related to climate technologies, from the raw materials needed to the finished wind turbines and solar panels.

Does that mean that the world is doomed to deglobalisation? Today, we mainly observe that an additional link between the US and China is being added to reduce political risk. Diversification of the supply chain may cause other suppliers to be sought in addition to – or instead of – China. Thus, we are moving towards a deepening of globalisation, with more (developing) countries getting involved. Alongside a slowdown in the trade of goods, we also see that services are flourishing, courtesy of accelerating digitalisation. Think, for instance, of digital administrative services being outsourced to countries with much lower labour costs. That is not deglobalisation. We call it multiglobalisation. And that certainly need not have a pernicious effect on global growth; quite the opposite. The winners here will mainly be the emerging countries, just as in the earlier period of globalisation. With the uncomfortable question of whether not only factory workers' jobs, but also service jobs in the West are now under threat.

> From an investment perspective, it is clear that if the world breaks up into multiple blocks, we need to ask ourselves which of these blocks we want to participate in as investors. At the moment, it is not difficult to tell a horror story about China. The country has major economic and demographic problems, not to mention the upheaval in its real estate sector. But as investors, can we afford *not* to sit at the Chinese innovation table? It is true that emerging countries, with China as the prime example, have been doing remarkably worse than their more mature counterparts since 2008. However, this results in a relative undervaluation of biblical proportions.
>
> And what about the hegemony of the US dollar? There has been a lot of talk lately about the erosion of its status as a world reserve currency. In the distant future, that may be a possibility. But right now, our reptilian brain says the greenback is still king. And if it falls from its throne, it won't be the yuan or the euro that will be the escape currency, but rather... gold. Anyone who says gold almost automatically says bitcoin, and anyone who says bitcoin quickly thinks of NFTs (non-fungible tokens). Progressive insight and interactions with students of the younger generation have led us to refine our views on this a bit.

Another threat to that important productivity is high energy prices. These are not entirely the fault of Russia's war in Ukraine. The – necessary – rapid climate transition results in a mismatch between the slow rollout of renewable energy and a too-rapid phase-out of fossil-fuel energy. Combined with geopolitical games, this increases price volatility for energy and commodities. The next few years promise to be chaotic.

The silver lining of the Russian-Ukrainian war cloud, insofar as there is one, is that it accelerated the climate transition by about a decade. We were massively behind on a net zero emissions scenario for 2050. Today, we are just way behind. The climate transition is the only one of the five trends covered that we consider 'new'. As such, the challenge is colossal. All previous energy transitions – from wood to coal to oil – were driven by technological and economic advantages and took 100 years or more each time. The current one is driven purely by policy. 'The objective of this transition is not just to bring on new energy sources, but to entirely change the energy foundations of what today is a $100 trillion global economy – and do so in little more than a quarter century,' explains resource specialist Daniel Yergin of S&P Global. That will require massive investments – now! The longer we delay investments, the faster our carbon budget – to keep the temperature increase below 1.5 degrees Celsius – is used up. The war jacked up investments sharply. Energy independence is suddenly right at the top of the priority list, with renewables as the saving grace. But most estimates assume another doubling of current investments of $2.4 trillion (2.5% of GDP) to meet climate goals. In developed countries, this is a matter of political will. Emerging countries depend on money from those developed countries and the private sector.

Besides green investments, emissions will simply have to go down. The most efficient way to achieve that is through the 'polluter pays' principle. This can be done by introducing a carbon tax or through an emissions trading system, like the one in Europe. The minimum carbon tax to reach net zero by 2050 will cost a Belgian family of four around 2,200 euros annually. In France, where per capita emissions are lower due to the higher percentage of nuclear power, this is 1,200 euros. The French yellow vest protesters took to the streets in 2018 in protest against an increase in fuel taxes with an annual cost of 20 euros for the poorest families and 160 euros for the richest families. Such an incendiary reaction over relatively modest amounts shows that good communication about the purpose of a carbon tax becomes crucial. In addition, a climate dividend for the least well-off families could keep everyone on board.

The climate challenge is also a tough one for businesses. It is up or down. Companies that do not react quickly enough risk having to write off a lot of assets. But there are also opportunities. The world is moving from a consumption-driven to a more investment-driven economy. The winners are found in manufacturing, construction, service providers and transport companies. Mining companies without the 'green minerals', along with oil and gas producers, are the big losers.

For investors, the energy transition is possibly the biggest opportunity in the past 100 years. As the world evolves from *big oil* to *big shovel* – where the raw materials for electricity production have to be hauled up by spade – huge amounts of metals will be needed. Due to years of underinvestment, future supply and demand can currently only be balanced at substantially higher prices. In any case, the climate transition is better guided by wizards who seek solutions, than by (false) prophets who only see salvation in catapulting our civilisation back to the era before the industrial revolution. It will be a matter of becoming as energy efficient as possible, as soon as possible.

The climate transition has another consequence: the rising debt trend will continue. The mountain of debt has never been higher in peacetime. But it is pointless to look only at those high debts. Ultimately, it is debt portability that creates crises. And that portability has steadily increased over the past 40 years thanks to persistently falling interest rates.

Average interest rates paid have recently started to climb again, and this will not change any time soon. Nominal interest rates in particular will rise due to structurally higher inflation, but real interest rates (adjusted for inflation) may also slowly creep higher. The huge demand for money to finance the transition in the coming years will be a driver of those higher interest rates. The hefty jump in interest rates following the expansionary fiscal policy announced by UK ex-premier Liz Truss illustrates that we are approaching a tipping point. Bond traders did not trust the situation: they sold UK government paper and interest rates promptly rose. The UK was close to a financial crisis. According to Martin Barnes, the former chief economist of the reputable research firm Bank Credit Analyst (BCA), there is a 75% chance that the US, with its high debt and huge budget deficit, will undergo the same reality check as the UK within five years. Shock therapy is needed to restore fiscal discipline. The 'bond vigilantes', the guardians of debt sustainability, are awakening from their years of hibernation.

In short, the whole debt story is extremely complex. Maybe we'd better play a game of monopoly, with debt.

The latest trend is an ageing population, which is a headwind pushing against economic growth. Labour force growth, together with productivity growth, is the source of economic growth. When that first engine sputters, developed countries have to rely on accelerating productivity to keep growing. Emerging and developing countries still enjoy the demographic dividend of a rising labour force. In the top six largest economies by 2050, there will be five growth countries. That is, if they don't screw up. By 2100, the global population will have stabilised and eight out of ten people will be living in Africa and Asia. Entrepreneurs know where growth can be found.

Anyone talking about ageing is also talking about rising costs for pensions and healthcare. How vulnerable are Western countries to those rising costs, taking into account the current debt situation and tax burden? Not coincidentally, Anglo-Saxon countries are the least financially vulnerable to ageing. This can be explained by their limited public pensions, counterbalanced by a large share of private pensions and savings. Japan, the UK and most Nordic countries show medium vulnerability. High vulnerability is found among northern and southern European countries. Italy and Belgium take the crown. Everyone knows the remedy for rising pension and health costs: work longer and put more people to work.

The baby boomers were, and remain, the pig in the python. They determine which products and services are consumed more or less. Baby boomers invest slightly more conservatively as they get older. But the 'asset meltdown' theory that postulates a collapse of stock markets due to 'dissaving' baby boomers will not materialise. Why not? Because baby boomers are not 'dissaving'.

More sensitive to that theory is real estate. The death of the baby boomer generation will undoubtedly have an effect on it. Their houses will then, on a massive scale, enter the real estate market, which will therefore come under pressure in ten years' time. While demographics have been driving house prices in the past decades, the ageing population is slowly threatening to put a brake on property values.

As we all move towards a, hopefully healthy, centenary life, not only are there huge investment opportunities that go well beyond healthcare, caravans and cruises; this will also reshape our society beyond recognition. In short, the coming decades present us with a host of challenges, but also just as many opportunities. We hope this book will help you seize those opportunities, surf the waves, or at least not get swallowed by the tsunami.

'It often seems that trends create events more than events create trends. The event itself is usually a reflection of everyone getting it as Ed (Seykota) calls it, an aha. By this time, the trend followers usually have well established positions.'

———

JASON RUSSELL

INTRODUCTION

'It all comes and goes in waves, it always does.'

———

DEAN LEWIS, *WAVES*

A new adventure

It is not easy to predict the future, let alone that of our economy and the stock market. And yet we like to make an attempt. On paper. In this chapter I, Philippe, kick off and tell you a bit more about the angle, context and underpinnings of this book.

'The beginning is a very delicate time.' This is the first sentence from the film adaptation of the book *Dune* by Frank Herbert. I am talking about the 1984 film version by David Lynch, not the more recent one we all know. It is the primal version from my childhood, in which Sting still plays a supporting role. I was 14 at the time. A strategic video game followed a few years later, a bit of a distant precursor to *Age of Empires*, linking strategic war engagements to an economic reality. You had to collect resources to buy buildings and weaponry. Around this time, my interest in economic developments and, above all, the stock market also developed. The fact that my father had always been involved in the stock market, and that it was regularly discussed at home, certainly gave me a boost. I have been reading books about history since I could read, or maybe just after comics. Then came literature, fantasy, philosophy and just about anything that had a cover and pages.

And yes, I have been lucky enough to have been able to turn my 'interest' into my profession, first at Generale Bank, then Fortis and now BNP Paribas Fortis. After an internship of just under two years, during which I went through just about every division, and a relatively short commercial period in the Hageland, where I learned what a customer was but also learned to eat and drink and live, I soon found myself in the markets room. In fact, I never left it. I threw myself into analytical work on just about every possible asset class, from equities to bonds to commodities. Then, about ten years ago, I was also given the responsibility for the strategy of Wealth Management, the private bank and specialist teams.

As such, I also got to know Koen a good six years ago. Or rather, got to know him better. Because we had known each other since his days at that other bank. We started as acquaintances, we became friends, and we started working together more and more often. It culminated in the podcast *Stand van zaken* (*State of Affairs*), which we enjoy recording every month with Francesca Vanthielen. This in turn led to many requests to tour business centres and private banking centres as troubadours to talk about the state of the economy and markets. Somehow, our audiences find the interaction between us fun and perhaps even instructive. And that is also the thrust of this book. When Koen suggested it, I did not hesitate for a moment.

In this book, we engage with each other. Koen provides the serious, reasoned economic work. And I do what I always do. I talk about markets, give direction where I can, say what I think I know and what I think I don't know, and tell stories. Because that's just the beauty of markets. Markets are made by people and words: stories and feelings are at least as important as numbers and calculations. In the end, all the rational considerations, as well as people's feelings and dreams, come together in one point, and that is the price of a stock or other asset. This makes that price the point where all disciplines converge: economics and mathematics, but equally or even more importantly psychology, technology, sociology, philosophy, geology and politics.

We thought long and hard about the form of the book. To keep it in line with the podcast and our presentations as much as possible, we opted for a somewhat unusual structure. I take charge of the first chapter. In it, I launch into some basic general ideas about how we look at markets and the economy. It is a look under our bonnet. What ideas and indicators provide a good basis for an analysis that should help us understand the world, or at least understand it a little better than what the consensus believes? In that last nuance already lies the first opportunity for gain.

We then look at trends, a crucial element in markets and the economy. Why are there trends and what are their building blocks? The answers will probably surprise you. In the chapters that follow, Koen explores some of the key megatrends that will shape the world over the next 20 to 30 years. I engage in dialogue with him, and with you as readers, in the form of boxes that float above Koen's subject matter. Often those interludes contain questions (and sometimes an attempt at answers) about what the investment implications of the trends are. We try to answer not only the questions we grapple with ourselves on a daily basis, but also the questions we get from readers and clients on a daily basis. Is the dollar going to lose its status as a reserve currency? Is it a good time to invest in gold or perhaps bitcoin? And when will growth markets finally start to live up to their lofty expectations?

Inevitably, a lot of books will come into the conversation. We will travel with Prometheus, Keynes and the philosophers from the Salons on Rue Saint Roch in Paris. I am quite a book fanatic. My wife calls it a midlife crisis; I keep it to, as Nicholas A. Basbanes puts it, a gentle madness. So, the whole of this book is indebted to writers, economists, traders and thinkers such as Robert Shiller, Jack Schwager, Michael Covel, Jim O'Shaughnessy, Nicolas Thaleb, Tom Basso, Mark Minervini, Peter Zeihan, George Friedman, Robert Kaplan and, closer to home, Jonathan Holslag, Geert Noels and Peter De Keyzer. Or to anyone whose name appears under the titles of the books that pile up in my house, even on the stairs.

Gamboni

We start with a story.

It is a sunny Friday afternoon just before dusk. Jack, a top trader at a major US investment bank, is driving home in his sports car in good spirits. The markets have been volatile. But Jack has managed to catch the right waves and his gains are substantial. Moreover, just about all his open positions have been closed, so he can look forward to a quiet weekend.

Just then, when everything in life seems to be going too well and not enough sacrifices have been made to the trading gods, disaster strikes. Jack suffers engine trouble. He only barely manages to get his car to a small garage in an grimy small town whose name does not otherwise matter. The verdict is disappointing: the garage will have to order the broken parts and the car will not be ready until the following day at the earliest.

In slightly dampened spirits, Jack books a room in a small hotel. Boredom strikes and he walks down to the bar and drinks a few whiskies. Then he notices a poker game going on in the adjoining room. Jack is a more than decent player, or at least he thinks he is. And what can a few locals do against a top trader who trades many millions every day? *Right?* He wriggles through the bystanders – and the thick cigarette smoke – buys himself a stack of chips and starts playing.

An hour later, Lady Fortuna's tide has gone from ebb to flood and back several times. Jack's stack of chips has remained about the same. But then he gets a hand of three aces and two kings, a full house, which is one of the better hands in poker. With a substantial pot already on the table, he raises the bet by $5,000. This is too much for most of the other players and they discard their cards with a sigh. But one last player, pretty much halfway between a lumberjack and Bill Gates, raises by another $20,000. Our trader, meanwhile, is through his chips and cash, but since he has a particularly good hand and assumes his opponent is bluffing, he bets his Rolex after some hesitation.

The cards come to the table, the lumberjack puts down a mishmash of cards that look like not much, a two and a three of diamonds, a five of spades, a ten of clubs and jack of clubs. Jack shows his full house and wants to start raking in the pot.

'Wait a minute,' says the Bill Gates lookalike, while the murmur and a few mock laughs should already have set all the alarm bells ringing at Jack. 'I have a Gamboni here.'

'Gamboni, I've never heard of that,' Jack replied in bewilderment.

'Just look at that paper on the wall,' ripostes the opponent, smiling his teeth, at least what is left of them, exposed.

Jack reads: 'Two diamonds, two clubs and one spade together form a Gamboni, which is the highest possible combination in this establishment.'

Jack looks around angrily, but rules are rules. And right now he is not the man to give up after a setback. He pawns his gold pinkie ring, buys another stack of chips and the game goes on.

Again, a few hours pass, during which he manages to make up a small chunk of his losses. Until he gets his hands on a Gamboni. At that point, two other players, including the lumberjack with Jack's Rolex on his wrist, are in the game. Confidently, he bets everything. The two opponents show a pair of sevens and three ladies respectively. Triumphantly, Jack throws his Gamboni on the table. Justice has been done and he prepares to rake in the pot.

This time the laughter in the room is no longer suppressed but exuberant. Jack looks around desperately.

'Look at the back of the paper,' says a voice that seems to come from very far away.

Jack turns the paper over and reads: 'Only one Gamboni is allowed in this establishment per evening.'

Trader Jack leaves with the proverbial tail between his legs. The next day, he picks up his car and leaves town, a Rolex, a pinkie ring and a fair amount of cash poorer, but a life lesson richer: 'Don't play games if you don't know the rules.'

This is an adapted version of a story from the book *Trader Vic, Methods of a Wall Street Master*, written in 1991 by Victor Sperandeo, described by the well-known investment weekly *Barron's* as the ultimate Wall Street pro. I used this story as an introduction to a number of presentations many years ago. Investing and trading can perhaps be seen somewhat irreverently as a game. But if you want a chance at success, there are rules, and this first chapter is about those. What does the chessboard look like on which our strategy unfolds?

That does not mean it will be a walk in the park. It is sometimes said that there are thousands of ways to beat the market. Unfortunately, they are all very hard to find. But take it from me: markets are not efficient. This means trends emerge that we can use to our advantage. The most important rule here, though, is: let your winners run as long as possible and cut your losers off as soon as possible. Only in this way can you be successful in what management guru Simon Sinek calls an 'infinite game': a game that goes on until you quit. In our world, this means you give up or you run out of money to continue 'playing'. In this book I hope to give you some insights on to avoid this. Fortunately, markets usually follow a certain constantly recurring pattern. This is because the world around us changes, but human nature always remains the same.

The market is going down: where is the news?

A first important observation is that big shifts in prices do not just happen on 'big news'. The 1987 crash is a good example. On Monday 19 October 1987, the US S&P500 lost more than 20% of its value for no apparent reason. Financial reporters had to go to great lengths to get something to the surface.

After many months, the most likely explanation was found in a hedging technique that went by the name of 'portfolio insurance' at the time. In short, it amounted to quasi-automatic, or fully automatic selling of stock futures to protect a portfolio from further losses if its value fell below a certain level. A perfect example of how sales leads to further sales, as we often see during a crash. Each further drop triggered new sales programmes. Because of the structure of the market, or the machinery behind it, market history was made that day. Pushing against one domino caused many others to fall in a market that, it has to be said, was overvalued.

But even when important news hits our screens, such as Russia's invasion of Ukraine or the outbreak of a pandemic, it can take days or even weeks for the market to correctly assess the gravity of the situation. In both cases, the market fell as it became clear to more people what the impact would be. This is at odds with the idea that all news is immediately reflected in prices. In this view, spreading news is a lot like the adaptation curve for a new product in the markets.

Tipping point

2,5%
Innovators

13,5%
Early adopters

34%
Early majority

34%
Late majority

16%
Laggards

And the similarity is not accidental. When a new product enters the market, there are innovators and leaders (*early adopters*) who are the first to start using the product. Then follows an *early majority*, a *late majority* and finally the *laggards*. It is the same with the emergence of a new trend, the rise of a company or a new investment opportunity. It starts with a select group of people recognising a new trend and trying to ride the wave. As the wave gains momentum, more and more believers join in. Until the trend inevitably stops and comes to an end on the beach.

One might conclude that it is always a good idea to be among the innovators or the frontrunners. But if we take the metaphor of a trend as a wave emerging, growing and breaking on the beach a little further: not all waves grow big before they turn over. Not all ideas grow into a new consensus or paradigm.

As we will see further along in this chapter, the ideal time to bet on a new idea is when the early majority comes on board. This corresponds to phase 2. It comes down to being quick with a new trend. But not too quick either. I think that is called timing…

All this makes it clear that, although news can enter the market very quickly, it usually takes a long time for the idea to catch on (or not catch on) and replace an older idea, becoming a new consensus or trend.

Three windows on the world

'There can be as much value in the blink of an eye as in months of rational analysis.'

———

MALCOLM GLADWELL

It is due to this fascination with trends that Koen and I spend all day looking through our proverbial windows at the world and the waves. Hoping to understand the world just a little better, or at least a little better than the consensus.

From the first window, we look out from our desks onto a gigantic library. Mountains of books and research with all human knowledge are stored there. I see it as a fascinating maze and the reward is the emergence of a new idea, a new insight with which we can return to our desks. In my mind, it is one of the underground ports of libraries on Erin Morgenstern's Starless Sea, from one of the most beautiful fantasy books of all time.

From the second window, we look at the sea, at the waves, at the trends rolling in and the stories and ideas they bring. I like that image. Trends that we can use to invest for our clients. This window is a metaphor for our screens, our charts of stocks, indices, commodities, interest rates and currencies. They are my screens in the markets room, anything that can draw lines on which we can follow the movement of prices. This is a constant dialogue with Mr Market. As a now-retired journalist from the newspaper *L'Echo* used to say, '*Le marché nous parle.*' The market tells us stories at any time, shows us trends. The market is always right and it is a laboratory that allows us to test the hypotheses we develop in our library. Both must be in agreement. The hypothesis and Mr Market, a metaphor for market movements, must go hand in hand. Otherwise, something is structurally wrong and we have to go back to the drawing board.

The third window looks out onto a huge conference room. There, at round tables, are our customers, business leaders and investors, along with our colleagues, with whom we are in dialogue on a daily basis. But strategists, economists, analysts and researchers from around the world are also invited. It is a big conference hall. And for us, like our second window, it is a laboratory where we can test our ideas against reality.

If Koen says that the global economy or the European economy or the Belgian economy is strong and is only going to grow in strength in the coming months, but the people from the port of Antwerp or the big exporters in Limburg say that there is hardly any trade, maybe there is something wrong with the analysis. For me, conversations with people from as many disciplines as possible are very enriching because they provide oxygen and ideas. They also allow me to feel the market sentiment. And often a sentiment can be so prevalent, a consensus so strong, that you can almost feel the wave turn and something totally new emerge. This window is perhaps not only the most fun, if some coffee or wine is involved, but perhaps even the most important, as market prices are still set by people.

Narrative economics

*'Stories was everything
and everything was stories.'*

———

HARRY CREWS

For that human factor, we cross the Atlantic and travel further to Yale and Michigan and then towards California to visit two Nobel Prize winners in Economics: Robert Shiller and George Akerlof.

Yale professor Robert Shiller is probably best known for the book *Irrational Exuberance*, in which he warned about the irrational optimism in stock markets and especially technology stocks back in 2000. His timing was perfect. When, in the months that followed, tech gods lost 50–80% and sometimes more of their value, a new guru was born. A status that was reinforced when, a few years later, he made a similar call on the overvalued real estate market, and a status he still enjoys today. Professor Shiller believes that the so-called 'animal spirits', also the title of a book he co-wrote with George Akerlof, professor at the University of California in Berkeley, are having a huge impact on the economy and financial markets. People's emotions, mostly greed and fear, make us see wild and often unpredictable movements in both.

An interesting fact is that George Akerlof is married to Janet Yellen, ex-chairwoman of the US central bank and currently the US Secretary of the Treasury. I imagine they have interesting discussions at the breakfast table. And it will often boil down to saying, over the toast and the bacon and eggs, that markets are irrational, that they are driven by human emotions, animal spirits, and that occasional Keynesian stimulus is a particularly good way to pull a flagging economy out of the doldrums. Animal spirits is a term used by John Maynard Keynes in his 1936 book *The General Theory of Employment, Interest and Money*, to describe the instincts, tendencies and emotions that ostensibly influence and drive human behaviour, and which we can measure in terms of things like consumer confidence. It also means that, as a policymaker, you can provide fiscal stimulus to the economy. That may make interest rates rise a bit, but the idea is that businesses make their decisions mostly based on their gut feelings and by looking at what others are doing, and less based on those interest rates.

Stories also drive markets, as Professor Shiller explains in his best book, *Narrative Economics*. People need stories to give meaning to their lives. People tell stories about markets, and those stories influence how people think and act. Those actions move markets. It is almost a perpetual motion. When a story becomes particularly powerful and goes viral, the speed and impact can be compared to a pandemic.

A pandemic has something like a *contagion rate*, a *recovery rate* and a *death rate*. When a pandemic takes off, the contagion rate, the sum of all recently infected people, exceeds the recovery and death rates. This continues until the disease wave declines in strength and recovery rates and, unfortunately, death rates become greater than the contagion rate.

We see the same pattern in 'contagious' economic or market narratives. Contagion occurs through conversations between people, physically or nowadays increasingly online, or slightly more ambitious talk shows or multimedia. As the story gains momentum, the rate of contagion exceeds the number of people who are no longer interested and drop out. At some point, even the most sticky, haunting and compelling story loses momentum and the number of people who drop out becomes greater than the newly infected. And then it is time for yet another new story.

It also happens that an old story, sometimes in a new guise, resurfaces after a while and goes through the viral life cycle again. And you can feel me coming: this is all very similar to an adaptation cycle in marketing, or to a wave or trend in financial markets. An idea has innovators, early adopters, an early and a late majority and some more laggards, trying to jump on a wave when it is already close to the beach. Waves like stories that roll to the beach, and on which we try to surf, not too fast, but not too slow either, preferably just before the majority picks up the story and jumps on the trend. I think that is a powerful and, above all, very beautiful image.

But perhaps we should ask Mr Keynes what he thinks of all this.

Interview with a dead economist

Chief strategist Philippe Gijsels interviewed none other than the late star economist John Maynard Keynes.

I was a bit nervous; conversations with living economic gods are one thing, but with a dead one...

I was just about to order a second espresso when a tall man joined me and sat down opposite me. He looked like the pictures in his biography, but a lot younger, and in his eyes there was the look of someone who has found peace, of someone who no longer searches but knows.

'A coffee, or something else,' I started to ask.

But he beat off the almost-question with a friendly flick of his long arms.

'We don't do things like that anymore after we, you know.'

'So then what...?' I blurted out in an attempt to get the bizarre conversation going.

'We are. But, I thought we had agreed to talk about the economy and the markets. Because I admit, I do miss those a bit.'

Where do you start when you suddenly find yourself at the table with Keynes? How do you come up with a question that hasn't already been asked a thousand times? How do you make an intellectual heavyweight of this calibre feel that you've done your homework and are more or less worthy of having a conversation with him? One point that had always struck me in Keynes' many biographies and writings was his fascination with Newton. So why not start there?

'Do you ever talk to Newton?' I asked as slowly as I could.

'Yes, quite often. He doesn't immediately give you the sense that he has a highly developed sense of humour. But now he can sometimes even laugh at the fact that I bought into the whole package, including the stuff that nobody was interested in, because it didn't fit the world's image of him, that of the progenitor of modern science. I prefer to see him as he is described in that book by Michael White, as the last magician.'

'Aren't you also a little bit in the field of economics?'

'Now you flatter me, but everyone naturally tries to be like their heroes. In that respect, I have always loved the expression: the dwarf standing on the shoulders of a giant sees more than the giant himself.'

He adjusted his long raincoat and it struck me again how tall he was, now almost as tall as the giant from *Twin Peaks*. After death, do we all get the stature the world assigns us?

'You know, we all try to make an all-encompassing model of reality, a mechanical clock like Newton tried to build of the universe. From where I stand now, I can tell you what a difficult and almost absurd exercise that is, especially if you can't manage to even come close to a definition for the concept of "reality". But I can say that I'm more convinced than ever that economics belong more to the field of social sciences than to the natural sciences, no matter how much we might wish otherwise.'

'Are you referring to the fact that you once lost a lot of money on the stock market?'

'Partially. But you know, that doesn't bother me anymore. I see it as a necessary learning process. When the material falls away, there are only the experiences and the ideas. My friend Newton once put it very nicely, *"I can calculate the motion of heavenly bodies, but not the madness of people."* So in terms of losing money on the stock market, I was in good company.'

'You say partially...'

'Yes. What bothers me more in this respect is the almost dogmatic way my work is summed up as Keynesian with all possible derivations of it: Keynesian stimulus, Keynesian politics and so on. Admittedly, it's quite flattering to have an entire school of economics named after you. And I still believe it's not a bad idea for the government to lend a hand to the economy every now and then when things are a bit off. Unfortunately, it invariably leaves out the part where I argue that the holes created by stimulus should be filled up again when things improve. But I guess that's peculiar to politics, right?'

'Does that also apply to central banks?'

'You'll have to ask Mr Friedman about that. The monetarists now clearly have all the power in their hands,' he said in a slightly harsher tone, showing that under the affable brown raincoat, the sacred fire was still burning somewhere.

I was happy about that. Because it made him, and thus our whole encounter, a little more human. Emotions provoke emotions, but sometimes also reassure.

'Are central banks inflating bubbles globally and how will that end?' I tried again against my better judgment.

'Clearly, when you keep certain economic variables, like interest rates, currencies and so on, off balance for a long time, you run certain risks. But as I said, the central bankers are clearly more followers of Mr Friedman and he clearly has no problem with it. Maybe you'd better invite him over. Bubbles always run much longer than anyone thinks possible. Timing is extremely difficult, if not impossible.'

After this last sentence, he seemed momentarily lost in thought and a silence fell. Was he remembering something from his material existence or was he thinking? I instinctively raised my empty cup to my lips to have something to do.

'Do you know how to go bankrupt?' he asked suddenly, without warning.

'Slow at first and then suddenly.'

Would that also be the case when dying? Was that the thought he was pondering just before?

'Do you mean that in the long run we need to protect ourselves from the monetary devaluation that an overly aggressive monetary policy can cause?'

'Protecting possessions is of course very deeply ingrained in you mortals, when all you really take with you are impressions, ideas and memories. But who am I to blame you? And yes, if we limit our discussion to the material, it is clear that if you keep increasing the money supply in your system, prices must rise. In other words, inflation begins to rise. Of course, there are many different types of inflation. Central banks would love to see inflation in the real economy. But instead they get it largely in assets. This almost inevitably leads to bubbles. But paradoxically, buying assets, such as real estate, stocks and even art, is the only protection against that money devaluation. But that's how we got back to Friedman...'

'Forgive me. But does gold offer good protection against the effects of central banks' money creation?'

For a moment, a boyish smile played around his lips. And he was that Cambridge boy again, long before the world made him an economic god.

'In the long term very much so. But your long term is a bit different than mine.'

And then he stepped away, first slowly and then suddenly. ●

Contribution by Philippe Gijsels, published in *De Tijd* on 3 December 2015

THE NEW WORLD ECONOMY

Reflexivity

The Alchemy of Finance by super-investor George Soros was one of the first books
I read about the markets. The central idea is that there is a two-way interaction
between market participants (the thinking entities) and the situation they participate in, the economy or the market. Participants try to understand the (market)
reality and take advantage of it. They act on what they think reality is. But by that
action, they also change reality. The interaction between the situation and the
participants is, in a nutshell, what Soros calls 'reflexivity'.

This insight has far-reaching implications. If everyone thinks a company is
great and drives up its share price, this gives the fictitious company a lot of advantages. For instance, it can attract cheap capital by issuing shares at a high level.
It can attract good employees because the company is cool. Or ultimately, it can
use its high share price or easy access to capital markets to buy out a competitor.
AOL's acquisition of Time Warner at the end of the internet hype in March 2000,
for an easy $182 billion, is perhaps the most striking example of this. The media
giant, then considered old-fashioned, was bought by the poster boy of new media.
The rest is history. At some point, AOL was sold out of the new group for next to
nothing. This story could never have become reality if investors had not believed
that old media was going to disappear and new companies like AOL would take
over the entire industry. And if they hadn't acted on it and driven up AOL's share
price to the point where it became almost inevitable that they would also use the
mountain of casino chips they got their hands on in the form of market capitalisation to rake in the under-funded media group.

The reverse reasoning also applies, of course. If a company falls out of favour
with the investment community because its results are disappointing, or because
an alternative seems more attractive at the time, its share price will fall. Falling
share prices automatically lure more bears out of the woods, who use their claws
to knock the prices down even more. If share prices fall enough, there will inevitably be negative consequences for the company in question. Banks will be less
inclined to lend to the company or the interest rate will at least have to be higher.
Customers might start looking for an alternative. Suppliers might start demanding
constant payment. In the most extreme cases, it may sound the death knell for a
company that in other circumstances, in a different reality, could have survived
perfectly well, even flourished. Everybody loves a winner.

It is what Phil Rosenzweig describes in his book *The Halo Effect*. When a company can boast rising sales and profits and the share price goes up, we easily conclude that the company has a brilliant strategy, a visionary leader, capable employees and a great corporate culture. When the share price drops and results are a bit disappointing, the perception quickly turns around: the strategy was wrong, the leader has become arrogant, the corporate culture and employees have caused this 'failure'. In reality, little may have changed. But perceptions of reality were thoroughly shaken. The halo of unapproachability has fallen away. Everything that was good only a short while ago is now bad. Indeed, consumers, investors and, yes, people in general are hardwired to form an opinion based on a general impression, and proclaim it. It is difficult for most people to have an independent opinion on separate elements that are linked together. There is a strong urge to take them all together. With the halo effect, our brain tries to create a coherent and consistent picture of a complex situation. Thus, it reduces or avoids cognitive dissonance. Our brain seeks peace and harmony.

An example Rosenzweig cites is that of George Bush Jr., who saw his popularity rise after the attacks on the Twin Towers on 11 September 2001. It is not illogical for the population to rally behind its leader in the face of a terrorist attack of that magnitude. But it was not only the president's overall popularity that went up. Public approval also rose for his steering of the economy; but this pretty picture didn't last long. By 2005, George W. Bush Jr.'s popularity had fallen sharply under impact of Hurricane Katrina and the increasingly unpopular war in Iraq. Americans judged that now his economic policies also left much to be desired.

We also use the halo effect to form an idea about things that are difficult to estimate. We take in information that seems relevant, tangible and objective to us and use it to delineate vague and ambiguous concepts. And what is more objective, relevant and tangible than a share price or, in derivative order, the price of an asset? If the price goes up, all will be well, surely? And if the price falls, something structurally negative is probably going on.

And so we are back to Soros. Our perception, through our actions, influences the price. And the price influences our perception. And meanwhile, halos are swung from one company to another. And the herd runs with every toss. A direct consequence of this is that markets are much more about performance in relative rather than absolute terms. It is not just how well the price of a stock or asset is doing in absolute terms, but mainly about how strong the percentage rise or fall is relative to the competition. This reminds me of the late 1990s, just before the internet bubble burst, when investors sold good-faith stocks, because they were 'only' rising 20 or 30% a year, to buy stocks on the East or the Nasdaq that could double in a day. Reflexivity and the halo effect, seasoned with some human emotions like fear and greed, combine to make a powerful and, for a while, sometimes even wonderful cocktail.

When, while writing this book, I took out Soros' work, which has since yellowed, I found another sheet in the book with some notes I wrote a long time ago. It's like walking on the beach and finding a message in bottle that you once threw into the sea. It was almost impossible to decipher my own writing, but even though wind, sea and sand had blurred the letters, it said something like:

'Investors' behaviour influences prices in markets, but prices also influence investors' behaviour. This creates an infinite interaction. That interaction is what George Soros calls reflexivity. Trends emerge as a result of the interaction. It is a process that sets itself in motion, but already carries the seeds of its own decline from the beginning. A wave reaches its peak and then breaks on the beach. The surf sings us a song of change, of evolution, revolution and progress. To the tune of this song, fortunes are made and lost, empires created and swallowed again by the sea. It is a story of ebb and flow, rise and fall, gain and loss, waves and trends.'

The emergence of trends:
take two

'Patterns repeat, because human nature
hasn't changed for thousands of years.'

———

JESSE LIVERMORE

Perhaps at this point it is not a bad idea to take the bull by the horns. What is a trend? It is one of those words that we use every day, but is not so easy to define. In *Trend Surfing*, Bert Van Thilborgh gives the following definition: 'Trends are processes of change in human behaviour situated in a social context and manifesting themselves in different ways among certain groups in society and striving to improve our quality of life through innovation. Trends are dynamic, evolutionary, influential and impactful and leave traces in society. Trends are observable and manifest themselves through ideas, language, culture, (life) style, taste, behaviour, products, services and events.'

That is already a mouthful and only one of many interpretations that have been given to the term over the years. Another is that of trend-watcher Herman Konings. He describes trends as civilising processes that carry and steer social developments. Some time ago, I had the opportunity to give a lecture with Herman Konings to a group of clients. What he calls the civilisation processes is very similar to what we call themes and trends, and corresponds with many of the topics we will cover in this book. Statisticians and economists, in turn, tend to see a trend as an upward (positive) or downward (negative) movement of a curve.

In this book, we will talk about trends in markets, but also about major macro trends, such as demographic trends, (de)globalisation, climate trends and trends in innovation. Perhaps it is good to make a distinction between market trends and everything else. A market trend is determined by how supply and demand change. That is also how prices are established in a free-market environment. This applies to trends as well, because a trend is a sequence of prices moving in the same direction. Supply and demand can then be traced back to people's behaviour. Why do they want to pay/get a certain price for an asset today? And why will it be different tomorrow?

Trends arise not only when change occurs, but also when perceptions of reality change. And that, as with Soros' reflexivity, can in turn cause the change and reinforcement of the existing trend, but just as easily its reversal or the emergence of a new trend. Non-financial trends do not come about through the laws of supply and demand. But human behaviour, which can change at any time, still underlies them.

Let us pause to consider that human behaviour. Humans are and remain vessels full of emotions, often driven by fear and greed, with a tendency to overreact in every possible direction. This is why the two concepts of 'underreaction' and 'overreaction' are crucial. Entire libraries of academic papers have been written over the years trying to answer the question of whether stock markets are underreacting or overreacting.

I think the stock market is both underreacting and overreacting and this is because it takes a while to change ideas. Let's take the example of share X. The company has been announcing only poor results for years. There is disappointment every quarter. Investors are fed up with the story. Sentiment is ruined to the core. And then suddenly a particularly positive quarter comes along. However, those figures are not believed. It will probably be a one-hit wonder again. The share does go up, but the market is so negative that everyone is waiting to see what happens. In other words, there is an underreaction to the good news. As confidence returns and more good news follows, the company begins to win people back little by little. And this is slow going. But just because it is slow, a nice trend emerges. You don't necessarily have to buy at the first positive news. All the good news is not factored into the price all at once. You get a number of entry points in the upward trend. Let us hope for the desperate and patient investors that the uptrend lasts for a very long time. After a long time, investors start overreacting to yet another positive result. In the meantime, there is so much positive confirmation that there is now great belief that it will remain this way forever. At that point, more positive news is priced in than the numbers justify. The market is exaggerating. There is overreaction. But trees don't grow to the sky. At some point, another unexpected setback blows in. Disbelief is high. How can such a brilliant company with a halo around its management now disappoint? It must be a one-off setback, which is possible, of course. But that is precisely why there is now another underreaction, this time to the bad news. A lot of investors believe things will be fine. And so begins the downtrend that can be exploited again. The same reasoning applies to all assets and, in a derivative order, to trends outside the financial sector as well.

What makes detecting and analysing trends so difficult is that there are very often many different causes that also influence each other. In doing so, it is always difficult to work out whether two things are correlated (they move together) or whether there is causality. Indeed, in practice, we often encounter the so-called 'butterfly effect'. The butterfly effect is derived from a metaphor used by Edward Lorenz in 1961 to show that the wing beats of a butterfly in Brazil can cause a tornado in Texas months later.

Often, the shocks that hit the (world) economy and/or financial markets midstream are a little bigger than the flapping of a butterfly's wings. Just think of the recent Covid-19 crisis, the invasion of Ukraine or the 9/11 attacks. Nicholas Taleb has used the term 'black swans' when there are very large and unexpected shocks. These can be of natural or human origin. Perhaps the biggest in history was the meteor that triggered the extinction of the dinosaurs somewhere in the

Cretaceous Period, 66 million years ago. The dominant species disappeared and mammals gradually took over the planet. In market terms, this means that you should buy when others are selling their stocks out of panic over a black swan event. But sometimes you have to be patient. With the 9/11 attacks, the wait-to-win (WTW) was shorter than the extinction of our Jurassic Park friends. But good things come to those who wait.

Positive black swans: we cannot call them white swans because that term has already been taken, so let's call them pink. Often these are technological developments that turn society upside down. Like when Prometheus stole fire from the gods to give to humans. But even pink swans sometimes have negative side effects.

As we will explore further in our chapter on innovation, every new technological development is accompanied by fear of the unknown, fear that the world will change too fast or that all jobs will disappear. I have a lot of sympathy for this. I have been thinking about change my whole life, trying to develop strategies that take advantage of change – I am fascinated by it. But anyone who knows me a little bit, knows that I am not good with change and that change scares me. Or in the words of Joseph Campbell, the expert on myths and author of *The Hero with a Thousand Faces*: 'The cave you fear to enter, holds the treasure you seek.'

This path inevitably leads us to the debate raging fiercely today regarding AI. Is this a pink swan, a black swan or a totally different animal? Do we want to enter this cave? Is this a fire or a meteor? We will pay plenty of attention to it further on in the book.

The madness and wisdom of crowds

'The test of a first-rate intelligence is the ability
to hold two opposite ideas in mind at the same time
and still retain the ability to function.'

————

F. SCOTT FITZGERALD

So far, we have seen that it is mainly human behaviour that underlies most of the trends we observe in financial markets. People live in a society, or somewhat less reverently, in a herd. In this section, we will consider how the behaviours of an entire group of people drive the movements of financial markets, and more importantly, whether it is wise as an investor to follow the herd. The answer will probably surprise you.

The books *Extraordinary Popular Delusions and the Madness Of Crowds*, an early study of mass psychology by Scottish journalist Charles Mackay, first published in 1841, and the much more recent *The Wisdom of Crowds* (2004) by James Surowiecki sat side-by-side on my desk for months. The two clearly contradictory ideas swirling around in my head crystallised again and again into the question: are the masses smart or stupid?

In his book, James Surowiecki gives us some very plausible arguments as to why, under the right conditions, a group can be more intelligent and come to better decisions than a single smart individual with expertise, whatever that means. Some examples are very telling, though. For instance, there is an annual fair where participants who can best estimate the weight of an ox win a prize. In all, there were eight hundred participants, including a number of specialists in the field, such as farmers, butchers and livestock buyers. But there were just as many participants who had never seen an ox, a bull or a cow up close, so to speak. The scientist Francis Galton, who did not think very highly of the intelligence of the herd, did a little research after the competition and averaged the weights guessed by all the participants. He came up with 1,197 pounds. This was not only just a fraction away from the actual weight, but also better than any figure an individual had written down.

Another interesting example is found in the deep sea. A number of specialists from different fields went looking for a missing submarine in 1968. They were mathematicians, engineers specialised in building submarines, specialists in currents, topographers, etc. Each of them had to indicate individually with a cross on a sea chart where he or she thought the submarine was located. And eventually the submarine was recovered less than 200 feet from the average of the indicated locations. This last example also has to do with innovation, which we will return to later in this book, and the fact that groups that are diverse and multidisciplinary turn out to be much better at innovation.

What James Surowiecki and other scholars put forward does not just contradict what Charles Mackay asserts in his monumental work that spans many centuries. It is also in apparent contradiction to many hundreds, if not thousands, of years of market history. Because when the herd runs wild, bubbles are inevitably formed, which then just as inevitably burst, with all the nasty consequences. Then the question bubbles up again: are large groups of people intelligent or not? Is it wise to run with the herd or not? It certainly is on the savannah. If the herd runs away, the chances are very high that there is a predator or some other danger lurking somewhere close. The herd has more eyes than the individual. So there is a good chance that a risk will be assessed better collectively than by a single animal. Today, we are at the top of the food chain. But long ago, we started very much less ambitious as the food of larger predators. That is why it is in our DNA and in the functioning of the brain to almost always opt for the safety of the herd when we need to make a quick decision in the face of danger.

Most books on investing will say that 'herd behaviour' is a bad idea and leads to terrible investment results. This view is too one-sided though. A compromise can be found to reconcile Charles Mackay and James Surowiecki over a good glass of wine. The herd sometimes shows wisdom, but is not too savvy at other times. But the most important thing is that in many cases, if not almost always, it can be followed. That is why it is important to keep a close eye on our second window on the world, the waves. How do the prices of the things we keep an eye on, that we try to gain insight into, evolve? Do they rise, fall or stay horizontal? Take the dotcom bubble, or all the bubbles before it in history. No investor would have particularly minded having internet stocks in his portfolio in 1996, 1997 or 1999. More so, a fair number of analysts and strategists lost their jobs in those years because they did not understand that a new technology of that magnitude would bring about such a big change that the sky-high valuations were certainly justified. Or to put it another way, while a trend becomes particularly powerful and leads to a bubble, which we can always ascertain only afterwards, it is good to be in the midst of the herd.

Benign and not so benign bubbles

'When I see a bubble forming, I rush in to buy.'

———

GEORGE SOROS

Another misconception is that inflating and imploding bubbles will always have extremely negative social consequences. Of course, losses are never pleasant for those invested in the bubble. But there are relatively benign and particularly malignant bubbles. This distinction depends largely on whether the bubble formed in a productive or non-productive asset and how it was financed.

Very often a bubble is already created when new, promising technology sees the light of day, especially if this moment coincides with loose to very loose credit conditions and/or the presence of a lot of liquidity. Investors want to participate, en masse, in the new and profitable world. Optimism drives prices and valuations to levels that can no longer be justified and then even higher. Until the inevitable happens. Prices fall, the herd flees in the other direction, an unstoppable negative spiral ensues and many investors lose money. But that is the financial side, the money side of the economy.

Needless to say, it also has an impact on the real side of the economy. Because when prices collapse and losses mount, it is also often accompanied by a general aversion to risk and a 'credit crunch' (when no one wants to extend credit anymore). If you are losing money as an investor, you might start being more cautious on other projects, delaying investments and even consuming less. Banks and other lenders may also put the brakes on new commitments or lending for a while.

The good news is that the investments that were made are not lost; they just change hands. During the railway boom, many companies went bankrupt. But the tracks remained and were restructured into new companies. These generated money for their shareholders and opened up whole new areas in the UK and especially the US and enabled massive innovation and wealth creation.

The same thing happened more recently with the internet bubble. Lots of money flowed into new technology and lots of ideas got funded. But a lot of those ideas turned out not to be viable. Capital, people and resources were reallocated to companies that had a business model that could stand the test of time. With Joseph Schumpeter, it is both Eros and Thanatos. There is tearing down to build back up, harvesting to sow again and weeding to keep the whole thing viable in the long run. Importantly, cables were also left in the ground, as were railways, for future productive purposes.

In 17th-century Holland, the price of tulip bulbs reached unseen heights, only to collapse after rampant speculation. Tulip bulbs are perhaps slightly less productive assets in this respect. Therefore, the tulip bulb mania can be better classified in the category of less benign bubbles. Still, the implosion of the tulip bulb craze did not prevent the Netherlands from experiencing its Golden Age at the time (technically more like half a century, as it only really took off after the Peace of Münster in 1648).

The reason for this can be found in the second criterion for classifying bubbles, namely the way in which the financing took place. More specifically, whether that financing takes place largely within or outside the banking sector. As for the tulip bubble; it was largely done with private funds, i.e. outside the banking sector. When the bubble bursts, it is accompanied by the loss of much of the money invested. I am by no means suggesting that the loss of money for private investors would in any way be less bad than the loss of money in banks. But if the funding is in the banking sector and the banks run into trouble because of the losses, it almost inevitably has a very negative impact on the entire economy, as lending stops or at least slows down. Whether we like it or not, the banking sector and the liquidity it provides are and will remain the lifeblood of a well-functioning economy. In short, if a bubble does need to be inflated somewhere, let it be in a useful, productive activity with funding that largely flows outside the financial sector. The internet bubble is perhaps the best example of this. Unfortunately, we often don't have a choice.

Some other bubbles tend to be a little harder to compartmentalise. The first tech bubble probably took place in London in the 1690s, when everyone got particularly excited about diving bells that could be used to retrieve treasures from sunken ships. But you guessed it: the 1690s were not coincidentally also a period of extremely low interest rates. Two things should always be present for a solid bull market or a more extreme bubble: sufficient liquidity and a good story. But history also tells us that if there is a lot of liquidity, the story is usually found quickly too. Or to put it another way: there is often a technological aspect, always a psychological aspect, but the monetary aspect is the fuel that makes the whole process possible.

Technical analysis: the black arts

A while ago, I had the honour and pleasure of giving a lecture on technical analysis for KU Leuven's student investment association Greenhill Capital. I started the lecture by saying: 'If this were Hogwarts, you would now be in a Defence Against the Dark Arts class and I would be Snape, who, by the way, has always been my favourite character.' With that, the ice was broken and I could tell them, while I had their attention, what technical analysis is to me and, above all, what it is not. Technical analysis has a bad name, and not only among supporters of efficient-market theory. A lot of fundamental analysts subscribe to this view because, according to them, it is just some line-drawing.

By far the most important thing is to know what we are talking about and not talking about. First of all, as with fundamental analysis, you cannot predict the future with technical analysis. You can make a hypothesis with all the information from room one and room three, and with everything you know or think you know. But ultimately, only in room two can you tell whether the future will or should unroll the way you think it will. And the techniques of technical analysis can help you do that. They help you define the trend. In doing so, the possibilities are seemingly endless, and going into this in depth would lead us too far. There are countless books on this subject for self-study; I recommend *Technical Analysis Explained* by Martin Pring as a standard work. The idea is to have a method by which you can decide objectively for yourself whether something is in an upward, downward or horizontal trend. The word 'objective' is particularly important here. Because if a wave threatens to turn, and if this means taking a (small) loss, you will go out of your way to convince yourself that the trend is still upwards and that it is better to wait a little longer. It's the same with me, it's the same with you, it's the same with everyone, even the Market Wizards – not the ones from Hogwarts, but the ones from Wall Street.

This book follows a number of megatrends that we think will have a good chance of developing over the next five to ten years or beyond. The analysis work happens mostly in the library of room one and the conference hall of room three. But we cannot turn these potential trends into actual investment decisions without room two. There are worse things than staring at the sea on a beautiful summer day, or when it is stormy, because then the waves are bigger.

The four phases of the market

'You've got to know when to hold'em, know when to fold'em,
know when to walk away, know when to run.'

———

KENNY ROGERS, *THE GAMBLER*

When talking about trends, it is impossible to avoid Stan Weinstein's four phases a market can go through. All the details are described in his bestseller *Secrets for Profiting in Bull and Bear Markets*. It is extremely important for any trend – stocks, commodities, currencies, interest rates or whatever – to know which of the four phases they are in. Let us take the example of the Nasdaq Biotech Index.

Nasdaq Biotech Index

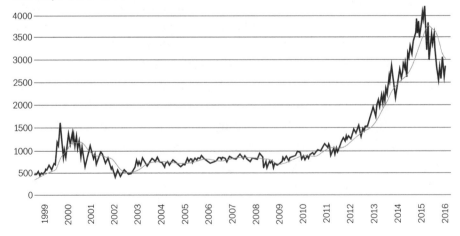

Phase 1: The basing phase

For the Nasdaq Biotech Index, the basing phase began in 2002 after the sharp decline following the implosion of the technology bubble. You can clearly see that the downward moment of the previous phase 4 (the falling phase, see below) is starting to recede and the price is starting to move horizontally instead. During the declining phase, sellers had the power. But in the first phase, buyers and sellers start to become more balanced. Very often, you see volumes drying up. Everyone who really wanted to sell has sold and there is still insufficient buying interest to start the advancing phase. Gradually, assets move from weaker hands to stronger hands. The 150-day average (this is the average usually used by Stan Weinstein. It is calculated by adding up the last 150 prices and dividing by 150. But nothing prevents us from using, say, a 200-day average) gradually goes from strongly declining to flat. The price of the asset, or in this case the index, moves alternately below and above the average. This process can take months or even years. From a technical perspective, it makes little sense to enter the market at this point. Because since this phase can take a very long time, it often means dead money, money that would be better put into another asset. However, there is also an unwritten rule that the longer the base, the stronger the advancing movement when the time for phase 2 finally arrives.

Phase 2: The advancing phase

The start of phase 2 is the best time to start capitalising on the developing uptrend. Possibly, initial positions can be increased further into phase 2, which can last for years. In phase 2, the asset finally leaves phase 1 and breaks out 'definitely' above its 150-day average. In the case of the Nasdaq Biotech Index, this was at the end of 2010, which immediately shows how long a basing phase can take. In theory, this sounds easy, but in practice, the transition is not always obvious. Therefore, it is sometimes easier to try to ride the trend if phase 2 has been going on for a while, because the 150-day average has turned from horizontal to upward. If the breakout to phase 2 is accompanied by a strongly increasing volume, this is another good indication that a new phase has started. A commonly used definition of an uptrend is also a sequence of higher tops and higher bottoms. So a nice phase 2 looks like a staircase being climbed, with steps where each advance may be followed by a smaller decline.

Phase 3: the topping phase

Even the longest and most powerful upward trends come to an end at some point. This is accompanied by a loss of upward momentum and price movements become more volatile and horizontal. The price starts to test the 150-day average a number of times and even falls below it a number of times. The topping phase can be short or long, but is often a lot shorter than the basing phase. If the basing phase is of the slightly longer type, the 150-day average also starts to peak and level off. In our example of the Nasdaq Biotech Index, the basing phase at the end of 2015 was rather short and there was little time between the upward and downward phases (phase 2 and phase 4). In the previous phase 3 at the end of 2000, the basing process was rather long. In phase 3, as in phase 1, there is again more or less a balance between buyers and sellers. None of the camps have enough strength to gain the upper hand. Hence the volatile but rather horizontal movements. Unlike phase 1, where volumes dry up, in phase 3 volumes are high, reflecting the fight between the bears and the bulls. Lots of shares change hands. There are profit-takers getting rid of their shares. But these are bought by market players who missed the rally and still jump on the bandwagon in extremis. In the adaptation model, these are the late majority or laggards. When these latecomers enter the market, the time has usually come to kiss the wave goodbye, beautiful as it was. And this while, on a fundamental level, the news about the asset is likely to be good and we will often see it on the covers of leading (investment) magazines. From a trend perspective, we are usually in the exaggeration (*overreaction*) phase here, where all the news seems good and the halo wave shines like never before.

Phase 4: the declining phase

This is the phase where sellers clearly take over. The price goes through all support levels and finally dives below the 150-day average, which turns from horizontal to declining after a while. While the transition from phase 1 to phase 2 is usually accompanied by high volumes, this is not always the case with the transition from phase 3 to phase 4. It may be that a particular news event suddenly turns sentiment around to such an extent that we see a sharp price drop on high volume. This was the case for the Nasdaq Biotech Index at the end of 2015. Here, the decline was very rapid. But if phase 3 lasts longer, phase 4 may kick in as the asset comes down under its own weight. Suddenly, buyers are no longer willing to take over the sellers' shares, except at lower prices. In such a situation, volumes are usually a lot lower. If, as an investor, you hadn't jumped off your surfboard in phase 3, the start of phase 4 is usually the last chance to do it without too much damage.

This, of course, is the theory. The Nasdaq Biotech Index is an example where the phases are (reasonably) clear. Sometimes it is more art or alchemy than science to determine which phase a trend is in, even though this is of vital importance. It is often challenging to work out whether a lull in an uptrend is indeed a lull (i.e. still phase 2) or the beginning of phase 3, which is the harbinger for decline. Analogously, it is not clear whether a rest or sideways move in phase 4 means we are looking at a pause in the decline (still phase 4) or have started the basing (beginning of phase 1).

The former is more problematic than the latter. If we are looking for the start of a new trend, we basically have no position yet and can quietly wait for the start of phase 2. If the trend is long enough, it is not a problem that we are a bit late. It is different with the advancing phase (*uptrend*), where we already have a position and the issue is to get out quickly when things turn bad, as phase 4 is usually fast, violent and without mercy. At the end of a basing (phase 1), shortly before we move to the uptrend (phase 2), we often see a powerful drop first, often on high volume. This is done to lose the last weak hands holding the asset, after which the uptrend can begin.

Surfing in practice: *grit or quit*

Psychologist Angela Duckworth wrote the bestseller *Grit: The Power of Passion and Perseverance*. The basic thesis is that the best way to predict whether someone will be successful in any field is not talent but grit. This is somewhat along the lines of books such as *Talent is Overrated* by Geoff Colvin or *Outliers* by Malcom Gladwell.

There too, the central thesis is that perseverance is more important than talent. Malcom Gladwell often talks about deliberate practice, at least 10,000 hours of training with the right coaching and guidance to become really good at something. In other words, if you spend 10,000 hours hitting golf balls without anyone telling you what you are doing wrong or how to hold your golf club, you are unlikely to win a major tournament.

In psychology, grit is a positive, non-cognitive trait based on a person's perseverance combined with passion for a particular long-term goal or end state. So giving up is not an option. Those who never give up will be successful in the long run and achieve their goals. In fact, our language is laced with expressions that express the same idea. 'Winners never quit and quitters never win.' All films and books that exhibit a modicum of heroism have heroes or anti-heroes who achieve their goals against everything and everybody or die trying.

In 2022, former poker player Annie Duke published her latest book *Quit*. It contains a story about a group of mountaineers who set out to conquer Mount Everest and at a certain point have to decide to abandon their mission and return to their base camp. There is a rule that states that if at any point you think that you will not make it to the summit, it is better to abort the mission and return. In jargon, these are called turnaround times. They are meant to protect climbers and give them enough time on the way back, as descending requires more skill than climbing. To cut a long story short, the leader saw that they would not reach the top within the predetermined time and decided to abort the mission. A lot of people will call this giving up. And this, of course, makes the story not heroic or spectacular or even worth telling. Many would probably have preferred to hear that they had kept going anyway, overcome all setbacks and still achieved their goal against unbeatable odds. Everyone loves heroes – even anti-heroes like Don Quixote.

The whole story is somewhat uncomfortable and would not meet with much acclaim at cocktail parties. But Annie Duke's book is just about how sometimes it is better to give up in an unfavourable situation. By the way, it is also described in Sun Tzu's *The Art of War*. Indefensible positions should be given up. Or to put it in poker terms: nobody obliges you to go out and play hero with a two of spades and a three of clubs. It is better to wait for a new and better opportunity and go for it again in full force. Angela Duckworth's grit lies precisely in not giving up after a number of losing hands at poker, or disappointing investments, and returning to the table with courage, fresh ideas and perhaps an adjusted technique or strategy. Like an investor who still manages to catch a big wave after several small losses, thereby not only erasing his small losses, but also adding a nice return. But above all, don't forget to follow your star.

Surfing in practice: the alligator principle

We return to the question: how do you know which waves to catch? *Trend Following* by Michael W. Covel is the book I recommend to people who ask me the question: which book should you absolutely read as a starting investor? It is a standard work that demonstrates what it means to surf a wave, hoping it is a life-changing wave, and jumping off at some point when it turns. There will be many small, disappointing waves among them that initially look good, but very quickly turn over on the beach. These lead to small losses in markets because a position is closed again relatively quickly. But every so often, there is a very nice wave that keeps going. And that one comes with its own challenge, because perhaps even harder than saying goodbye to an idea that very quickly becomes nothing is to keep going on this big wave. The time-honoured 'stock market wisdom', 'You can't go bankrupt by taking profits,' is wrong. You just need big profits, big waves, to offset the losses of would-be trends that end up not becoming trends after all. And how big a wave becomes, or just doesn't become, is difficult, if not impossible to estimate.

Let's take the surf metaphor a step further and make it a bit more interesting. Suppose we are still trying to surf the waves. We lie in the sea and wait for a nice one. Every wave that comes along we try to ride for as long as possible, knowing that there will be some waves that will fairly quickly prove to be a serious disappointment. No problem, we paddle back to our starting point and wait for the next opportunity. In the real world, of course, the trick is to make sure you are still able to take advantage of the next opportunity. To do so, we need to ensure that when disappointing waves occur, the losses do not mount to the point where we cannot or dare not surf any further. Let us therefore introduce some alligators that come at us every time we fall off our board.

The term 'alligator principle' is based on the way these animals feed. The more the victim struggles, the more the alligator gets. Imagine an alligator holding you by your leg. It holds your leg firmly clamped between its jaws and waits for you to start struggling. The moment you bring your arm near its jaw to release your leg, it also grabs your arm. The more you flounder, the more body parts you lose.

As harsh as it sounds, the only way to make it out alive is to sacrifice your leg and try to get yourself to safety. Translating this to the market, it means: when you see that the trend you are on is going in the wrong direction, act immediately and don't let the losses mount. Don't play the hero, don't rationalise, don't hope, don't pray, don't increase your position, or whatever you think you are doing. Get out of there. There will always be a new wave and with it a new opportunity. Or in the words of trading legend and *Market Wizard* Larry Hite, 'If you bet nothing, you can't win. And if you don't have more, you can't bet anything.'

Of course, you will say: there are no alligators in the sea. But I'm just taking a bit of poetic licence. And because of this contrast, the image of the waves, the sun, the feeling of paradise and the alligators will be even more strongly imprinted. So, it is one of perhaps the two most important ideas in this entire book. Stick to your winning trends for as long as possible, but get out of there when things go wrong. Let your profits run and cut your losses short.

TEN
to REMEMBER

1   Don't play games whose rules you don't know enough about (and certainly not Gamboni).

2   Markets can move perfectly well (quickly) without any 'new news' having appeared.

3   Fundamental, objective figures move markets, but markets also move those objective figures. In other words, nothing is objective, everything is perception. This mutual influence is what George Soros calls reflexivity.

4   John Maynard Keynes would surely classify economic sciences with the social sciences rather than the natural sciences. He thus agrees with Isaac Newton, who is purported to have said that he could calculate the movement of heavenly bodies, but not the minds of people.

5   Sometimes the masses are intelligent, sometimes a little less so. But following the masses is usually a good idea.

6   There are benign and evil bubbles. If one bursts, let it be from a productive asset, not financed through the banks.

7   It can be a long wait for the right big trend wave. Enjoy it, but also remember to jump off in time, before it plunges thunderously downwards.

8   Trend analysis and technical analysis are two different things. The latter supports the former, but it cannot predict the future (which is particularly unfortunate).

9   According to Stan Weinstein, try to buy stocks, commodities, interest rates... when the price finally rises above its 150-day average. If it then starts flirting with that average again, look to sell.

10 Being able to persevere, or having grit, is more important than having talent, or at least sometimes. Because occasionally, giving up is necessary.

ONE TREND
to RULE THEM ALL

'Our earth is degenerate in these latter days: bribery and corruption are common;
children no longer obey their parents; every man wants to write a book,
and the end of the world is evidently approaching'

———

ASSYRIAN TABLET, CIRCA 2800 BC.

It is 16 March 2020. The world is in lockdown. The Covid-19 pandemic has the world in its grip. A lot of our certainties are being pulled out from under us. Stock markets are plummeting. I sit with our head of private bankers in lockdown waiting to reassure our clients via a live audio recording. Telling them that the world will not end and that crises like this in the past have always been great opportunities for long-term purchases. But most of all, I sit and wait for the Fed. History teaches us that in times of crisis, central banks, with the US Federal Reserve in the lead, support markets with lower interest rates and massive liquidity injections. When our presentation begins, I keep an eye on my Bloomberg screen. And as I talk about what might happen in the coming days and weeks, run over scenarios, the Fed springs into action. You can see it in the price movements in the bond markets. There is a big buyer at work. It is like an attack, a bombardment of B-52 bombers. Raid after raid is being carried out. But when the big market reaction fails to materialise and equity markets do go lower again after a few rally attempts, I doubt my view for a moment. Will they manage it again this time? That day, the market's bottom has not yet been found. But the day after, central bankers will come back into the market. And the day after too. And the day after that. Until balance sheets are so swollen and there is so much money in the system that we will see a sharp rise, not just in equity markets, but in just about all asset classes. We hit bottom on 23 March, barely a week later, but a week that seems to last for years. It is something I have experienced many times. When markets crash, time seems to slow down, everything slows down. According to Hedderik van Rijn, professor of neuro and cognitive sciences at the University of Groningen, excitement changes your perception of time because your body goes into an excited state. If you find yourself in a life-threatening situation, you become more alert. As a result, the internal clock in your brain starts ticking faster, which makes 'real' time seem slower.

In our world, interest rates are both gravity and a time machine. With rising inflation, interest rates also rose and we have arrived at a pivotal moment in time. In this chapter, we will look at how we got into the current complex, and not immediately favourable, situation and what the possible consequences could be. The main question we will have to ask ourselves with each subsequent theme of this book is: is the money tap open or is it closed?

And eternally pounding elephants

"Cause it was 1989, if it was any other time
I'd know'

————

dEUS

With March 16 in mind (and this is just one of many examples), it is clear that the moment has come to dwell on the monumentally important idea of why interest rates are so important to our continuing story. Before we get to that, let's enjoy a zoological diversion to one of the most imaginative metaphors about how the financial system works. We find it in Mark Faber's book, *Tomorrow's Gold: Asia's Age of Discovery*, written over 20 years ago now.

On a bendable pole made of bamboo is a large container of water with a tap. At the bottom of the pole is a large herd of elephants, some with attendants, some without. Between the elephants are buckets. When the water tap is turned all the way open, the big basin overflows and the water falls down into the buckets. The elephants try to reach the water, but this causes them to push against each other and against the bending pole, causing the water to follow an erratic, constantly changing path. Sometimes the elephants push against a bucket and the water spills from one bucket to another, while also ending up on the ground and being lost.

In this metaphor, the water represents the liquidity that central banks inject into the system. The central bankers control the tap. They can determine how much liquidity is generated in total. They do this by raising or lowering interest rates, but also through other tools in their arsenal, such as quantitative easing or tightening (using their balance sheet to buy or sell bonds or other assets in the market, thereby increasing or decreasing the total amount of liquidity). But they cannot determine, or at least have great difficulty determining, where the liquidity ends up. That is what the elephants, the investors, the traders and company managers and their handlers, the advisers, the press, and the commentators, do.

When central banks drop a lot of money, just about every bucket gets filled. These are the investment themes and the various asset classes. Some of the buckets also represent the real economy. When the money tap is open as it was, say, in 2021, all asset classes rise together and the world overflows with money. Some of it also ends up in the buckets of the real economy, for which the money was actually intended. But with all their power, the central bankers cannot prevent much of the money, which they would like to see go into the real economy, from pushing up asset values. On the upside, they don't even mind. Because the 'wealth effect' (when people feel richer because the value of their real estate, art, stocks or bonds has gone up) ensures that overflowing buckets of assets partly enter the real economy. Part of it therefore falls directly like manna from the central bank's heaven into the real economy in the form of lending by banks. Another part flows indirectly from the overflowing asset buckets into the real economy. That said, these are fun times for the elephants and their handlers, as there is so much water filling all the buckets and it is not that difficult to invest, as everything is increasing. The money flows from bucket to bucket, but there is enough for everything and everyone.

It becomes less fun when central banks turn off the tap because prices (inflation) in the real economy have risen too much. The idea is to let less water flow into the real economy, but this also means less water gets into the asset buckets. In extreme cases, such as recently in 2022 (the beginning of the fastest interest rate hikes made by central banks in four decades), the tap gets turned off altogether. An asset class or a theme can only rise if water flows into it from another bucket. And water is certainly no longer flowing from assets towards the real economy. In fact, we have a negative wealth effect. It is a period of drought, with most asset classes struggling and declining.

In the first chapter, we talked about waiting for a wave, a trend, with the idea of trying to surf it for as long as possible. Here, the idea is to be the first one there when water starts flowing into a bucket. But if there is no water, there are no nice upward waves. Looking at it this way, interest rates and, in derivative order, the amount of liquidity in the system are a bit like gravity. If interest rates are low and the quantity of liquidity is high, there is no gravity and all assets can fly. If interest rates are high and the quantity of liquidity is low, then everything is pulled down. In this view, we can see 2022 as the year gravity returned.

In fact, history teaches us that big trends, big investment themes, seem to occur over time spans of about a decade.

Investment themes by decade Source: MSIM, Bloomberg, Factset, Haver

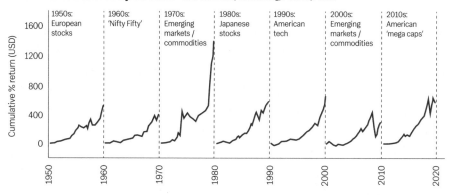

From 1950 to 1960, it was European equities that led the world (indeed, it's been that long). In the 1960s, a limited number of stocks, the US Nifty Fifty, did particularly well. These were the IBMs, Xeroxes, Polaroids, Eastman Kodaks, McDonalds, Walt Disneys, General Electrics and JC Pennys of this world. It was a difficult period for the stock market, not coincidentally with high interest rates and high inflation. However, it was also a period when one Peter Lynch was hugely successful as a fund manager. His books *Beating the Street* and especially *One Up on Wall Street* are well worth reading even today. Not only do you get a unique insight into his investment strategy, but also a picture of the times that, as we will point out in the book, could be eerily similar to today.

Going through the list of Nifty Fifty stocks again, a few things should stand out. First, a number of companies are still alive and kicking after all these years, such as Disney, McDonalds and IBM. Other companies were once leaders but failed to adapt and have disappeared, or are greatly reduced in market value (Eastman Kodak, Polaroid). Secondly, there is a rule – but rules are meant to be broken, of course – that says the winners of one decade are not the winners of the next. Because after the Nifty Fifty came the growth markets and commodities, before ending up in Japan's great decade in the 1980s. Tokyo saw its peak in 1989, after which the property market and then the stock market imploded. Then we come to the themes that are even fresher in our memory. The 1990s were for tech and especially the internet. The 2000s were for growth markets and commodities with China's entry into the WTO (World Trade Organisation) in 2001. The most recent decade was again for US mega-technology values.

The logical question that always comes up when I show this chart at a presentation is what's next? What is the next big theme? That is by definition unpredictable, no matter how long we study in our library. But regularly peering at the waves can give us some clues. We will review possible contenders for the next few years in this book. And just as naturally, those themes might well be related to the major geopolitical, social, technological and economic developments we will discuss.

Interest rates as a time machine

'Compound interest is the eighth wonder of the world.
He who understands it, earns it; he who doesn't understand it, pays it.'

———

ALBERT EINSTEIN

A very long time ago, there was the loan, and interest was paid on that loan. We know from history books that people have been borrowing and borrowing against interest for more than five thousand years. The custom was not always popular, quite the contrary. In the ancient world, charging a fee for capital was often seen as exploitation and, in case of non-payment, a sure path towards prison or slavery.

As the idea of capitalism became more established, say from the late Middle Ages onwards, interest was seen for what it is or can be: something that is necessary to persuade owners of capital to make their capital available for relatively safe or even less safe ventures; or, for the many other roles it fulfils. Interest on capital, for instance, encourages people to save. More importantly, interest is a means by which capital can travel through time. In other words, a means of comparing different capital flows at different times. Interest lies at the heart of calculating the time value of money. After all, all economic and financial activities take place over time. Interest is often described as the price of money. I prefer the definition given to it by Edward Chancellor in his particularly instructive book *The Price of Time*: interest is the price of time. In life, time is more important than money. Time is the most important currency. We only have a limited number of units of it (at least until science manages to stretch life almost infinitely). Money can be gained, lost and regained. But time that has passed can never be regained. Time is scarce, time has value. So interest is the time value of money.

Today, the idea that interest rates are necessary for our financial system to function is widely accepted. If we want to value an investment project or an asset – think of a bond, a share or real estate, all things that generate cash flows – we simply have to list all the cash flows and calculate them back to today.

$$NPV = -C_0 + \frac{C_1}{1+r} + \frac{C_2}{(1+r)^2} + \dots + \frac{C_r}{(1+r)^T}$$

$-C_0$ = initial investment
C = cash flow
r = discount rate
T = time

If we knew all the cash flows in the numerator and the appropriate discount rate r perfectly, there would be no discussion about the value of an asset. Then it would just be a matter of arithmetic. But in the real world, there is a large degree of uncertainty. With a bond, the coupon (in the numerator) is basically fixed, but the r can vary greatly due to the up and down of interest rates and cause the value/price of a bond to fluctuate considerably.

With a stock, the uncertainty is even greater. As here, both the numerator (dividends that depend on future earnings) and the denominator are difficult to predict. It partly explains why equities are more subject to sentiment than bonds. When investors look at the world through rose-tinted glasses, future profits are invariably set very high. When pessimism is rampant and the bears have the upper hand on Wall Street, those same profits are estimated (too) low, leading to a much lower valuation of equities.

Let us now focus on the denominator for a moment, the discount rate, which is largely determined by interest rates. If the r is very high, it means that the future is worth relatively little when calculated back to today. Because of the principle of compound interest, after a time, we soon find ourselves with a 5th or a 10th or a 15th power. This means that if we calculate the 10th, 11th or 15th year back to today, it will not be worth as much in today's money. Let this sink in for a moment: high interest rates mean that when time travels from the future to today, that future becomes worth less. The reverse is true when interest rates are low. Then future cash flows back to today are worth a lot. It becomes very extreme when we have extremely low or negative interest rates, as we saw a while ago. In short, this means that there is hardly any discount rate on the future and that the future becomes infinitely valuable. This has two major consequences. First, many more investment projects are accepted because the future cash flows become worth a lot. Second, the theoretical valuation of just about all assets becomes very high. In our investment world, this translates into (sharply) rising prices of stocks, real estate and bonds, among other things.

Viewed this way, it is not so difficult to see how central banks, by raising and lowering interest rates, can not only boost or slow down the economy, but also have a huge impact on the value of all assets. This explains why 2022, the year when interest rates rose sharply and thus gravity returned, was a difficult year for both equity and bond markets. It also explains why technology and biotech stocks are a lot more sensitive to interest rates dancing up or down than, say, a food company. (Bio)tech stocks have a lot of their cash flows sitting (far) in the future. That is why the discount rate is so important. The food company, like all companies, also has a lot sitting in the future, but the cash flows of the next few years still carry a lot more weight. When you look at it this way, it suddenly becomes a lot more reasonable that the more speculative piece of the technology puzzle is the first to take major hits when interest rates rise. After all, these are technology stocks that will hopefully be very profitable in the future, but still burn a lot of cash in the coming years. They will also bounce back strongly if there is even a slight indication that interest rates will fall again.

The interest rate cycle is more important than the economic cycle

This brings us to a concept that is not always easy to grasp. For equity markets, the interest rate cycle is often more important than the economic cycle. There is often a perception that a recession is particularly bad news for stock markets. And of course a recession is no fun. The economy cools down, consumption and investment fall and unemployment increases. In the real world, this is undeniably not good news. In the financial world, in our formula, this means that a large number of the counters are decreasing and as a result, *ceteris paribus*, the value of the stock must therefore decrease. But there is more than just the numerator. A recession invariably pushes interest rates down as well. That means the discount rate in the denominator decreases and future cash flows continue to increase in value. I cannot stress this point enough. If you had bought every time the economy was doing well but interest rates were firmly increasing over the past 30–40 years, and sold every time there was a crisis or recession but against the backdrop of falling interest rates, the timing would have been massively wrong in the vast majority of cases. It leads to a golden rule: when you see the bottom of the recession, at a time when interest rates are probably still falling, it is usually not a bad time to become more active in the stock markets. This may seem counter-intuitive, but it is what the stock market history of the past years teaches us...

The Maestro, the Nobel laureate, the reverse kaizen

All this makes the role of central banks and their impact on both long-term and short-term interest rates even more important. To understand how we got to the current situation, we need to go back in time.

Over the course of five thousand years of widely fluctuating interest rates, they have never gone as low, and even negative, as during the aftermath of the 2007–2008 global financial crisis and the 2020 global pandemic. Governments and central banks undoubtedly had good reasons to shore up and provide liquidity to the system through extreme policy on interest rates, and when they could no longer go any deeper, quantitative easing (massive buying of government and, to a lesser extent, corporate securities to depress long-term interest rates) as well. Without those interventions, the financial crisis and/or pandemic would probably have ended in a depression similar to that of the 1930s.

But the story actually begins with Alan Greenspan. Once the world's most admired central banker, he became chairman of the Federal Reserve in August 1987. He was immediately put to the test when, on 19 October 1987, the US stock market crashed by more than 20% during 'Black Monday'. Alan Greenspan then firmly cut interest rates. Looking back at a long-term stock chart now, that gigantic one-day drop is barely visible. The loss from the crash was made up in just a few months. Nor did the US economy go into recession. From that windy autumn day in 1987, the US Federal Reserve, and with it all the world's leading central banks, followed a new mantra: use the interest rate weapon – and later the liquidity weapon – whenever the real economy gets into trouble and/or a crisis of any kind breaks out (war, pandemic) and/or financial markets come under too much pressure.

In the 18.5 years Greenspan held the reins, the interest rate weapon was deployed with the regularity of a Swiss watch. Greenspan emerged as the patron saint of Wall Street's bull crowd. He became the ultimate provider of liquidity to the economy and the markets. To use our elephant metaphor, he was not afraid to open the money tap. Paul Volcker got inflation under control. But under Alan Greenspan, his successor, the idea arose that the economic cycle should also be abolished and recessions were out of the question. The world and its political rulers saw that it was right. Greenspan was awarded the Presidential Medal of Freedom and knighted in the UK.

Sir Greenspan's successors, Ben Bernanke and Janet Yellen, bravely continued down the same path. But they had to be inventive. At a certain point, there were no interest rates left to cut because interest rates were already zero and sometimes even less than zero. There is still a limit today on how far you can drop interest rates. If a bank charges you too negative an interest rate, you can decide to take all your money away and put the cash in a sock or under the mattress. That's not really safe. But it does set a lower limit somewhere on how low one can go. This is why a digital currency and the complete abolition of cash is not without its dangers. Because then, one bad morning, when central banks find it necessary to stimulate the economy, we could all face a negative interest rate of 5 or 10%.

Since this was not yet possible, new liquidity weapons had to be brought into play. The technicalities of all these weapons, such as QE (quantitative easing by buying government and other bonds), ZIRP (*zero interest rate policies*) and TARP (*Troubled Asset Relief Program*) to name a few, are beyond the scope of this book. What is important to note is that they are all ways of further easing monetary policy and flooding the world with liquidity, when interest rates have sunk so deep that they cannot be lowered. And once again, the world saw that it was right. Ben Bernanke was awarded the Nobel Prize in Economics for a number of by no means undeserving papers. And also, in part, for defusing the 2008 financial crisis.

Central bankers' liquidity injections can be seen a bit like 'negative kaizen'. In the mid-1980s, when the Japanese stock market was riding high (the peak of the Nikkei225 index was in 1989), we were inundated with Japanese management books containing wonderful concepts. One of them was 'kaizen'. You have the water that forms the surface of a river, or a lake. As you lower that water surface, you see pointy stones sticking out of the water. Those are your problems. You take away those stones. You solve the problems. You lower the water surface again and so on. In this way, the system gets better and better, more and more robust.

But what central bankers have been doing for many years is reverse kaizen. Every time a problem occurs, of whatever nature, a lot of liquidity (thousands of billions) is thrown over it. Until we no longer see the problems. When problems reappear after a while, the water level is raised again.

'How long can this go on?' business leaders and investors regularly ask us. Our answer has always been: almost indefinitely. Or until what happened in 2022 occurs: inflation suddenly starts rising. And then central bankers are forced to downsize their balance sheets and raise interest rates. They will be obliged to lower water levels. If you do that in a river like the Dijle in my college town of Leuven, there are bicycles sticking out of the water besides stones. And two such bikes were Silicon Valley Bank and Credit Suisse.

Perhaps one of the most important conclusions we can already draw here is: if inflation returns structurally, if we return from a world without gravity to a world with gravity, if TINA (*There is no alternative*) and TRINA (*There really is no alternative*) leave the building, and central bankers can no longer do what they have been doing since October 1987, then we will be living in a structurally different investment world.

The law of unintended consequences

In the coming years, we will undoubtedly face the unintended consequences of central bankers' actions over the past few years. In 2012, Canadian economist William White published a research report entitled *Ultra Easy Monetary Policy and The Law of Unintended Consequences*. In it, White argued that extremely low interest rates encourage households to spend more, to consume and therefore to save less. Pulling consumption from the future to the present has the disadvantage of being less likely to accumulate savings for the future, not to mention retirement, while lower interest rates actually make it necessary to set aside more to reach a certain amount.

Interest rates that are too low also misallocate capital: it prevents capital from flowing from less profitable to more profitable projects. As a result, productivity falls and so-called zombie companies (weak companies that survive only because they are constantly fed with almost free money) persist. As a result, the process of renewal and regeneration in the economy cannot take place sufficiently.

It encouraged speculation and risky investments. Even among pension funds and insurance companies, which have to take more risks to achieve sufficient returns. It is often rightly noted that financial markets have been limping from bubble to bubble and crisis to crisis in recent years. The seas of liquidity circulating in the system, which are reduced from time to time, are at least partly responsible for this.

It may sound like a paradox, but precisely because central banks try to guarantee stability and banish the economic cycle at all costs, they themselves become a major source of instability. No one studied and described this paradox better than Hyman Minsky. This American economist, who died in 1996, became best known for his 'instability hypothesis'. His central idea is that stability destabilises, that in a stable economy everyone tends to take ever greater risks, which eventually undermine stability. As the economy continues to do well for longer, memories of a past crisis fade. Increasing optimism during years of economic growth and stability leads many to believe this is normal and act accordingly. Indeed, optimism causes almost everyone to start believing that trees grow to the sky. More and more people want to take advantage of rising prices in the financial markets. This means they no longer see any danger, become reckless and take more and more risks. Then a spiral begins in which the prices of financed assets – stocks, bonds, houses – rise faster than the actual production of goods. Minsky argues that as a result, an economy with a good, robust financial structure with mostly normal financing slowly but surely turns into an economy with a 'fragile' financial structure, where speculative and Ponzi financing dominate. Share prices rise very rapidly in this phase, without being supported by economic fundamentals.

Minsky sees three stages in the growth of financial markets, each with its own type of financing. In normal financing, there is sufficient income to pay the interest and repay the debt, often with long-term bonds. In speculative financing, income is sufficient to pay the interest but not to service the debt. In this case, a funding risk arises because borrowers in this debt often have to roll over short-term debt or sell other financial assets to repay that debt. With Ponzi financing, there is insufficient income to both repay the debt and pay the interest, which only increases debt, as well as financing risk. The term is named after Charles Ponzi, who set up a pyramid scheme in the US in 1920, where the 'profit' for existing customers was paid out with the money new customers put in. Once existing customers started withdrawing their initial deposits or the accretion of new customers stopped, the fraudulent system collapsed. These three stages are not independently operating units. They often reinforce each other, blend smoothly into one another, and both lenders and borrowers are to blame.

Governments also saw their cost on their debt fall sharply, which removed the brakes on taking on more debt. Why should a government put its fiscal house in order when central banks provide low interest rates? Kicking the proverbial can down the equally proverbial road is the name of the game.

A final point not to be underestimated is that central banks increase inequality in society by driving up the value of all kinds of assets through their actions. To benefit from an increase in the value of assets, one must of course own these assets. And if possible, own many real assets. On the other hand, it becomes difficult for young people to buy a piece of real estate when its price seemingly rises faster than the value of their savings. All this could create social unrest and fuel populism, as a part of the population no longer believes that the economic system or the world order benefits them.

An important conclusion for investors is that when central banks' actions drive up the price of assets, it is best to own as many real assets as possible and that it can be very useful to put some loans against them (without exaggerating, of course). In such a world, the value of those real assets will rise systematically, while the real value of debt will fall rapidly due to inflation. On the other hand, if central banks are forced to turn off the money tap and the value of assets falls, the opposite effect may temporarily occur. But since governments themselves have accumulated quite a lot of debt, this is obviously something the central bankers will not continue for too long if at all possible...

The most important thing to take away from this chapter is how crucial interest rates and liquidity are for all asset classes. Whether the money tap is turned on or has just been turned off has the power to override, in the short term, all the other long-term trends that we will discuss later in this book. Therefore, no single trend, theme or idea can be separated from whether we are in an environment where monetary conditions are tight or money is flowing abundantly. The second situation is clearly preferable from an investment perspective, at least in the short term. But always beware of the unintended consequences...

TEN
to REMEMBER

1   The stock market crash caused by the Covid pandemic was actually a very
    good entry moment.

2   When markets crash, time slows down. A week seems like an eternity and
    that requires investors to have nerves of steel.

3   Due to the increase in inflation since 2022, central bankers can no longer
    do what they are used to doing. They have to reduce their balance sheets
    and let interest rates rise. This means that we live in a structurally different
    investment world.

4   Central bankers can open and close the tap of market liquidity. But it is the
    elephants, especially investors and companies, who determine where the
    water ends up.

5   Interest rates are like a time machine, allowing cash flows to travel through
    time and different capital flows to be compared.

6   Interest rates are like gravity. If interest rates rise, it pulls down all assets.
    If interest rates fall enough, then even the heaviest assets can fly.

7   The interest rate cycle is much more important to (equity) markets than
    the economic cycle. If you see the bottom of the recession then it may be
    a good idea to buy.

8   The more stability is sought, the greater the risk of instability becomes.

9   We will have to live with the unintended consequences of central banks'
    actions for years to come.

10 As we analyse the megatrends that are reviewed in the following chapters
    and try to assess their impact on financial markets, it is vital to determine
    what the liquidity situation is like. Is the tap open or closed?

1

INNO VATION & PRODUCT IVITY

Rosy scenario for productivity confirmed

Quantum computing changes everything

15 March 2042, *The Global Times* – by Julien Maes

The 10% productivity jump from 2040 doubled to 19% by 2041, according to the US National Bureau of Economic Research (NBER). The breakthrough of quantum computing continues to create efficiency gains, spreading to all sectors. Poorer countries also benefit.

'Spectacular!' exclaimed Professor Bloom at the Economic Forum Congress. 'We had expected an acceleration in productivity but the past few years have exceeded all our expectations.' For the third year in a row, the Forum, the global economic event of the year, was all about productivity. 'It reminds me of Ernest Hemingway's novel *The Sun Also Rises*,' Bloom said. 'How did you become bankrupt?' ask Bill. 'In two ways,' said Mike. 'Gradually and then very suddenly.' That's how productivity went.

General artificial intelligence

The evolution over the past decade is indeed spectacular. Since 2032, productivity growth slowly crept higher from less than 1% to 4% in 2039. 'Over that period, productivity climbed more or less as we predicted,' explained brand-new Nobel Prize winner for Economics Brynjolfsson. 'Thinkers became almost a quarter more productive over this period with the help of general artificial intelligence. They produce almost 60% of total US added value, bringing the overall increase in productivity for the whole economy to 15% over this period.'

Then came the breakthrough of quantum computing. In the US, productivity growth shot up to 10% by 2040. By 2041, that doubled to 19%, according to the latest figures from the NBER. Suddenly, complex problems that were almost unsolvable on traditional computers could be solved. Calculations that used to take months with supercomputers now took barely a few hours. 'No one could have predicted the enormous impact this breakthrough has had on almost all sectors. Not even me,' joked the 84-year-old emeritus professor from MIT.

Quantum computers

News of the breakthrough spread quickly. 'When solving complex problems, exponential calculations have to be performed on huge amounts of data,' explained Laure Le Bars, research director of the Worldwide Alliance on Quantum Computing. 'Classic computers have problems with that. Quantum computers don't. We knew that combining these computers with artificial intelligence (AI) and machine learning algorithms would create fireworks.'

Business investment doubled in less than a year. Quantum computing was deployed across all sectors to solve sector-specific challenges resulting in downright spectacular productivity gains. During the panel discussion, UPS boss Bala Subramanian testified to huge efficiency gains and cost reductions through route optimisation, reduction in transportation costs and order bundling. The CEO of General Electric estimated productivity gains in his materials division at nearly 30% since the breakthrough. New materials were developed, ideally suited for innovations in renewable energy, electronics and specialised industrial processes. The BNP Paribas CEO pointed to major improvements in high-frequency trading, risk analysis and portfolio optimisation as an explanation for the 50% higher profits last year.

Developing countries

Productivity growth is manifesting itself in all western countries. Will developing countries follow? Roland Sachs of the Global Development Institute has no doubt. 'Huge investments in renewable energy and infrastructure led to an average annual productivity growth rate of 5% in the 2030s. A chunk of the wealth gap with western countries has been closed as a result. Quantum computing will provide almost free energy, breakthroughs in batteries with much larger and longer storage capacity and much more. This will create a cascade effect, enabling unlimited desalination, for example. That alone will stop further desertification, bring drinking water for all, and increase agricultural productivity.' Many things that were not possible until now will become possible with cheap energy. And, according to Sachs, we are on the eve of the commercialisation of nuclear fusion. 'The era of poor versus rich countries will soon be a thing of the past.'

Professor Bloom closed the conference with a tribute to Nobel laureate Paul Krugman, who died earlier this year. 'Productivity is not everything, but in the long run it is almost everything, Paul said a very long time ago. Paul, you were wrong there. Productivity is just everything!' ●

the
PRODUCTIVITY
BOOST

KEY POINTS

✓ Increased productivity is the only source of growth for ageing Western economies. Human hands are not involved, if at all. New General Purpose Technologies are needed for this. These lead to fundamental changes in the production process, new laws and regulations, and a differently skilled workforce. This will take time though.

✓ AI with ChatGPT (GPT) as its flagship may be one of the standard-bearers of a (some say explosive) acceleration in productivity. AI as GPT does take time – at least another decade, experts estimate – before showing up in productivity figures.

✓ The problem with the digital product innovations of the past decade is that productivity gains are passed on in the form of consumer surplus - more wellbeing - but not in producer surplus - more welfare. Only the latter is included in GDP.

✓ Alternative calculations to measure realised consumer surplus suggest an increase in annual GDP of between 0.1 and 0.9 percentage points. The problem remains that such theoretical productivity growth does not address the high global debt levels.

QUESTION: How will productivity evolve globally?

ChatGPT: It is difficult to predict exactly how global productivity will evolve in the future. However, there are some factors that will potentially affect productivity.

First, the increasing automation and digitisation of the economy is likely to lead to an increase in productivity. This can happen through reducing human error, increasing efficiency and reducing costs.

In addition, the increasing globalisation of the economy can lead to an increase in productivity, as companies can take advantage of cheaper labour costs and other benefits of international cooperation.

Another factor that could potentially affect productivity is the development of new technologies and innovations. These can lead to new ways of producing products and services that are more efficient and effective.

Finally, the development of employees' education levels and skills can also affect productivity. Companies that invest in training and development of their employees may be able to increase productivity through improving the skills and knowledge of their employees.

In general, it can be said that global productivity is likely to continue to increase in the future, but this depends on a number of complex and unpredictable factors.

The breakthrough of AI

ChatGPT is just one of OpenAI's developments that shows the general public what AI is capable of. It is a chatbot that can write accurate text at lightning speed, but you can also ask the super brain to write poems, recipes or computer code. Or children's books, as design manager Ammaar Reshi did by combining ChatGPT with Midjourney and some other AI tools. Midjourney is an image programme that generates a unique combination of pixels based on a command. That programme won a local art competition in the state of Colorado in early September 2022 based on input from digital artist Jason Allen. Allen had fed the model with a description of the image he wanted to see.

The negative reactions to Allen's artwork and Reshi's children's book are misplaced. Some people accused Reshi of 'stealing' other artists' work, as AI art programmes often train themselves on copyrighted data. But that seems no different from an average artist finding inspiration by studying Picasso or Gaudi. And shouldn't we welcome tools that open up creative fields to more people? The other side of the coin also quickly became clear. Publication submissions of science fiction and fantasy stories for the online Clarkesworld Magazine, usually about five a month, skyrocketed after ChatGPT was launched in November 2022. By February 2023, the tally reached more than five hundred.

OpenAI is the standard-bearer of generative artificial intelligence, which made a complete breakthrough in 2022 and has since pocketed a billion-dollar investment from Microsoft. Elon Musk, along with Sam Altman, the current CEO, founded the research centre in 2015. According to Altman, with AI, we are moving 'on an exponential curve' that will turn society upside down and create enormous wealth. According to Sundar Pichai, Google's boss, this is 'the most profound technology humanity is working on – more profound than fire or electricity or anything that we've done in the past.'

Will AI become one of the drivers of a new productivity boom, just as the PC was in the 1990s (especially in the US)? 'At its core, AI, like computing in general, is about saving mental labour,' argues blogger Noah Smith.[1] 'If it extends the powers of our minds the way physical technology extended the powers of our bodies, another productivity boom is probably ahead.'

The importance of productivity

Tom Davidson of financier Open Philanthropy expects artificial intelligence (AI) to have a huge impact on idea generation.[2] The idea-based theory of long-term growth attempts to explain 10,000 years of gradually accelerating growth. More ideas resulted in more people (new agricultural techniques fed more people) generating more ideas. Until, in the late 19th century, people decided to become even more prosperous but stop having children: the per capita growth rate of the most advanced countries remained more or less constant from then on.

AI could boost that growth again, according to Davidson: 'Imagine if AIs could generate new ideas just as well as humans. They could come up with better computer designs (better hardware), and more efficient ways of running AIs on those computers (better software). As a result, more AIs could run on each computer. In addition, the AIs' ideas could create wealth that is invested into creating more computers on which to run AIs.' That positive feedback from AI catapults annual economic growth towards 30%. Fellow researcher Ajeya Cotra estimates the chances of developing such a transformative AI before 2100 to be 80%, and 50% before 2050.

Peter Berezin, the Chief Strategist of Canadian research firm BCA Research, also seems convinced of the potential. When I presented him with the above figures, he replied: 'If we achieve artificial general intelligence like this, AI that AI learns and evolves itself, then we have to start thinking exponentially. Then we have to go back to the agricultural or industrial revolution. Then we can even go towards a period of 50% productivity growth per year! When? I think it can be done in the next 10–15 years!'

Besiroglu and his colleagues at MIT Future Tech hold out for a doubling of productivity compared to the past 70 years.[3] Deep learning, the key technique in AI, must become good enough to be widely used in research and development (R&D). It can then fuel knowledge production through more thorough and better research and recombination of a wider range of ideas than human scientists. According to the authors, its implementation leads to an increase in deployed physical capital where deep learning significantly increases processing power and permanently increases the production of ideas as well as growth. Scaling this up is easier than finding more scientists. To illustrate: today, capital investments such as computers account for barely 6% of all STEM research centres funded by the US National Science Foundation. Scientists are the main expense and idea generators. But for how long?

AI's entry into the pharmaceutical world is already under way through collaboration contracts (Bristol Myer Squibb and Exscientia) and acquisitions of AI companies (BioNTech's purchase of InstaDeep). During the Covid crisis, AI discovered that an Eli Lilly rheumatoid arthritis drug also has an effect as a coronavirus inhibitor. AI also helped develop UCB's psoriasis drug Bimzelx. The promise of AI is that increasingly powerful computers and self-learning algorithms, which you feed and train with data, can comb connected databases. As a result, they will discover new disease targets and ideal drug candidates faster.

'Productivity is not everything, but in the long run it is almost everything,' said Nobel laureate Paul Krugman.[4] Economists Alan Blinder and William Baumol share the same view.[5] According to them, small differences in productivity growth add up over long time periods, like compound interest in a bank account, and can make a huge difference to the prosperity of a community. Nothing contributes more, they say, to reducing poverty, increasing leisure time and a country's ability to fund education, public health and environmental care and the arts.

Economic growth is the sum of the growth in the number of workers and the number of hours they work, and their productivity. With an ageing population, keeping the number of workers stable in developed countries is already becoming a tall order. Therefore, it becomes all the more important that each worker can deliver as much output as possible. In the European Union and Japan, future economic growth will at most equal that productivity growth.

The first (1700 to mid-1800s) and second (mid-1800s to mid-20th century) industrial revolutions saw an explosion in productivity. In the third, the computer revolution, productivity growth was the great absentee. From 1891 to 1972, US labour productivity grew by 2.3% a year, according to Professor Robert J. Gordon.[6] The returns achieved on the inventions of the second revolution slowly died out, causing productivity to fall to 1.4% over the period from 1972 to 1996. Meanwhile, by the 1960s, the computer age had arrived. This produced a surprising observation: 'You can see the computer age everywhere but in the productivity statistics,' American economist Robert Solow articulated the paradox in 1987.

The productivity paradox

How is it possible that there was no impact on productivity despite all these technological advances? One explanation is that in the 1970s and 1980s, computers and information technology (IT) represented too small a fraction of total capital equipment to have a significant impact on productivity. Critical mass was only built up afterwards. Investment in IT and software (expressed as a percentage of gross domestic product or GDP) multiplied to 4.6% over the period 1960–2000. This eventually resulted – in the US – in a spectacular acceleration in labour productivity to 2.5% over the period 1996–2004. This late visibility should not be surprising. Growth accelerations do not coincide with industrial revolutions. The steam engine was invented in 1705 and widely deployed in the second half of the 18th century. But the full impact of railways on productivity and US growth followed between 1850 and 1900.

This characterises *General Purpose Technologies* (GPTs).* They lead to fundamental changes in the production process and manufacturing infrastructure of industries using the new invention. These new technological systems change almost everything. They change what we produce, how we produce it, how we organise production, the location of production operations, the infrastructure and personnel required, the laws and necessary regulations. This takes time.

Railways enabled catalogue sales in the second half of the 19th century, transforming retail trade. Before that, they already had a significant impact on agriculture, now that perishable goods could be transported over longer distances. In turn, cheap computers and telecommunications equipment led to an increasing flow of complementary inventions. In wholesale and retail distribution, just-in-time stock management led to much smaller inventories. But in addition to ICT investments, companies need to build up know-how and expertise, which is very slow. Consequently, productivity acceleration came only in the second half of the 1990s. And only in the US.

Scepticism about the ICT revolution

Professor Gordon uses an example to illustrate the fundamental difference between the inventions of the second industrial revolution and the innovations coming from the ICT revolution since 2002. Suppose you have to choose between option A and B. With option A, you retain all access and use of the electronic technology that was available in 2002, including your Windows 98 laptop and access to the internet. On top of that, you retain running water and indoor toilets. But you no longer have access to things developed after 2002.

---

* General Purpose Technologies are innovations that engage and move an entire economy. Most GPTs play the role of enabling technologies, offering new opportunities rather than completely finished solutions. For instance, the productivity gains associated with the introduction of electric motors were not limited to lower energy costs. The flexibility of electricity inspired more efficient plant design, with machines placed side by side rather than plants several floors high.

In option B, you continue to use X (Twitter), Facebook and WhatsApp on your iPad to your heart's content. With that option, your access to indoor plumbing (and therefore running water and the indoor toilet) is cut off. The water now has to be carried in and the waste out every day. At 3am on a rainy night, your only toilet option is a wet and muddy trip towards the outside toilet. Which option do you choose?

This imaginary choice, according to the professor, always elicits roaring laughter from listeners because of the obviousness of choice A. The listeners suddenly realise that just one of the many inventions of the 19th century was far more important than the portable electronic devices they have become addicted to over the past decade.

This did not resolve the paradox. The internet-linked 'New Economy' died a quick death. Over the period 2004–2012, US productivity growth fell to 1.3% a year, the same level as during the 1972–1996 period. 'The productivity impact of third industrial revolution evaporated after only eight years, compared to the 81 years (1891–1972) required for the benefits of second industrial revolution to have their full impact on productivity and the standard of living.' Since 2012, US productivity has slowed further to an average of 0.6%.

Yet today, innovation is moving faster than we can keep up with. How is it possible that we do not see that reflected in economic growth? According to Gordon, it is because the focus of the current industrial revolution is not so much on labour-saving innovations, with computers replacing and supplementing humans. Innovations, until recently, were mainly in leisure and communication devices. These have the same functionalities as before, but are now available in smaller or different formats. Think of mp3 players, which have eventually been replaced by streaming services on your smartphone. Or the iPad, which has become the new competitor to traditional PCs. These are product innovations that have been enthusiastically welcomed by consumers. But unlike before, they have not – yet – created a more efficient production process (so-called process innovation). Or as venture capitalist Peter Thiel put it: 'We wanted flying cars, instead we got 140 characters', in a reference to posts on X, formerly known as Twitter.

Columnist John Thornhill writes in the *Financial Times*: 'Listen to the critics and you would get the impression that Silicon Valley has produced little more than one big metaphorical banana slicer in recent years.' He is referring to one of 7,000 (!) reviews by a user of the Hutzler 571 banana slicer. He used to slice a banana with one knife, then wash the blade with water. 'But now, thanks to this device, I have to clean 17 individual blades every time I slice a banana.'

'While trumpeting their own creative genius,' Thornhill continues, 'the giant tech companies stand accused of pursuing innovation for innovation's sake, solving few real world problems while generating new ones. The tech writer Brian Merchant has even declared the end of the Silicon Valley myth, arguing the big tech companies are now more concerned with extracting rents and crushing nascent competition than creating anything usefully new.' Indeed, it is not yet clear whether innovations such as cryptocurrencies, the metaverse or social media contribute anything positive to humanity.

Yet Thornhill sees at least two reasons to believe that we are entering a new phase of more productive use of technology. There will be 150,000 redundancies in technology companies worldwide by 2022. This is not good, but this is offset by a sharp increase in tech profiles at banks, retailers and healthcare companies. The number of US technology workers rose 12% to 6.4 million. So they are deployed more widely across different business sectors.

Second, some of the most powerful technology tools, such as AI, cloud computing and low-code/no-code software are now accessible to all enterprises. It is not only a company's chief technology officer who understands and uses these technologies. The head of the product and marketing division has also started using them.

Personally, I am also optimistic about future productivity growth. But before giving you the reasons for that, let's look at why productivity growth has remained so – seemingly – low over the past two decades.

Measuring productivity

'The crux of the matter is that productivity gains used to be passed on via producer surplus in the form of extra profits,' Professor Theo Peeters, emeritus professor of International Economics at KU Leuven, explained to me a few years ago in an interview for my book *De winnaarseconomie*.[7] 'This was then distributed to employees, resulting in an increase in their income and wealth. Today, the increase in productivity is leading to consumer surplus, resulting in an increase in wellbeing.' But wellbeing is not counted in GDP.

Consumer surplus from digital goods often does not translate into a GDP increase

Consumer surplus or welfare is defined as the difference between the value a consumer experiences when consuming a good – what would be the maximum price I am willing to pay for it? – and the price he actually paid for it. Due to market competition, consumers often pay less than they are willing to pay. This abstract measure quantifies the economic welfare of a consumer who consumes a product. Producer surplus refers to the real income for a firm from the sale of a good. It refers to the real cost of producing the good and the selling price. Only the producer surplus of final goods is included in GDP. No problem arose with classic physical goods from the 20th century, such as cars, books and cassette tapes. Consumer surplus – more people enjoying their cars – increased proportionally to the car producer's income. Doubling the number of cars sold doubles the producer surplus and therefore the contribution to GDP, but also the consumer surplus.

Then came the purely digital goods, such as search robots, social media and digital maps. These have zero marginal cost (whether one person uses a search robot or one million people, the cost to the robot remains identical). As consumers use more of these free goods, consumer surplus increases. But this change in welfare did not result in, or at least resulted in much less of, a change in producer surplus and GDP.

Finally, digital goods are replacing physical goods and services. Encyclopaedias are a good example. We used to spend hundreds of euros buying a paper encyclopaedia, such as the *Encyclopedia Britannica*. Today, all that information is available for free on Wikipedia. At 3.9 billion words, Wikipedia's content is 90 times more words than the online *Encyclopedia Britannica*. *Britannica* pulled the plug on its printed – money-making! – version in favour of the free alternative. As a result of the transformation from a money-making physical product to a digital good, consumer welfare is rising but the encyclopaedia's contribution to GDP is falling. Many of the digital goods we use today are free, such as digital maps, but also online software or streaming music services, online educational resources, social media platforms and apps. 'Free' is the key word here, although sometimes providers still generate income through online ads. The changes in GDP and consumer surplus here are clearly disproportionate and often even opposite.

The speed of a free online payment via scanning a QR code and signature with facial recognition frees up time to do fun things. A smartphone replaces several devices, including (video) camera, alarm clock, music player via streaming service, calculator, computer, navigation device, landline phone, gaming console, video player and recording device. Moreover, a smartphone has new apps and features, such as search engines, social media and instant messaging, which did not exist before. According to one estimate, the total cost of some of these replaced devices exceeds $5,000.[8] Not even the most expensive iPhone is that expensive.

The average American spent about 6.3 hours a day on digital media in 2018, up from 2.7 hours in 2008. By 2020, as a result of Covid-19, that number had risen to 7.9 hours and by 2024 we are heading towards 8.5 hours a day.[9] Most of this time is spent on apps on mobile devices, more than 90% of which are free. As consumers consume more free digital goods, their consumer surplus, and hence wealth, increases. But this is not reflected in producer surplus and GDP. The information sector's share, as a percentage of GDP, remained stable around 4–5% for a long time since the 1980s. Until 2016, when the share slipped to 5.2%, and since Covid-19 towards 5.6%. Technology clearly plays a much bigger role in our lives than it did 40 years ago, but we don't measure it. Nobel laureate William Nordhaus found that companies barely capture 3–4% of the total social returns from technological innovations.[10] The remaining 96 to 97% flows to consumers. To measure the real contribution of digitisation, we need to move away from just measuring production.

Hal Varian, chief economist at Google, calculated the time saved by Google for random searches.[11] On average, it took 22 minutes to answer a random query without Google's help. With Google, that took 7 minutes. That time saving multiplied by the number of searches per person per year at an average hourly wage of $22 results in a saving of $500 per person per year. Although the question is of course whether Google really saves time or not. After all, before the search robot was invented, we simply asked fewer questions.

In 2019, Brynjolfsson introduced a new method by conducting large-scale online choice experiments.[12] Consumers can choose to continue using certain goods or give them up for a certain amount of time in exchange for monetary compensation. For example, the average American values access to Wikipedia for one year at $150, representing an annual consumer surplus of $15 billion. Facebook is valued at an average of $48 per month. Search robots and email are particularly popular. If we include this consumer surplus in US GDP, it would contribute an additional 0.05 to 0.11 percentage points annually. Brynjolfsson uses this method to estimate the consumer surplus generated by the most popular digital goods in the US. For the median American, this is an estimated value of $32,000 for 2017.

Value attributed by median user to online goods (annualised)
Source: Erik Brynjolfsson, Felix Eggers, Avinash Gannamaneni et al.

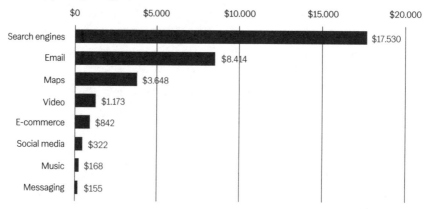

The problem with high or low estimated 'theoretical' productivity growth is that this does not provide a solution for the real high global debts. When consumer surplus is not reflected in producer surplus, it does not translate into a commensurate increase in VAT or corporate tax revenues. So it does not help the government in reducing its debts. An increase in those government debts with GDP growth sharply lower every year due to unmeasured productivity gains results in a higher debt ratio. The fact that consumers attach considerable value to these free products is little consolation for governments.

The crucial question is therefore whether this digital revolution will lead to real productivity gains among producers, resulting in higher profits and higher wages. Again, technology optimists believe we are on the cusp of a growth spurt. They refer to a study by Professor Chad Syverson.[13] He noted that the pattern of productivity growth, since the start of the third industrial revolution in 1970, can be compared to the first 50 years of electrification from 1890 to 1940 (the first part of the second industrial revolution). For the first 25 years, labour productivity grew slowly, as it did in the period 1970–1995. This was followed by an acceleration that lasted a decade: from 1915 to 1924 during the electrification period and from 1995 to 2004 for the IT period. Then productivity slowed down again for ten years (1924–1932) to record a final growth spurt averaging 2.7% over the period 1932–1940.

Perhaps such a growth spurt is closer than we think. My colleague Arne Maes showed that the share of the digital economy* in Belgian GDP has doubled since 1995. It achieves that 5% with barely 2% of employment. We see the same trend in other European countries, by the way. 'If this trend continues, the digital economy will represent a fifth of total Belgian GDP by 2050,' argues Arne. 'That's more than the construction and industrial sectors combined.' So don't despair.

Importance of sectors in Belgian GDP (% of GDP) Source: Arne Maes (2023)

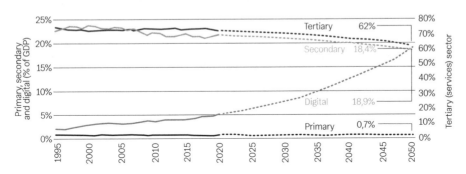

* Included in that digital economy, according to the narrow OECD methodology, are publishing, audiovisual and broadcasting services; telecommunications; computer software, consulting and computer services; computer, electronics and optical products. The latter category, which comprises mainly physical production, was not included.

CHARACTERISTICS
of the
DIGITAL REVOLUTION

KEY POINTS

✓ The new economy is mainly based on intangible assets (IVA), such as Research & Development and patents, building customer and supplier networks, computerised data and software, and human capital.

✓ Features of IVA are scalability, combinability, spill-overs and sunk costs. In such a world, there is more uncertainty, but there are also more ideas that spread faster and on a much larger scale. Because of the complexity, there is a winner-takes-all effect.

✓ These unique features of IVA come on top of exponentiality, the lightning-fast successive doubling, found in digital technologies, among others.

✓ Technology develops according to the law of accelerating returns. Good computers process more and more data faster and faster, helping to make different and better chips. Different technologies also feed off each other, resulting in a constant acceleration of technological change.

✓ People do not grasp the power of exponential growth.

'Most of the gains are still ahead of us,' Brynjolfsson and McAfee argued some five years ago. Progress continues to be exponentially rapid. New technological developments based on existing technologies, they say, are leading to an even wider range of new combinations, which in turn are forcing new breakthroughs. 'In the next 24 months, the planet will add more computer power than it did in all previous history. Over the next 24 years, the increase will likely be over a thousand-fold.'

With those bold statements, the authors of the brilliant book *The Second Machine Age* (2014) expose two of the key features of the digital revolution: digital innovation happens exponentially and combinatorially. Furthermore, the new economy is driven by intangible rather than tangible assets. This too produces specific characteristics.

The non-tangible economy

Let's start with intangible assets, assets without physical form. The use of both intangible assets and digital technologies is often characterised by high fixed costs and network effects (*see sidebar*). Both bring economies of scale that are often unique and cannot be replicated by companies other than the pioneers, leading to a slowdown in technology diffusion. The more complex technologies also create additional barriers. All this leads to the winner-takes-all effect and slows productivity growth coming from efficiency gains.

The death of accountancy

For an industrial company working with tangible goods, the balance sheet gives a reasonable picture of productive assets. Not so for digital companies. According to accounting rules, assets on the balance sheet must be physical in nature, owned by the company and within the company's boundaries. But digital companies mostly own non-tangible assets, and numerous companies have an ecosystem that extends far beyond the company's boundaries. Examples include Uber's cars or Airbnb's rental properties.

The building blocks of Facebook and other digital companies are R&D, developing brands, building customer and supplier networks, computerised data, along with software and human capital. Many of these intangible assets (IVA), such as the estimated value of an internally developed brand, are not found on the balance sheet. They are not capitalised, but recorded directly in profit and loss as an expense. Traditional companies are also increasingly investing in IVA. One consequence is that profit and loss figures and the balance sheet have lost their importance for valuing companies. The correlation between a company's market value and its book value (asset value on balance sheet) and operating profits has fallen from 90% in the early 1960s to less than 25% over the past decade. In the US, investment in IVA exceeded that in fixed assets in the late 1990s. In Europe, the gap is narrowing, but tangible assets still have the upper hand.

Not only are some IVAs often not recognised on the balance sheet, but unlike physical assets, where assets decrease in value with their use, the value of some IVAs increases with their use. Take Facebook: its value, the brand value, increases as more people use Facebook. The more people do, the more interesting the Facebook network becomes for the next user. That is the network effect. However, there is no place in financial accounting for the concept of network effects, where the value of something increases the more it is used. The core idea behind the success of a digital business, the increasing return as one reaches a larger scale, thus goes against a fundamental principle of financial accounting.

All this makes investing even more difficult. Digital companies are much more uncertain than 'physical' companies about their underlying value, as well as about the real drivers of their value creation. Only by interviewing company leaders can the investments in IVA and their hidden value be clarified. Companies could accommodate investors by including additional information in the notes to the annual report. Only then will financial statements remain relevant and avoid the death of accountancy.

On the rise of the non-tangible economy, Jonathan Haskel and Stian Westlake wrote *Capitalism without Capital* in 2021. In 2022, they published the sequel, *Restarting the Future: How to Fix the Intangible Economy*. In the first book, the authors used the four S's to describe what makes intangibles so unique: scalability, synergies, spill-overs and sunkeness, (or 'sunk costs').

Scalability and synergies

An example of scalability – S1 – is Toyota's lean production system, which allows it to quickly spread around the world. Coca-Cola's main asset is the recipe of its secret syrup and the brand name. The formula and the Coca-Cola brand operate similarly, whether it sells a thousand colas a day or one billion (the counter currently stands at 1.7 billion a day). Music and the rights to it are also scalable. Once the first single is printed, you can print as many as you want at a low cost. With digital music, an extra single no longer even needs to be printed and the extra costs are zero.

The low reproduction cost of digital information almost allows it to afford itself the status of a collective good. Because almost everyone can use it at the same time, making it 'non-rivalrous'. Rival goods can only be used or consumed by one person or thing at a time. If I sit on a chair, no one else can sit on it. If I listen to my smartphone with headphones, no one else can use it. But someone else can listen to the same digital music at the same time. This is non-rivalrous. The most important consequence is that digital information does not run out through use.

Number 2: synergies. What happens when you combine the mp3 protocol with a miniaturised hard disk, Apple's design skills and the licensing agreements between Apple and the record labels? The result is the iPod. 'Innovation is what happens when ideas have sex,' British science journalist Matt Ridley stated in a widely watched TEDTalk.[14] These synergies correspond to the 'recombinant' aspect we already talked about. '"Recombinant innovation" refers to the way that old ideas can be reconfigured in new ways to make new ideas,' explains economic historian Martin Weitzman.[15] New things are invented by combining existing techniques. And that development, in turn, forms the building blocks for new development. Major technological innovations therefore first require several smaller technologies to evolve. Today, these are the latest developments in computer chips, communications, the expanded infrastructure of the internet, cloud computing and software applications.

Digitalisation allows millions of creative minds to work with all these new technologies simultaneously and very cheaply. This leads to an explosion of new applications, all of which are combinations of existing technologies. For example, the Google Car combines the capabilities of GPS, sensors and cameras. And an innovative navigation app like Waze uses GPS technology, machine-to-machine communication and sensors. Both also rely on the cloud as an elastic infrastructure. 'The ultimate limits to growth may lie not so much in our abilities to generate new ideas, as in our abilities to process to fruition an ever-increasing abundance of potentially fruitful ideas,' concludes Weitzman.[16]

Spill-overs and sunk costs

The third 'S' stands for spill-overs. IVAs are difficult to protect, to shield. For a self-designed machine, this is easy: you close the factory door and no one can copy your invention. This does not apply to your ideas. While intellectual property rights via a patent, trademark or copyright provide protection, the risk of copying remains: change an idea enough and at some point the patent no longer provides protection. An example is Apple's iOS operating system, which, according to a furious Steve Jobs, was copied and 'transformed' into Google's Android operating system. Ideas are non-exclusive. Therefore, in a world of IVA, new ideas spread more quickly.

A final feature of IVA concerns sunk costs. You invest a lot of money in your idea, brand or management method, but selling it is less obvious. Suppose your company goes under; the machinery can usually be sold quickly. Tangible things are easier to sell because they are standardised and mass-produced, and because they are less uniquely linked to the company. This is not the case with the Lean Production System, in which Toyota has invested millions. How can it split this off from its factories and sell it?

In summary, in a world dominated by IVA, sunk costs lead to more uncertainty. If things go wrong, IVA will be worth less. But if all goes well, they will be worth much more because of their scalability. It is all or nothing, which is annoying for banks when it comes to giving loans. The economy as a whole benefits from successful IVAs because of their easier combinability with other ideas. The spread of all those new ideas, ways of working and software goes much faster because they are harder to lock away. That should ultimately lead to faster growth.

Innovative monopolies

Interview with Joseph Schumpeter: theory is the theatre of the mind

I sit on my bed in Hotel de Meredien on the Opemring in Vienna and once more read the letter's graceful handwriting, from another world and another time.

Dear Sirs De Leus and Gijsels,

As you are writing a book where you will be talking about innovation and my name will inevitably be mentioned, I would like to invite you for a conversation. This is to avoid you doing even more injustice to the truth than you already do. Come to the Burg Kino cinema on the Opemring on January 8 at 9 p.m. When they ask your name when making the reservation, say John Maynard Smith.

Of course this is a joke. But the story is too beautiful and the writing too ornate not to accept the invitation. Koen, as usual, declares me crazy and has refused to come along. But I have a weakness for mysteries. And here I am at a quarter to nine, a stone's throw from a lame joke or a nice story. A lot of snow fell last night and it's at least 30 centimetres deep, maybe half a metre. I cross the street and in the glow of the streetlights, which reflect a thousand times in the snow, I am face to face with some strange-looking creatures and drawings in an art gallery on the corner. This is in stark contrast to the small movie theatre a few buildings down on my right.

But I am out of luck: the cinema is closed. Who goes to the movies in such weather? Of course, I will be laughed at by everyone back home, and rightly so. Just when I'm about to turn around and go for a drink in the hotel bar, the door opens and a young man, dressed in a slim-cut suit along with a tie and hat, comes out.

'Do you have a reservation, Mr...?'

'John Maynard Smith,' I can exclaim, determined to play the game.

The young man nods at me to follow him. We step through the doorway into a dark corridor with sparse lighting here and there and enter a small cinema with red seats.

'Which film would you like to see?' the young man asks.

This setting lends itself to nothing less than Milos Forman's *Amadeus*.

Immediately, the film starts playing. The young man comes and sits next to me. But even before Antonio Salieri can get the story off to a good start, the picture stops. I look at the man next to me and realise he is not so young. I also notice now that he is wearing white gloves and holding an umbrella.

Professor Schumpeter...

'You're not as stupid as I thought,' he says in perfect English with an unmistakable German accent. 'While you are recovering from your surprise and before you can ask a few sensible questions, let me explain a few things that will certainly enhance the quality of your book. You are on the eve of one of the most important waves of innovation, or rather innovation clusters, in history. This in itself is nothing new. But the speed at which it will happen will be greater than you may be able to handle mentally, psychologically and socially. The process of creative destruction will be pretty fast this time. Not least because you have not had a purging of the economy for years: by far too lenient monetary policies, you have kept alive armies of zombie companies...'

I bite down with an initial question.

'In your works *Capitalism, Socialism* and *Democracy* and your two volumes of *Business Cycles*, don't you argue that credit is essential to the innovative process? It is what allows entrepreneurs to get innovation going.'

'Ah, you know your classics. Indeed. Money is the lifeblood; you might say the engine of the process. But at some point, that money has to stop flowing and the ideas that are not viable have to be allowed to fail.'

He takes a dramatic pause that's just a little too long, which gives me time to organise my thoughts.

'Professor, a question that concerns me very specifically at the moment is the following. You say that the creative process brings new innovations in clusters every time. That is the progress that creates wealth. In the process, new companies often emerge to replace the old ones. These new monopolies have a lot of market power and can make very nice profits as a reward for innovation. But today it doesn't look like the established tech giants, like Google, Microsoft and Apple, will be replaced immediately...?'

'Do you want investment advice from me now? "Should I buy Apple?" How uninspiring.' He starts waltzing through the empty cinema. 'The important thing is that progress is free to do its thing. New players will force the big tech giants to be innovative, otherwise they will be replaced. It doesn't matter who wins and is the first to reach a market value of 10 trillion dollars. As long as it...'

Then he stops abruptly, as if he realises he is giving me too much information. He takes a piece of paper from his pocket, unfolds it, writes down a few things, folds it again and carefully tucks it into his inside pocket.

I stare at the hushed screen for a moment and say: 'May I ask one more question, professor? In your work on economic cycles, you build on the work of Kondratiev and his waves. At the moment, I am struggling to count the cycles. If the deflation of recent years was winter, why haven't we had a purge? And if we are now in full inflation, it is summer. Then where is spring?'

'First of all, young man, let me say that I did not build further on Nikolai's work. He merely established that the cycles were there, plain and simple. I gave them a substantiated framework. Schumpeter waves would have been better. But this is an intelligent question. And the answer may surprise you. For the first time in history, winter did not bring a purge. You skipped spring through massive liquidity injections. And you now have an inflationary summer, but still with a gigantic mountain of debt. That's no fun. I lived through the inflationary period of the Weimar Republic...'

'Perhaps at the end of the day, it all comes back to Darwin after all. It is not the strongest, the fastest, or the most intelligent who survives, but the one who can best adapt to change.'

'Yes, yes, yes,' shouts an ever-shrinking figure with ever-more dramatic theatrical gestures. 'I am the Darwin of economics. If you don't kill the planet, you have won. But with that winning comes a huge responsibility. And you must also let the economy take its course. Recessions are like pit stops in your Formula 1. By the way, if I had lived in this era, I would have been the world champion,' he says, stepping back in my direction and taking a slight bow. 'I always wanted to be the best lover in Vienna, the best horseman in Austria and the best economist in the world. Only that second one I did not achieve. But you need the pit stops to recharge for the next rounds. Recessions are part of the creative process. Write that in your book.'

Then suddenly he is gone and I continue watching *Amadeus*, which starts playing again. But I think of Darwin, giant market capitalisations and a year without spring.

Value stocks, growth stocks or unicorns and phoenixes?

What I take away from my alienating encounter with Joseph Schumpeter is that we should bet on companies that manage to create a fresh monopoly through innovation. The zombie companies that displace them are to be shunned.

This is not to say that we should immediately banish all the established names, the companies that have had some years on the clock, from our basket of possible buy candidates. Indeed, some have a very strong market position, a near-monopoly. A 'moat', super-investor Warren Buffett calls it, protecting their corporate profits from possible intruders. Coca-Cola and Microsoft are two examples. Coca-Cola has a rock-solid brand. Who doesn't love the sleds and Father Christmas that come back on the screen around this time every year? Microsoft has its operating system that enabled it to generate enormous cash flows for years and become – and remain – dominant in other fields. But no monopoly lasts forever. It comes down to these companies constantly reinventing themselves. Writer and influencer Peter Hinssen calls these companies phoenixes. They are companies that rise from their ashes through transformation. The unicorns, unlisted companies worth at least a billion dollars, are then the newcomers that may grow into the new leaders.

Some companies, by the way, can get surprisingly old. Currently, the oldest operating company in the world is Kong Gumi, a Japanese construction company founded in 578. The next three are St Peter Stifts Kulinarium from Austria (803), Staffelter Hof in Germany (862) and The Royal Mint in the UK (886).

Both unicorns (after they go public) and phoenixes can be good investments. But both are also subject to Schumpeter's 'creative destruction'. The scythe of innovation mows down young companies as much as older ones if they fail to perform. It is a tough but a fair world. The freshly sharpened blade does not know the distinction.

In short, it is actually the eternal debate between growth stocks and value stocks in a different guise. Mature companies tend to be value stocks. Not always, as an established value can pull off another growth spurt through a radical turnaround. Younger companies coming to the market are usually growth stocks. Not always, because more mature shares can sometimes also float on the stock exchange.

If we look at the long-term picture and plot the performance of growth against value, we see that both have long periods of outperformance and each do deserve their place in the sun in a portfolio.

Growth vs. value, S&P500

So we should not be blind to the beautiful potential of phoenixes. Apple is probably the most imaginative example here. Apple was founded in 1976 by Steve Jobs and Steve Wozniak. It went public on 12 December 1980 at $22 per share. This would convert to $0.1 for all share splits today. Considering where the share price is today, that's far from a bad investment. But it didn't just happen in a straight line. In 1985, the two Steves left the company after disagreements with management over the strategy to follow. Many difficult years of endless battles with Bill Gates' Microsoft, IBM and many others followed. In 1997, Steve Jobs came back on board, made peace with Microsoft and the rest is history. The phoenix rose and created mountains of gold for those lucky enough to own some shares. And not just to own, but to hold. That too is trend following. A lot of investors will have had Apple in their portfolio at some point. But who has experienced a big chunk of the ride? Personally, my biggest misses in investing are not picking stocks that dipped down. Or not even keeping up with these losers for too long. But rather taking profits too quickly on strong risers before the trend had reversed. This is how I have missed a lot of Apple-like moves in the past.

This is a thought I constantly repeat to myself as I sit and watch my screens in the evening or at night. I don't look at lists of stocks that are low or in a clear downtrend. I look at stocks, groups, sectors, themes that are rising and setting new 52-week highs or even all-time highs.

Because when you look at these kinds of stocks, you automatically come across the Apples and other huge risers. Apple cannot possibly go from $0.1 to its current share price without having hit a new high many times along that trajectory. You can go first to your library, read and study, make analyses and develop hypotheses about which stocks, sectors or themes should do well. Then head out into the sea of your screens to see if Mr Market agrees with your conclusion and the idea in question also shows a favourable wave. Maybe you are too early and the movement is yet to come. Waiting a while won't hurt. If the trend is strong enough, the wave huge like with Apple, it doesn't even matter if you are in the late majority. There are entry points enough. But maybe the trend is so negative that it's better to put your idea on ice. The opposite way of doing things also applies and may even be better. You first check which waves are favourable. And then head to the library to try to find out what is driving the movement.

This may present another problem. A lot of investors have a hard time buying stocks that are optically high. Investing in an index such as the S&P500 can certainly help. Call this progressive insight. Because for a very large part of my career, finding the next Microsoft or NVIDIA was pretty much the pinnacle of investment happiness. But sometimes with age comes some sense. The S&P500, the Nasdaq100 or other indices that are regularly reweighted and rebalanced can be seen as a trend-following perpetual. Very regularly, stocks that have not performed well recently are thrown out of the index and replaced by companies that have done well recently. Or to put it in the simple words of Ralph Accampora, one of the most legendary technical analysts ever, 'Good things go up and bad things go down.' And because you buy a basket of stocks, you automatically buy the ones you would never want or dare to buy individually because optically, their price is too high. And those might just be the shares you want for the next few years.

The great master Schumpeter would have found the S&P500 a very nice tool to put his theory into practice. On top of that, the creative destruction at this index seems to be accelerating.

The period that a stock stays in the S&P500 after its entry is now 15 years on average, compared to more than 30 years in the 1960s and even as late as the mid-1990s. Yet another far cry from the exponential age we live in.

But of course, all this is not to say that we should stop looking for the next Apple. Locations for this, as mentioned, are the 52-week high or all-time high lists. From experience we know that we often encounter technology and biotechnology stocks, alongside fast-growing retailers. Remember, when Sam Walton's Walmart went public in 1970, the supermarket chain had just 24 stores and $46 million in annual sales. Every new retailer starts small, but of course not everyone makes it to the finish line so successfully. Along the way, there have been some K-Marts, for those who remember. What is also striking, by the way, is that in every bull market, a shoe manufacturer manages to sprint to the podium spots somewhere. There have already been Adidas, Nike, Reebok, Crocs... I wonder who will be next...

Exponential growth

These unique characteristics of intangibles come on top of the exponentiality found in digital technologies. Underlying this is hardware that constantly cranks up computing power, at an ever-decreasing price. This is the legacy of Moore's Law. In 1965, Gordon Moore, co-founder of chip maker Intel, noted that the number of transistors (the building blocks of a computer chip) on a chip was doubling every year.[17] 'If the auto industry advanced as rapidly as the semiconductor industry,' Gordon Moore once remarked, 'a Rolls Royce would run half a million miles per gallon [or 177,000 kilometres per litre] and it would be cheaper to throw it away than park it.' His law remained in place for 40 years, although today we know that the doubling actually happens once every 18 months.

By the late 2010s, growth in the number of transistors per chip slowed. IBM developed 2-nanometre-sized transistors in 2021, which allowed the company to assemble 50 billion (!) transistors on a chip the size of a fingernail. But that was a full four years after it developed its 5 nanometre chips. The transistors have become so small – barely a few atoms wide – that they will soon be subject to the laws of quantum physics. Then they begin to behave like waves, where they can move through physical barriers and end up in places where they should not be. Moore's Law is reaching its limits.

But this does not mean that the growth of computing power will slow down. According to futurist and Google director Raymond Kurzweil, technology develops according to the law of accelerating returns. Good computers allow us to process more data, which helps us make better chips. And this process, according to Kurzweil, is going faster and faster, and moreover, simultaneously in different technologies.

Historically, technology follows a predictable life cycle with three distinct phases: research and development, adoption of the technology by the masses, and maturity. The first phase is slow, gradual and expensive. Until the technology reaches an inflection point, becomes more cost-effective and adoption increases rapidly. After the invention of electricity, it took 46 years for a quarter of the US population to embrace the new technology. With the PC, it was 16 years. And since 2000, the short tail of the S – the period from R&D to mass adoption – has been reduced to an average of ten years. For the internet, it is seven years. Open AI's ChatGPT already counted more than a hundred million active users two months after its launch. Are we facing a new acceleration?

The evolution of technology

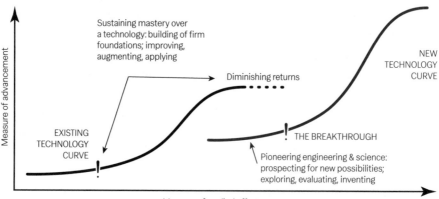

The development of several S-curves simultaneously ensures that when the 'old' technology reaches its maturity (its limits), the newer technology enters its explosive phase. As a result, we end up in a new acceleration phase. More importantly, the different technologies 'feed' each other: innovations in one sector inspire developments in another. The result is a constant acceleration in the pace of technological change, even if the development of individual technologies slows down. And while Moore's Law is indeed reaching its limits, this theory suggests that new ways will be found to meet increasing user demand. However, more computing power will no longer be based on cramming even more transistors onto a chip.

That is exactly what has happened with the development of AI. 'Between 2012 and 2018, the computing power used to train large AI models increased about six times faster than the rate of Moore's Law,' explains author Azeem Azhar.[18] The reason was that just at the right time – as Kurzweil had predicted – traditional computer chips were replaced by (larger) AI chips. These have design features specially optimised for AI, for example, logic gates and parallel computation systems more suitable for typical AI tasks, such as image processing, machine vision, artificial neural networks and so on. Due to this new type of chip, computing power will simply continue its exponential growth in the near future. These graphics chips will reach their limits in a few years or decades, so a completely new approach is now being prepared in the wings: quantum computing.

'Quantum computing represents a step change in our ability to solve difficult problems, in the same way that the development of the modern computer did back in the 1960s,' says Azhar in his podcast with Chad Rigetti, founder and former CEO of Rigetti Computing. Huge amounts of data could then be processed and analysed simultaneously, because in such computers the processor uses the principles of quantum mechanics. Such a processor can perform the same calculations at once – in parallel – over a very large amount of data. This makes the computer up to 100 trillion times faster than a conventional one, but only usable on very specific tasks. 'It is a disruptive form of computing that is going to bring solutions to problems that are today well out of reach of any ordinary or what we might think of as classical computer,' Chad Rigetti believes.

The power of exponential growth

American futurist Ray Kurzweil illustrated sustainable exponential growth with an old story about the invention of chess in 6th century India. The particularly clever inventor of the game travelled to the capital Pataliputra to present his brainchild to the emperor. The latter was so impressed that he asked him to name a reward.

Praising the emperor for his generosity, the inventor said: 'I am only asking for some rice to feed my family.' He suggested using the chessboard to determine how much rice he would get. 'Put one grain on the first square of the board, put two on the second, four on the third and so on,' the inventor suggested, 'so that each square gets twice as many grains as the previous one.' 'Let it be done,' replied the emperor, impressed by the inventor's apparent honesty. After 32 spaces, the entire first half of the board, the emperor had given the inventor

4 billion grains of rice. That is a reasonable amount, about a large paddy field. But the emperor was beginning to pay attention. At this point, the emperor was still the emperor. And the inventor still had a head.

Only when they crossed over to the other side of the chessboard did at least one of them get into trouble. Because that's where the numbers turn into billions, trillions and quadrillions. Then we lose count as the numbers become too big to comprehend. According to Kurzweil, today we are at the second half of the chessboard.

Imperceptible growth

Exponential growth is mind-boggling. People don't grasp it. It takes us by surprise. A characteristic of exponential growth patterns is that the growth is almost imperceptible for a long time. Imagine: one drop of water – 1 millilitre – falls into a football stadium. The number of drops doubles every minute. How long does it take to fill the stadium to the brim? Weeks? Months? Years?

The answer: about 44 minutes!

And the scary thing is that somewhere around the 40th minute, there is still only a little water on the playing field. You are sitting at the very top of the stand, wondering what all the fuss is about exponential growth. Barely four minutes later, you are swimming – or drowning. The situation only becomes alarming just before the water reaches you.

'Academics from fields as diverse as finance and psychology have uncovered reams of evidence that we are hopeless at understanding exponential growth,' argues Azeem Azhar. 'Psychologists who study how people save for the future have identified the "exponential growth bias", which makes us underestimate the future size of something growing at a compounded rate.' People are therefore consistently blown away by the compound growth rate of savings or retirement plans.

The speed at which we are inundated with new technological developments is overwhelming. This is not only true in computing. In 2016, SpaceX and Blue Origin managed to perform a vertical landing with their rockets. Launch. Land. Repeat. Barely five years later, in September 2021, SpaceX put four space tourists into orbit for three days. The launch of the Starship spacecraft costs 97% less than Russia's Soyuz in the 1960s. In 2024, it plans a manned flight with six to eight top people in their fields, plus one or more astronauts, around the moon.

Another example of exponentiality can be found in the mapping of the human genome. The first time, it took more than a decade and cost $3 billion to complete. In 2019, it cost $1,000 and one day, and in the foreseeable future it will be a matter of minutes and one $100 bill. DNA analysis allows cancer drugs to be customised, allowing for more personalised and effective medicine. In turn, diagnosis of hereditary diseases could save many lives.

Sometimes exponential growth is terrifying. If you place a living organism in an environment with unlimited resources, with neither enemies nor competitors, it will always grow the same way: exponentially. Consider Covid-19. At the end of August 2020, we counted 450 additional infections daily in Belgium. In the following weeks, that number doubled to 1,000 in mid-September and almost 2,000 in early October. From then on, it rocketed to 4,000 on 10 October, 8,000 on 17 October and a peak of 17,802 new infections at the end of October.

Our AI future

Is AI 'for real' this time?

'Ships have already set sail on the open sea.
To find the gateway to the Indies.

...

to new ideas
that will sweep everything away.'

———

VICTOR HUGO, *NOTRE-DAME DE PARIS*

Is AI for real this time? Of all the questions we get on the subject, I find this one the easiest to answer positively. Yet the question is certainly not unwarranted, as AI has been talked about for more than 50 years. We have already seen four to five false starts.

So why now? What makes this different? It has everything to do with the way innovation happens. The best book I have ever read on innovation is *Where Good Ideas Come From* by Steven Johnson. He depicts innovation as a round table surrounded by smart people. On that table are parts. Let the smart people play with the parts and new things are invented. But there is a catch, which is the concept of the 'adjacent possible'. This means you have to do inventions in a certain order. For an aeroplane or a car, you need an engine. For a computer, you need semiconductors. Visionaries like Leonardo da Vinci, who were ahead of their time, were already drawing submarines, aeroplanes and parachutes. But they didn't have the parts to build them. And what are the parts, the components, the building blocks for AI? Answer: a lot of computing power and big data. We didn't have those for the last 50 years, or at least not enough. Today we do. Especially if the computing power of quantum computing is added in the coming years, an (investment) trend to keep an eye on. The AI train has left and will not look back.

The consequences for people and society can hardly be overestimated, even though they are particularly difficult to assess at the moment. There is little that divides hearts and minds so much today. We see a broad spectrum, ranging from extremely positive visions to outright doomsday scenarios. Some see the potential for productivity to skyrocket by 30–40%. Others, like economist Nouriel Roubini, warn of the enormous dangers.

Exploding unemployment is undoubtedly one of the biggest concerns. Economic history shows that in the past, new technology always eliminated jobs, but created new ones. In the process, prosperity and comfort also increased. But is it different this time? Until now, new technology has always been a tool, a way to work more efficiently. This is what AI can also become. Perhaps the analysts who argue that jobs will not be replaced by a computer but by a human who knows how to use AI intelligently are right. But computers programming themselves – that's still a bit scary....

Past waves of innovation invariably brought winners and losers. One group of winners were the investors, entrepreneurs and the highly skilled. The relative losers were actually everybody else. At least initially. Because even the lowest-income people in the West live far more comfortably than an average Roman emperor. Fortunately, that's how progress works. But it is clear that the labour market and the way tasks are fulfilled will never be the same again. Take programmers, for example. Not so long ago, it was said that if you could code well, you were set for life. Is this still true today? These are difficult questions, fortunately with a purely economic slant, so I can leave them for Koen. Be sure not to forget to talk to him about it at the next opportunity.

Is AI threatening to become a new internet bubble?

'Stock market bubbles don't grow out of thin air.
They have a solid basis in reality, but reality as distorted
by a misconception.'

———

GEORGE SOROS

In the first chapters, we described in detail how bubbles form. We also pointed out that while a bubble is forming, a lot of profit can still be made. Although of course it's best to leave if it eventually bursts.

To inflate a bubble, you need two things: a great idea or theme that captures the imagination and makes one dream, and fuel – liquidity – to fuel the fire. The former is evident with AI. Any advanced new technology looks like magic to its users. The things AI can do with a few simple commands must feel like some kind of superpower to less experienced computer users. Not to mention computers that will be able to program themselves better than humans can, computers that will do all the work when things are going well and take over the world when things are a bit tough. That's where you want to be as an investor, right?

As for fuel, the story is less rosy for the bubble blowers. In 2022, central banks abruptly turned off the money tap in their fight against inflation, a process that resonated into 2023. Unlike the internet bubble in the late 1990s, when the money tap was wide open, this time there is less cash to keep the tech bonfire blazing. This is not to say that AI-related stocks cannot rise: they suck in cash from other parts of the market and the real economy. But if the AI party had erupted in 2021, when central banks flooded the world with liquidity to fight the negative effects of the Covid pandemic, the flames would surely have flared much higher. But what hasn't happened yet can still come.

It is of course not easy to assign an exact timeframe to this. Some analysts and observers argue that, by analogy with the internet bubble that burst in March 2000, we are only in 1995. Others argue that it is already 5 to 12, or December 1999. My hunch is that we are in 1998 and so will see the bubble grow for another two years or so. But don't quote me on this. Everything in investment land these days has a habit of moving faster, and this is certainly true for AI.

How to invest in AI?

'There will be life and new life, life everywhere on earth.
That was the end: and this is the beginning.'

———

KEVIN CROSSLEY-HOLLAND, *THE NORSE MYTHS*

How can we as investors best participate in the AI theme? To answer this question, it is important to understand how a new industry emerges. It starts with a new, promising idea. That idea gets picked up by investors, who provide massive amounts of money. You can imagine it a bit like a sandbox where new ideas are tested and massive amounts of liquidity are brought in. What is important in this phase of experimentation is that there is sufficient funding to test all possible ideas. A huge number of new companies is also emerging. At the birth of the car industry, there were some eight thousand car companies at one point. In Belgium, we then had Minerva. Other examples are the railway industry and, more recently, the semiconductor sector. The standard work on this was written by Geoffrey A. Moore. You will find a wealth of information in his book *The Gorilla Game*.

The big picture is always the same. At some point, the new sector goes through a shake-up in which all less viable ideas disappear. In the High North, we would call this Ragnarök. But instead of Heimdall, it is Schumpeter blowing the horn and having his heyday.

This phase is quite disruptive and usually accompanied by a sharp decline in all stocks in the industry, as it is often difficult for investors to assess who will survive and who will not. The sentiment around the industry is very negative; what predominates is disappointment. The good news is that at the moment, investors can often pick up very interesting companies at bargain prices. Companies that survive and succeed are often the leaders. They will be the winners in the stock market for many years to come. Think of Amazon and Google, which you could have picked up after the internet bubble imploded and the internet industry came of age. This pattern repeats itself over and over again and is inherent to the birth, growth and maturation of a new industry.

Translating this to today, there are two possibilities. Either we still participate in the first phase and assume it still has a few months or years to go. With the full understanding that at some point there will be a shake-up, it is best to invest as soon as possible. Or we wait until the horn is blown and the winners emerge from the dust. On the one hand, this is not so difficult, as anything that bounces back sustainably is likely to be a winner. On the other hand, it is difficult, because the blows that have been dealt before often mean that no one dares to buy. We are talking about Ragnarök and not the mess that needs to be cleaned up after a party that got out of hand.

What is different this time is that the market currently assumes that tech giants such as Microsoft, Google and Apple will be the big winners of the entire AI story. That's what their share price increases teach us. But a few hundred years of financial history argue against this conclusion. A new industry typically involves new companies and new leaders. The process of creative destruction replaces old monopolies or near-monopolies with new monopolies. That is the reward for the entrepreneurs who build the new industry and survive the shake-up.

Or could it be different this time? That is a very difficult question. Never before in history has there been a club of companies with such impressive market capitalisation, mountains of cash and economic power as those of the current generation of tech giants. Is it possible that they are strong enough to repel the attacks of anyone trying to disrupt them? Or will it still be a few new companies in a student's dorm room or cosy old factory hall in Croatia, New Mexico, Singapore or maybe even Silicon Valley, Chicago or Leuven, that will prevail? I dare not comment on this.

Fortunately, there are other ways to get a piece of the AI story. When everyone is digging for gold, some of the gold miners will become new star companies. But many will fail. With any new gold rush, it is therefore a good idea to invest in the suppliers of shovels and pickaxes. During the internet bubble, these were the so-called equipment makers, the suppliers of cables, servers and routers, the Ciscos of this world so to speak. Today, they are the semiconductor manufacturers and equipment makers for the semiconductor industry. But beware: when the bubble bursts, although these companies will not go bankrupt, they will see their sales fall sharply. Cisco shares moved horizontally for more than a decade after its fall in 2000.

In addition, there are less obvious places to look for AI gold. AI is undoubtedly an exponential technology. Its rapid growth can also help a lot of other technologies grow faster. A good example is the biotech sector. With AI, you can map proteins very quickly. Proteins are very important in medicine because they are often used to attach drug molecules. In doing so, their spatial structure is particularly important. Mapping those easily took several years, and that while there are tens of thousands of different proteins. With AI, the whole exercise could be done in a few months. The data was then made available to the pharmaceutical industry, which helped its growth rate. Drugs tailored to patients will thus become possible faster.

Clearly, the whole AI thing will create yet another mountain of data. This needs to be stored and processed somewhere. Storage and cloud computing will undoubtedly benefit from this. With the crucial caveat – inherent to the internet age – that the quality of what AI produces will depend to a very large extent on the quality of the dataset on which it is trained.

Quality and proprietary data then immediately become very valuable. The investor in me then asks who has the data. I think of Bloomberg, Spotify, Netflix, Uber, Meta, Google, Apple, Airbnb, Visa, Amex, insurers, banks and, yes, the government too. In each case, though, we have to ask which companies can, may and want to use that data.

Then there is the security aspect. After all, you don't want your data to be just up for grabs. The medical profession needs your data to customise medicines. But do you want a future employer or partner to know that you have an increased risk of cancer or another disease? That potentially reduces your chances of getting a job or a relationship. It can also result in having nowhere to get health insurance at an acceptable price.

The same goes for the energy that will have to power the whole circus. Chat-GPT consumes even more energy than crypto mining. This will have to come from somewhere. Therefore, an investment in (alternative) energy is indirectly also an investment in AI. But more on that in the chapter on climate change.

Finally, I want to reflect on something very close to my job. Will artificial intelligence help us predict trends? Will there soon be an AI-powered machine looking through my windows at the world and able to draw better conclusions than me? If trend detection is partly advanced pattern recognition, that might just be possible. After all, trends are often about patterns that occur frequently and within more or less the same time period in different places in the world. It is sometimes already interesting to check which searches are the most common on Google. How often is the word 'inflation' googled, or 'deflation', or 'recession'? Or which stocks are cited most often on Reddit? But it can go a lot further. AI can also look for connections that we cannot name with our vocabulary. In fact, our AI friend looks at the world not through three, but through infinite windows. Though for now, it may not be able to adequately describe what it sees and probably does not realise how beautiful, fascinating and interesting everything it sees is. Or maybe it is laughing, albeit into its electronic hand, at so much human incompetence.

NEW TECHNOLOGIES
& PRODUCTIVITY
ACCELERATION

KEY POINTS

✔ There will be exponential technologies that improve at a rate of 10% a year, at a constant cost, for several decades. The beauty of these is that as their price falls, they pop up everywhere.

✔ Exponential technologies can be found in AI, 3D printing, energy and biology. These technologies have shown spectacular growth rates in the past and will continue to do so.

✔ Important for accelerating productivity is not only that new exponential technologies are available, but also that there is demand for them from households and businesses. A positive sign is the recent surge in investment in intellectual property.

✔ A trend reversal in productivity growth often follows wars, global financial crises, supply shocks and major political changes. With the 'war' on Covid and the Russian invasion of Ukraine, we have been 'spoilt' in recent years.

Besides AI, there is another tidal wave of new developments coming our way. It is the exponential technologies that will have the most impact on society and the economy. According to author Azeem Azhar, these improve at a rate of at least 10% per year, at a constant cost, for several decades. 'The threshold of 10% per year is important. A 10% compounding improvement in the price and performance of a technology would result in it becoming more than 2.5 times more powerful for the same price every 10 years. Conversely, the cost would drop by more than three fifths for the same level of performance. [...] For a technology to be exponential, this change should hold true for decades – and not just be a short-lived trend.' A technology that advances at a rate of more than 10% a year for a few years and then stops would be much less transformative than one that evolves constantly. For this reason, according to Azhar, the diesel engine is not an exponential technology. In contrast, the computer chip industry, with its estimated 50% annual improvement over five decades, does have a claim to the title.

The beauty of exponential technology is that as the price drops, the technology suddenly appears everywhere. Computer chips were first used by NASA and defence missiles. Today, they are attached to packaging, simply to track the movement of products. Along with the falling price, the technology's power and capabilities are exploding. The computing power of a smartphone today is about 100,000 times greater than the computer used for the Apollo moon missions.[19] Exponential technologies are found in AI, 3D printing, energy and biology.

3D printing

According to Jeffrey Immelt, chief executive of General Electric from 2001–2017, 3D printing is already as promising as the internet of things.* 'If you look at what's the common thread between gas turbines, an MR scanner, a jet engines, a locomotive... It's material technologies. Now the way that it is made today is subtractive. You get a block of something and you weld it. You arch it and you take the scrap and it goes someplace and that's how you make those parts today. 3D printing

---

*　In the Internet of Things, machines and robots are connected to each other and to large databases. Big data should make that dream of the bulk of business leaders a reality.

allows you to make that product right the first time. It allows you to make it from the core up and that is the Holy Grail,' Immelt said in 2013.[20]

Meanwhile, parts are already being 3D-printed in aerospace. 'For example, we make interior parts for Airbus,' says Fried Vancraen of Nasdaq-listed Materialise in an interview with Trends magazine.[21] 'Many parts are expected to be 3D-printed when the next generation of aircraft will fly on hydrogen: because of the complexity of the engines, but also to save a lot of weight. Today, 3D printing is already very important in the drone sector, where regulations are slightly less strict and weight saving is crucial.'

3D printing involves melting layers upon layers of material with a laser or a tool that works like an inkjet printer. In 2019, 3D printing was used in Dubai to erect the then largest 3D-printed object: a 232 sq. m single-storey building. The job was completed in 17 days with 75% less cement. Vancraen says the waste issue helps integrate 3D printing into the manufacturing industry.

Until recently, 3D printing was mainly used to print prototypes. Where does the industry stand today? 'It is difficult to give an unequivocal answer to that,' answers Vancraen. 'Many see 3D printing as a kind of one-size-fits-all, while it involves lots of variants of technologies for different materials in various application domains. In a way, you could say it is still in its infancy. Less than 1% of global manufacturing is done via 3D printing. It will never become 100%, but we believe 10–15% is achievable. That is a huge growth potential, which will also provide us with double-digit annual growth.'

Technological developments such as AI and machine learning illustrate the combinatorial potential of new technologies: they make 3D printing more accessible by allowing automated printing in an efficient production process. In 2020, Mordor Intelligence estimated the total 3D printing market at USD 13.7 billion. By 2026, the study firm projects a total market of nearly $64 billion, a compound annual growth rate of 29.5%.

Energy and biology

Besides computer chips and 3D printing, Azhar notes similar exponentiality in energy and biology. 'Each of these technologies is undergoing a spectacular, thrilling transformation. The costs of the key technologies in each area are falling dramatically, by the equivalent of a factor of six or more every decade.' In 1975, solar panels cost about $100 per watt of power produced. Because of their high cost, they were only used on satellites. But between 1975 and 2019, the price of solar panels fell by a factor of 500 to less than 23 cents per watt. In the decade to 2019, the price of electricity generated by solar panels fell by 89%. This meant that the cost of solar panels – like wind power – fell below that of the cheapest fossil fuel: a gas power plant.

Unlike fossil fuel, renewable energy is not an energy carrier. Energy carriers, like electricity or batteries, do not produce energy; they simply contain energy from another energy system or substance (fuel). Batteries are also on the same exponential path. The storage cost of a lithium-ion battery fell by 19% a year since 2010. Large-scale batteries were almost as competitive as coal and gas power plants in 2021. It is highly likely that this falling cost of renewable energy and its storage capacity will continue over the next decade.

With the emergence of the PC, smartphone, the internet, cloud computing and software as a service, AI and so on, we have so far only experienced the transformative power of computer chips in our daily lives. The resulting digital services offer huge benefits for traditional industries, healthcare, finance, tourism and mobility alike. As 3D printing, energy and bioengineering become cheaper and more performant, the tentacles of these GPTs will spread to all aspects of our lives. We are far from there yet. But the productivity gains from, say, (almost) free energy for industrial processes, transportation, agriculture, data centres and so much more are simply beyond our comprehension.

Productivity acceleration

Exponential technologies, such as AI, 3D printing, energy and biology, hold promise. But do they definitely translate into an acceleration of growth? What are the conditions for finally seeing productivity rebound? We often get a trend reversal after major shocks such as wars, global financial crises, supply shocks and major political changes, argue Antonin Bergeaud *et al* of the Banque de France.[22] These are often accompanied by major institutional reforms. Productivity rose sharply from 1939 to 1973, but also after World War I, thanks to the spread of new technologies and demand recovery. The new technologies often emerged from the second industrial revolution, but their widespread rollout and impact on productivity took decades. The 1920s saw the rapid spread of electricity and the automobile, the 1950s automation. These were general purpose technologies that revolutionised daily life. By 1929, 70% of US buildings were electrified compared to 30% immediately after the war. Refrigerators and freezers appeared in homes. These GPTs improved transport connections, facilitated the rapid expansion of cities (and their expansion into the suburbs), created new forms of entertainment, and so on.

Over the past decade, we have seen an acceleration of innovation and dynamism in major technology companies. But increasing productivity requires wider diffusion of new technologies, which has not been the case so far. Weak growth after the Global Financial Crisis put the brakes on IT investment in companies. Supply-side growth of new technologies, which has certainly been there in recent years, is not enough. We also need demand growth through household

Investment in intellectual property vs productivity (in US)
Source: BNP Paribas Fortis, Macrobond

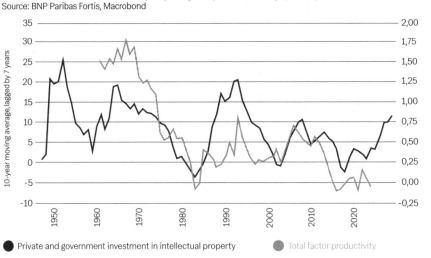

Private and government investment in intellectual property · Total factor productivity

THE NEW WORLD ECONOMY

consumption and business investment. Rising inequality and deleveraging have hampered that in the past decade.

This seems to be changing. The chart shows the relationship between US private and government investment in intellectual property (IP) and total factor productivity (TFP, see legend). Investment, especially in IP, has been at the root of accelerating productivity in the past. In the US, spending on IP grew by about 8% a year over the period 1980–2000. Since then, it slowed down, and from the Global Financial Crisis of 2007–2008, it went down altogether. US productivity followed that movement with a lag.

In recent years, overall investment in intellectual property picked up again. If the past is a guide for the future, productivity will follow. Research by investment bank Goldman Sachs shows that productivity always returns to its average.[23] In the long term – over the past 140 years – it appears that TFP is stable in the US, with alternating cycles of acceleration and deceleration around an annual average of 1.2%. After a long trek through the desert, fruitful years lie ahead. By the way, note that in Europe and in the UK, even more than in the US, productivity growth has only dipped lower in recent decades.

The study by Bergeaud and his co-author refers to shocks that led to trend breaks in the past. And we have not been spared shocks in recent years. At the beginning of 2020, the coronavirus turned the world upside down. In 2022, the war in Ukraine, primarily in Europe, led to a new supply and energy shock.

The Medici Effect

How diversity and inclusion
accelerate the innovation process.

'To steal ideas from one person is plagiarism.
To steal from many is research.'

———

WILSON MEZNER

Everyone today is talking about diversity and inclusion, two sub-trends of our multicultural society. Despite the sometimes uncomfortable discussions, everyone more or less agrees that everyone should be included on the path to a better world and greater prosperity. That everyone regardless of origin, gender, age, skin colour, ethnicity, social background... should be given the same opportunities. In practice, this all seems to be a lot more difficult.

A more inclusive world starts with the realisation that diversity and inclusion inevitably lead to more innovation and thus more prosperity. In our metaphor in which we depict innovation as a table with parts, I have so far mainly focused on the parts on the table. It is high time we looked at the people around the table. I have conveniently called them inventors, engineers, scientists and *bricoleurs*. Of course, this definition is far too narrow. Innovation happens not just at that metaphorical table, but in the minds of everyone connecting ideas and concepts, or in a group of people developing new ideas.

It is therefore time to bring in one of the best books on innovation: *The Medici Effect* by Frans Johansson. The central idea in this groundbreaking book, which is now some 20 years old, is that innovation and creativity happen at the intersection of different domains, ideas, people and cultures.

I always love it when books or films begin with an image that lingers for quite some time. The image Johansson (son of a Swedish father and an African-American/Cherokee mother) conjures up is that of a vision in which bright, colourful rays of light dance around each other and begin to overlap, to intersect.

Each ray of light represents a different domain or culture. But when Johansson looks at each ray of light with his mind's eye, he sees that they are composed of different pieces, like atoms or molecules. Each of these pieces represents a specific piece of knowledge, a concept in the domain.

And this is where it gets extremely fascinating. There are two kinds of ideas: directional and intersectional. Directional ideas arise in one light sample, intersectional ones when the light rays cross each other, when cultures, domains, different perspectives come into contact with each other. Johansson calls these overlaps intersection. And it is here where the magic of innovation is created. Most leading, groundbreaking inventions span different branches of science and are done by groups of people from completely different backgrounds.

Just think of Darwin, who conducted geological research on his ship *Beagle* that eventually sowed the seeds of evolutionary theory. Or the entrepreneur Richard Branson and the somewhat shy musician Mike Oldfield, who put their heads together to cross beams of light from classical music and rock. The result was the masterpiece *Tubular Bells*, and, as a by-product, the record label Virgin.

We know from the film *Ghostbusters* that the rays should never be crossed. But for innovative ideas to emerge, we need to do just that. Let as many rays intersect with each other as possible and at the intersections, new ideas emerge. In the end, it's all maths. After all, there are many more possible combinations between all the concepts of the different rays than between the concepts within a single ray. It is also not difficult to see that the number of possibilities for success increases exponentially every time you add a new ray.

There again is that magical word for innovation and investors: 'exponential'. We are always looking for the new Microsoft, Apple or NVIDIA; things that grow exponentially. To grow exponentially, you need exponentially intersectional ideas. Many people will take issue with the fact that chance plays a big part in this. But there is also good news: the more the rays intersect, the more likely it is that a revolutionary product or process will roll out.

If you more or less accept all this, we have something that not only has enormous implications, but can also be modelled. After all, the next logical question is: how do we as companies, as entrepreneurs, create a situation or environment where the magic is more likely to happen? And as investors, how do we find the situations and companies to participate in?

Let me start with the no-brainer. In order for as many rays to cross as possible, we need to encourage everyone to make as many connections as possible. As always, the theory is simple, but the practice is slightly more difficult. All this is elaborated in great detail, and practically, in Johansson's book. How do we create the Medici Effect and what are the barriers?

As so often, these barriers are in our heads. For a start, there is what is known as an associative barrier. This is a consequence of how our brains have evolved over millions of years. We look for structure in our environment and in our heads. We like order. People with high associative barriers do evolutionarily well because they arrive at a solution quickly. The reason is that their thought process is focused; they very quickly remember how something was successfully solved in the past. When a sabre-toothed tiger comes, you have to run away quickly. That works quite well on the savannah, especially if your neighbour is still thinking about how he will react.

Hearing a word or seeing an image creates a chain of associations in our minds. The image of a fish will evoke a very different set of associations for a chef than for an angler. Scientific research shows that when you put similar profiles together in a group, similar associations tend to emerge. They are less likely to think outside the box.

Another survival instinct ingrained in our DNA is to have faith in what we know, our own species. This can be reflected in the networks that we all develop. But here too we must strive to make our network as diverse as possible. Because here too we are looking for more of us, for a group of like-minded people, for confirmation. In the investment world, this is the famous confirmation bias. We selectively go through all kinds of data to find confirmation of what we already think or think we know. Everything else is neatly swept under the carpet. When I step through my first window on the world, the one from the introduction, into my vast library, I actively look for arguments that contradict my investment thesis. If I am positive about the market or an industry, I look for the biggest gloomy prediction I can find and go through that person's arguments with an open mind. If I am very negative about the market, which also tends to happen, I do the opposite.

A final tip from Frans Johansson: take some books and magazines haphazardly and try to make links with what you are working on at the time and between the books themselves. In practical terms, this is not particularly difficult for me, because in our house there are mountains of books randomly mixed together. I only have to pick up a few somewhere that happen to be lying together. It also often happens that, looking for a book that I definitely have but can no longer find, I bump into something else and thus make a new connection. My wife calls it disorder. Scientists call it serendipity: finding things you are not looking for. But Johansson is right: the more books you read, the more connections you start to see.

As investors, we need to look for innovative companies that can make such numerous and original connections that they can grow exponentially and almost inevitably see their share price rise over time. In practice, this is not always easy. It is impossible to follow all companies and look inside a company as an outsider. But there are clues. Does the company pay attention to diversity? How many women are on the board of directors? Are employees allocated time to engage in side projects? What percentage of sales or profits goes to R&D? How many patents are filed annually? How many collaborations are there with other companies or academia? And the bottom line: does the company have its own research institute or lab? It is things like this that we are looking for.

Fortunately, innovation has a habit of clustering. This means that innovative companies that make lots of connections and grow nicely as a result have an above-average chance of continuing to do so, at least for a while. Nothing succeeds like success. Companies that wear the halo of growth company and innovative workplace are more likely to attract talent. Not just for financial reasons. Companies that are seen as boring and not innovative see their best people leave. That's Schumpeter in action again. The strong get stronger. The weak get weaker and disappear. People and resources flow to the places that show the most promise. But that always takes a while. There is therefore a momentum that we can see. When a company starts growing exponentially, it is not for a single quarter but often for years. And we can capture that momentum. One of the best books on markets ever written is *How to Make Money in Stocks* by William O'Neil. His brainchild, the Investor Business Daily (IBD), has an index of 50 values, stocks of what they call 'The New America'. This is one, but certainly not the only place to hunt for new growth companies and exponential growth.

By the way, humans are very bad at estimating exponential processes. We think linearly. Law is orderly. But that has many drawbacks, including in the investment sphere. One is that we systematically underestimate the growth of fast-growing companies. That is why the valuations of many of the new growth companies seem too high to us, often causing us to miss out on the new Apples and Microsofts. Anyone who resolves never to pay more than twenty times earnings for a share will never have these types of shares in their portfolio. Even worse is to wait until a negative quarterly result or series of them makes one of these companies a lot cheaper. Then you often buy a loser, or at least a company whose growth is declining solidly. The two best books I can recommend for trying to understand exponential growth are *The Exponential Age* by Azeem Azhar and *The Future is Faster Than You Think* by Peter Diamandis and Steven Kotler. These are works to read and re-read, giving courage and hope that we are on the cusp of a period of unprecedented growth. Ideal at times when the Nasdaq index loses 30% or more in six months. Because there will be those too.

As (real estate) investors, we can also look for so-called smart places, places where lots of innovators congregate. Look for places around universities, with good accessibility, with plenty of water and lots of greenery. Places where it is reasonably easy to get a residence permit. I could add: where taxes and duties are reasonable, but I won't. In short, places where digital nomads, who can go anywhere, like to stay. Perhaps America is or was so successful in part precisely because so many different influences and ideas came together. And especially because people managed to make themselves feel American immediately or after just one generation. The inscription above the suitcases in the museum on Ellis Island, for a long time the gateway to the new world and a new life, reads: '*Where we came from*'. It gives me goosebumps every time. It reminds me of the book *American Gods* by one of my favourite writers, Neil Gaiman. Everyone who came to America from all over the world brought their own gods with them. But the gods fell into disuse. The Egyptian gods found nothing better than to go through life as undertakers. But then they set their sights on revenge under the leadership of none other than Odin, who calls himself Wednesday in the book. To grasp that pun does require a few connections.

Perhaps we should now explain why bringing together the different perspectives is called the Medici Effect. It is named after the Florence of the Medicis, a place where lots of fascinating figures from different disciplines came together and gave birth to the Renaissance. At that time, we still had the true *uomo universalis*, whose patron saint was Leonardo da Vinci, who was truly a jack of all trades. Since then, knowledge has become highly specialised and fragmented. But I am convinced that we are moving back to a world of generalists, who can make connections between the specialists, who can unite the rays and ideas. These are the new translators we will need, from one domain to another. I am also very curious about the role AI can play here. At the same time, I worry about the fact that if the world becomes less globalised, or otherwise globalised as Koen calls it, there will also be fewer opportunities for connections, innovation and ultimately prosperity.

I want to end the story of innovation with a powerful image. In the early 1950s, Albert Einstein and the 27-year-old Kurt Gödel regularly walked to and from the Princeton Institute of Advanced Studies in New Jersey. Einstein later explained that what had pleased him most during that time were his conversations with Gödel. Two rebels who had each changed their respective fields, physics and mathematics, beyond recognition, walked together across a beautiful lawn and exchanged ideas. Both were refugees from Nazi Germany, underlining once again that totalitarianism and innovation do not mix well. Both were themselves geniuses with lots of interests. Einstein played the violin, for instance, and Gödel was a big fan of fairy tales. In my mind's eye, I see two giant beams of light moving across Princeton's grass, dancing around each other and constantly making connections. And the investor in me then asks from a safe distance: how can I buy a stake in this?

the IMPACT
of COVID-19

KEY POINTS

✓ Companies accelerated the digitisation and automation of business processes during the Covid pandemic, especially in the service sector and SMEs. These are the traditional laggards in productivity, which means there is now a wider spread of new technologies.

✓ The introduction of homeworking can bring significant productivity gains, especially in the service sector. Less time is wasted commuting and there is more efficient time management and much cheaper accommodation.

✓ Covid particularly affected the least productive sectors, reducing their share of the economy. In a few years we will know whether that shift has lasted and boosted overall productivity.

✓ In contrast, the number of zombie companies has increased. These debt-laden companies have lower average productivity, invest less and siphon money away from start-ups.

Productivity rose sharply after the First and Second World Wars with a long period of economic renewal. Which way will things go following the war against the coronavirus? Business investment, especially in sectors large enough to have an impact on overall productivity, is already an important prerequisite.

Accelerated digitisation

During the Covid pandemic, companies took great strides in the digitisation and automation of business processes.[24] The chart shows that service companies made a leap in digitising their customer contacts in two years, which would normally have taken 4.5 years. Huge leaps have also been made in digitising administrative work. In sectors such as ICT and finance, where staff could work from a distance and companies were able to take advantage of new digital solutions, productivity increased after the initial lockdown. In wholesale and retail trade, manufacturing and accommodation, productivity went up a bit later, but remained strong until quite far into 2021. A temporary boost or a sustainable rise?

The Covid-19 pandemic accelerated the digitisation of businesses
Source: BNP Paribas Fortis

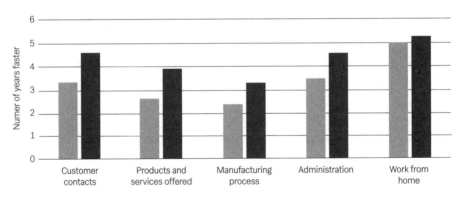

It is striking that progress in the services sector was faster than in industry. Manufacturing has been constantly automating over the past decades. The service sector, which is quite a bit larger, caught up a bit during the period of the Covid pandemic. The same goes for the small and medium-sized companies versus their big competitors. They too are taking bigger steps forward, as the BNP Paribas Fortis survey showed. This is good news for productivity growth, which depends on a wide distribution of new technologies among companies. To this end, the pandemic has certainly contributed.

Paloma Lopez-Garcia, a consultant at the European Central Bank specialising in productivity and the labour market, confirms (via email): 'Yes, there has been a boost in technical update during Covid, in particular in technologies related to connectivity. But I do not think that we are going to see the productivity impacts in the short-run as they need some time and complementary investments to increase the efficiency of production processes.' To take advantage of the most promising digital applications mentioned by the companies – big data analytics, cloud computing, AI – we must wait for the rollout of a high-performance 5G network in Belgium. The cybersecurity risk also needs to be resolved.

Lopez-Garcia refers to technologies related to connectivity. Service companies, characterised by more contact-intensive occupations, were forced to approach their customers differently. E-commerce flourished and consumers followed suit. In the financial sector, the rollout of banking applications, and their acceptance by customers, suddenly went up two gears.

The entry of working from home

In terms of connectivity, the biggest change was undoubtedly the introduction of working from home. Before, employees were allowed to work from home an average of half a day a week at large and medium-sized companies and barely at all at small enterprises. Today, medium-sized Belgian companies are at a fifty-fifty ratio and small companies at two out of every five days. Working from home is here to stay. The different perceptions about the impact of homeworking on productivity are striking, though. According to the bulk of the most technologically advanced firms and large companies, there is no impact. On the other hand, a majority of SMEs see a negative impact.

A study by Barrero, Bloom and Davis estimates the potential increase on US productivity at 5%.[25] Economic blogger Noah Smith fully subscribes to that optimism.[26] 'Reduced commutes, efficient time management, and much cheaper housing will batter down the main costs of service industries – human beings' time and space. Asynchronous management and the blurring of boundaries between companies will allow production processes to be radically reorganised, perhaps to the degree that electricity allowed factories to be broken up into little independent workstations.' Working from home will push productivity higher, especially in the service sector, according to the former Bloomberg columnist. That is by far the largest sector and also the one in which average productivity is lowest.

Besides working from home, companies have also become more aware of the power of data. Improving data quality is crucial in this regard. The better the data is, the more useful it is and the more it helps in making decisions and approaching customers. Process transformation and automation of repetitive tasks also offer great opportunities. As in past surveys, companies indicate that this digitisation and automation will lead to restructuring and job losses. But very positively, almost two in three companies now believe that automation and digitalisation will help the company solve the labour shortage.

Innovation versus employment

'A dystopia is when robots take half of all jobs,' argued Noah Smith. 'A utopia is when robots take half your job.' Innovation and automation caused millions of jobs to disappear in the past. But at the same time, new jobs were constantly being created. We kept pace through continuous training and the growing knowledge economy.

According to McKinsey, the breakthrough of AI means that between 2030 and 2060, some half of current work activities could be automated, a decade earlier than their previous estimates. In 2020, the World Economic Forum estimated that 85 million jobs would disappear by 2025 due to a new generation of smart machines. With 97 million jobs being created at the same time, this leaves a net job creation of 12 million jobs.

Who will be affected? Usually it is the employees at the companies that do not invest in these new digital technologies. You don't lose your job because of AI. You lose your job because of a company using AI. This is also shown by our 2019 survey of 148 corporate clients of BNP Paribas Fortis and 13 Factories of the Future (FoF).[27] The FoFs of technology federation Agoria are forward-looking manufacturing companies using the most advanced digital technologies. When asked about the impact of automation and digitalisation on the number of jobs, almost twice as many corporate customers expected net job destruction in the short term (< three years) rather than job creation. That ratio rose to three to one for the long term.

By contrast, at the FoF, twice as many expected job creation rather than job destruction, regardless of the timeline. The better prepared companies are for the future, the more they see the opportunities of digitalisation and automation, rather than just its dangers. And we also notice this in practice. Over the period 2015–2020, the average turnover growth of all FoFs in Belgium was 14%, well above the 2% industry average. Their productivity growth over that period was almost double that at 9.7%. And despite their advanced digitalisation and automation, employment increased by 13% compared to +1.5% for their competitors.

Automation is increasingly seen as something positive, as a tool for companies. And they could use that help, given the ageing workforce in developed countries. 'Productivity-enhancing AI applications could be precisely what is needed to counter damaging economic trends, such as population ageing,' agrees British economist Jim O'Neill, who thinks the constant stream of warnings from AI experts is exaggerated. 'The UK national health system needs a dramatic uptake of modern technology,' the Times Health Commission member believes.

In the US, during the pandemic, 'The Great Resignation' phenomenon came on top of an ageing population. Millions of people quit their jobs, partly as a result of lockdowns and the new opportunities of working from home. These lifestyle choices about which jobs to do or not meant that companies had, and still have, difficulty finding employees. The choice is then simple: not automating means taking on few additional assignments and limited growth potential. Automating and digitising the production process and services keeps the growth opportunities intact. This also makes us optimistic about future productivity.

Will more technology lead to more prosperity for all?

'A thousand years of history and contemporary evidence make one thing abundantly clear: new technologies do not automatically bring broad prosperity. Whether or not they do is an economic, social and political choice,' Acemoglu and co-author Simon Johnson, both economics professors at US university MIT, write in *Power and Progress*.

'If technology is purely used for automation and tighter control of workers, you will not get a widely shared increase in prosperity,' explains Acemoglu in an interview with *De Tijd*. 'That's lazy automation, which yields few productivity gains anyway, but it pads corporate profits at the expense of stagnant wages.' The hopeless chat robots trying to help your customers are a prime example. AI is in danger of taking that path today: reinforcing the decades-long trend in which digital technology is mainly aimed at gradually automating jobs.

'Another kind of automation is this one that puts machines at the service of human goals by giving us better tools,' says Acemoglu. 'We call that machine utility. That approach has led to some major innovations: the computer mouse, clickable hyperlinks, Google's first search robot.' This kind of innovation enhances human productivity. It leads to robust productivity gains, which are translated into higher wages and thus boost broader welfare. Past examples include Ford's first car factories, which created all kinds of new tasks (machine operation, design, administration). Thanks to their large productivity gains and cheaper car production, they also drove other sectors (oil, steel, chemicals, transport, travel). The choice between replacing humans or enhancing their productivity is a socio-economic and political choice. The further development and implementation of technology can be controlled. 'We have already regulated countless complex technologies. And we are lagging behind in regulating AI because we have chosen not to invest in the regulatory apparatus, in expertise and a strong civil service culture.' Additional obstacle: the technological elite is more powerful than ever.

A more inclusive AI can give us the potential for a new leap in prosperity, Acemoglu argues, with education and healthcare as attractive targets. Think personalised education or digital tools that extend the role of nurses, up to and including diagnoses, resulting in a quality boost. It would boost demand for teachers and nurses as well as their salaries. But that dynamic can only take off if the current obsession with cost-cutting disappears.

Dynamics in the economy

Low productivity, high impact

The dynamics of an economy is another important factor that can boost productivity... or slow it down. 'There is a lot of churning in the economy, with many firms expanding/contracting and entering/exiting the market simultaneously. This churning results in large reallocation of resources across firms, not only during recessions, but at any point of time, in any sector or country', explains Lopez-Garcia.

That redistribution was significant during the Covid crisis. There was – and this is exceptional – more of a significant shift between sectors, less between companies. Those most affected by the Covid pandemic, especially sectors with face-to-face interaction, were those with the lowest productivity, such as hospitality, leisure and culture and certain branches of real estate. Less hard-hit sectors, such as manufacturing or technology-intensive sectors, actually benefited from the necessary online solutions. The contraction of the least productive in favour of the most productive sectors accounted for 30–40% of the productivity increase since the start of the Covid pandemic until the second quarter of 2021, according to ECB[28]. During the five years prior to the pandemic, the contribution of shifts between sectors was negative.

Does the shift of capital and labour towards the most productive sectors permanently jack up productivity? Lopez-Garcia and her colleague Béla Szörfi urge caution in the ECB Bulletin. 'First, it is not clear to what extent the contribution of sector reallocation will persist over time.' Will people remain undiminished fans of e-commerce or will shopping make a comeback? Will the hospitality industry fully recover from the blows? 'Second, reallocating jobs and capital across sectors is always harder, and takes longer, than within sectors, which might weigh on the recovery.' Only in a few years' time will we know the definitive share shifts between sectors that the Covid pandemic has triggered.

More zombie companies

The pandemic certainly increased the number of zombie companies, which failed to cover annual debt repayments with their profits. Their share rose as governments bailed out all companies during the period of the Covid pandemic, regardless of their long-term chances of survival. Before the pandemic, the Bank for International Settlements (BIS) estimated the percentage of zombie companies at 20 and 15% of all listed US companies and all companies globally, respectively. That percentage is certainly higher now.

The upward trend of 'zombification', with their rate tripling since the 1980s, is undoubtedly related to ever lower interest rates. The more zombie companies there are, the more difficult and painful it becomes to eliminate them. In the long run, they hurt productivity and growth potential. Zombie companies are less efficient because they have more debt and therefore invest less. They are also utilising loans that are continuously rolled over and therefore do not go to promising young companies.

the ENERGY TRANSITION

✔ The 750 billion European NextGenerationEU plan is leading to a tidal wave of productive investments, partly because far too little has been invested in recent decades. In contrast to subsidies and cheap loans, there are reforms.

✔ Breakthroughs in climate technologies can create cascade effects with benefits in the most diverse domains and sectors.

✔ These productivity-enhancing factors are counterbalanced by a flood of new green regulations. These gobble up a bunch of non-productive adaptation investments and assets that need to be written off early.

✔ The low carbon economy we are moving towards is more likely to be linked to labour-intensive activities with predominantly lower productivity.

✔ Two very important negative elements for productivity are the (temporarily high) cost of energy and deglobalisation. Both force production in a different way.

The coronavirus slowly faded out at the beginning of 2022. The world, and certainly Europe, was not granted a period of peace, however. On February 24, Russia invaded neighbouring Ukraine. One recovery plan followed another.

Post-Covid recovery plans

When talking about productivity drivers as a result of Covid, Paloma Lopez-Garcia of the ECB argues that we should not forget the NextGenerationEU plan and related reforms. Europe allocated 750 billion euros to help the economy emerge from the pandemic stronger. The initial 672.5 billion euro Recovery Fund (Recovery and Resilience Facility), which awards grants (40%) and loans (60%) to the Member States, is the cornerstone of the plan. After the Russian invasion of Ukraine, the European Commission launched the REPowerEU plan. This should encourage investment in the energy transition, diversify supply and boost energy savings. The money needed for this – 210 billion euros by 2027 – is to be found in the funds not yet allocated under the NextGenerationEU plan. Energy security is now at the very top of the ranking of priorities, though.

Critics are sceptical about the impact of the huge Recovery Fund. They point out that public investment has little impact and often leads to waste. They are wrong this time. This matters little for the short-term boost after the economy climbs out of the Covid trough. As Keynes pointed out, during recessions, even borrowing money to pay people to dig ditches and fill them again is stimulating. Nothing is created, nobody gets better from labour, but incomes are created where there was unemployment. The multipliers do their job, the money earned is spent, new loans are taken out and growth ensues.

This time, mother-in-law, the European Commission, is watching for a favourable effect on long-term growth and productivity. Europe critically examines the submitted proposals and makes adjustments where necessary. Investments must be accompanied by reforms and be at least budget-neutral. That was not the case for Belgium's pension reforms, which blocked the first tranche of almost €1 billion. Meanwhile, the adjusted reform does comply. Even further along in the process, when agreed investment targets are not met, the Commission may again withhold funds.

There is a vision behind the recovery plan: at least one third of funded projects should be green (and including the new REPowerEU initiative, that climate share will increase), 20% should contribute to further digitalisation. R&D, one of the main drivers to boost productivity, is a key component in climate investments. 11% of the EU Recovery Fund has been allocated exclusively to the 'Power Up' flagship programme for the development of clean technologies and renewables. 'Moreover, as a portion of the proceeds from CO_2 taxes and windfall profits of fossil fuel electricity producers will be used to subsidise green R&D,' explains economist Spyros Andreopoulos of BNP Paribas London. 'This will help improve EU productivity. Unifying the electricity grid should also help somewhat, but this process is likely to take an extended period of time, possibly decades.'

Finally, the timing was ideal to get plenty of value for money. The fiscal measures taken since the outbreak of the pandemic were remarkably effective in cushioning the shock. The main reason was that the noses of all countries were pointed in the same direction, and the extremely loose monetary policy at the time further amplified this effect. Public investment spending is also extremely growth-positive: 1 euro of investments generates an average of 1.2 euros of additional GDP output in the following two years, according to a hundred or so academic studies. For tax cuts and transfers, that return is three times lower. That effect is probably even larger now for two reasons. First, these estimates do not take into account the specific effects of digital and green spending. The IMF estimates that every million dollars of investment in renewable electricity creates eight new jobs. For conventional electricity, this is limited to three. In addition, following decades of heavy underinvestment in public infrastructure, interesting and productivity-enhancing projects are up for grabs (*see climate section*).

New green laws

In parallel with the investment plans, the European Green Deal is also rolling out a tidal wave of new regulations requiring companies to invest in reducing pollution. However, adjustments to do so drain resources from other productive investments and also do not generate added value for the company. The result is a short-term decline in productivity growth. The same applies to the billions in future stranded assets, which we talk about in detail in the climate chapter. Moreover, some companies are unable to make such investments for financial reasons, forcing them to cease operations or leave them to an acquirer. In countries with many SMEs, a wave of consolidation is likely to present itself. Retiring baby boomers add to this. In the US, 51% of business owners were 55 or older in 2018.[29] Would you still make the investments and effort to join the climate transition, especially if you had no heirs? The effect on overall productivity growth depends on the relative productivity of exiting and acquiring firms.

And what about new 'green' businesses? BIS notes that a low-carbon economy is more likely to be linked to labour-intensive activities (such as the circular economy).[30] Low productivity is often typical of such activities, which amplifies *Baumol's cost disease* effect* and slows overall productivity and economic growth. Green policies can also increase the barriers to entry for new activities.[31] This may shift certain polluting activities to other countries with less stringent environmental legislation. Europe plans to counter this through the introduction of a carbon border tax from the end of 2026 (see climate chapter).

Green policies also restrict the choice of products and production processes used, requiring the use of sub-optimal inputs and reducing synergies. This also leads to lower productivity growth, especially in the short term.

Cascade effects of climate innovation

But the effect of green regulations on productivity can also be positive, especially in the long run. The Porter hypothesis (Porter and van der Linde, 1995) argues that well-designed environmental policies can promote innovation and productivity, resulting in long-term benefits that outweigh possible short-term costs. Empirical analyses support a weak version of the Porter hypothesis. They show that in the short term, tightening green policies has a positive effect on the productivity growth of a third of companies and a negative effect on the rest.

---

* *Baumol's cost disease*, or the baumol effect, is the negative effect on aggregate productivity due to rising wages in sectors where there was no or hardly any productivity growth. Those wages rise in parallel with rising wages in sectors where labour productivity did increase.

The companies that benefit are the technology leaders in the industry. They are best able to seize new opportunities and quickly deploy new technologies. Less sophisticated companies need relatively more investments to comply with new regulations. That is where productivity drops temporarily. Green policies can also foster the emergence of new sectors or activities with positive spill-overs to the rest of the economy (*see sidebar*).

Savings and new business models in a circular economy

The circular economy is a promising new ecosystem. In such a system, European GDP would grow by 7% and 12% more than in the current linear model by 2030 and 2050, respectively, according to the Ellen MacArthur Foundation. According to Peter Lacy and Jakob Rutqvist, authors of *Waste to Wealth* (2014), a circular economy could generate an additional $45 trillion in economic output by 2030 and $25 trillion by 2050. By comparison, the IMF estimated global GDP at just over $100 trillion by the end of 2022.

The circular economy reduces demand for virgin resources by reusing, repairing and recycling products and materials, bringing down production and distribution costs. For the EU-27, McKinsey calculated a €1.8 trillion (25%) reduction in production and use costs of primary raw materials in the mobility, food and construction sectors by 2030.

New business models are evolving from purely selling products or services related to products (consulting, leasing, product sharing/pooling, outsourcing and so on) to purely services. Often, the producer retains ownership of the product and then offers its use as a service. This shift prevents the producer from simply selling away its responsibility, which is what happens now. Producer, consumer and product thus enter a new relationship with important implications for product performance and longevity. We are moving from 'supply chain to supply circle, from toys to tools and from fashion to function', says Walter Stahel, the founder of the circular economy. 'If you want to reach 100% recycling rate, don't make your Coca-Cola cans out of aluminium, make them out of gold.'

Breakthroughs in climate technologies can also create cascade effects in a wide variety of fields.[32] More than 8 million people die annually – just under one in five of the global number of deaths just before the pandemic – as a result of breathing air polluted by fossil fuels.[33] Better health leads to fewer long-term illnesses and increases input labour productivity. Cheap and abundant energy opens the door to pollution clean-up, cheaper production, et cetera. It brings down the current stratospherically high cost of desalination. Besides quenching thirst, fresh water expands food production and lowers costs. And innovations in agricultural technology – such as vertical farming or lab-grown meat – reduce the consumption of water and polluting fertilisers in food production.

Energy cost

'It is difficult to predict where productivity growth will be in the medium-term, unfortunately,' says productivity expert Paloma Lopez-Garcia. 'There are several tailwinds […], but there are also powerful headwinds. Most importantly, in my opinion, is the increase in energy prices and deglobalisation forces. Both developments will trigger a structural change, a need for a different way of producing.' Or even not to produce at all. In the second half of 2022, electricity and gas prices were at such high levels that it was no longer profitable for many European companies to continue producing. Energy-intensive companies, such as brick manufacturers, chemical, fertilizer and glass companies, shut down a portion of their production capacity.

High European electricity prices are not forever

European electricity prices hovered around 50 euros per megawatt-hour (MWh) between 2018–2020. Due to the war in Ukraine and the subsequent gradual cut-off of Russian gas supplies - almost 40% came from Russia - Europe had to quickly look for other gas suppliers in 2022. It has succeeded in this, in combination with a decrease of 10 to 15% in consumption. Gas supplies to get through the winter were filled to 95%, especially with LNG imports of the previously challenged US shale gas. The hefty premium that had to be paid for it pushed electricity prices to an unprecedented peak of 600 euros-MWh in summer 2022. In winter, the price hovered around 400 euros/MWh.

Gas supplies in 2023 are high compared to the past. Yet uncertainty for the coming years remains high as well. Projected European electricity prices for the winter months are fluctuating on the European futures markets between €100 and €150/MWh until at least 2027. That is well below the peak, but still triple the 'normal' electricity price. That weighs on European competitiveness and productivity.

As Europe adopts more alternative energy sources, the shortage is shrinking. With the construction of additional gas terminals and LNG ships, the tightness in the gas transportation market also decreases. The current regional gas markets, with pipelines as the main means of transport, then turn into a global market. Price differentials between the US and Europe will fall. European industry is not doomed.

Price of electricity in Europe Source: Intercontinental Exchange (ICE)

Average electricity price 2018–2020: 50 euros per megawatt hour

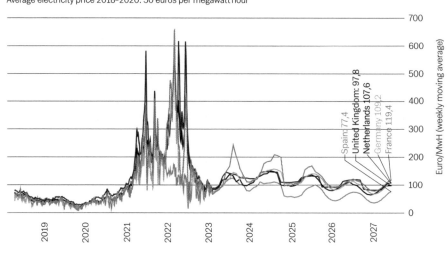

Global European players were pitted against international competitors. With gas prices five to six times higher than in the US, competing was impossible. On top of that came the at least $380 billion US Inflation Reduction Act (IRA; *see Climate, Multiglobalisation*). A consequence: German chemical giant BASF announced in late October 2022 that it would permanently cut its investments in Europe. BMW chooses South Carolina for its new battery plant, Norwegian battery company

Freyr does the same in Georgia. China also continues to fully subsidise its own climate and high-tech industries. Europe risks losing its energy-intensive industry.

In light of this 'distortion of competition', Europe launched its own green industrial policy. By the way, the NextGenerationEU plan was already well underway. The Green Deal Industrial Plan extends a regulatory framework to the NextGenerationEU plan to create a more favourable environment for the production of net zero emissions technology and products that enable it.

Launching industrial policies in numerous regions will accelerate the climate transition. But free-market advocates despair. The state has a poor record of choosing the most productive investments. Rising protectionism is also another step towards deglobalisation. Are we inevitably heading in that direction?

TEN
to REMEMBER

1   Increased productivity is the only source of future growth for ageing Western economies.

2   The problem with recent digital product innovations is that productivity gains are passed on in the form of consumer surplus – more wellbeing – but not in producer surplus – more welfare. Only the latter is included in GDP.

3   Alternative calculations for realised consumer surplus boost annual GDP by 0.1 to 0.9 percentage points. But such theoretical productivity growth does not address high global debt levels.

4   Artificial intelligence with ChatGPT fuels hopes of productivity acceleration. But the general spread of new technology takes time.

5   The new economy is built on intangibles with the characteristics of scalability, combinability, spill-overs and sunk costs. There is more uncertainty in such an economy, but there are also more ideas that spread faster and on a much larger scale.

6   Rapidly developing exponential technologies can be found in AI, 3D printing, energy and biology. As their price falls, they are popping up everywhere.

7   A trend reversal in productivity growth often follows wars. This is promising, as with the 'wars' against Covid and in Ukraine, we have been 'spoilt' in recent years.

8   The Covid pandemic accelerated digitalisation and automation most among the least productive companies and sectors. In contrast, more zombie companies emerged.

9   The tidal wave of productive investments by the European NextGenerationEU plan is being neutralised by new green regulations, leading to accelerated depreciation.

10 High energy costs, deglobalisation and new green regulations are forcing production in a different way and are weighing on productivity.

TEN
to INVEST *in*

1   Monopolies are lucrative to invest in (surprise, surprise).
2   Also keep an eye on companies that constantly reinvent themselves, the phoenixes. They are worth money.
3   It usually doesn't pay to be a frontrunner in the stock market.
4   The S&P500 is secretly a trend-following index, which is why it is so successful.
5   AI is for real, the computing power and data are on the innovation table. Applications will therefore not take long to appear.
6   If we compare AI today to the internet bubble of 2000, it is 1998. So invest quickly, and be careful to spot overvaluations in time.
7   After the inevitable collapse, look for opportunities in the rubble.
8   Whoever owns data has the power and gets the profits.
9   Creativity happens at the intersection of different domains, ideas, people and cultures.
10 Look for companies with diverse boards, with many patents and their own laboratory to expand their knowledge.

CLI2
MATE

2039 marked by climate disasters

Catastrophic year with a glimmer of hope

3 January 2040, *Brussels Capital* – by Jos Vansteeland, editor of Climate

As the world leaves behind the disastrous year of 2039, the mega financing deal between the Big 4 (US, China, India and United Europe) offers a single ray of hope. This deal should get the world out of this vicious global warming spiral. The devastating climate catastrophes did not spare a single continent this year.

'It's heartbreaking to see how our world is gripped by climate change,' US President Celine Johnson said after the climate summit in New Delhi. 'This deal should get us out of this negative climate spiral.' The deal struck between the US, China, India and United Europe includes virtually unlimited funds to develop technology to capture methane. It is estimated that tens of thousands of tons of the gas are being emitted annually from the melting ice caps of Antarctica and Greenland, negating all climate efforts elsewhere. Funding for the energy transition in emerging economies is also being scaled up sharply.

'This is a turning point for humanity, a moment when we must work together and put aside our differences,' said Ding Xuexiang, the new Chinese leader. 'We have no choice but to act together to save the planet.' It is too late to stop the ice caps from melting. The rising concentration of CO_2 is acidifying the oceans and threatening corals, crustaceans and molluscs with extinction as well as resulting in dramatic consequences for other food chains. 'It's not five to twelve; it's quarter past twelve,' argued Rudy Alvarez. The Greenpeace chief executive was invited to the conference.

Heat waves

In 2039, the world once again faced the painful consequences of past government leaders' procrastination, with Africa being the biggest victim. Temperatures in Mali and Ethiopia soared to 54°C, resulting in tens of thousands of deaths. Hunger and war plagued the continent. Millions emigrated between African countries, but many also ventured further towards Fortress Europe, often with fatal results.

But Europe was not spared either. Southern member states were hit by heat waves. Devastation undermined tourism in Spain and Portugal. House prices plummeted. In the north, with Belgium and Germany in the lead, major rivers turned into trickling streams. After repeated flooding of various coastal cities, France finally launched its own Delta Program, following the example of the Netherlands.

Commodities drive inflation

Globally, floods have led to crop failures and skyrocketing grain and wheat prices. European inflation climbed to an alarming 8%. In emerging economies, average inflation reached 20%. Commodity wars and export restrictions are complicating the climate transition in the West.

Destruction hit insurance companies and claims rose to their highest level ever. Several insurers, including juggernaut Insurance First, collapsed. 'Climate change is a reality we face every day,' explained Simon Dupont, top executive at Allied Insurance Group. 'We just no longer can cover certain risks.' ●

There is an old joke about a driver stopping to ask a villager for directions. 'Ah,' says the villager, 'well, if you're going there, I wouldn't start from here.'

That describes our starting point for saving the planet. Ideally, we should not start from here. Sea levels are rising globally (the last time the concentration of greenhouse gases (GHG) in the atmosphere was as high as it is today, sea levels were 20 – twenty! – metres higher), the oceans are acidifying and the world may well be closer to abrupt and irreversible environmental changes – or 'tipping points' – than we think. The average global temperature is currently 1.2 °C higher than during the industrial revolution some 250 years ago. Each successive decade since the 1980s has been warmer than the previous one. The last eight years have been the warmest ever, with 2022 at number 6. The climate is changing and human activity is probably the main contributor to this trend.

Humanity is not doomed, not now and not even in the disaster scenario of 2040 outlined earlier. First and foremost, science should never become dogma. As humble economists, we know this all too well. The 'open mindedness' of the brightest economists should also characterise climate scientists, especially as they are dealing with even more complex phenomena than markets and economies. That being said, the scientific probability that something is seriously wrong with the climate is more than strong enough to change our human behaviour on a global scale. Even if much alarmism turns out to be exaggerated, we would still do well to accelerate the process of treating our planet in a much more sustainable way. Therefore, the best we can do is limit warming to 1.5 °. The many ill effects of climate change worsen as we exceed that temperature.

To do so, we need to ramp up our climate efforts very quickly. We are left with a carbon budget of barely 250 gigatonnes (Gt = 1 billion tonnes). At current annual emissions of 38 Gt, this will be used up in six years. To keep temperatures stable by then, we must have achieved net zero emissions, thereby keeping the GHGs emitted and removed in the atmosphere in balance. To limit warming to 2 °C instead of 1.5 °C, we may emit an additional 350 Gt on top of that 250 Gt. But even that will be a challenge. During the economic disaster year 2020, emissions fell by 5.4% thanks to lockdowns and freezes. Suppose we manage to reduce emissions linearly by 5.4% annually, then after 26 years, around 2050, the budget will still be used up. And 12 Gt of GHGs will still be spewed out every year. Good luck! Talking about net zero emissions, so-called negative emissions, where CO_2 is removed from the atmosphere, are also included in the calculations. For that, we have to count on carbon capture and carbon use (where captured carbon is processed and reused as much as possible), which is still in its infancy today. We will also need to implement reforestation on a mammoth scale.

Naive? It is technically and economically possible. The use of wind and solar energy that avoids emissions has grown exponentially in the last decade – and especially in the last two years. The prices of these energy sources have fallen sharply and are now among the cheapest. But energy storage and decarbonisation of energy-intensive industrial processes, such as steel and cement production, still require more research. Their prices still have to fall before the technologies can be widely rolled out. As do those of carbon capture and use.

It is also politically possible. The progress made at the annual climate conferences, known as COPs, was admittedly disappointing. But awareness is growing. In 2020, former EU Trade Commissioner Pascal Lamy said: 'If you compare the world today with that of 18 months ago, the big difference is that back then only a quarter of the world set a decarbonisation horizon. Today, three-quarters of the global economy has such a horizon.' By 2023, that will have risen further to more than 90% of global GDP.

We are also at an inflection point socially. The Global Climate Strike movement mobilised 7.6 million people in 185 countries worldwide. They want to see actions, not just words. School strikes then turned into global climate strikes. The history of revolutions shows that social movements evolve slowly, but then suddenly accelerate massively. The urgency permeates the world. With an increasing number of catastrophes, the momentum will accelerate in the coming years.

WAR
and
ENERGY

✓ The war in Ukraine accelerated the climate transition by a decade. High energy prices halved the payback time of green energy sources. Annual investments increased dramatically, but should soon double again.

✓ A transition to green energy sources reduces dependence on imported energy. The aim is also to reduce dependence on the minerals and metals needed for the green transition.

✓ The energy transition will only succeed if low- and middle-income countries join in. CO_2 emissions will rise fastest in those countries due to their need for growth to get out of poverty and their rising populations. But investments for the green transition in those countries are sorely lacking.

✓ Rich countries urgently need to fulfil their promise of at least $100 billion in funding annually – and preferably (much) more.

✓ That money can be leveraged to attract private money. Voluntary credits traded on a standardised and regulated carbon market will complete the financing package in the future.

Catastrophes are sometimes tipping points, and the war in Ukraine is one of those. The world has changed. Energy transition now goes hand-in-hand with energy security. The speed of transition has suddenly shifted several gears. The great North-South contradictions were further exacerbated.

Energy transition accelerated by necessity

Energy security first, and that includes a giant finger pointing at naive European politicians. They – and especially the Germans – misjudged Putin, who they thought of as a teddy bear but who turned out to be a grizzly. That ruthless bear turned the European gas tap off without batting an eyelid. 40% of the gas needed in Europe no longer flowed in. The desperate search for other energy sources turned a local miscalculation into a global problem. Europe paid extortionate prices to bring in gas and oil from elsewhere at the expense of low-income countries.

This first energy crisis of the energy transition was not (exclusively) due to Russia. Already in 2021, a year before the war, money was flowing freely into the oil- and gas-producing countries. Extreme weather and resurgent demand after the lifting of the Covid lockdowns doubled and quadrupled US and European gas prices respectively, and oil prices also doubled. The shock had a huge impact on a market without a buffer. This was due to limited oil and gas investments because of low prices in 2015–2016 and 2020, uncertainty about future demand for fossil fuels and public pressure to invest less in them. A pre-famine feast for the oil-producing countries.

Energy security – sufficient supply at a reasonable price – is back. Accelerating the climate transition increases that security. Renewable energy is produced locally. The war in Ukraine reinforced that idea. In the slightly longer term, Russia is shooting itself, and OPEC+ countries, in the foot.

The Economist estimates that war and subsidies shortened the transition timeline by a decade. The global economy became 2% less energy-intensive in 2022, measured by the amount of energy needed to produce 1 unit of GDP, the steepest decline in a decade. Investments in alternative energy sources soared. At a market price of €50 per MwH – pretty much the maximum price for electricity until early 2021 in most European countries – the payback period for a German solar farm is 11 years. Since then, prices have gone up five times and more, pushing the payback period under three years. Notwithstanding the drop, electricity futures in mid-2023 point to a price range of €100–150 for the 2024–2026 period and just under €100 thereafter. That is still at least half the payback period.

Price signals worked (despite the €800 billion that European countries spent to shield businesses and households from skyrocketing energy prices). Governments worldwide accelerated transition plans. The US introduced its Inflation Reduction Act (IRA), which earmarked $370 billion in subsidies for green technology. According to Goldman Sachs, the final cost could be up to three times that, depending on the extent to which the private sector makes use of the unlimited investment credits. In response to IRA, the European Commission added the Green Industrial Plan to its already €750bn NextGenerationEU fund (one-third of which is for green investments). State aid will be relaxed under certain conditions, and licensing for energy projects will be curtailed. The planned doubling of installed solar capacity has shifted from 2030 to 2025. In its fourteenth five-year plan, China is putting forward a target for the share of renewable energy in the total energy mix for the first time: 33% by 2025. Meanwhile, Japan introduced its Green Transformation Plan.

The International Energy Agency's (IEA) report on estimated global energy investment from 2021–2023 is hopeful for the first time in years. Renewable energy capacity should increase by 2,400 gigawatts (GW) over the period 2022–2027. This corresponds to China's entire installed capacity and is a third more than was forecast in 2021. Investments in green energy are increasing faster than investments in fossil fuels by a ratio of 1.7:1. If the former continue to grow at the current pace, by 2030 more than enough will have been invested in infrastructure and electrification to meet the climate promises.

The IEA report also notes that just under 50% of the fossil fuel industry's excess profits in 2022 were diverted back to oil and gas exploitation and exploration. Five years earlier, 82% still flowed back (albeit from significantly lower profits). It indicates that investors are taking into account that climate policy makes such investments much less profitable. Once the transition is complete, the bulk of those assets will be put on hold.

That risk also applies to the 25 planned LNG terminals in EU member states since the Russian invasion. That additional capacity corresponds to about 41% of total EU fossil gas demand. It also exceeds the total past Russian gas imports. If all 25 were built and used, it would increase total carbon emissions by an estimated 1.9 Gt a year, according to Climate Action Tracker (CAT). Option one is that the assets are not used and stranded. Option two is that they are used and we are stuck with fossil fuels for longer.

The energy transition and prosperity through an EROI lens

We are facing one of the greatest transitions in human history. That is both scary and exciting at the same time. Few topics have had as much written and as much nonsense told about them as climate change. It is not my ambition here to add much to that. Except that it is abundantly clear that climate, even more than financial markets, is a complex, chaotic and very difficult system to predict. There are lots of elements that impact it. CO_2 is clearly one of them. And the consensus has grown that CO_2 emissions need to come down and preferably as soon as possible. This fact alone makes both traditional and alternative energy sectors particularly interesting to follow from an investment perspective.

In doing so, it is important to gather as much accurate and well-founded information as possible. History is a good starting point for this, as always. I can heartily recommend all the works of scholar Vaclav Smil. His books are eye-openers in every way. By the way, if you read his work, you are in good company: none other than Bill Gates is constantly peddling his books on social media.

Everything around us is energy. From the first law of thermodynamics, we know that in a closed system, energy can neither be created nor destroyed. Energy passes from one form into another. This brings me to a concept often used by Adam Rozencwajg, a well-known commodity strategist and fund manager: the EROI (*Energy Return on Investment*). Some comparison can be made between EROI and the better-known ROI, which indicates how much return you achieve on an investment. In this case, it becomes: how many units of energy do I get out of an invested unit of energy? Very concretely for our early ancestors: how much energy do I put into making a spear, running after a mammoth, killing it, cutting it up and cooking it versus the energy that my body ultimately extracts from the food? Rozencwajg calculates that the ratio of energy extracted at that time was five to one. So the EROI here is five. With an EROI of five, you should not expect miracles in terms of economic and population growth, as the energy gained from activities is only just enough to earn a living. There was little or nothing left to invest in the future. Of course, there were kings, emperors and pharaohs who built palaces, temples and pyramids. But this was always at the expense of others: slaves, serfs or whatever you want to call them. Famines were commonplace. For a long time, there seemed to be only room in the world for one or a few great empires. Those empires eventually collapsed, because subjects got tired of doing all the work without getting much in return.

But then we get to 1650. In England, they start burning coal instead of wood as a source of fuel. Coal has an EROI (and we round up again) of around ten. Suddenly, the world is ready for the industrial revolution. There is now room for investment and growth. There is more time to think about the world. Philosophy flourishes, the age of enlightenment begins. And of course it is all very polluting, there is a lot of inequality, and terrible things happen, for example child labour, as described in the books of Charles Dickens. But an important step has been taken towards a better world. Koen and I often discuss the so-called trickledown effect. In this, prosperity flows down after a time, perhaps sometimes too long of a time, making everyone better off. By the way, it was the time when Adam Smith laid the foundations for the study of economics with his *Wealth of Nations*. Without an EROI of ten, there wouldn't have been much of an economy, there would have been no *Wealth of Nations* and certainly no Adam Smith. In itself, that would be a shame.

Fast forward to the mid-19th century. Oil is found in 1846 in Azerbaijan, and in 1859 in Pennsylvania in the United States. The EROI once again skyrockets, to no less than thirty. There is even more room to invest in what we now call the modern world.

The crucial lesson is that all our prosperity is built on a growing energy lever. Everything we eat, do or make is energy. The unimaginable challenge on the table today is to try to maintain or increase EROI, while significantly reducing the amount of CO_2 emitted.

It brings us to the key question: what is the EROI of solar, wind and hydrogen, for example? How much energy should you put into these technologies, and how much can you get out of them? I deliberately don't mention an EROI figure here, because I don't want to get bogged down in a discussion about what exactly you do and don't include in the calculations. But let's take the example of a wind turbine. For a 4.5 megawatt wind turbine, you need about 60 tonnes of copper, 200 tonnes of steel and 1,600 tonnes of cement and concrete. You need energy to make all that, in the process also emitting CO_2. Same goes for solar panels, where the shopping list in terms of materials is shorter, but you need to install a lot of them to get to the efficiency of a gas or nuclear plant. And then we get to the electrical grid. There you must ensure that you have sufficient capacity to store energy for when the wind does not blow and the sun does not shine. In practice, backup production is certainly needed today that is still conventional in nature.

Securing energy

Option three is that this creates an (expensive) buffer that can be used in the next energy crisis. The goal of 100% energy from renewables should be maintained. But price shocks are almost guaranteed during the transition. There is a mismatch between building up renewables too slowly and phasing out fossil fuels too quickly. And once the transition is realised, buffers will still be needed when, for example, extreme drought makes net zero carbon energy production (no cooling water) impossible.

It is not just Europe with its total lack of fossil fuels that is susceptible to this. In recent years, the US was the world's largest oil producer and believed it could now do without Saudi Arabia. High oil prices in 2022 again pushed the US to its knees for additional production. But the Saudis did not give in.

Reducing US investments in oil and gas increases dependence on OPEC during the transition period. Its share increases from 30 to 50%, albeit in an ever-shrinking global oil production. US strategic oil reserves become more important than ever. 'The OPEC+ snub of Biden – as part of the broader geopolitical fragmentation – opens the door for a bipartisan "grand bargain" for the sake of energy and national security,' believes Grace Fan of research firm TS Lombard.[34] Such a deal involves subsidising a minimum supply of fossil fuels in exchange for even more carbon-cutting measures. The former pleases Republicans, the latter Democrats.

Graphite, cobalt, lithium and rare earth metals are needed for the production of electric cars and battery cells. 50% of these come from China. The production of solar panels, ranging from polysilicon over wafers and solar cells to the panels themselves, is always at least 80% in Chinese hands. It gives China an immense advantage over its western rivals, possibly until the end of this decade. It is a geopolitical weapon, which it will use in its technology war with the US (and other countries). These will then have to choose a fast and cheap energy transition with China, or a slow, more expensive but safer transition, with friendly countries and without China.

The super cycle in commodities

When we look back at the resource landscape in a decade, we will call the period starting today 'the period of resource shortages'. We are at the early beginning. Commodity cycles are perennial and, like all trends, governed by supply and demand – thus, actually, by fear and greed. We can already hear the scepticism about this message. After all, we live in the age of semiconductors and AI, so who cares about something as basic as raw materials? On top of that, the last major commodity cycle is some 40 years behind us. Few investors active today have actually experienced it. Warren Buffett and his comrade Charlie Munger are two notorious exceptions. Therefore, it should perhaps come as no surprise that they are firmly on the buy side today.

The story is always the same. Let's start with supply. A saying you hear at every presentation on commodities is: 'The best remedy for high prices is high prices and the best remedy for low prices is low prices.' This means that when commodity prices are high, companies flock to those handsome profits and invest more money in the sector. As a result, supply increases and prices eventually go down. If prices are low, logically, there will be less investment and some less profitable players will go out of business. As a result, supply falls and prices rise. The reason why cycles are typically so long is that it takes at least five years for an investment decision to result in real increased supply. If you have found a new resource reserve, it still takes a long time to get the permits and financing in place and build the mine or oil field in question.

The reason why I think we are on the brink of a giant cycle is the massive underinvestment in commodities over the past decade or longer. Since 2010, energy has seen a huge drop in prices, as shale oil and gas suddenly entered the market from America. Prices of most metals were also low, so there were few incentives to invest. Add to that the fact that many big oil and mining giants had overinvested and overpaid for certain assets in the previous cycle, it is not so exceptional that investments have been at historic lows in recent years. Moreover, the energy transition means that investments in fossil fuels and mining are not particularly popular. Even with rising prices, we still do not see money flowing into the sector; on the contrary.

What about the demand side? That is very difficult to predict in the short term because demand depends very much on the economic cycle. But in the slightly longer term, the trends are clear. The chart below shows demand for a number of metals over the next few years. The strong increase is, of course, largely due to the energy transition. If you want to go from *big oil* to *big shovel*, or an expansion of mining, you need a lot of metals.

Estimated demand for metals Source: Bloomberg NEF

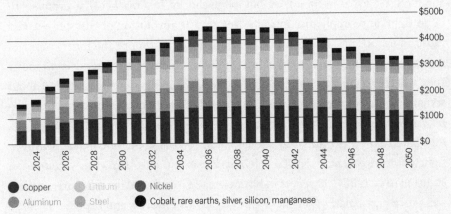

The impressive demand facing us is offset by a supply that is not increasing or, in many cases, is decreasing because the mines are becoming exhausted. Add the two together and it is not too difficult to predict what will happen to commodity prices in the coming years.

Of course, there are a few 'buts'. It is almost impossible to make predictions about total demand over such a long period. Even more difficult is predicting what the demand for metals will look like. Take battery metals, for example. Today, cobalt is needed in batteries, but no one knows whether this will still be the case in the future. It is very difficult to predict what the batteries of the future will look like. Maybe the magicians will find a way to make them in which no cobalt is needed at all, or at least much less. Maybe we will actually need more nickel. Or maybe not. The same goes for lithium, which is very difficult to recycle and of which we are predicted to need much more than we use today. That is, until a method is found to replace lithium with sodium. Remember that at one point aluminium was more expensive than silver because there was no good way to extract aluminium from bauxite.

We are most confident in copper. Copper will still be needed if you want to get electricity from point A to point B, something that will come in handy with the electrical revolution. According to some estimates, several hundred new mines will be needed in the coming years to meet soaring demand. And of course, if only for environmental reasons, we should commit to recycling as much as possible. But that alone will be insufficient.

When we look back in ten years, we will see the next ten years not only as a period of shortages, but possibly also of shocks. We will not then be talking about oil shocks, as in the 1970s, but metal shocks. In a market that promises to be so tight, any supply disruption – due to war, revolution or disaster – could cause enormous price swings. It is no coincidence that more and more countries are calling not only rare earth elements but also copper a strategic commodity. They will try to secure supply. Moreover, copper supply is concentrated in about six countries. Countries such as Chile and Peru are already making efforts to take more control of lithium production within their borders and let the profits flow back to their people. Why shouldn't they do the same for copper? Maybe at some point we will have an OCEC (*Organisation of Copper Exporting Countries*) in addition to an OPEC. Reserves in places located in safe and friendly jurisdictions will prove particularly valuable. However, always ensure a good spread. Because nationalisations, expropriations or failure to obtain permits due to environmental issues are not just imaginary risks.

Three factors are therefore at play for future energy security. First, there is the return to rival superpowers, this time with the US and China in the lead. This makes for a more multipolar and fragmented international system. Applied to the energy market, the West no longer likes Russian fossil fuel, but the Chinese and neutral India do. Further fragmentation of the global energy market reduces the security of energy supply for all and ultimately results in rising prices. This fragmentation is offset by the globalisation of the LNG market, however. Huge investments in terminals and ships are transforming the market from a local to a global one.

A second new reality is the desire for autonomy and diversification of the supply chain among many countries. The Russian war, as well as the Covid pandemic, illustrated the vulnerability of having only one supplier. An accelerated energy transition also increases autonomy through reduced dependence on globally-traded fossil fuels that are subject to changing geopolitical factors. But autonomy simultaneously increases uncertainty: it encourages domestic industries, but thereby increases the risk of protectionism and even more fragmentation.

Third, climate change itself brings uncertainties. Global net zero carbon emissions by 2050 will only be achievable if 50% of global energy consumption is covered by electricity. Today, that figure is 20%. Nearly all that electricity must be produced from carbon-free sources, compared to just 38% today. However, the infrastructure needed for this electricity generation, transmission and distribution is at greater risk of being hit by storms, forest fires or other climate catastrophes. Climate change may also have a negative impact on renewables: by 2100, the Intergovernmental Panel on Climate Change (IPCC) expects a 10% drop in wind speeds as climate change reduces differences in atmospheric temperatures that generate wind.

In summary, in the short and medium term, giant investments push the prices of used materials higher. The mismatch between renewable energy and fossil energy, in combination with geopolitical games, increases price volatility. The next few years will be chaotic. But ultimately, once the most important investments have been made, we will enter calmer waters.

The North must help the South

Governments have to keep a lot of balls in the air to secure the energy supply and transition. Massive investments in solar and wind power have doubled the share of low-carbon-intensity energy – renewables and nuclear – since 2000 to... 8% of primary energy needs. For the first time, this surpasses the 7% share of traditional biomass, especially wood, as a fuel in emerging economies. The share of fossil fuels, meanwhile, remains stable at the remaining 85%.

This exposes another pain point in our quest for net zero emissions: just scaling up renewables is not enough. The use of fossil fuels must also be reduced. This is where emerging economies play a crucial role. Per capita energy consumption has peaked in most developed countries. But in emerging economies, it will continue to increase as the need to lift people out of poverty and raise their living standards will also continue to increase. Low- and middle-income countries also have the highest population growth.

For 72 emerging economies, the IMF calculated that a 1% annual increase in growth has been associated with a 0.7% increase in GHG emissions since 1990. In China, emissions spurted from 3.6 Gt in 2000 to 11.5 Gt in 2021. With more than double the emissions of the US, this makes it the planet's biggest polluter in absolute terms (but per capita it emits half that of the US; in Europe, it averages a third). It is estimated that, by 2030, two other fast-growing countries, India and Indonesia, will emit 800 million tonnes more CO_2 every year. That corresponds to additional emissions equal to those of Germany.

Emerging economies accounted for 42% of total emissions in 2000 (28% excluding China). By 2023, they will account for 65% (34% excluding China). 'The Paris agreement is not at stake in the US. It is not at stake in Europe. They are doing their part,' Francesco La Camera, director-general of the International Renewable Energy Agency, argues in the *Financial Times*.[35] ' The Paris agreement is at stake in the developing world, like Africa, like south-east Asia.'

A truly green transition will require $2.4 trillion in annual investment (or 6.5% of their GDP) by 2030. The Grantham Institute, a think tank affiliated with the London School of Economics, previously estimated that amount at $2.8 trillion, with an additional $3 trillion annually for sectors such as health and education to lift them out of poverty. In 2019, the last year for which reliable figures are available, the combined amount invested stood at $2.4 trillion, not even half that. The think tank suggests an investment of $1 trillion that developed countries should at least match annually. The remaining shortfall will then come from the private sector and developing countries themselves.

Why should the West step in? Because North America and Europe have been responsible for more than 70% of the current GHGs in the air over the past 270 years. Because the average American or Australian emits as much CO_2 in 2.3 days as the average inhabitant of Mali or Nigeria does in an entire year. Because the whole transition fails miserably if emerging economies are left to fend for themselves, even if emissions in the West fall to zero. In 2009, rich countries promised to provide – barely – $100 billion in additional funding annually by 2020. In 2020, funds did not exceed $83 billion.

The consequences of the Russian war rubbed extra salt into this wound. At the 26th climate summit in November 2021, Western countries pledged to halt new fossil fuel projects and fuel subsidies. As a result of the energy crisis, Europe restarted several coal plants in 2022, Brussels and Washington announced a new deal for US LNG and European countries invested in new gas terminals, the UK promised the restart of shale production and European governments implemented energy subsidies. Emerging economies rightly accused Western governments of hypocrisy.

Solutions are available, but first of all they require that Western countries fulfil their agreement. Professor Raghuram Rajan, who in addition to being ex-chief economist of the IMF is also ex-governor of the Reserve Bank of India, came up with an interesting mechanism for a fair carbon tax. The regions that emit the most per capita – the most affluent – contribute to a fund that finances green projects in the regions that emit the least (*see sidebar*) and are most vulnerable to the impact of climate change. Such a global carbon market operates alongside mandatory national carbon markets (e.g. the European Emission Trading System (ETS), see below) and voluntary carbon markets. In the latter, companies finance, for example, reforestation in Guatemala, or a piece of a major renewable energy project in Mali. For this, they receive CO_2 offsets. This is how emerging economies find financing for their projects. Very promising, but today the legal uncertainty for companies in those markets which are not yet regulated or in standardised voluntary carbon markets is still too great.

Global carbon tax proposal

'We need a global carbon tax,' Professor Raghuram Rajan explained in a speech to the IMF. 'And it makes sense. All economists say it makes sense. But it's a one size fits all solution.'[36] Politically, the introduction of a carbon tax in the US today is unfeasible. And for Tanzania, it is unfair because its CO_2 emissions per capita are barely 0.2 tonnes compared to 16 tonnes in the US.

'So the US, which is an over-emitter, would pay [for] 16 [tonnes], which is its average, minus 4.6, which is the global average,' calculates professor Rajan. 'That's the excess that it does, times 325 million US people, times what I call the global carbon incentive. Let's set that at $10 per ton. Think of that as equivalent to a global carbon tax.' That $10 can be increased later, if necessary. 'If that is the case, the US would pay $38 billion into this fund. And when you do the math, it turns out globally, the fund would get about $100 billion. Why does the number resonate in your ears? That is a number that rich countries promised to pay poor countries to help them deal with climate change. Tanzania, an under-emitter, would receive around $2.4 billion by the same calculation. A completely self-financing mechanism.'

That public money can be used to cover the biggest risks of certain projects. This attracts additional money from the private sector. 'Nine to one leverage would get you close to a trillion a year. That's the kind of financing that starts making sense for the climate action we need.,' the former IMF chief economist calculates.

Justice is served. A second advantage of this system is that it sets the right incentives. 'Tanzania has no incentive to increase emissions because it loses out on what it gets. In the same way as the US also wanted to reduce emissions, because that would reduce the amount it pays into the fund. Everybody has the same incentive.'

Finally, it is a decentralised system: countries decide how to limit their CO_2 emissions. Are Tanzania and the US not interested in proposing a carbon tax on their citizens and businesses, unlike the European Emission Trading Mechanism and other carbon taxes in place? Then Tanzania can reduce CO2 emissions by, for example, banning coal. The US can provide incentives instead of a carbon tax, as it recently did with the *Inflation Reduction Act*. 'Different strokes for different folk. All you need to do is make your payments at the national level. What you do domestically is your choice.'

What is also interesting about this system is that it assigns responsibility to other countries. 'What we need is a system of allocating property rights in emissions. This does it.' There is a common budget, an average level of emissions you are allowed to emit. If you emit more, you pay. And you pay as long as you emit more than that average.

To channel additional private investments towards emerging countries, the cost of financing also has to come down. In Western countries, 80% of the financing for green investments comes from private money compared to barely 14% in low- and middle-income countries. The average financing cost for building a solar farm there is excessively high; the average interest rate paid is 10.6% compared to 4% in the European Union, calculated emeritus professor Avinash Persaud. According to Persaud, this is a market failure. He suggests the creation of a joint agency of multilateral development banks and the IMF, which would bring down that cost through hedging techniques. As a result, he says, many more renewable energy projects could be financed.

The conclusion? The war has shifted the transition up two gears. On a scale of 1 to 10, we have accelerated from 3 (way too slow) to 5 (too slow). An additional doubling of the effort is necessary, with the emerging economies in particular having to come on board. But let's take a step back and look at why it is so important that we make this climate transition as soon as possible.

CLIMATE RISKS
UNDERMINE GROWTH

KEY POINTS

✓ In assessing macroeconomic impacts, there is the physical impact of climate change damage, and the transition risks associated with the transition to low-carbon energy sources.

✓ Regarding physical damage, there has been a trend increase in insured damage of 5–7% annually since the 1990s.

✓ Both excessive heat and cold undermine labour productivity and hence growth.

✓ A major risk during the transition period is that certain technologies and products will become explicitly excluded and worthless.

✓ Global warming suffers from the 'tragedy of the horizon': the costs are felt immediately, while the benefits lie further in the future. As a result, policymakers delay action for too long.

Climate risks are not new, but we are now getting to the point where they are imminent and concrete. The macroeconomic impacts of climate change, and governments' attempts to mitigate its damage through 'decarbonisation', will have an increasing impact on the global economy, interest rates and inflation, as well as the performance of financial markets.

In assessing macroeconomic impacts, we distinguish between two effects: the physical impact of climate change damage on the global economy, and the transition risks associated with the transition to low-carbon energy sources. There is obviously a trade-off between the two: the more successful the transition, the better we can suppress the physical risks. The slower our response to climate change, the more both effects are magnified.

The economic toll of natural disasters

Within physical risks, we distinguish between those related to gradual global warming versus the increasing frequency of certain types of extreme weather events. Extreme weather disrupts agriculture, damages international trade and destroys physical capital. It can also affect demand by destroying wealth, undermining confidence and discouraging business investment. Uninsured losses cut into the wealth of property owners. Insured losses hit the financial health of insurance companies and banks. This in turn affects overall financial stability and the cost and availability of credit to the economy. Even a credit crunch cannot be ruled out.

In 2022, natural disasters caused $275 billion in economic damage worldwide, of which $125 billion was insured, according to reinsurer Swiss Re. This is the fifth highest amount since the 1990s and confirms the annual upward trend of 5–7% over the period. Weather-related loss events have tripled since 1980; related insured losses have increased eightfold – in real terms – as urbanisation has led to more assets being concentrated in vulnerable areas. Due to inflation, the replacement cost of buildings in 2022 was also almost 40% higher than in early 2020. These trends are continuing. Without adjustment and in case of a temperature increase of 4.3 °C, the coastal area (and population) subject to flood risk will increase by half by the end of the century. So does the number of assets at risk in those coastal regions, which rises to a fifth of global GDP.[37] Most at risk are coastal regions in the Asian tropics, but also in North-Western Europe. Think before you buy that spot on the coast!

Losses from natural disasters will continue to rise faster than global GDP, according to Swiss Re. In addition, there are tomorrow's liability risks. Parties suffering loss or damage from the effects of climate change may sooner or later demand compensation from those they deem responsible. Compare it to the asbestos protests of the past. In the United States alone, ultimate net claims are expected to cost insurers $85 billion. That is equivalent to almost three times the claims filed for Superstorm Sandy or Hurricane Ida.[38]

Finally, insurers will no longer want to insure a lot of risks, or only at exuberantly high premiums and/or with government intervention. By 2100, $250–500 billion worth of US real estate will be below sea level.[39]

Negative impact
on labour productivity

The economic effects of extreme weather are very visible. But over time, more subtle effects also manifest themselves. For instance, numerous studies show that higher temperatures lead to lower labour productivity. Hot weather and hard work do not mix. Using differences between districts within the US over a 40-year period, Deryugina and Hsiang (2014) found that productivity falls by 1.7% for every 1°C increase in average daily temperatures above 15°C. Persistent heat waves collapse productivity altogether. At 34 °C, workers lose 50% of their work capacity.[40] The global economic damage due to heat stress was estimated at $280 billion in 1995. By 2030, this would increase eightfold to $2.5 trillion, accounting for 2.5% of current global GDP.

Air conditioning may provide relief, but it does not help the climate. Moreover, the more capital goes towards adaptation and repairs due to damage suffered, the less capital flows towards other sectors, like research and development. That in turn undermines the total productivity factor – how efficiently we do things.

There is much less 'learning by doing' in the case of repairs and replacement investments than in the case of investments in new productive capital. There, there are innovation and efficiency gains. The physical impact of climate change can thus undermine productivity, the key driver of economic growth.[41]

In 2015, Burke et al. brought everything together in one model and estimated the impact of temperature on the growth rate of GDP per capita. They assumed that both excessive heat and extreme cold are detrimental to growth. They found that the growth rate of output per capita peaks at an annual average temperature of 13°C and falls sharply at higher temperatures. A projection of the results into the future in a catastrophic climate scenario with a temperature increase of 4.3 °C would then globally result in a fifth less income in 2100 compared to a world without climate change.

Business loss during transition

Governments are increasingly determined to limit the physical impacts of climate change by accelerating towards net zero emissions. But that entails major transition or transition risks. Some sectors of the economy will become obsolete or redundant with new technologies. Governments will also make deliberate attempts to shift resource allocation. They may do this through the stick, for example by banning cars with internal combustion engines by a certain date. Or, as in London, through the introduction of an ultra-low emission zone. Its recent extension to the outskirts of the city costs drivers of the most polluting cars £12.5 ($16) a day! The carrot can also be brought out: promising subsidies to encourage investment in new technologies.

This affects investment, employment and financial markets. There is a high risk of 'stranded assets'. These are companies' assets that become worthless because they are no longer in demand due to the greening of the economy. For instance, to meet the 1.5°C target, 80% of remaining fossil fuels must remain in the ground. For 2°C, it is 60%. That realisation, and the prospect of increasing taxes on fossil fuels, has led to a collapse in investments in exploration and exploitation since 2015.

The transition to a low-carbon economy also suffers from a 'discounting problem': economic costs come first, benefits lie far in the future. Mark Carney, United

Nations Special Envoy for Climate Action and Finance, calls this 'the tragedy of the horizon'.[42] 'We don't need an army of actuaries to tell us that the catastrophic impacts of climate change will be felt beyond the traditional horizons of most actors – imposing a cost on future generations that the current generation has no direct incentive to fix,' Carney explains. 'The consequences are beyond the business cycle, beyond the political cycle and beyond the horizon of technocratic authorities, such as central banks, who are bound by their mandates.'

That is why governments are too slow to respond to climate change. Being slow might result in being too late. There are extreme tipping points that, when crossed, lead to exponential consequences. Economists tend to underestimate that risk. William Nordhaus, who received the 2018 Nobel Prize in Economics for his influential models that intertwine climate and economics, is getting wind of the situation, claiming he underestimates the damage of climate change and overestimates the cost of necessary efforts. 'According to Nordhaus' optimal policy, we could ideally accept a temperature rise of 3 degrees Celsius by 2100, because more ambitious efforts to limit temperature rise to, say, 2 degrees would cost too much in relation to the damage avoided,' writes *De Tijd* journalist Kris van Hamme. 'Except that climate scientists have since agreed that a planet 3 degrees warmer by the end of this century would be catastrophic.'

ECONOMIC
DISASTER
or OPPORTUNITY?

KEY POINTS

✓ With currently announced policies, temperatures will rise by 2.7°C by 2100 compared to the pre-industrial era, according to the CAT.

✓ According to 'degrowth' advocates, we need to slow economic growth to limit temperature rise. But that would have dire economic and social consequences.

✓ We must quickly reduce emissions, especially through a rapid doubling of investments in energy infrastructure and technologies. Investment increases growth until 2030. After that, a gradually rising carbon tax just takes over.

✓ Putting a price on carbon emissions either through direct charging of a carbon tax or through the introduction of an emissions trading system is the most efficient way to bring down emissions.

✓ Today, the average global carbon price fluctuates between $3 and $10 per tonne of CO_2. A minimum price of $50 to $100 is needed to meet the net zero emissions target.

✓ Without a global carbon price, Europe should introduce a carbon border tax.

The Paris climate agreement (2015) aims to limit warming to 1.5 °C. Immediately after that conference, the NGO Climate Action Tracker (CAT) created an indicator that measures the total effect of all emission reduction targets and different countries' other policies and what that means in terms of warming. In its latest update in November 2022, that 'tracker' points to a 2.7°C temperature rise in 2100 compared to the pre-industrial era, the same as in November 2021.

Consuming differently

Will appropriate political policies and technological ingenuity suffice to keep emissions within the carbon budget, or will economic growth have to come down? Global policymakers are planning huge investments to make the transition to net zero a success. According to the degrowth advocates, only fools and economists believe that unlimited growth is possible on a limited planet. 'We should not consume more, we should consume less.'

I think we should change our consumption, not diminish. That is a world of difference.[43] It is the difference between throwing in the towel versus taking up the gauntlet to achieve 'Green Growth' based on a different way of producing goods and spending money. It is an expression of faith in humankind's ingenuity and sense of responsibility.

How do we address this? One interesting way to look at the challenge is by reformulating the production of GHGs. These are due to four factors: the population, the prosperity of that population (the more prosperous, the greater the emissions), the energy intensity of growth and the emission intensity of energy. Assume that we cannot change anything about population growth and prosperity (GDP per capita). Increasing GHG emissions must then be offset by the other two factors (energy use + emission intensity = GHG emissions per unit of GDP). This requires an absolute decoupling of GDP and GHG: GDP continues to rise, but GHG emissions fall. Is this feasible?

$$\text{Greenhouse gas emissions} = population \times \frac{GDP}{population} \times \frac{energy\ demand}{GDP} \times \frac{GHC}{energy\ demand}$$

Until now, GHG emissions per unit of GDP (-1.8% annually) did not fall enough to offset global GDP growth (annual +3.8%). To limit climate warming to less than 2°C, global annual GHG emissions need to fall by 45% by 2030, to zero by 2050 and negative emissions thereafter. With no limit on population growth and projected population welfare growth, this means an annual decline in GHG emissions per unit of real GDP of 9% until 2050. That is a five-fold increase from the contraction of the past 25 years. Unachievable according to the degrowth advocates. According to them, global growth and consumption should be limited or kept equal. The fairy tale of eternal growth must be shattered.

Is that realistic? I think not, and for at least five reasons.

1   The world needs growth. Families, businesses and governments are in debt because they count on growth in income, profits and tax revenues. Defaults increase during recessions. Imagine what happens in a social model based on degrowth?

2   For investors trying to accumulate enough capital for retirement, a huge shock awaits in such a world: stock prices fall without growth.

3   There are huge questions about the feasibility of a degrowth strategy. If a single country decides to do this, companies will migrate to neighbouring countries. Unemployment and economic malaise will undermine the goals of the utopian country.

4   There is little chance of creating public support for this. The strategy amounts to freezing what exists in terms of income and wealth. Effort, hard work and a drive to innovate would no longer be properly rewarded.

5   There is no support internationally either. Governments of emerging economies are not going to deprive their populations of hope for a better future. And Western countries will not accept contraction to make developed countries grow faster.

These considerations do not take away from the fact that the degrowth advocates accuse the 'Green Growers' of dreaming. Some crucial technologies, such as carbon capture and storage, green hydrogen and advanced batteries, are not yet available. In theory, these should account for almost half of the emissions reductions between 2030–2050, according to the IEA. We should not take that into account, according to the degrowth advocates. The IEA agrees that significant efforts are needed to get these technologies up and running by 2030. However, one positive message from the Covid period should not be forgotten: when huge research and development funds are made available, human ingenuity is almost unlimited.

The world needs more magicians and fewer prophets

'Yer a wizard, Harry.'

———

RUBEUS HAGRID

So what is on the table is not small. On the one hand, CO_2 emissions have to go down. On the other hand, this has to be done in an EROI-efficient way. There are two ways to deal with this. Either we can stand around shouting that the Earth cannot handle 10 billion people, that we all have to consume less because otherwise we will die. Or we can try to find a solution.

It is sometimes said that prostitution is the world's oldest profession. But the oldest profession in the world is prophet of doom. Predicting the end of the world has been going on since the dawn of time and has often been lucrative, too. Optimism often seems like a sales spiel, while pessimism is seen as thoughtful, wise and full of good intentions. But let's be clear: today we definitely need more magicians – people who look for solutions – and fewer prophets.

We believe that the future will be better than today. We will have more technological capabilities. Except for a few tonnes of stardust that falls to earth every year, all the atoms have been here since the Earth took the shape we know today. Progress is ordering and controlling that matter differently. A piece of wood becomes a chair. A number of very complex molecules become a drug. Lots of parts form a car. But everything requires energy. Investments in both traditional and alternative energy – and especially the technologies that make the transition possible – will therefore be more interesting than ever. The next Apple or Microsoft might well be a battery or *cleantech company* that finds a method somewhere to improve the EROI of our entire system. If we want to match rising energy demand with greater care for the environment, technology will play an important role anyway. It is once again very important for an investor to diversify properly. A lot of money is being pushed towards new technologies; there is a lot of experimentation going on, and there will be breakthroughs that we do not think possible today. But that also means that a new, highly efficient technology, such as nuclear fusion or irradiating solar energy from space, can make countless other investments virtually worthless in one fell swoop. So investing in the climate transition will not only be one of the biggest opportunities ever, but also a particularly volatile one.

An absolute decoupling of growth and GHG emissions is no illusion. In the European Union, CO_2 emissions fell by 0.8% a year between 1990–2016, think tank Bruegel calculated.[44] In doing so, the decline in GHG per unit of GDP was greater than GDP growth. In particular, the falling energy intensity of growth contributed to this (more services, more energy efficiency), more than the emission intensity of energy. In the slightly longer term, it will be energy that becomes fully decarbonised rather than growth becoming 'energy-free'. The drastic fall in the price of renewable energy technologies suggests that accelerated decarbonisation of energy is possible, provided massive investment happens in storage capacity and distribution. And a change in behaviour is needed as well, for instance by going to Southern Europe by train instead of by plane. Or eating less beef, which accounts for a third of total emissions from food production.

Passing on the real price of products would also have a big impact. The climate footprint of what we buy, how we move, how we travel, is still insufficiently reflected in the cost price of the product or service. Raising that price is difficult. Low-income families find it harder to bear that extra burden and drop out. But raising awareness is possible and helps. In concrete terms: when we buy something, let us make it clear what its carbon footprint is. The chance that we will then buy Kenyan beans flown by plane or Fiji water transported by ship will then be much smaller.

Investing to grow

The path of 'Green Growth' is one of massive investments, faith in new technologies and an adjustment of our behaviour, based on awareness as well as price signals. Investment has already been firmly jacked up. With the IRA ($369 billion) and the Infrastructure Investment and Jobs Act ($1.2 trillion, a third of which is for climate), US green investment exploded in 2021 due to the realisation of the high dependence on Chinese green technology (*see sidebar*). The IRA significantly increased the chances of meeting the Paris climate targets, according to most studies. Europe introduced the 'Fit for 55' package, which aims to cut GHG emissions by at least 55% by 2030 compared to 1990. With the Green Industrial Plan, it relaxes subsidy rules for governments and shortens approval times for solar and wind farms. This comes on top of the previously approved NextGenerationEU plan (€750 billion, a third of which is earmarked for green investments). The CAT judges that European investment initiatives are almost sufficient to keep temperature rise below 2°C.

In 2021, even before the approval of some of the above investment flows, the IEA estimated global economic growth to 2030 at a cumulative 40% at 7% lower energy consumption. Even that will fall short of the targets. In 2022, global energy investments reached $2.4 trillion, 2.5% of GDP. These should peak at $5 trillion annually (4.5%) by 2030. There they stabilise for a while to fall back to $4.5 trillion by 2050 (at that point again 2.5% of global GDP).

China leads the energy transition

'If you talk about the clean energy technology race, in many ways, it looks as if the race has already been run,' says climate specialist Thijs Van de Graaf in an interview with the *Financial Times*,[45] 'and the winner is China.'

The transition to net zero will not be easy for China. It is by far the world's largest emitter of greenhouse gases and relies on coal for 58% of its electricity production. But Chinese companies enjoy huge domestic subsidies for the energy transition. They will also benefit from growing demand for clean technology products. China produces more than 70% of all solar photovoltaic panels, half of all electric vehicles and a third of all wind power. Any country trying to meet its net zero targets must buy solar panels, batteries and rare minerals from China.

Beijing controls the entire supply chain: from mines in the Democratic Republic of Congo (China now controls 10% of global cobalt supply) to the final production of lithium-ion batteries. Chinese companies control more than 85% of the world's refined chemical capacity for cobalt, essential for most lithium-ion batteries. It also mines almost all the world's rare earth metals used in electric motors and wind turbines.

Battery manufacturer Contemporary Amperex Technology (CATL) is the prime example of China's strategy. CATL grew from producing 6.2 GWh (gigawatt hours) of batteries in 2016 to 34 GWh by 2020, a third of the world market. It is now the world's largest producer and has contracts with Daimler, BMW and Tesla, among others. Making an electric car without involving China is almost impossible.

The graph shows the initially very limited positive and subsequently negative net effect on global annual GDP growth of the increasing investment subsidy flow until 2030 versus the increasing cost of the carbon tax. For the first 15 years, the additional annual growth averages around 0.1%. From the mid-2030s to 2050, the impact of the carbon tax exceeds that of the investment flow, squeezing growth by a tenth of a percentage point on average. The package of measures reduces total emissions by 75% from the current 38 Gt to 9 Gt by 2050. Without action, annual emissions rise to a catastrophic 57.5 Gt per year by then.

Impact investment boost on global real GDP (percent deviation)
Source: IMF World Economic Outlook 2020

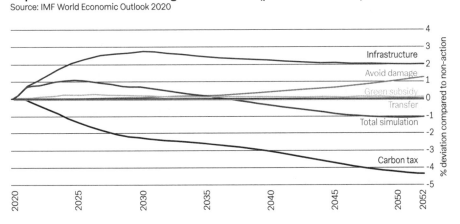

The investment boost comes at the ideal time. It compensates for decades of austerity, in which infrastructure investments in particular have suffered. In the US, government investment (excluding defence) has halved since 2000 to 1.4% of GDP. In Belgium, it plummeted from 4–5% during the 1980s fiscal consolidation to well below 2% of GDP in the early 1990s. Since then, it has hovered around 2–2.5%. In the European Union, it is 3% following a solid hit since the Global Financial Crisis. Outdated infrastructure leads to crumbling productivity over time. Fighting global warming could be a long-term growth catalyst to get us out of the secular stagnation we have been trapped in for the last decade or so.

The main gap in the investment story is the absence of financing for low- and middle-income countries. This is absolutely necessary for their future growth to be as emission-free as possible. Due to the carbon budget used up by the West, they can no longer follow the carbon-intensive growth path. On the other hand, it allows them to make giant strides in rolling out a modern, clean energy infrastructure in a short time. In the not-so-distant past, mobile phone technology also made the installation of telephone lines obsolete.

The polluter pays

A successful transition to net zero will require three sets of policy measures. One obvious one is the immediate removal of fuel subsidies, amounting to $5 trillion over the period 2010–2021. Second, low-carbon energy sources must be made cheaper and more abundant. Productivity in these sectors needs to increase further, with a focus on adapted infrastructure and radical technologies as well. Investment and subsidies help there. Finally, there are the measures that slow down current GHG emissions. This can be done through tighter regulation and the introduction of emission standards for cars, for example.

Reduction can also be achieved by increasing the cost of emissions. For most economists, including 27 US Nobel laureates, this is the most important piece in the solution to the climate puzzle. Price signals cause us to adjust our behaviour. No change in behaviour without an invoice. And it sanctifies the 'polluter pays' principle. Because politicians are reluctant to pass the bill to their constituents, current climate politics consisted – and continue to consist – of introducing discrete but expensive measures, such as granting far too high a compensation for installing solar panels, or excessively high emission-reducing standards for cars and insulation for houses. Consumers barely notice, but pay the cost in their electricity bills, or in the price of their cars and homes, or ultimately through higher taxes. A carbon tax levied on, say, polluting diesel, on the other hand, is immediately visible and instantaneously discourages its consumption. It also weighs on the family budget, but the cost per ton of CO_2 reduced is many times higher than with those devious methods.

Charging a carbon price can be done in several ways. One is to charge for the consumption or production of CO_2. A carbon tax then replaces the pre-existing tax on diesel or petrol. But a carbon tax can also be charged on that nice juicy steak, which suddenly becomes a whole lot more expensive. If you don't want to pay that, eat chicken. Or even better, switch to vegetables that have a minimal carbon footprint. In Europe, meanwhile, 18 countries have introduced such a carbon tax. Belgium has not. That tax fluctuates from €0.07 per tonne of carbon emissions to €116 in Sweden. Spain taxes only the use of fluorinated gases, which account for 3% of Spain's total GHG emissions. Carbon taxes in Norway – at €58.6 per tonne – cover 60% of total GHG emissions.

A second way of charging a carbon price is through the introduction of a quota system and then allowing trading through emissions trading schemes. This is the cap-and-trade system. They impose a maximum number of emissions through the issuance of a limited number of allowances. That number is slowly reduced in subsequent years. The allowances are distributed to targeted sectors, and within those sectors to companies. Those who emit too much buy additional allowances on the emissions market. Those who emit less than required sell their allowances. The higher the carbon price, the more companies will be inclined to reduce their emissions and invest in ways to do so.

In this cap-and-trade system, it is the government that sets the pace for reducing emissions. It sets a CO_2 target to be achieved for all sectors included in the emissions trading system. Each year it gradually reduces the number of available allowances. The price of an allowance, the market price, increases as fewer allowances are available. The difference with a real carbon tax is that there is no emission target there. Of course, the higher the tax – the more expensive the steak – the more the market will look for alternatives and emissions will fall. But here, the market decides the speed at which CO_2 emissions are reduced.

	Cap and trade	Carbon tax
Emissions	Government reduces gap between emissions target and current emissions	Total emissions based on market
Price	Market price	Increasing tax determined by government
	Government places the target CO_2 first and thus achieves it	Market decides on reducing CO_2

Both carbon taxes and the creation of emissions trading markets are increasing globally. The World Bank states that almost a quarter of global GHG emissions are covered by 73 instruments compared to barely 7% a decade ago. The best known is the European Union Emissions Trading Scheme (EU ETS). It started in 2005 specifically for industry and electricity production, the two biggest polluters. That system did not work perfectly because too many emission allowances were handed out free of charge at the start so as not to penalise participating companies against non-European competitors. Nevertheless, the companies included managed to achieve a 41% emission reduction over the period 1990–2020, far more than the 20% target.

In recent years, we have gained momentum in Europe with the introduction of the Fit for 55 programme. Emission reductions for the EU ETS have now been raised to 55% by 2030. The phase-out of emission allowances allocated free of charge doubles to 4.2% per year. The system is also being expanded to the maritime transport sector. This means more companies are allocated fewer emission allowances. The price to emit 1 tonne of carbon exploded. Until 2018, it had remained below 10 euros. Since then, an emission allowance has fluctuated between €65 and €100 per tonne. An additional separate emissions trading system for buildings, transport and fuel use for some other sectors is in the pipeline.

The ideal price

A key question when introducing a carbon price – via an emissions trading system or a direct carbon tax – is how high the price should be for companies to reduce their carbon emissions or, for example, start installing a carbon capture and storage system. When does producing green hydrogen or installing a solar farm become profitable? The global average price was barely $10 in 2021, the Peterson Institute for International Economics (PIIE) calculated. The World Bank put it at $3 per tonne in 2022. Economist Christian Gollier, in his book *Le Climat après la fin du mois,* argues for a carbon price of €50 per tonne, while a group around Nobel laureate Joseph Stiglitz puts forward a minimum price of $100.

The risk of a local carbon price, either through a tax or a cap and trade system, is that it encourages the private sector to move polluting activities to places with less stringent regulations, or lower carbon taxes, and then import their products towards the region with the higher carbon price. The EU wants to close such 'leaks' in the system through a carbon border tax. Imported products from countries with no carbon tax and a carbon footprint greater than the applicable European standard must pay a tax according to that difference. This encourages the company to reduce the carbon intensity of its non-European production. These countries are thus drawn into the pool.

Ideally, the European Union would agree on a carbon price with some like-minded countries. This would result in one universal price for a tonne of CO_2 that could then be traded between these countries. Where there is the most pollution, the greatest effort would be made for a rapid reduction in collective emissions. Companies in countries that are already further along in their transmission could sell their allowances. Countries that do not want to participate would pay a border tax. This would have to be high enough so that they too want to join the alliance. The Bertelsmann Foundation simulated such a set-up.[46] The foundation calculated that if the EU on its own raises the carbon price per tonne by $50, global emissions fall by barely 2.5%. Actually, they fall sharply in Europe – and especially in carbon-intensive Eastern European industries – but rise slightly in other countries due to carbon leakage. Introducing a carbon border tax significantly reduces 'leakage' but hardly increases global emissions reductions. Now suppose we set up a global climate club with the same carbon price everywhere. If the carbon price is raised by $50 for the whole club, emissions fall by 38.6% or 11.5 billion tonnes! Those are numbers that make a difference!

WINNERS
and LOSERS

✓ The (necessary) introduction of a minimum carbon price will cost a Belgian family of four 2,200 euros annually, according to a conservative estimate. A climate dividend for the least well-off families should keep everyone on board.

✓ Companies that do not join the transition face worthless assets. Creative destruction, the development of new, environmentally friendly technologies, often also creates stranded assets... and businesses.

✓ The Western world is moving from a consumption-driven to a more investment-driven economy. Winners are industry, construction, service providers and transport. Mining companies without the 'green minerals', like oil and gas producers, are the big losers.

✓ Most of the countries can potentially become energy independent. Winners are countries with plenty of metals and minerals used in green technologies, as well as those who can export green energy through an abundance of sun and wind.

✓ The challenge for emerging economies remains enormous given the huge investment required relative to their GDP and limited access to capital markets. Physical and transition risk in these countries is also above average.

Keeping consumers on board

'*Le concept d'une transition énergétique heureuse est une utopie*', Christian Gollier writes in his book.[47] At its (low) minimum carbon price of 50 euros, the cost, with a direct consumption of 6 tons of carbon dioxide per French person, amounts to 300 euros per year. For a Belgian with emissions of almost 11 tonnes (mainly due to fossil energy-intensive electricity production), that rises to 550 euros per person per year. For an average family of four, this amounts to an additional expenditure of 2,200 euros. Acceptable? In 2018, France increased taxes on fuel by 20 euros a year for the 10% of poorest families and 160 euros for the richest 10%. The yellow vests took to the streets with a clear message: '*NON!*'

The European Commission wants to set up a separate emissions trading system for road transport and heating systems in buildings by 2025. Citizens will be charged this carbon tax when they refuel or when they heat with fuel oil or natural gas. But a chunk of the revenue from the new trading system will fund a 72 billion euro social climate fund over the period 2025–2032. It thus discourages carbon consumption and is at the same time a dividend that goes to climate investments, research and development of necessary technologies and support for the least well-off.

In addition to a carbon price, efficient regulation is needed. Otherwise people will not make major investment decisions, such as renovating old, energy-guzzling homes. 'In Belgium, barely 4% of private homes are futureproof from a 2050 climate perspective,' environmental economist Johan Albrecht calculated. 'Most owners are looking at an average energy climate renovation of 50,000 to 65,000 euros to achieve energy label A [very low energy consumption]. A hefty investment, but precisely because of the renovation, the house retains its value while also reducing the annual consumption bill.' The 2022 and 2023 inflation surge increased that bill by a fifth. The Social and Economic Council of Flanders (SERV) estimates the payback period of such investments to be 30 to 60 years.

No problem for higher-income households, 'but about half of owners do not have the financial capacity to renovate.'[48] And a large proportion of lower-income households today live in energy-guzzling rental properties that offer a low quality of life. They too must be given a full place in the energy transition. 'Who gets warmed up by energy transition with 2050 hyper-efficient homes for higher incomes alongside inefficient homes with high consumption bills for lower incomes?'

The government needs to eliminate this imbalance. 'Flanking climate policy with government regulation therefore has an important social dimension. Without this dimension, the bill for social tension [increasing protests] risks exceeding that of the carbon tax.'

Fast but not too fast

The clock is ticking, but policymakers must also keep voters on board. 'Do not overestimate support for climate policy,' warns Pierre Wunsch, governor of the National Bank of Belgium in an interview with *Trends*. 'Many people were led to believe that the transition is a great economic opportunity, whereas it is a supply shock that costs us money.' If people have to insulate their house or install a heat pump without enough builders or installers to do so, they drop out. The same applies to the purchase of an electric car without sufficient charging stations. 'People understand bottlenecks that are the result of the war, but not for bottlenecks that we've created ourselves.'

The challenge we face is unique. 'All previous energy transitions were driven by technological and economic advantages, not policy,' explains Daniel Yergin of S&P Global. From wood we moved to coal and then to oil. Those transitions took more than a decade each time. 'The goal of the current transition is not to add a new energy source as it was then. We want to change the entire energy underpinnings of a $100 trillion global economy, and in just over a quarter of a century.'

Given the scale of the challenge, economist Jean Pisani-Ferry says we first need to better understand the macroeconomic impact. Raising net zero carbon emission targets too quickly could then lead to a 'negative supply shock [due to a sudden shortage of oil or gas] similar to the shocks in the 1970s.' The costs and benefits of such acceleration must first be clearly identified.

In addition to escalating social tensions, generational conflicts also threaten if older generations continue to block drastic measures. To limit the temperature rise to 1.5°C, the 'average' global newborn has a personal carbon emissions budget for their lifetime that is one-eighth that of their grandparents. 'Think about that the next time you hear "OK, boomer",' Marc Carney sneers in his book *Value(s)*.

And then there is the migration challenge that climate change will bring. An analysis of asylum applications in Europe combined with weather changes in 103 countries from 2000–2014 predicts an increase of 98,000 in asylum applications on top of the 351,000 annual average by the end of the century with a 2–3°C temperature rise and 660,000 at a 4.3 °C higher temperature.[49] Climate warming and associated natural catastrophes result in more social conflicts and wars, with more migration from affected areas.

And now for the winners:

...

So much for the list of winners.

Companies have to switch

To meet the 1.5 °C target, the bulk of current fossil fuel reserves must remain in the ground. These are stranded assets, or worthless investment assets. An illustration of the impact? The combined market capitalisation of the four major coal producers has fallen 99% since 2010, including some bankruptcies.

Stranded assets are not limited to fossil fuels. Commercial agriculture is responsible for 70% of tropical deforestation. The main culprits are palm oil, soya, livestock and logging. Some of these agricultural activities are slowly becoming unsustainable as governments limit deforestation. About 28% of Indonesia's territory – more than 6 million hectares – has become stranded assets since the government stopped issuing new palm oil licenses and imposed a moratorium on forest and peatland licensing.[50]

Stranded assets are also often a consequence of creative destruction. Waves of disruption took place during historically significant transitions. In many cases, it is not the established companies that adapt to the new market conditions, but the newcomers that overtake the current market leaders. The established values become redundant due to the technologies that the newcomers develop. Electric cars no longer need gearboxes, or petrol stations. Sustainable food production needs less packaging and fertilisers.

The disruption of the European electricity sector in the first half of 2010 illustrates this dynamic (*see sidebar*). And according to a 2016 report by consultant

Materials Economics, many other sectors are following suit. It identified €750bn worth of European assets at high risk of becoming worthless in three industries: automotive, textiles and electricity. That corresponds to a fifth of the total market capitalisation of the DJ EurostStoxx-50, a group of 50 leading European listed companies. In the automotive sector, potential write-downs amount to €240 billion due to three trends: electric vehicles, driverless driving and shared cars. Investment in the design of new internal combustion engine models is being halted. Associated patents and skills lose their value much earlier than anticipated. Factories producing redundant gearboxes, for example, will have to close. Note that workers will also have to retrain. But according to McKinsey, for all sectors combined, more jobs will be added than lost due to the climate transition: 200 versus 185 million.[51] By comparison, the consultant estimates job losses from the digital revolution over the period 2018–2030 at 270–340 million (but the same number of jobs will be created).

How to disrupt an industry?

The dramatic development of the European electricity industry since 2010 is a textbook example of assets becoming worthless due to the rise of disruptive technologies,[52] in this case solar and wind power. Between 2010–2016, seven of the top 10 electricity companies lost 65% of their value. This is surprising for an industry that 'on paper' should be highly predictable. Electricity demand is stable, power plants have a lifespan of 25–60 years and electricity generation is a stable B2B industry. Electricity shares were safe stocks.

The 'surprise' was the rise of renewable technology. This led to a declining demand for energy generated from gas, coal and nuclear energy. This is another textbook example of creative destruction. What is striking, and disturbing, is that neither financial analysts nor the major credit agencies saw this coming. Of course, it is easy to say in hindsight, but there were plenty of warning signs. The realisation that drastic changes were coming could have prevented many investment projects. These had to be written off as stranded, worthless assets!

We said nobody wins. However, some sectors may profit in the end. An innovation-driven net zero transformation scenario results in a $3.7 trillion larger global economy by 2050, according to research firm Oxford Economics.[53] Who benefits from this? Mainly industry, construction, service providers and transport. Mining companies are the big losers, as are oil and gas producers. The world is moving towards more investment-driven growth. Huge investments in solar and wind farms, transmission infrastructure and other equipment are driving the electrification transition. Machinery manufacturers, producers of basic materials (despite higher energy prices) and minerals are the suppliers of the spades and picks of this gold rush. Construction companies must also make huge investments to adapt to rising temperatures. Consumer spending is slowing due to rising inflation, which is eroding disposable income.

The analyses made always relate to large companies. They have the money and staff to meticulously monitor and implement rapidly changing legislation. This is much less true for SMEs. In Belgium, these account for 99.4% of the total number of companies and represent two-thirds of total Belgian employment. This is also the average in Europe. Despite their greater flexibility, SMEs are hit harder by the tsunami of new regulations. In the corridors of the ECB (European Central Bank), they fear an unspecified giant bankruptcy wave.

The unfair impact on countries

What is the damage if we do (much) too little? Swiss Re estimated the economic impact of a temperature rise of less than 2 to 3.2°C by mid-century.[54] In the first scenario, global GDP in 2050 is 4% lower than in a world without climate change. In an extreme scenario we head towards 3.2 °C of warming and GDP is 18% lower. The regional differences are enormous, but there are no winners here.

In that extreme scenario, the negative impact on GDP (compared to no climate change) rises to almost 50% in some South Asian countries. In the Middle East and Africa, GDP drops by a quarter. In South America, shrinkage of 17% is on the cards. The richest countries, North America and Europe, limit the economic damage to 10%. Two conclusions: the world is not fair, and doing nothing is not an option (which is the title of the study).

What is the impact if we do intervene? The introduction of a carbon price reduces the supply of fossil fuels and derivatives. The peak demand for fossil fuels is situated in the coming years. 'Gradually the power of those states that were big players in the world of the fossil-fuel economies, or big corporates like the oil companies, will fritter away,' says Ólafur Ragnar Grímsson, chairman of the Global Commission on the Geopolitics of Energy Transformation in the *Financial Times*.[55] According to the commission's report, energy supply in the future will no longer be the domain of a limited number of countries.[56] The majority of countries have the potential to become energy independent, benefiting their development and security.

New winners will emerge. First, these are countries with large reserves of metals needed to produce green technologies, such as Australia, Chile, Peru and Indonesia. Countries that export green energy are also potential winners. Africa, South America and Australia, among others, enjoy an abundance of sunshine. Most countries in sub-Saharan Africa are also benefiting from decreasing dependence on fossil fuels. Nigeria and Angola, two major oil exporters, are exceptions. African countries, and quite a few South Asian countries, have a golden opportunity to skip expensive investments in fossil fuels and centralised grids. They can immediately switch to mini-grids and standalone solar and wind power.

Notwithstanding this opportunity, the transition challenges in emerging economies remain enormous. The investment needed in infrastructure relative to their GDP is almost double that of developed countries, McKinsey calculated. However, accessing capital markets to finance the transition is much more difficult and expensive. The know-how to implement projects is also lacking. Opposition due to fear of job losses can slow down the transition: in these countries there are relatively more jobs in energy-intensive industrial activities compared to the larger number of service jobs in developed countries.

As if that were not enough, for some low-income countries there are increased physical and transition risks on top of this (*see graph*). In India, for example, the likelihood of deadly heat waves increases year after year. In the Sahel region, there is accelerated desertification. In South Asia, home to a quarter of the world's population, the risk of a water crises looms.

Countries with lower GDP per capita and fossil fuel resource producers have higher transition exposures

Source: McKinsey, The Net Zero Transition

Archetype of physical risk through transition exposure vs GDP per capita by country (logarithmic scale)

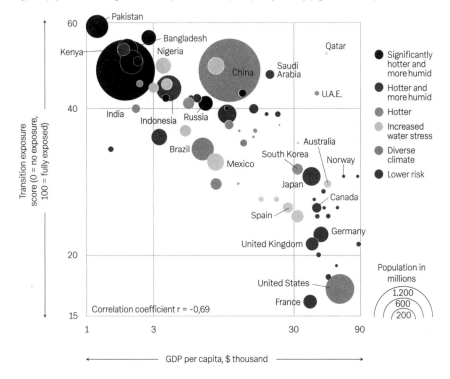

INFLATION,
INTEREST RATES
and DEBT

✔ The demand for resources needed for the energy transition exceeds supply in the short term, while the supply of fossil fuels risks falling too fast. This results in volatile, higher inflation during the transition period. Food prices will also rise.

✔ If the transition is too slow, a sudden increase in the carbon price will lead to an additional inflationary shock.

✔ In the short and medium term, I expect slightly higher growth, interest rates and inflation.

✔ In the longer term, productivity growth offsets stable to slightly declining investment.

✔ More than half of climate investments – and even more in emerging economies – will be financed by the private sector. Government investments will push debt ratios slightly higher by 2030.

A typical battery pack for an electric car contains about 8 kilograms of lithium, 35 kilograms of nickel, 20 kilograms of manganese and 14 kilograms of cobalt. Charging stations, in turn, require significant amounts of copper. Copper is also the metal of electrification. Solar panels are full of copper, silicon, silver and zinc. Wind turbines require iron ore, copper and aluminium. These are a lot of raw materials for which demand will increase spectacularly.

The accompanying IMF chart illustrates the shortage of a lot of raw materials at current production levels relative to projected demand over the period 2021–2050. In the net zero scenario, the share of fossil fuels shrinks from 80 to 20%. The share of renewable energy increases from 10 to 60%. A structural shortage of necessary resources increases the volatility of inflation during the transition period and potentially pushes it sustainably higher.

Metals in a net-zero scenario   Source: International Energy Agency, US Geological Survey 2021, IMF
Current production rates of some important metals, including copper, are likely to be inadequate
to satisfy future demand (supply/demand ratio, energy and non-energy demand coverage)

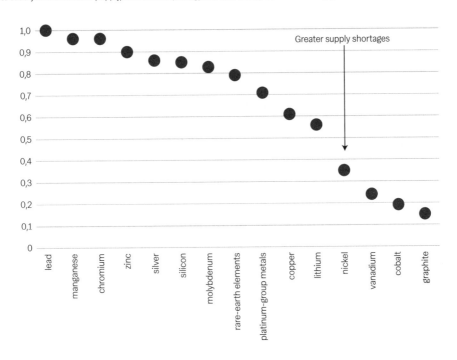

Green inflation in rapid transition

The same applies to energy prices. Some are calling for an immediate end to the use of fossil fuels. We are not ready for that. Demonising fossil fuels increases the likelihood of price shocks, which would quickly erode public support for the climate transition. Since 2015, global capital investment in oil and gas has more than halved.

The price spike in oil and gas in late 2021 and early 2022 illustrates the problem. The total of European wind energy generated in 2021 was highly disappointing, while hydroelectric power stations worldwide generated less energy due to drought. Countries therefore had to rely more on fossil fuels, resulting in lower stocks. Then, in late August, Hurricane Ida disrupted oil supplies in the Gulf of Mexico. That perfect storm led to an acute shortage of fossil fuels, which Russia then gratefully exploited.

'By the way, higher natural gas prices also increase the prices of basic materials whose production is highly energy-intensive,' argues research firm Bank Credit Analyst (BCA).[57] And ultimately we end up in the perverse situation in which less natural gas and oil do not lead to a faster, but rather a slower and more expensive energy transition. Countries and regions – like Europe with its 25 newly announced terminals – are competing for more spare and replacement supplies in global LNG markets. The ongoing switch between oil, gas and coal translates volatility in European natural gas into global volatility. Higher and more volatile energy prices also lead to higher food prices (nitrogen fertiliser is made using natural gas). These will also rise due to crop failures and a reduction in available arable land (desertification).

Energy efficiency and renewable energy price drop

The total weighting of energy in the European consumer inflation index is around 10%, making it a major contributor to inflation. A carbon price will push overall energy prices higher. The persistent decline in the price of renewable energy creates an opposite trend. New technologies, productivity improvements in the green sector and energy savings will also eventually reduce inflation. But it may be some time before these effects prevail.

Environmental economist Professor Johan Ekman also believes in more efficiency and cheaper renewable energy: 'Renewable energy involves high initial investments but then very low additional costs.' Wind and sun are free, unlike oil, gas and uranium. 'The revenue model for electricity products has to change. We will probably no longer pay per kilowatt-hour. Customers who can be flexible in their demand – retailers who set up their freezers at night and use less energy during the day – will get a lower price.'

Among private individuals, hopes are pinned on the 'smart grid', a smart energy system where solar panels, electric cars, wind turbines, water pumps and home electronics, among others, 'work together' to distribute energy as smartly as possible. With apps, consumers can optimally respond to a temporary shortage or surplus of energy. 'Consumers might play for a while with, say, an app indicating that now is the best time to turn on your dishwasher. But that effect quickly fades away. Something like that needs to be automated.'

Disorderly transition leads to stagflation

Those temporary price shocks risk being amplified in what the ECB calls a 'disorderly transition scenario'.[58] In an orderly scenario, carbon prices and taxes are raised very gradually. The impact on inflation thus remains zero. A transition shock occurs when governments are forced to suddenly raise the 'price' of GHGs sharply, after initially being too slow to respond to climate change. Companies pass on the higher emissions costs in their prices. This is accompanied by higher inflation expectations among consumers and an inflation shock of 0.5–2% in the following years. Jean Pisani-Ferry of the PIEE sees similarities here with the 1970s,[59] when the supply shock of expensive oil resulted in stagflation: a sharp slowdown in world growth coupled with high unemployment and high inflation.

Is stagflation once again written in the stars? Pisani-Ferry points towards some mitigating factors. First, a global price on carbon is not realistic. Even if the European Union fully implements its plans, the bulk of global emissions [unfortunately] remain without a price. Second, the oil shock was completely unexpected.

This is not true for carbon pricing or similar legislative initiatives. The more gradual the transition, the less capital suddenly has to be written off.

Third, the oil shock of the 1970s led to an income transfer from importers to oil exporters. The latter spent much less of that extra income, which had an additional impact on growth. Today, the initial demand effect of a gradually (!) higher carbon price is probably neutral and may even stimulate demand in the long term. The carbon tax is a domestic transfer from the private to the public sector, which can be used for climate investments or distributed through a carbon dividend. Finally, a wave of new technological advances can be expected, possibly driving growth.

Technology also reduces inflation. Energy efficiency compensated for part of the higher energy costs for companies during the energy crisis of recent years. In the medium and long term, productivity gains from the transition will emerge. Oxford Economics, in its net zero transformation scenario, estimates global industrial energy consumption at minus 30% by 2050 with a three-quarter increase in the added value of industrial activities in return. Electricity is much more energy-efficient than fossil fuels.

Four types of shocks and their impact on growth and inflation Source: BNP Paribas

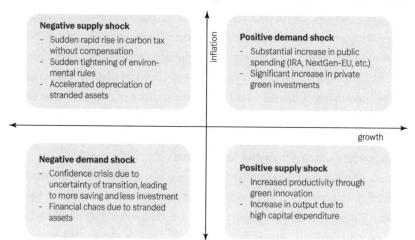

THE NEW WORLD ECONOMY

This chart shows different supply-and-demand shocks and their impact on growth and inflation. The final scenario will be a combination of the four. In the short and medium term, I expect an upward inflation impact and minimal growth impact. I continue to believe that governments will do what is necessary. In that race, price shocks will come from all sides. In the long run, productivity gains and the net zero cost of energy will depress inflation.

Towards green monetary policy?

Structurally higher and much more volatile inflation is a challenging environment for central bankers. They need to keep inflation around 2%. But does it make sense to push higher inflation towards 2% if the price increase is the result of a supply shock – higher prices due to the carbon price and declining supply of energy/raw materials – and not from higher demand? Besides, there will also be a significantly higher demand due to the required investments. Is it wise to slow down that demand if that slows down the energy transition? That only increases the likelihood of even more (inflation) shocks. A more flexible interpretation of the inflation mandate is required.

Should central banks also 'green' their monetary instruments by favouring 'green' bonds in future bond purchase programmes? The risk of blowing green bubbles is real. The BIS recently warned of a dotcom bubble in investment products with an ESG (*Environmental, Social and Governance*) objective due to the sudden popularity among investors.[60] Central bankers have other options but opinions are divided. '[…] we are ready to further step up our efforts in the fight against climate change,' stated ECB board member Isabel Schnabel at a symposium on central bank independence in Stockholm in early 2023. Barely three hours later, Fed chairman Jerome Powell countered: 'We are not, and will not be, climate policy makers.'

Even within the ECB, there is disagreement. 'There is not much we can do,' NBB (National Bank of Belgium) governor Pierre Wunsch said during a webinar for think tank CEPS. 'According to Article 3 of the EU Treaty, the ECB must, without jeopardising its core mandate of price stability, also take into account other considerations such as financial stability, employment and sustainable environmental management. But that Article 3 also includes promoting scientific and technological progress, countering social exclusion and discrimination, and much more. If you go along with that, you open Pandora's box. Should we or should we not buy bonds from companies that may or may not go along with the transition? I don't think so. Carbon pricing is the main tool. And each should focus on their specific task.'

What is the impact of the climate transition on the equilibrium R* rate (*see abbreviations*)? Huge public and private investments drive the demand money. If this is matched by stable savings, the neutral interest rate rises. But that rise is neutralised if uncertainty about the climate transition were to arise and hence savings increase. Besides, those massive investments could push real growth higher, and so R*. The same goes for higher productivity as a result of those investments. 'But if all investments flow to the transition, or if that transition attracts all the bright minds, who is going to provide the innovation in other areas?' wonders Wunsch in *Trends*. 'This could weigh on productivity increases and potential growth. That is perhaps the largest cost of the transition.' Here the impact on interest rates and growth is negative.

In any case, the climate transition forces central bankers to think more long-term than before. Quickly reducing inflation to 2% in the event of a temporary inflation slippage ensures that inflation expectations remain under control. But that is a Pyrrhic victory if such a restrictive monetary policy slows down the construction of a low-carbon economy and therefore increases the risk of a chaotic transition. On the other hand, there is the challenge of distinguishing between temporarily and structurally higher inflation. This is not easy, as demonstrated by the 'temporary' inflation of recent years, which ultimately turned out not to be so temporary after all. Once it has been reduced, discussion about a possible temporary increase in inflation targets arises.

Who will pay?

It is important that the investment flow quickly reaches cruise speed. The doubling of the current annual investment of $2.4 trillion referred to in the IEA scenario corresponds to 2.5% of GDP. More than half of this should go to developing and emerging countries. Besides the rich countries' contribution, the bulk of that funding will have to come from the private sector. New environmental require-ments for international companies will force them to make green investments throughout the supply chain. Companies will also have to buy carbon credits on the voluntary carbon market to achieve net zero emissions. But the traded volume of $2 billion in allowances on that voluntary carbon market is much smaller than the $900 billion on the mandatory – or *compliance* – carbon markets organised by national governments such as the European ETS. According to Carney, the market potential – once standardised and better regulated – will quickly reach $100–150 billion annually.

What is the effect on the budget? That will worsen during the coming years. Carbon revenues from carbon taxes and carbon fees will be smaller than infra-structure spending, subsidies and carbon dividends for poorer families. After 2030, the revenues are more than sufficient to finance the reduced green infrastructure bill by then. So until, say, 2030, public debt will rise. A recent report for France estimates a gradually increasing investment bill at an additional 2.5% of GDP on top of current investment expenditure by 2030. That pushes France's debt ratio – barely – 9 percentage points higher. Boosting that investment will be a challenge, though: 'We have to do in ten years what we barely managed to do in the previous 30 years,' say the report's authors. In Belgium, the NBB estimates the additional climate investments needed at 2% of GDP annually. But only a quarter to a third of that expenditure is borne by the government. 'For Belgium, with a total of annual government expenditure of more than 50% of GDP, the extra 0.5% is not insurmountable', said governor Pierre Wunsch in a speech. On top of that, member states were already given a boost with the 750 billion euro NextGenerationEU plan and a relaxation of the Growth and Stability Pact.*

In any case, climate investments are a powerful argument for allowing gov-ernments to incur debt. Future generations prefer a legacy of a protected climate and slightly higher financial debt to healthy public finances and irreparable envi-ronmental damage.

---

* The Growth and Stability Pact provides for, among many other rules, a maximum budget deficit of 3% of GDP and public debt to be reduced to 60% of GDP over a maximum of 20 years. For a lot of European countries today, this is absolutely unachievable.

Where can I go?

In the approximately 60,000 years that humans have been spreading across the continents, there has been one constant: change, mobility. Hunter-gatherers, as well as long-time sedentary city dwellers, have been constantly in search of food, water, resources, political stability and often a better life. Major events such as wars, revolutions, pandemics and certainly climate change have always accelerated this process. Therefore, the imaginary lines we have drawn on the world map are never fixed and never acquired.

If futurists like Parag Khanna are to be believed, we may be on the brink of another migration wave. Trying to estimate which areas will be (partly) abandoned and where people will migrate is very difficult. In addition to climate variables, there are also quite a few geopolitical and deeply human questions at play. Which countries are willing to accommodate the climate refugees who will, almost by definition, be economic refugees? Our world population today numbers some 4 billion restless young people, often in areas where the prospects for a better life are not too bright.

Moreover, if the slowdown in globalisation means we will have more hard borders and walls again, it is clear that there will be some serious pressure. Those borders are physical, legal, psychological and historical in nature. As a thought experiment, let's try distributing the current world population efficiently over the Earth's surface of some 150 million square kilometres, like the first move of armies in a game of *Risk*. You would soon find that this is not easy, even if you don't have to consider the limitations of borders. Do you leave parts of the world completely empty? How many people do you put in more favourable locations and how much space do you allocate to each person? By the way, we also need to put the overpopulation of the world in perspective. If you were to adopt New York's population density for the entire state of Texas or Alaska, the entire world's population would fit in each of these states. It shows that very large chunks of the world are unpopulated or barely populated. It is immediately clear that efficient distribution is anything but simple.

In addition to places that will have a difficult time in terms of climate in the coming years, such as large areas in the South and cities in the richer North such as New York and Miami (sea level rise), Los Angeles (water shortage) and San Francisco (forest fires), from an investment perspective, we should also be looking for locations that can benefit from the new waves of migration. The latter can also be internal waves, especially for large countries such as the United States.

One place that might not seem obvious, but could do well, is the US state of Michigan, with its empty factory towns. There is plenty of water there, a relatively healthy political system and potentially affordable real estate.

It is what Parag Khanna calls the New North in his book *Move*, where regions like Canada and Scandinavia, which are now relatively sparsely populated, have the perfect climate to attract new residents. From an investment perspective, cities that act as 'gateway communities' (a stopover from which further travel is possible) may be a good idea. We can add to this the Great Lakes region of the United States. No wonder Chicago is on the rise.

We should not forget that cities and real estate are ecosystems that decline at a certain point, but can also revive, just like coral reefs. These are characterised by their ability to form a hard exoskeleton that provides protection for themselves and other marine animals. Stony corals can only do this in symbiosis with so-called zooxanthellae, single-celled algae concentrated in the tentacles of coral polyps that also give corals their often beautiful colours. Under the influence of sunlight, zooxanthellae convert carbon dioxide from the coral into oxygen, which is needed to keep the polyps alive, through photosynthesis. A change in quality or a warming of the seawater can cause the zooxanthellae to die off and with them the whole ecosystem. The corals then look chalky, colourless and lifeless.

A city or a region can also be seen as a coral reef. As an ecosystem where all parts interact and depend on each other, but also as a situation where, when certain creatures 'die' – think of businesses or individuals leaving their buildings – new inhabitants or activities can take their place.

In doing so, it is often a good idea to follow the artists. They use vacant (factory) buildings and dilapidated residential houses as studios. Then follow the museums, boutiques and restaurants. The neighbourhood is becoming hip again. Young creatives and slightly less young artists follow, and the coral reef regains colour.

This does not go unnoticed by companies eager to establish new industries in old, abandoned locations. Local governments are assisting them in this. In this respect, a new Detroit-Toronto corridor seems to be in the making, where it will be good to live and invest. In this respect, in the longer term, I am also less worried about offices, of which fewer may be needed because of people working from home. They will be put to other uses.

Unfortunately, movements in the other direction are also possible. For years, Hong Kong was a thriving and dynamic city. Now it is seeing more and more (young) residents leave as Beijing curbs their freedoms. Long before 2047, the time when Hong Kong will be officially fully integrated into China, the youth and thus the future will pack their talent into a suitcase and look for more promising places. We need to be well aware that today, young people worldwide are much less rooted and perhaps less patient.

The departure of part of the population with perhaps the greatest potential will always have its impact on a city and its markets. The Hang Seng index (Hong Kong's stock index) has quite a lot of real estate in percentage terms. It is not surprising that this index has not been doing too well lately. And from the experience of Japan's Nikkei 225, we know that when a property bubble bursts, it can take a very long time to make up the losses. After the fall of the Berlin Wall in 1989, German real estate, especially that in the former East Germany, entered a boom period. A boom that almost inevitably turned into a bust, which caused the German real estate market to have a different cycle to the rest of Europe for years. There was a lot of commotion recently because artists complained that real estate in Berlin had become unaffordable for them. If anyone knows where the artists are going, let me know. In addition to an art tip, we might suddenly have an investment opportunity. The route New York has already taken from this perspective was from downtown across New Jersey to Williamsburg. With each stage, a new region blossomed.

Equally interesting is where the 'high potentials' from Hong Kong will go. Will they help build a new Asian golden age, like the people from Antwerp who migrated to Amsterdam after the Fall of Antwerp? Two places that come to mind are Ho Chi Minh City and Singapore.

To develop an overall investment strategy that takes into account which cities, countries and regions will succeed or fail in the coming years, we must try to understand political, economic, technological, social and climate-related factors.

Let's start with climate and its expected impact on the Belgian property market. In terms of climate, things don't seem too bad here. If the coast, where

I enjoy spending time and can often be found with a book in a beach bar, gets a few more hours of sunshine, we won't complain. Unless, as some predict, the Belgian coast were to become one big flood plain. And our beautiful forests in the south will certainly bring some cooling. But even if flooding doesn't turn out to be as acute a problem as in other places in the world, it is still a concern. Our sewage system is built to drain water as quickly as possible, just like so many other places around the world. In the future, it might be a better idea to hold the water longer. For that, we need a separation of the pipe system for wastewater from that for rainwater. And you can guess what I am about to say: this requires a lot of infrastructure investment. You can see future construction sites everywhere. Infrastructure remains a very interesting investment theme for the coming years just about everywhere in the world, together with the materials and raw materials it requires. Did we mention that we are in a mega bull market for commodities? Perhaps the biggest in history? Then you know where the laws of supply and demand will ultimately drive prices. Hopefully recycling and the circular economy can do some of the work there. It will be desperately needed.

But let's get back to real estate. Belgium will not have to complain about the climate. And there will be times when we are happy with the rain. 'Life is not about waiting for the storm to pass, but about learning to dance in the rain.' Taking this wise saying to heart will become increasingly easy in the future.

In addition, the Belgian property market has a lot of longer-term strengths. We remain a small country with a solid population density. Or as my sidekick Herwig Jaspers always says: 'Belgium has too few roofs.' By which I think he means there is more demand than supply. From a price perspective, this is not a bad situation to be in.

Moreover, despite the sharp rise in house prices in recent years, partly driven by years of extremely low interest rates, those price increases still remain very reasonable compared to other countries. Also, the level of debt financing is still low; relatively little has been bought with too much debt. This means that if things were to go less well, there should be no fear of foreclosures. Housing crashes usually happen when investors or, unfortunately, homeowners can no longer repay their loans and have to throw their property on the market at any price. That is not the kind of market we see in Belgium.

In terms of renovations, Belgium probably has more work to do than other countries to achieve environmental standards. But that will also bring investment opportunities. Belgium, until further notice, is still one of the nicer pieces of lithosphere floating on the lava asthenosphere. And an investment in a nice piece of real estate, even at current prices with a loan, is still an excellent protection against the higher inflation and interest rates to come in the years ahead.

TEN
to REMEMBER

1   The war in Ukraine has accelerated the climate transition by ten years.

2   The transition to green energy sources reduces dependence on imported energy. The dependence on minerals and metals needed for the green transition should also be reduced.

3   The next few years are likely to be chaotic. The mismatch between renewable energy and fossil energy and geopolitical games increase price volatility for energy and commodities.

4   The energy transition can only succeed if rich countries and the private sector finance climate investments in poor countries. That is not happening today.

5   Global warming suffers from the 'tragedy of the horizon': the costs are felt now while the benefits lie in the future. As a result, policymakers delay action.

6   According to the 'degrowth advocates', we need to slow down economic growth to limit temperature rise. This would have dire economic and social consequences.

7   We need to cut emissions fast by doubling investment in energy infrastructure and technologies. Investment increases growth a little until 2030. After that, a gradually rising carbon tax just takes over.

8   The most efficient way to bring down emissions is the 'polluter pays' principle. This can be done by introducing a carbon tax or through an emissions trading system. A minimum carbon tax costs an average Belgian family 2,200 euros annually. With a climate dividend for the least well-off families, we keep everyone on board.

9   The world is moving from a consumption-driven to a more investment-driven economy. Winners are industry, construction, service providers and transport. Mining companies without the 'green minerals', such as oil and gas producers, are the big losers.

10 In the short and medium term, we expect slightly higher growth, higher inflation and higher nominal interest rates. Too slow a transition will lead to an additional inflation shock.

TEN
to **INVEST** *in*

1 The energy transition is one of the biggest investment opportunities ever. Don't miss your chance.

2 New, highly efficient technologies can kill other promising projects. Those investments can become virtually worthless.

3 If we do not keep a close eye on EROI (*Energy Return on Investment*), we will go back to the Dark Ages. Industry always involves energy.

4 The next Microsoft or Apple might well be a battery or cleantech company.

5 We are on the brink of a super-cycle in (new) raw materials. So set your sights on the raw materials for the energy transition: metals.

6 The oil shocks of the 1970s will find their successor in today's metal shocks. Alongside OPEC, an OCEC (Organisation of Copper Exporting Countries) may emerge to pull the strings.

7 Beware of nationalisations and expropriations. These will have a major impact on businesses and investments.

8 The 21st century will be one of migration and climate refugees. Some countries, regions and cities will benefit, while others will not. Look at the North.

9 A city is an ecosystem like a coral reef. What goes into decline can also rise again. If you want to invest in real estate, follow the artists. They are catalysts.

10 The Belgian property market is still very reasonably priced and loans are still being repaid as they should be.

3

MULTI GLOBAL ISATION

Global economic growth gears up

18 April 2044, *The Financial Standard* – by Robbert Schoormans in Geneva

The IMF expects further stabilisation of growth and inflation during the coming year. The Great Depression is behind us for good, says chief economist Laurence de Groodt. During a final meeting, 100 world leaders decided to abolish all import and export restrictions, bringing a definitive end to a decade and a half of deglobalisation and self-destruction. Global funding for the climate transition in developing countries quintuples to ACU 5,000 billion ($1,000 billion).

The stabilisation of inflation is especially good news for the IMF. 'I can report that we are finally rid of "The Spin",' said De Groodt. For the third year in a row, inflation hovered between 3 and 4.5%. Central bankers who had travelled to Geneva also expressed satisfaction. 'The Great Divide is a thing of the past. It's time for the big march forward,' said Chandrakanta Devi, Indian chairman of the Asian Currency Unit, the common currency of the Asian Union.

The Great World Depression

The Great Divide of course refers to US President Jeremy Kudller's dramatic decision in 2028 to ban all Chinese imports. On top of the ban on Chinese goods, inputs of Chinese raw materials and intermediate products could no longer be processed. With that promise, the 'accidental president', as he has since been called, came to power in a country where barely 5% of the population had a positive outlook on China. America's partners were forced to take sides, resulting in the Western Alliance. China created a southern front with mostly Asian countries (including India) – soon renamed the Asian Union with the introduction of the ACU – and a pack of resource-rich African countries. The southern front banned imports of many western products, as well as exports of minerals and metals crucial for the climate transition and the production of advanced chips.

The consequences were catastrophic for both camps: growth collapsed and inflation completely derailed the global economy. Real growth during the Great World Depression of the 2030s averaged 0%. Inflation peaked at 10% and above in several regions, only to fall into deflation in the following years. Over the past three years,

The Spin – named after an uncontrolled downward rotation in aircraft – appears to be stabilising. Productivity has also shown positive growth.

Financing for developing countries explodes

At the subsequent summit of the 100 world leaders, the last import and export restrictions were lifted. Co-chairs Eneko Daniel Gutierrez of the IMF and Bai Wáng of the Asian Infrastructure Investment Bank also managed to lift all export restrictions on metals and minerals. 'If we still want to have a chance of keeping global warming below 2.5°C, we need massive investment in infrastructure in the least developed countries, now,' Gutierrez argued. 'That's why the five-fold increase to ACU 1,000 billion in annual development funding is imperative.'

'We're seeing the first results of renewed cooperation,' US President Harold Kazinsky said in the closing press conference flanked by Chinese President Xing Huáng. 'There's still a long way to go, but this time, we'll go the distance together.' Both leaders had two long private meetings during the three-day conference. This clearly paid off. 'We're forced to work together. There is no Planet B,' said Xing Huáng. 'So we'd better make the best of it together.' ●

why GLOBALISATION MATTERS

KEY POINTS

✓ Globalisation increases productivity through knowledge diffusion and increased competitiveness between countries and firms.

✓ The international disaggregation of the production chain accelerated during 1990–2007. Countries participating in such offshoring developed faster, especially when they shifted from exporting simple goods to more sophisticated industries and services.

✓ Lower prices due to increased trade with China caused a sharp increase in the purchasing power of an average global family.

✓ Cross-border trade has increased since the Bretton Woods Agreement of 1944 and accelerated with the fall of the Soviet empire and the opening up of India and China in the 1980s. This further lowered labour costs and hence inflation.

Scattered knowledge
fuels productivity

The benefits of globalisation are similar to those of technological progress: both increase output and productivity in countries, raise wages and lower the prices of products – and increasingly of services – in the global economy. Real income and wealth are increasing. We sometimes forget that the variety of products is also increasing (imported tea in the UK, cocoa beans for Belgian chocolate). Countries' growing exports go hand in hand with rising per capita income.

But how does globalisation contribute to higher productivity? One way is knowledge diffusion. In today's hyper-integrated world, innovation spreads like wildfire. Globalisation fuels that fire. When companies invest in overseas factories or services, they export their knowledge. That transfer of foreign knowledge and expertise to these locations drives domestic productivity and growth.

The intensified global knowledge exchange did not harm emerging economies. Available foreign knowledge accounted for 0.4 percentage points of annual productivity growth each year between 1995 and 2003. Domestic research and development and a better-educated population contributed an additional 0.3 percentage points. From 2004 to 2014, trade flows intensified, pushing the contribution of foreign research and development to 0.7 percentage points.

Knowledge and technology do not flow in one direction. Technology leaders also benefit from new innovation in emerging countries. The inclusion of those emerging countries fuels competition. This in turn spurs companies, both in the 'old' economies and the emerging countries, to further innovate and develop new technologies. As China and Korea increasingly contribute to exploring the technological frontier and file new patents, there will be more positive spillovers from these new innovators to the traditional inventors: the US, France, Germany, Japan, and the UK.

Foreign money
for domestic improvements

Knowledge diffusion and increased competition are just two of the channels through which productivity is being driven. 'Financial openness matters because it has the potential to catalyse development of the domestic financial sector, improvements in institutions, and better macroeconomic policies,' says Eswar Prasad of US think tank, the Brookings Institution. 'These factors should improve allocative efficiency and, by extension, total factor productivity (TFP) growth.'[61]

The global value chain developed at lightning speed, particularly in the period 1990–2007. Technological developments in transport, IT and communication allowed the production process to be split up. Moreover, trade barriers were demolished. In 2008, global value chains peaked (*see graph: the percentage of products in global trade that cross a border at least twice*) and represented more than half of global trade.

Global value chains Source: World Development Report 2020

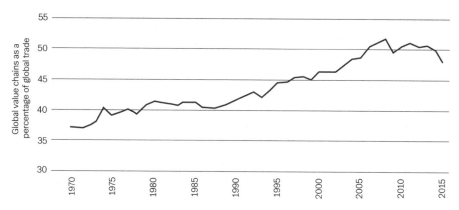

Countries that participate in this expanding global value chain grow faster, import skills and technology and create more jobs. Global value chains allow local firms to accelerate their development. 'The biggest growth spurt typically comes when countries transition out of exporting commodities and into exporting basic manufactured products (for example, garments) using imported inputs (for example,

THE NEW WORLD ECONOMY

textiles) as has happened in Bangladesh, Cambodia, and Vietnam,' explains the World Bank.[62]

Sustaining such rapid growth rates is difficult, but not impossible. A systematic upgrade to an increasingly sophisticated form of participation in the value chain is crucial: from simple industrial processes to more sophisticated industry and services to eventually innovative activities. Vietnam is showing Cambodia and Bangladesh the way forward with its real cumulative growth of 390% since 1990. How? The production of Samsung phones is a prime example of what such a global value chain entails. Its components come from 2,500 suppliers around the world. Vietnam produces more than a third of these phones, and it reaps the benefits.

More purchasing power through lower prices

United States, price evolution of goods and services (Year 2000 = 100)
Source: World Development Report, 2020

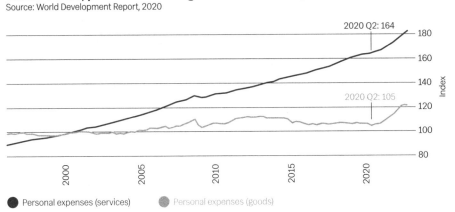

2020 Q2: 164

2020 Q2: 105

Index

180
160
140
120
100
80

2000 2005 2010 2015 2020

● Personal expenses (services)   ● Personal expenses (goods)

The beneficial effect of globalisation on poverty is not limited to developing countries. 'So if you look at day-to-day things that you purchase, in terms of washing machines, or cars, or even clothing, because of international trade we've had a decline in prices of these goods, so they have become far more affordable for a lot of people in the world,' explains Gita Gopinath, chief economist of the IMF in a blog. From 2000 until just before the 2020 Covid-induced price shock, US goods prices barely rose. The main reason? International trade. It allowed most Americans to buy more goods (we'll come back to the increased inequality and stagnant wages among the least advantaged later). It also helped offset the 60% rise in services prices. These were harder to trade until now. In the Eurozone, the difference in price increases between goods and services was more limited, at 30 and 46% respectively, but still significant.

Jobs versus prosperity

Through globalisation, companies bring down the cost price of goods by moving production to countries with lower labour costs. More imports also increase competition and push domestic producers to lower prices. This was the conclusion of a study by Xavier Jaravel and Erick Sager of the Federal Reserve Board of Washington.[63] They looked at the positive effects of increased US trade with China since 1990. A single percentage point increase in the share of Chinese imports in US domestic demand reduced consumer prices by about 2%. And yes, jobs fell. But for every job that disappeared, there was a consumer surplus/welfare gain of as much as $400,000, six times the average US annual wage. 'Another way to put it,' writes Xavier Jaravel, 'is that due to trade with China the US economy lost about 1 million manufacturing jobs on the one hand, but on the other hand purchasing power increased by about $1500 for each American household.' And with some 84 million American families, that number runs high. That high benefit per job loss is first explained by the fact that the product categories under Chinese attack were not that labour-intensive. The number of jobs lost was therefore limited. In addition, those product categories did represent significant consumer spending (especially for the least well-off families).

Hyperglobalisation

Central bankers are very attentive to the price effects of globalisation. These affect their mandate to keep inflation stable at around 2%. In late 2021, Fed chairman Jay

Powell referred to 'persistent disinflationary forces, including technology, globalisation and perhaps demographic factors'. One of his predecessors, Alan Greenspan, described the salutary effect of globalisation on inflation in 2000. 'A lowering of trade barriers, deregulation, and increased innovation, cross-border trade in recent decades has been expanding at a far faster pace than GDP. As a result, domestic economies are increasingly exposed to the rigors of international competition and comparative advantage. In the process, lower prices for some goods and services produced by our trading partners have competitively suppressed domestic price pressures.'

That dismantling of trade barriers resulted from the Bretton Woods Agreement of 1944. The IMF, the World Bank and the General Agreement on Tariffs and Trade (GATT) were born. The IMF oversaw financial flows, the World Bank gave loans to countries for reconstruction (and, over time, development aid) and the GATT oversaw global trade. This culminated in the Washington Consensus. The IMF and World Bank were slowly seen as the shock troops of US capitalism. Globalisation was driven by privatisation, deregulation and free trade. Reagan replaced the GATT with the World Trade Organisation (WTO). This simple agreement became a veritable regulatory institution with participating member states. US negotiations with Canada and Mexico led to the North American Free Trade Agreement (NAFTA) in 1994. In Europe, the systematic expansion of the European Union since the establishment of the European Coal and Steel Community in 1952 resulted in the dismantling of barriers.

The fall of communism freed Central and Eastern Europe from the centrally planned economy of the Soviet empire in the early 1990s. Not long before in the 1980s, China and India, together 2.6 billion people, or two-fifths of the world population, opened their markets to market capitalism. Both events created an influx of billions of new participants in the global economy, resulting in a dampening effect on inflation via wages.

In the US, the price effect was impressive. Import prices of capital goods have fallen almost constantly since the 1990s. The rise in consumer goods prices slowed from more than 4% annually in the 1980s to just over 1% in 1990–2010 (the graph shows the fall in both goods and services prices). Price evolution in the euro area is similar: from an average of 6% in the 1980s to 2.6% (1990s), 2% (2000s) and 1.4% (2010s). Besides globalisation, technological innovation also plays an important role in falling prices.

Will there come an end to the disinflationary effects of globalisation? According to Greenspan, the positive growth effects and pressure on inflation were probably a function of the degree of acceleration of the globalisation process, rather than the degree of globalisation. 'If so, that stimulus will gradually die out as we reach the limits of globalisation.'

United States, import prices and core inflation Source: BNPP Fortis

THE NEW WORLD ECONOMY

from GLOBALISATION *to* DEGLOBALISATION

KEY POINTS

✓ Steamships and railways propelled the first wave of globalisation and a huge rise in prosperity in the G7 countries. China and India's share of global GDP shrank from more than half to barely a few per cent.

✓ Their share recovered from the late 1980s onwards. Information and communication technologies made offshoring irresistible to industrialised countries.

✓ An initial period of deglobalisation took place in the 1930s. The Great Recession of 2008 does not kickstart deglobalisation 2.0.

First wave of globalisation drives wealth increase in G7

'Around 1800, the first wave of globalisation took place,' explains Professor Richard Baldwin, author of *The Great Convergence* and *The Globotics Upheaval: Globalisation, Robotics and the Future of Work*, two standard works on globalisation. Until the invention of the steamship and the advent of railways, most people's economic life took place in and around the village. The range of goods and people was limited by the high cost of trade and communication. But the more ships came, the more people bought goods produced far away.

That separation of production and consumption had enormous consequences. Baldwin shows that the first wave of globalisation accelerated wealth growth in the G7 countries (US, Germany, Japan, France, Britain, Canada, and Italy). A self-reinforcing cycle of industrial agglomeration, innovation and growth propelled the G7 countries' share of global income sharply higher. This happened at the expense of China and India, whose huge populations still accounted for just over half of global GDP in the year 1000. After the first wave of globalisation, India and China's share shrank to barely a few percent, Baldwin calculated. By 1990, the G7 countries accounted for two-thirds of global income.

In the late 1980s, the trend reversed. The revolution in information and communication technology depressed communication costs. Complex production operations could be organised modularly and from a distance. Effective trade costs also fell significantly due to fewer trade barriers. Low wages in emerging countries became irresistible to large international firms in G7 countries, which outsourced the labour-intensive and routine parts of the production process. The upward welfare spiral in industrialised countries came to a halt in favour of those emerging countries. The G7 countries' share of global GDP fell from 67% to 46% over the period 1990–2014, the same level as in the early 20th century. Today, it stands at 44%.

Resurrection of the emerging markets

This second wave of globalisation led to the accelerated industrialisation of half the world's population. The share in global GDP of India and (especially) China, at 21% – plus 5 percentage points since 2014 – is still far from the historical 50% share. But the trend has been set, according to Baldwin. And together with South Korea, Poland, Indonesia, and Thailand, they form the 'Industrialising-6' (I6): the six countries that by far benefited the most from the second phase of globalisation.

Find the trend barrier: share of world GDP, 1000–2021
Source: Richard Baldwin, *The Great Convergence*; own calculations as of 2015

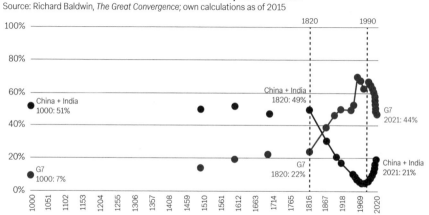

The New Globalisation created additional competition for the industrialised countries. The know-how that had been held by industrialised countries for almost two centuries since 1800 was transferred by international companies to emerging countries. If a European or American company transferred technological know-how to one of those countries, increasing international competition for these exporting companies, it may well lose workers in Europe of the US. The result was accelerated industrialisation in emerging countries and deindustrialisation in the Western countries.

Nobel laureate Paul Samuelson came to the same conclusion in 2004. '[T]his invention abroad that gives to China some of the comparative advantage that had belonged to the United States can induce for the United States permanent lost per capita real income,' he wrote. 'And, mind well, this would not be a short run impact effect. *Ceteris paribus* it can be a permanent hurt.'[64] And the data proves him right. From 1960 to 1990, US real income rose by 60%, roughly keeping pace with rising corporate profits and productivity. From the 1990s until the end of 2021, efficiency gains and especially cost declines drove US real corporate profits 260% higher. But median real income per household in the US barely rose 36%. Productivity gains rose 88%.

The evolution in other industrialised countries is similar. The New Globalisation has led to millions of losers in industrialised countries in addition to hundreds of millions of winners in emerging countries. International companies jacked up their margins by moving parts of production and their know-how to low-wage countries. Those economies flourished, and about 650 million people in emerging countries have been brought out of poverty since the 1990s. In industrialised countries, this led to deindustrialisation and polarisation of the labour market. This polarisation occurred mainly in the (Anglo-Saxon) countries without compensatory policies.

United States: labour productivity, median income and real corporate profits Source: BNPP Fortis, Macrobond

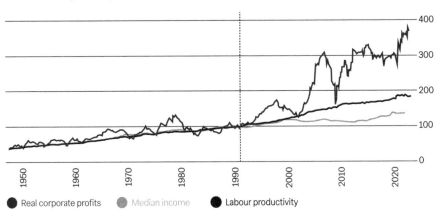

● Real corporate profits ● Median income ● Labour productivity

THE NEW WORLD ECONOMY

Deglobalisation 1.0 versus deglobalisation 2.0

With the digital revolution, the next wave in globalisation is upon us. We also find these waves in deglobalisation.[65] Peter van Bergeijk, professor of international and macroeconomics at Erasmus University in Rotterdam, wrote *Deglobalisation 2.0* on the topic. 'We can observe that during both the Great Depression of the 1930s and the Great Recession, the leading power of the time (the hegemon) deserted the rules of the game [...],' Bergeijk argues. The US market suddenly shut down.

In the 1930s, the US tried to seal off its market. Overproduction was huge due to falling domestic demand and the rebuilding of European industry after World War I. The Smoot-Hawley Tariff Act raised tariffs on more than 20,000 imported goods. Other countries responded. Average tariffs between countries rose from 14.5% in 1928 to over 22.5% in 1932. On top of those tariffs, quotas and other trade restrictions were introduced en masse.

In 2008, a severe macroeconomic shock hit the US. Global trade volume fell to 18% below its peak a year later. In 1930, that decline was limited to 8% over the same period. Knowing that the decline in global industrial production was similar in both periods, the obvious conclusion is that more protectionist measures were taken during the Great Recession than during the Great Depression.

That conclusion is wrong. Trade tariffs only temporarily went slightly higher. The sharp drop in global trade volume has mainly to do with the composition of that trade, as is revealed in an interesting study by Kevin O'Rourke. Until the 1960s, the global economy was divided into an industrialised North and a non-industrialised South, which mainly exported raw materials. Now Southern countries also export industrial goods towards the North. The share of those industrialised products in total trade increased from 44% in 1929 to 70% in 2008. But industrial production is more volatile than primary production – e.g. of agricultural products – and trade in those products. Because we must have food, and so we have to keep importing grain, even during a crisis.

The main explanation for the bigger fall in world trade in 2008 is the greater weight of that more volatile industrial production compared to 1929. This production also rebounds much faster after a recession, as shown by the rapid rebound in world trade since 2009.

GLOBALISATION
in TRADED GOODS
at its PEAK

KEY POINTS

✔ Following the acceleration since 1980, merchandise trade as a percentage of GDP has probably peaked. This is partly due to the different composition and price trends of the numerator (goods) versus the denominator (goods and services).

✔ In addition, outsourcing of the manufacturing process reached its limit in 2008 and companies want to reduce the complexity of the global value chain.

Commodity trading at its peak

The Great Depression in the 1930s and then World War II took global trade down completely. GATT, the IMF and the World Bank have led a spectacular recovery since 1950. An acceleration in trade followed, starting in the 1980s, and it rose even more in the early 2000s when China joined the World Trade Organisation. Despite the hiccup in 2008 and more recently due to the Covid pandemic, global trade volume increased by 4300% over the period 1950–2021. The average globally applied inter-country trade tariff fell from 17.2% in 1991 to 5.6% in 2020.

Has globalisation reached its peak? 'For trade in goods, the answer is probably yes,' Professor Baldwin believes.[66] The decline in goods trade as a percentage of GDP varies from region to region. China peaked in 2006, Japan and the US in 2011 and 2014. European goods trade, which accounts for 30 per cent (!) of global trade, has stagnated since 2012. On average, the peak happens to fall around 2008. Highlighting that coincidence – or falsity – of the peak is important, according to Baldwin, 'since attempts to associate the changes in globalisation with the traumatic Global Financial Crisis of 2008 − or the Great Trade Collapse that followed − are almost surely misguided.'

The decline in Chinese merchandise trade has been particularly spectacular. Between 2000–2006, goods imports and exports shot up from 40% to almost 65% of GDP. Today, that ratio hovers around 30% of GDP. China is thus converging towards the even lower ratios of other mega-economies such as Japan, the US and Europe. 'What is unusual is the asymmetric way China's globalisation is evolving in terms of selling to and buying from global supply chains,' Baldwin notes. Inputs produced in China for other countries account for almost 3% of total global output. This is a hefty percentage. 'China is rapidly becoming the "OPEC of industrial inputs" for the whole world. By contrast, China is scaling back its purchases of intermediate goods from the rest of the world, relying more on its own industrial base to provide the inputs.' Behold China's dual circulation strategy in practice.

China's engagement with GVCs 1995-2018
Source: calculations by Rebecca Freeman and Angelos Theodorakopoulos using concepts developed in Baldwin et al. (2022)

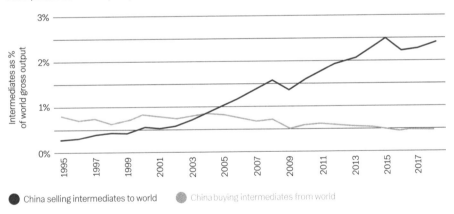

● China selling intermediates to world   ● China buying intermediates from world

China's dual circulation strategy[67]

Decoupling is a major concern for China. It recognises the importance of access to global trade, intellectual property and raw materials. On the other hand, it is aware of the risk of over-reliance on foreign chips and crucial commodities, such as soybeans. Hence the dual circulation strategy. This aims to reduce dependence on external inputs while maintaining a high market share in global trade.

In practice, this means an active import substitution strategy, especially for technology from the US. Crucial imports should be replaced by domestic production as soon as possible. Beijing allocates hefty government subsidies and other incentives to produce its own high-tech chips. This strategy differs from a passive substitution strategy, where China works its way up 'naturally' into a more sophisticated value chain and gradually uses more domestic inputs.

Another important part of dual circulation is rolling out the red carpet for foreign companies, especially those that still have much to contribute to China in terms of technology and knowledge. Examples include Tesla, BASF and Bayer, as well as financial institutions. The attractiveness for international companies remains high, even if China has long ceased to be a low-cost producer. Chinese exports remain competitive thanks to its huge, highly skilled and flexible workforce and superior infrastructure. In addition, the world's largest middle class exerts an irresistible attraction.

The decline in foreign direct investment (FDI) in China and exports from the country will therefore be very slow, notwithstanding the near collapse of those FDIs in the first half of 2023. That decline, according to China specialist Rory Green, is temporary and attributable to the economic dip China is experiencing and the relative unattractiveness for renminbi assets (which prevents foreign companies from investing their renminbi earnings in Chinese treasuries).

The 2008 peak and subsequent decline in the ratio of goods trade (not services!) to GDP must be treated with caution for another reason: the composition of numerator and denominator differ profoundly. Three-quarters of world trade in goods is made up of manufactured goods, with the rest divided roughly equally between agricultural and mining goods. Global GDP, in turn, consists of two-thirds services and only one-third goods. The goods trade-to-GDP ratio declined as GDP – especially the prices of services in it – rose relatively faster. The ratio has increased since the 1990s due to the price explosion of mining products and fuels in the denominator. Until it peaked in 2011. 'Sweeping analyses claiming that the 2008 peak is all about the end of multilateralism, or the end of the neoliberal regime, will struggle to account for the plain fact that 60% of the fall was due to a phenomenon known as the "commodity supercycle",' Baldwin concludes.[68]

From offshoring to reshoring

The fact remains that the upward trend of trade in industrial goods as a percentage of GDP has stopped since 2008. Why? Mainly reshoring (or friend-shoring, near-shoring, shortening supply chains...). A factory used to process almost everything, from raw material to finished product. ICT and better coordination allowed international companies to carry out manufacturing processes where they could do so optimally. Manufacturing processes with limited added value went to low-wage countries. Research and development and the more complex processes that required highly skilled personnel remained closer to home.

Chopping up the production process led to more complex production chains. Raw materials and intermediate products crossed several borders many times before rolling off the assembly line in a finished product. That breakdown of the production chain alone caused a robust increase in trade in industrial goods. Its consequence was a greater dependence on a smoothly running international production chain. A disruption in the chain can bring the production of industrial goods to a halt, as the Covid pandemic has shown.

The offshoring expansion phase has ended Source: Baldwin, 'The Peak Globalisation Myth: Part 3', VoxEU. Share of global industrial GDP, G7, I6 & Rest of World, 1990 to 2020

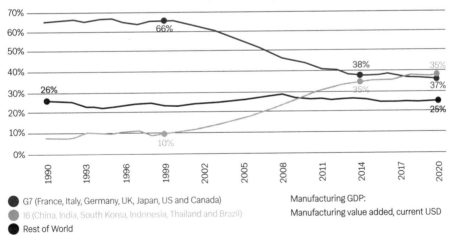

Reshoring involves two elements: stopping the outsourcing of the manufacturing process to cheaper producers, and reducing the complexity of the global value chain (both within and between countries). The accompanying chart illustrates the spiking offshoring process. The G7 accounted for two-thirds of industrial production until the early 2000s. That share almost halved by mid-2014 and has stabilised since then. The I6 ramped up their production share. They are China (+16.2 percentage points; ppt), India (+1.5 ppt), South Korea (+1.5 ppt), Indonesia (+1.0 ppt), Thailand (+0.5 ppt) and Brazil (+0.5 ppt). 'This pattern is suggestive of a transition between stable equilibria,' suggests Baldwin. 'In other words, the easy and obvious opportunities for combining high technology from G7 firms with low wage labour in emerging market factories were exploited and so the rate of offshoring slowed.' We think this applies to countries like China and South Korea, but less to other emerging countries like India or Indonesia.

The complexity of the global value chain is also hitting its limit and more value creation is being done within companies themselves. The importance of intermediate products from other companies declined again since a peak in 2013 until just before the Covid pandemic (*see chart on page 115*). Both elements of reshoring started around mid-2010. That is well before President Trump's declaration of war on trade and also before Brexit. It was also five years after the Great Recession, which indicates that this was a natural process rather than a tipping point prompted by a particular event.

The conclusion? Offshoring has reached its natural limit, and the overall complexity of value chains has declined. Both led to a decline in the share of trade in industrial goods in global GDP. However, they are not a sign of flaring protectionism.

GLOBALISATION
is FRAGILE

✓ The disruption of the supply chain due to the Covid pandemic and the Russian invasion of Ukraine exposed the vulnerability of globalisation.

✓ Globalisation has lifted hundreds of millions out of poverty. Big international companies have won. In some developed countries, the disappearance of factory jobs without compensatory social policies has increased inequality.

✓ The returns of globalisation decrease with a higher degree of globalisation for the world leader(s). Young countries benefit the most and threaten their position.

✓ The US, led by Joe Biden, remains negative towards free trade and trade agreements. China is the big bogeyman: it does not play the trade game fairly and threatens the US in its hegemony.

✓ The benefits of globalisation over the period 1950–2016 amounted to an extra income of $18,131 per US family. Jobs were cut, but these represent barely 1% of total annual layoffs in the US.

✓ There is growing resentment from the European Union over unfair Chinese trade practices. The symbiosis of past decades – technology in exchange for a huge market – is in jeopardy as China enters the European market with its own products.

Covid-19 and Russia
show our vulnerability

Globalisation and Covid-19 are intertwined. Its rapid spread was spurred by the global nature of economic activities and the value chain. The flow of people to other countries came to a near standstill. Export volumes plummeted. In 2022, the uppercut followed, at least for Europe: we discovered how dependent we had become on Russian (and Ukrainian) raw materials. If the disruption of the supply chain due to the Covid pandemic and Russia has made one thing clear, it is that over-dependence on one supplier is risky. The extent to which companies see supply chain disruption as a one-off will help determine the extent to which they will swap their just-in-time strategy for a just-in-case one.

In her book *Homecoming, Financial Times* columnist Rana Foroohar highlights the flaws of a globalised world.[69] According to her, it is dominated by profit-maximising multinationals, global supply chains focused only on efficient production and large countries like China that do not share the same values as the US. She points the finger at globalisation, the growing importance of the financial rather than the real economy and excessive concentration of corporate power for US problems such as rising inequality. To counter this, the US must prioritise 'the local versus the global, Main Street rather than Wall Street, special-interest groups rather than shareholders, and small rather than big'.

A global world is a more
unequal world... in the West

An increase in inequality is the most commonly heard argument against globalisation. The Covid pandemic increased that income inequality: the poorest countries and the least advantaged in rich countries were hit hardest. Everyone applauds the fact that hundreds of millions of people were lifted out of poverty over the past quarter of a century. On the other hand, the middle class with average wages was significantly eroded. Against the increased industrialisation and prosperity in emerging countries from the 1990s onwards, deindustrialisation manifested itself in Western countries. Extensive automation further reduced the number of industrial workers needed. Workers then sought refuge in low-paid service jobs.

'The spread of inequality is also geographically determined,' Jonathan Holslag, professor of international politics at the VUB, said in an interview. 'In the US and Europe, you see a rapid increase in wealth in globalised coastal cities. But the hinterland, the countryside, is lagging behind. And then there is often the clash between the rich cities on the one hand and, on the other, the villages, which want different accents.' Service quality has improved in the cities, but declined in the villages. You need proper education to participate in the global labour market, but where can you find it in rural areas with low-quality schools, as all economic activity has migrated away from them?

Other globalisation winners are companies. 'The big multinationals have certainly benefited from cheap labour and growing domestic demand in emerging countries. They cover the entire horizontal production chain, which was chopped up and optimised everywhere. That's where economies of scale come in,' Holslag explains. He says the same is also true for smaller players who have started to position themselves flexibly within that new production chain and in specific sectors. 'In Europe, there is the so-called *Mittelstand*, the SMEs, which have made themselves indispensable throughout that chain. And as long as they stay ahead of their competitors and ride the wave of change in those big companies, they fare very well.'

Can you blame those companies for anything? 'You can assume that the market is selfish and that companies seek short-term profit maximisation. You cannot ask a lion to suddenly become a vegetarian. If there are excesses, the responsibility lies with the government to correct them.' And that, according to Holslag, does not only apply to the decreased share of total income going towards labour and wages. Increasing reliance on Chinese products and Russian energy should also have rung the alarm bells in governments.

Today, inequality in the UK, but especially in the US, has risen almost to the same level as it was during the Great Depression. The 1% of richest Americans (before the redistributive effect of taxes) snatch 20% of total income. In the European Union, that hovers around 12%. The UK hovers in between. Not coincidentally, the US and the UK are the two Western countries that have already adopted the most protectionist measures. Globalisation is an easy scapegoat.

The redistribution of profits towards the 'losers' of globalisation also becomes more difficult with a higher degree of globalisation,[70] argues Peter van Bergeijk. Initially, productivity and wealth increase with the opening up of the economy, especially for developing countries, but also for the world leader(s). Then the costs of redistribution rise. There is the loss of jobs. On top of that come the burdens for that world leader so that an open, stable and peaceful world can function. Over time, those burdens exceed the benefits. The longer globalisation persists, the more the costs for the world leader increase. The more young, emerging and dynamic countries benefit from globalisation, the more the leader – the US – starts to feel threatened. 'That is also why strong globalisation carries within it the seeds of its own destruction,' Van Bergeijk concludes.

The United States is closing in

During our interview following my book *The Winner Economy* in 2016, Baldwin already predicted more backlash against globalisation. 'I fear a turbulent decade of social and political unrest in countries like the US and Britain. There, governments have failed to distribute both the pain and the gains of globalisation fairly.'

First Brexit, then Bregret

Brexit has not brought what Britons were promised. Brexit was mostly a vote against migration. A study by a think tank in late 2022 estimates the net loss of available workers and white-collar employees due to Brexit ('suppose Brexit had not taken place') at 330,000 workers, or 1% of the labour force. Combined with the shock of the Covid pandemic, this creates a dire shortage of workers... and high inflation.

Imports to and exports from the UK are stalling. Export volumes in the last three months of 2022 were more than 9% below the 2019 pre-coronavirus graph average. 'A disaster,' says trade economist Sophie Hale of think tank Resolution Foundation. 'It really leaves the UK at the bottom of the G7 pack.' Exports from the EU are down 20% two years after the divorce, estimates the Irish think tank Economic and Social Research Institute. An Office for Budget

Responsibility report concludes that 'weak growth in imports and exports over the medium term partly reflects the continuing impact of Brexit, which we expect to reduce the overall trade intensity of the UK economy by 15 per cent in the long term.'[71]

Import controls make everything more complex, but the most far-reaching measures are yet to come. The introduction of a UK rather than an EU marking will force importing companies to make two products. Controls on products of plant and animal origin are also in the pipeline. The UK imports about a third of its food and two-thirds of its medicinal and pharmaceutical products from the EU. Politicians are delaying these measures out of caution.

The Brexit is giving way to 'bregret'. Periodic polls by YouGov show that more than half of Britons favour turning back the clock. Barely a third continue to believe in it and only one in five Britons argue that the divorce will go smoothly. Gloating is inappropriate as all studies also point to economic damage to the EU. And in a multipolar world, an EU with the British is much stronger than one without. For the UK, this is even more true.

'Those who have become especially negative about the Brexit are the zoomers of Gen Z, who were too young to vote in 2016, and the undecideds of 2016,' tweeted academic Matt Goodwin. The largest proportion of 'leavers' (60%) was found among those over 65. Time thus plays in favour of the 'bregreteers'.

Baldwin's prediction soon came true. Brexit was voted for in June 2016, and President Trump seized power in the US late that year with his slogan 'America First'. 'We have rejected globalism and embraced patriotism,' Trump stated during a memorable speech to the United Nations General Assembly. The current Biden administration is also clearly not about to take pressure off any time soon. China-bashing is ubiquitous. The percentage of US citizens who view China positively has fallen to an all-time low of 15% against a long-term average of just over 40%. Biden is backed into a corner with his China policy. 'This is a dangerous situation,' Hank Paulson believes.[72] 'I strongly believe that Biden would like to stabilise the China relationship but both Republicans and Democrats in Congress have staked out a very strong line which complicates things for Biden.'

China as bogeyman

Has the US been too lenient with China? During his presidential campaign, Trump continuously lashed out against China, accusing it of 'one of the biggest thefts in the history of the world' and 'raping' the US economy. The red flag of Trump's wrath was the US trade deficit. For goods and services combined, it amounted to just over 2.5% of GDP. China was the big bogeyman, but Germany and the Netherlands, and by extension the entire European Union, also abused America's goodwill, so to speak. And Mexico. And Canada.

Simple messages are powerful slogans – as Trump knows better than anyone else. According to him, a trade deficit means you lose, a surplus means you win. But the underlying reason is that a country spends more than it produces, and it consumes more than it saves. A budget deficit encourages more spending. The dollar tends to be relatively strong as a result of its status as a world reserve currency. There is always demand for it. That keeps US interest rates 'abnormally' low. It increases the attractiveness of foreign goods. These become cheaper for Americans, but it makes US exports more expensive. A trade deficit is neither good nor bad. On the one hand, the US benefits from a wider choice of cheaper foreign products and investment. On the other hand, it has caused some workers to lose their jobs (but it is a political choice whether to ease that pain or not) and it increases the national debt burden.

From January 2018, Tump gradually increased import tariffs on 12,043 Chinese products from 2.6% to 16.6%, accounting for 12.7% of annual US imports.[73] Import tariffs on steel and aluminium from Canada, Mexico, and the EU also became more expensive, as did those on washing machines and solar panels. Average (weighted) US trade tariffs more than doubled to 3.5% in 2018 and rose further to above 5% in 2019.

Countries exporting to the US did not lower their prices, resulting in rising import prices. Fajgelbaum et al. estimated the annual loss to US consumers and businesses who bought these imports at $54 billion, or a quarter percent of GDP. Taking into account additional revenues for the government and some domestic producers, this leaves a net loss of $7.2 billion.

Raising trade tariffs was certainly not the first feat in Trump's fight against globalisation. A year before (2017), the G20 countries (the 20 largest economies and emerging countries), at the insistence of the US, had agreed to remove their commitment to free trade from the final declaration. 'This must be regarded as a historical moment,' economist George Friedman wrote in his blog for Geopolitical Future.[74] 'While many G-20 nations have practiced protectionism by formal or informal means when it suited them, allowing the commitment to free trade to be excluded from the agreement represents a fundamental shift in a concept that has been central to global economics for more than a generation, and sacred since Ricardo made the case for it.' But for Trump, free trade is not a principle, just a means to improve economic conditions. According to him, that remedy no longer works for the US. Many countries, such as China, did not apply free trade but benefited from it.

Free trade in Ricardo's era is not the free trade of today

Ricardo's theory of comparative advantage is simple and straightforward. If all countries concentrate on selling what they produce most efficiently and leave the rest to others, everyone wins. If the US produces computer code more efficiently than steel, it is more beneficial to stop producing steel and concentrate on computer code.

However, two problems arise. The first is the interchangeability of jobs. Ricardo wrote his theory in the 19th century. A farmer could retrain relatively easily to become a factory worker. If profitability or comparative advantage shifted from one product to another, new products would be produced and new jobs would emerge.

That interchangeability of jobs is less true today. Steel workers are not computer programmers. Writing more computer code and producing less steel contributes to GDP but increases structural unemployment. This creates discontent, and politicians are sensitive to it.

The second problem is timing. A favourite phrase of economists is 'in the long term'. That term applies differently to an economy than to a human being. Over the next 50 years, it makes sense to move from one industry towards another. But for a 45-year-old worker, this ruins his life. If it ruins enough lives, politics intervenes. 'We are depriving people 50 years down the road of the payoff,' writes Friedman. 'But our willingness to immiserate ourselves and our children for the wealth of the unborn doesn't exist. The political system is constantly intervening in the economic system and imposing suboptimal solutions on the economic system. But the economic system is constantly producing solutions that are politically unsustainable.'

Unfortunately, Biden's election does not herald a new era. 'Biden's approach to globalisation is Trumpism with a human face,' writes *Financial Times* commentator Edward Luce.[75] The Biden administration has not yet considered new trade agreements. In October 2022, six years after Trump cancelled the Trans-Pacific Partnership (TPP), US Trade Representative Katherine Tai set her sights on other trade deals. Those deals carry 'significant costs: concentration of wealth, fragile supply chains. De-industrialisation, offshoring, and the decimation of manufacturing communities'. If she saw any benefit in trade deals – or just trade – she was demurely silent about it. Those responsible for US trade policy believe that the liberal world order created under US leadership has turned into a new evil globalisation. Does free trade really bring more disadvantages than advantages to the US?

The benefits of free trade... for the US

With the protectionism of the 1930s and the deepening depression that followed, the US took it upon itself to create an open and regulated trading system. 'This policy created a more prosperous world economy, which became the foundation of western economic (and so political) success in the Cold War,' writes Martin Wolf,[76] chief economist of the *Financial Times*. 'They facilitated a staggering reduction in global poverty. They are the most important credential for the US claim to have been a benign hegemon.'

The enormous success of post-war US policy is not a matter of theory. It is a fact, according to PIIE. 'The alternative – a relatively closed, state-dominated system – was tried, in the Soviet Union under Stalin and by Mao Tse-tung in China,' writes Alan Wolff et al. of PIIE.[77] 'Both failed.' The Soviet Union collapsed and no longer exists. China lifted its isolation and, under Deng Xiaoping, integrated its economy into world trade.

Did the US, the architects of today's free trade policies, benefit from globalisation? In a 2017 study, the PIIE estimated the US gain from trade expansion between 1950 and 2016 at $2.1 trillion or 10% of GDP (in 2016).[78] That means an additional increase in GDP per capita of $7,014 and per household of $18,131. On the other hand, the researchers calculated an annual net job loss due to increases in trade (imports and exports) of 156,250 in 2001–2016. That represents less than 1% of annual layoffs in the US. And a more generous unemployment insurance programme could help affected workers.

The US does not have much of a problem with trade: almost two-thirds of Americans are favourably disposed towards trade. That affection is far from there for China: barely 15% of Americans are positive about China. China has been accused (and not just by the US) of not playing the trade game fairly. As Harvard's Dani Rodrik puts it: 'The Chinese used the world economy to advance their own domestic policy agenda.' The rest of the world 'crafted national policy to serve the global economy.'

China is also threatening America's hegemony. All predecessors of current President Xi Jinping spoke of a 'peaceful development' of China. Xi, on the other hand, promised in his first speech in 2012 to make China great again and realise the 'great revival of the Chinese nation'. His 'Made in China 2025' strategy, launched in 2015 to make certain sectors 70% self-sufficient by then, also provoked international ire (and is therefore no longer mentioned today). If China succeeds, German, South Korean and Japanese importers of high-tech products will rightly feel threatened.

A major miscalculation was that when China was admitted to the World Trade Organisation, it was assumed that the Chinese system would converge towards the market economy of its major trading partners. That did not happen. Is the WTO playing its role adequately? The organisation is currently a toothless watchdog. Its dispute settlement body – the Appellate Body – no longer works because of the blocking (by the US) of appointments. Consequently, enforcement of the rules has become impossible.

WTO director-general Ngozi Okonjo-Iweala warns: 'If you didn't have the WTO it would be the Wild West.' The movies might be more exciting, but life would be worse, as stated in the *Financial Times*.[79] 'These problems are compounded by the broader geo-strategic developments,' writes the EU in a draft note to the European Parliament. 'In essence, since 1995 the world has changed; the WTO has not.'

Sino-European trade relationship gets into a rut

Opposition to China was much less pronounced in Europe until recently. The huge sales market made politicians, especially those from Germany, grit their teeth and accept China's unfair market practices. Volkswagen sold 40% of its cars in China in 2019 and was the top-selling car brand there. But that's no longer the case.

How are China's trade practices problematic? The main issues are the (often forced) technology transfer, subsidies and activities of state-owned enterprises, building up overcapacity and then dumping the products in Western markets. The fate of German solar panel producers shows this too. In 2003, Germany held a quarter of the global market share versus 3% for China. In the following decade, China absorbed and copied foreign technical expertise, developed massive capacity and economies of scale with government support, and thus captured the global market. By 2021, Europe's global market share in solar panel production had shrivelled to 3% compared to 93% for Asia, of which 70 percentage points are China's.[80] But Europe is also constantly shooting itself in the foot, financial blogger Noah Smith believes.[81] 'Whether it's using China as a cheap production base or selling core technology to Chinese companies, France and Germany seem to consistently choose quick cash over maintaining their long-term technological lead in advanced manufacturing.'

Germany and China are less of a match

The German and Chinese economies complemented each other nicely over the past two decades. Investments by German companies in China provided the country with high-tech know-how. German companies were happy with access to 1.3 billion potential buyers. Questionable market practices were covered with the cloak of love. Europe followed suit.

That modus vivendi is changing, as the evolution in the car industry illustrates. One in two internal combustion engine cars sold in China is foreign. The German share in that is large, with Volkswagen being the best-selling brand for the past 15 years. However, this is changing.

Made in China EVs could turn Sino-EU automotive trade on its head (EUR billion) Source: Eurostat

● EU car exports to China   ● EU car imports from China
○ of which EVs   ○ of which EVs

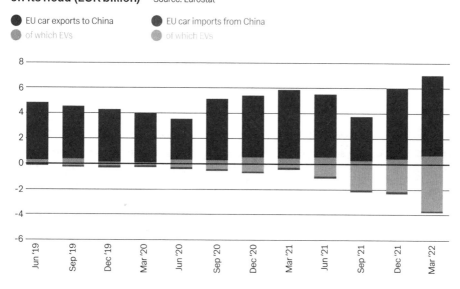

Since the first quarter of 2023, China's BYD has knocked Volkswagen off its throne. The bulk of BYD cars are fully electric or plug-in hybrid. The top ten best-selling electric cars in China included eight Chinese brands. Tesla was second with 10% (ranking 2023 to April). BYD has a 40% share. With its 2% share, Volkswagen risks tumbling out of that top ten at any moment.[82]

China is now succeeding with its electric cars where it previously failed with most other manufactured goods: building its own expertise and brand name to compete internationally. Hefty subsidies, pervasive knowledge of battery technology and a near-monopoly on raw materials to produce those batteries help. China will soon become the biggest exporter of electric cars, with an already significant market in Southeast Asia and a steep rise in Europe. German (and European) manufacturers will see the lucrative Chinese market go up in smoke and gain a formidable competitor on the home front. Demand for affordable electric vehicles is high there, supply by European manufacturers is limping along behind, and the Chinese are jumping into that gap. Will European politicians stand by and watch as China seizes the European market? When the first layoffs in the car industry occur, anti-dumping and anti-subsidy taxes will soon be introduced. Raising defences will be slower when Chinese

> factories appear in Europe. The impact on employment will then remain limited. New Chinese investment in Europe, especially in the automotive sector, has been increasing in recent years. The result? Reduced complementarity between the Chinese and German/European economies. We're curious to see how long Europe will continue to turn a blind eye to China's unfair market practices.

Should Europe reject cheap Chinese solar panels, wind turbines, and cars? If so, the cost of the climate transition is mounting. A 2022 study in the scientific journal *Nature* estimates that between 2008 and 2020, the globalised solar panel market reduced installation costs by $36 billion in China, $24 billion in the United States and $7 billion in Germany.[83]

Europe should insist on reciprocity. It should strive for a level playing field for European companies in China. But things are stalling there for now. 'Although Europe and China already sit at opposite ends of a shared continent, it seems they are drifting further and further apart,' writes president Jörg Wuttkes of the European Chamber of Commerce in China in his foreword to the annual report. 'Trade could represent the means of strengthening ties between the two sides, but currently it is lopsided. The European market's importance as a destination for Chinese exports is around double that of the Chinese market for Europeans,' – all as a result of large-scale regulatory barriers.

Global currencies

The dollar and the potentially transitory privilege of the reserve currency

'The dollar is our currency, but it's your problem.'

———

JOHN CONNALLY, TREASURY SECRETARY UNDER RICHARD NIXON

After World War II, the United States, with its entire intact economy, strong military and innovative growth, quickly became the world's leading nation. The Soviet Union tried to provide a communist alternative to that. But we learn from history how this kind of experiment ends. It might work for ants and bees, but not for humans. In geopolitical terms, China did not play a significant role at that time.

Against this backdrop, it is no big surprise that the US was at the inception of the new monetary system, Bretton Woods, and called the shots. The US dollar would become the lynchpin of this new world order. A world order where trade became increasingly important, even after Nixon closed the gold window in 1971 and de facto buried Bretton Woods. Even after dollars no longer became automatically convertible into gold, and the gold price consequently began a spectacular climb, the whole world continued to trade and invest in dollars. The role the so-called petrodollars played in this should not be underestimated either. Countries such as Saudi Arabia and what was then the Shah's Iran started trading their oil in dollars. The dollar became the trading currency for the entire world of commodities.

In the chapter about debts, we will certainly talk more about rising sovereign debt. But so far, rising US debt has played to the advantage rather than the disadvantage of the US dollar as the world reserve currency. At first glance, this sounds paradoxical. An initial logical reaction might be that if a country's debts are rising, the rest of the world will be less eager to hold that currency. But the willingness to hold a currency for the long(er) term depends overwhelmingly on confidence in debt repayment and interest rates. And despite several downgrades of the US debt rating – by S&P in 2011 and recently by Fitch, each time from the very highest rating to the level just below – this is still the case. Moreover, the fact that the debt is so large has even contributed to the dollar's status as a reserve currency.

To see the logic of this, we have to go back to basics, namely what properties something must fulfil to function as money. Money must fulfil three functions. The first is that of a unit of account. The other two functions are a little more difficult. One is the medium of exchange: you have to be able to trade with it. But for that, enough parties must be willing to see the currency as a means of payment and actually trade with it. It has to be practical, but it is mainly a matter of trust in the currency. From a historical perspective, this makes sense. Historically, you could exchange a spear for, say, a piece of mammoth meat, or a goat for an ornament. The problem with this was that if someone had a goat but did not find a counterparty willing to exchange the ornament for it, the transaction stalled. Selling the goat for money first and then buying the ornament from someone else was the solution. But the whole process does rely on the goat seller's belief that he will find someone who trusts the money enough to exchange goods for it. Moreover, the value of the money should not drop too much during the time he is looking for an ornament. The latter is even more important in the third function money must fulfil: you have to be able to store value in it. Sometimes you have sold much more than you bought and need to look for investments. You have to be able to store your surplus, your wealth, preferably somewhere where it does not lose too much of its value.

If we fast-forward to today, it is very important that there are large pools in which people with assets may temporarily store their wealth, where there is a basis of trust that they can get it back at some point with value more or less preserved. Deep, broad and liquid capital markets are significant too. The US not only still has the largest stock market with the most interesting (growth) companies, but also a very deep, large and liquid market for bonds, and especially government bonds. A crucial assumption here is that this debt is safe and will be repaid.

Fed chairman Jerome Powell's assertion that the financial crisis has fundamentally changed the financial system underlines this point. According to Powell, we live in a world where there will be constant and volatile demand for safe, liquid assets. Therefore, the Fed will not return to a scarcity policy of reserves. This has far-reaching implications, as it means there is a limit on how far the US central bank will reduce its balance sheet. It wants to have enough US government paper on hand itself to supply the market with enough paper in case of stress and volatility. This not only allows it to regulate the long term, but also supports the status of the US currency as a reserve currency.

Recently, however, more and more questions have arisen as to whether the US dollar is about to lose its status as a reserve currency. In the chapter about debt, we see that tremendous privileges hang on reserve currency status. It is not illogical that China, with its ambition to knock the US off the leadership throne, has its eye on that reserve currency status. But there is more. The US is increasingly using the dominant position of the dollar to hit countries that do not toe its line geopolitically. For instance, Russia was recently partially thrown out of the Swift payment network and saw part of its dollar-denominated assets frozen. As such, it should come as no surprise that the confidence a number of less-friendly nations have in the dollar as a store of value has faltered.

That is why it also makes sense to look at an alternative. This starts on the trade front. For instance, the BRICS (Brazil, Russia, India, China and South Africa) are looking at the possibility of trading with each other in their own currencies or even in a new, joint currency that would be convertible into gold. A kind of mini-Bretton Woods, so to speak. That may sound promising, but when trading in their own or joint currency, someone will have certain surpluses. Do you hold those surpluses in the counterparty's currency that you have received? Or will you invest them somewhere? If there are insufficient investment opportunities in the bloc and you do buy US assets again, you are back to square one, as you cannot buy US bonds or stocks without buying dollars. That is one of the important reasons why we always keep a percentage of dollars in the portfolios we manage: you always need them somewhere. All in all, the whole story hinges on whether sufficient investment opportunities can be created. Increasing China's sovereign debt could paradoxically partially solve this problem. Sometimes, financial markets work counter-intuitively.

Then there is the aspect of gold as a historical currency. Do you have enough gold to convert every coin into the yellow metal if it were in demand? You'd need a lot of it, probably much more than countries like China currently have. It also means that with growing trade, more and more gold would be needed. A lack of gold inhibits trade. It helps understand why countries like China and Russia are currently buying gold en masse. It is not just a way to diversify their reserves away from the US dollar. If you want to talk about a new world monetary order, a new mini-Bretton Woods, you better have some gold nuggets in your back pocket.

Adding all this together, it seems that a growing share of world trade will gradually happen in currencies other than the US dollar. 'Gradually' is an important word here. History shows that over long periods, the importance of a currency declines and increases, that new currencies can snatch reserve currency status from old leaders. This happened when the economic centre of power shifted from the Italian city-states towards the Netherlands with its guilder, then towards the United Kingdom with its pound, eventually ending up where we are today. There were also very long periods when there were several reserve currencies at the same time. In a world that is becoming more bipolar or even multipolar, it is not implausible that we are heading towards that. But we are talking about very long periods, not something for the next five or ten years.

I have a simple way to determine what the reserve currency is. To do so, we'll take an evolutionary biology approach. In the fantastic book *Mean Markets and Lizard Brains*, stock market specialist Terry Burnham tells us how people often react irrationally and how we can take advantage of this as investors. Again, the basic idea is that over millions of years of evolution, we have developed different types of thinking processes or brains. When we are not under pressure and have enough time, we mostly use our modern human brains. But when pressure or panic hits and it is a matter of life or death, as tends to happen quite often in financial markets, we are back on the savannah and our reptilian brains take over. These are ideally suited for things like reproduction and survival. Let us imagine the following situation. A giant black swan, an unpredictable extreme event, falls on our heads. All certainties are mown away from under our feet. We have five seconds to decide whether to put all our wealth in dollars or yuan. What we choose in that moment is the world reserve currency, even if it may not be rational. In these times, I know what I would choose....

This also means that if for whatever reason confidence in the dollar were to suddenly plummet, not everyone will quietly start thinking about which basket of other currencies is an alternative. At such a time, and let us hope it does not occur, things will go rock-bottom towards the ultimate reserve currency: gold. This also makes the dollar the Achilles' heel of our financial system in addition to being the reserve currency.

Is gold the ultimate reserve currency?

'Gold gives the ugliest thing a certain charming air,
for without it, it would be a miserable affair.'

———

MOLIÈRE

Few investments can capture, divide, and confuse hearts and minds as much as gold. Every day I speak to both strong believers, and possibly even stronger detractors. The latter, including Warren Buffett, consider gold a barbaric relic at best, and worse in other cases.

There are as many reasons to invest in gold as there are buyers. Two very obvious ones are protection against inflation and against just about any other calamity, such as wars, the collapse of civilisation or the end of the world. That protection against inflation is certainly correct, although we should add that it only applies in the very long term. Studies have been conducted that indicate that with the amount of gold it took to buy a toga in Roman times, you can buy a nice, sleek suit today. The statement also holds true over periods of more than 50 years. But there are quite a few periods of 20 years or more when gold does not offer proper protection, or even offers only poor protection, against the general rise in price levels. Moreover, gold does rebound when war breaks out or a major attack occurs somewhere in the world, but whether that rise is sustainable again depends on the situation at hand.

A third and possibly even more important historical reason for explosive increases in gold prices is not only the rapid devaluation of money – (hyper) inflation – but even more importantly the total evaporation of confidence in paper money. At such times, gold resumes its age-old role as money or medium of exchange in an economy. The main reason why gold is useful as money is that it is above all a store of value. The latter is due to the fact that gold is rare. All the gold that man has scraped together over the past 6,000 years fits into a cube of less than 25 metres. The fact that this cube is worth roughly $15 trillion illustrates its rarity and also its value. Gold, despite all the efforts and dreams of alchemists, cannot be made by human hands. Gold is an atom that was not formed on Earth itself. All gold on Earth comes from space, where it was forged in the nuclear blast furnaces of supernovas.

This means that if the world were to lose faith in the dollar for any reason, all roads would lead to gold and silver. As happened, for example, at the beginning of the 18th century, when confidence in paper money diminished after the financial experiment of the brilliant Scottish adventurer John Law, finance minister of France. It was no big surprise that Napoleon returned to a currency system based on gold and silver after the French Revolution.

Such a scenario questioning the financial system itself is fortunately never a likely or basic scenario. However, it does justify a particle of gold in portfolios at all times. But beware: the negative correlation of gold with just about everything else only works in very extreme cases. With a negative correlation, one rises when the other falls, which helps reduce your risk. There are quite a few misunderstandings about this correlation when it comes to gold. First of all, gold and the dollar are almost always negatively correlated. Gold is a commodity, and commodities are traded in dollars. There is therefore usually a negative correlation between the two. Even if commodity prices fall in dollar terms but the dollar rises, commodities can still become more expensive in their local currency for non-dollar countries. But the real reason for the negative correlation is more complex. The dollar usually does well when US interest rates rise. The latter sucks money into US bond markets. To buy US bonds or bonds denominated in US dollars, foreigners also have to buy dollars, which pushes up the price of the greenback. That in itself is mostly bad news for gold, which trades in dollars. More importantly, gold also becomes less attractive as an investment when interest rates rise – especially real interest rates (nominal interest rates minus inflation). After all, gold does not yield interest. As long as it competes with near-zero interest rates on a savings account, the opportunity cost of holding the yellow metal is virtually nil. But if interest rates on a savings account or in the bond markets become 6%, it means that the gold price has to rise by 6% a year to achieve the same return.

This has serious implications. When real interest rates rise, not only does gold tend to underperform, but so do equity markets. While equities often pay a dividend, they are also not impervious to the gravity that higher interest rates mean. At the end of the day, all investments are in competition with each other. And it also becomes harder for equities to compete with bonds when interest rates start to rise firmly. This means gold is not always a good security or diversifier for an equity portfolio. If interest rates rise, equities and gold may perfectly well plunge together. Or if interest rates fall, they can both rise. Only when equity markets drop sharply due to some shock that also causes interest rates to fall can gold benefit.

Still, the conclusion remains: putting a part of one's portfolio in gold is often a good idea. Investors are always surprised when I say that the price of gold could well double over the next few years. That would not be the first time in history. Until President Richard Nixon lifted the convertibility of the dollar into gold in August 1971, the gold price was $35 an ounce. Then came a doubling to $70, to $140, to $280, to $560, to $1,120, and recently it almost doubled again to around $2,000 an ounce. If my maths is correct, that's six doublings since I was born. Of course, timing remains a tricky business. And gold, like just about all asset classes, moves in big waves. But we could well be on the cusp of a big wave. As I said, a lot of countries are trying to diversify their reserves away from the dollar. Gold is also a way to play the growth markets. The biggest physical demand for gold comes from emerging markets. India and China account for half of all demand for gold. If the emerging markets are doing well, you can expect gold to do well too.

There is another indirect way to capitalise on a rise in the gold price, namely investing in gold mines. These very often have leverage on the gold price. Specifically, if the gold price rises by, say, 1%, mining companies will rise by a multiple of that. The same applies in the other direction, unfortunately. And let's face it: gold mines have structurally not been a good investment for many years now.

Philadelphia Gold & Silver Index

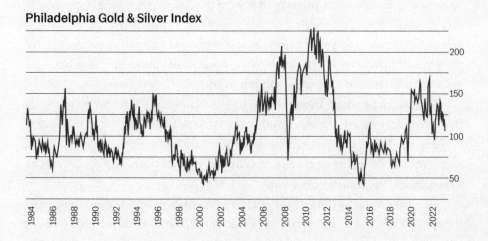

If we look at a gold mining index, such as the Philadelphia Gold and Silver Index, we see that we are still at the same level as in the early 1980s, and this even though the gold price has increased about fivefold over that period.

This story does deserve some nuance, as gold mines regularly paid dividends over that period that are not captured in the index. But even then, the underperformance is remarkable. You could even say that the gold mines destroyed value, because you also have to factor in inflation over those years. Often these companies made bad investments at the wrong times (when gold was (too) valuable and the sky seemed the limit) by simply overpaying for certain assets and also taking on too much debt. Added to this were setbacks such as accidents, production outages, power shortages and, more recently, the difficulties of obtaining operating licences. Mining projects also often turned out to be much more expensive than budgeted. To complete the horror story, finding gold at an acceptable price became increasingly difficult, as the large and 'easy reserves' were found in relatively stable jurisdictions. You already have to be a top expert and/or very lucky to get into this. Currently, 2,500 to 3,000 tonnes of gold are mined annually, barely 1.5% of the total amount of gold available. This immediately explains why changes in the annual quantity produced have little or no impact on the price of gold.

Still, there is something to be said for investing in gold-mining stocks today, at least for investors who can handle above-average risk for a piece of their portfolio. The leverage on the cycle is huge. If the gold price is indeed on the verge of a nice rise, the rise in the sector left for dead could well be spectacular. The cost structure, the price to mine an ounce of gold, varies greatly from company to company. For instance, projects that were previously absolutely unprofitable may suddenly become so with a higher gold price. It means that in an environment of a sharply rising gold price, the less profitable companies suddenly have the greatest upside potential. But beware, because of course they also have the greatest risk. The two tend to go hand in hand.

Overall, the balance sheets of the bigger players in the sector were firmly cleaned up and we are at the bottom of the cycle. A final asset left in the pocket of the much-hit sector is that many gold mines are also active in copper. And as we point out in the chapter on climate, copper is one of the better opportunities to respond to the climate transition.

So what should be the ratio of gold to gold mines in a portfolio? The simple answer is that there is no definite answer to this. It varies from investor to investor. But if I have to advise something, I stick to 75% in a tracker on gold and 25% in gold mines for the extra leverage.

For those 25% gold-mining stocks, an appropriate spread is important. The risk of investing in just one or a few gold-mining shares is extremely high. Therefore, investing via an active or passive fund with a spread is recommended. An additional advantage is that there are often a number of smaller and medium-sized companies in the fund in addition to the large well-known gold-mining stocks. These junior miners in particular, which are still in the exploration phase and often do not yet have a producing mine, can be interesting because of their huge leverage in case of success. This is also because the big companies will almost be obliged to expand their portfolio further. They can do so by looking for the precious metal themselves, or by buying out promising juniors with enough reserves. Currently, the entire junior mining sector is historically low priced. This means that in the not-too-distant future, a buyout wave could well be under way. That has been a long time coming.

What about silver? Or in derivative order silver mines? 'If you like gold, you should love silver,' is commonly said by gold and hence silver lovers. Gold has few industrial applications. The production of smartphones and circuit boards does require a small amount of gold. But unlike zinc, copper or aluminium, gold can hardly be called an industrial raw material. Gold is and remains first and foremost a precious metal. With an investment in silver, you are betting on two horses: one called precious (metal), and another called industry. Silver is at such historically low levels that it is probably the cheapest metal on the planet right now. But again, potential return and risk go hand in hand, as silver and silver mines are still a lot more volatile than their gold counterparts.

What about crypto?

*'When it comes to money,
everyone is of the same religion.'*

———

VOLTAIRE

Can crypto replace old-fashioned gold as the ultimate reserve currency? That's a question we are increasingly getting asked. There are certainly some similarities. Both are mined, one real and the other virtual. Both therefore require a lot of energy. Both have little or no real value in themselves, other than the value that stems from their relative rarity and from the faith investors place in them.

The crypto story is very cleverly marketed. Every strong story has a culprit, and the culprit here is the central banks, whose ever-faster-running money press not only undercuts the value of paper money but also fuels inequality. When their quantitative easing, the massive buying of (government) paper by central banks, reduces the value of money and therefore the value of everything denominated in money, the value of real assets skyrockets. To benefit from this, you obviously have to be a lucky owner of real assets. Moreover, every strong origin story has a hero, and in this case it is Satoshi Nakamoto, the man who, according to urban legend, gave life to bitcoin. The fact that it is the pseudonym of an unknown person or group makes the story even more powerful. Imagine: a new world order based on crypto coins is coming. The relative price of these coins is going to rise explosively, a thousandfold. And if you get there in time, you will suddenly be one of the billionaires of this new world. Now, that's a story.

There are currently thousands of crypto coins, most of which will go up in digital smoke over time. Crypto coins are also still young and must contend with the credibility of gold, which is anchored in a history counted in millennia. But young people see things differently.

I must admit that I also see things in a slightly more nuanced way now than I did a few years ago. Back then, I would have said that central banks have flooded the world with liquidity to such an extent in recent years that, when it no longer found a way out in the real world, it also partly flowed towards the virtual world. That remains part of the explanation. It explains why bitcoin struggles when interest rates rise and often moves along with gold, albeit more explosively and that both up and down. Rising interest rates create more attractive investment alternatives for bitcoin and co.

But if you give lectures to young people and students, you won't get away with this explanation alone. If you say you don't believe in bitcoin, they will tar and feather you or worse, you will lose their attention. Therefore, a slightly deeper analysis is needed. Are crypto coins money? To answer this question, we need to go back to the functions of money. Bitcoin is a unit of account, because you can count in it and it is also divisible. It is a medium of exchange, because you can trade in it, although the number of people who will buy a pizza with it can probably be counted on one hand. This is also understandable. Nobody wants to have consumed a $5,000 or more pizza a few years ago, when the price keeps rising. And then there is the most difficult feature: the store of value. Can you store value in bitcoin? Are you sure it will hold its value? The answer depends a lot on who you ask the question. We can at least agree on the fact that bitcoin is quite volatile. The value it has today may have changed positively or negatively tomorrow. And of a currency, surely you would prefer that it does not double or halve in a few months' time.

I therefore do not see bitcoin as a currency, but rather as a bet on something technological. Again, the correlation with technology stocks and the Nasdaq is striking. On days when the tech exchange Nasdaq is doing well, in the vast majority of cases bitcoin goes up and vice versa. Also, if you look at bitcoin's price movement, you come to the same conclusion. I sometimes take the test during presentations. I show the chart of bitcoin but remove the name from it. When I then ask what chart this is, I almost never hear a coin, but almost always one of the technology stocks and then one of the more speculative, volatile kind. Once someone said a Turkish lira expressed in euro, and admittedly, it does look a bit like that. But it is not a stable currency, nor a stable store of value. However, that does not mean that bitcoin cannot rise.

As an investor, what interests me even more than crypto currencies are a number of developments closely linked to them. One is blockchain technology, an advanced database system that allows information to be shared transparently in a network. The name 'blockchain' comes from the way that data is stored: as blocks in a chain. So much for the technology. The interesting thing from an investment perspective is its potential applications. First and foremost, there are massive productivity gains possible. Take the use of points. Those things have completely fallen into disuse in the banking sector because of the huge administrative hassle and labour intensity. But with blockchain, this whole process could potentially be given a new lease of life.

I also look with much interest at the opportunities that may arise from so-called smart contracts and NFTs. An NFT (non-fungible token) consists of a code incorporating a smart contract. This code may store digital applications of the NFT. For example, an NFT can refer to a digital artwork, such as an image, photo or video. But it can also be a key or an access ticket to do something, such as entry to a concert. It can also be a right to something, like an income stream. And that's where it gets interesting. Imagine if you could approach one of the most amazing artists – like Vincent van Gogh, who lived in terrible poverty during his lifetime – and say, 'Mr Van Gogh, I love your art. Let's draw up a contract. You will receive a certain sum from me on which you can live comfortably, and I get 10% of your future income stream.' A deal everyone can get on board with, right? So this whole story is less about trading strange digital creatures whose prices have equally gone through the roof due to the abundance of money in the system, and more about gaining access to markets that were previously impossible to access. In the future, you may be able to buy the future cashflows of artists, writers and inventors. Meanwhile, there are places where you can invest in wine or whisky where there are constant bid and offer prices. Or where you can buy a thousandth of a real painting (not virtual) by a Warhol or a Basquiat, which would normally be out of reach for most people. As a wine lover, art lover and markets person, I can only welcome new entrances to markets. This creates more opportunities and more possibilities to diversify into real assets. All this makes an investment in the technology that makes all that possible very worthwhile.

There is no doubt that the line between the real and virtual worlds will blur more and more, and from that perspective, we will live in some kind of multiverse in the future. This is probably why the whole metaverse story gets less attention and appreciation than it deserves. In the metaverse, our physical existence merges with the surrounding digital world. The metaverse as we define it today can be thought of as an upgrade of internet applications, where users enter 3D virtual environments via virtual reality (VR), augmented reality (AR), mixed reality (MR), or holography and engage in all kinds of activities in them, such as gaming, working, studying and trading. Currently, focus on the metaverse has languished in favour of AI. But the two are particularly complementary. AI will be used to create virtual worlds and video games of unprecedented quality and depth. It will make not only the line between real and virtual blurry, but also the boundaries between genres. There will be films about video games, video games about films, and so on. Perhaps *Tomb Raider* was a pioneer of that. Above all, the franchise will become much more valuable. The *Star Wars* films will not just be video games and theme parks, but everything will become much more interactive. Before long, you will be able to re-enact your favourite character on some kind of holodeck like in *Star Trek* in a virtual world that will be indistinguishable from the real one. Gaming platforms such as *Fortnite* and *Roblox* are currently creating a symbiosis where gaming, social media and other entertainment forms merge completely. They then become the setting for mini concerts by the likes of Ariana Grande and others.

In a world where everything fragments, the value of events that everyone wants to see will only skyrocket, as will the price tag of superstars. Advertising through our screens can be bypassed more and more easily. Advertising directly on the events will get more and more value. More than 80% of those events have to do with professional sports. The prices paid for certain sports clubs or for certain players often raise eyebrows. That's true if you calculate with past cash flows, but it is the cash flows from the future that matter. And those will only increase in a world where 'the winner takes it all'. We are more than ever in what statistician Nassim Taleb calls *extremistan*, which is the opposite of *mediocristan*. Imagine a sleepy Italian village with a piazza and a few restaurants around it, sometime before World War I. It is almost dusk. The atmosphere is exuberant, because tonight, Francesco, the local opera star, will give a performance. The fact that Francesco can't actually sing all that beautifully is not important. Every village has a Francesco. And they all earn a reasonable living and are world-famous in their village and some neighbouring streets. But then comes the gramophone record, and then the radio and Pavarotti. Suddenly everyone is watching and listening to them, they become world stars and collect all the income from the Francescos, who are suddenly out of work. We live in an *extremistan* that gets more extreme every day.

This also opens up unseen opportunities for young people. Suddenly, influencers get access to millions of followers. This can be extremely lucrative, and the technological barrier is very low today. Still, the world is tough. Today you can be an influencer with the world at your feet, while tomorrow, someone or something else will be much more interesting. Just like in trading, you are only as good as your last trade, your last deal. The pressure to keep posting becomes huge. So many people will drop out and only become users or consumers of products and services, which will only widen the gap with creators, as will inequality. Since AI and the metaverse are really Siamese twins that reinforce each other, the building blocks of the metaverse and hence the investment opportunities will be the same. Semiconductors and energy, anyone? A final investment idea we can add as a bonus track here is e-sports and related betting. As sports teams and top athletes become increasingly valuable, their counterparts in the virtual world will surf along in their slipstream. Of the giant video game events that are already extremely popular in Asia, we haven't even seen the beginning.

the DECOUPLING

KEY POINTS

✓ Another couple of years of good relations between the US and China would allow China to step into the club of developed countries. Then it can compete with the US. A detente is not on the cards.

✓ The two countries are now in a relationship that is confrontational in lots of ways. An acceleration of the decoupling during Xi Jinping's current five-year tenure is becoming the default business mode for US investors and other affiliates.

✓ The Pentagon has decided that chips are the hill they are willing to die on. Ring-fencing sensitive technology is stifling China's growth ambitions and accelerating the disconnect between Western and Chinese companies.

✓ China is doing all it can to become self-sufficient faster. It is taking targeted counter-measures with the 'nuclear' option of denying the US and its allies access to minerals and metals necessary for the climate transition.

✓ The West's response is to do everything possible to become more self-sufficient as well. Spearheading that strategy is the Inflation Reduction Act (IRA) in the US and the European Green Deal Industrial Plan, which builds on NextGenerationEU.

✓ Europe is providing more resources for its reindustrialisation than the US, but is not as effective in getting them sold.

Since the Ukraine war, China has sided with Russia. It is also no longer the developing country of four decades ago. By 2035, according to its own definition, it aims to be a moderately developed country, by 2049 a developed country. China is growing steadily, and its rise is seen by the US and the West – rightly – as a serious strategic challenge due to differences in ideology and political systems. 'It's not possible to pretend that [China] is just another big player,' says Lee Kuan Yew, the former prime minister of Singapore. 'This is the biggest player in the history of man.'

US opposition to China

After Biden's election, everyone was hoping for a detente in US-China relations. It hasn't happened. Democrats and Republicans agree on almost nothing, except that the basis for US foreign policy should be opposition to China's rise. From the US point of view, according to research firm BCA,[84] confrontation is justified. 'While another decade of US engagement with China would benefit the US economy, it would be far more beneficial to China.' It would give the country the necessary room for manoeuvre to make crucial technological breakthroughs. That would boost productivity and allow China to escape from the infamous middle-income trap, in which emerging countries struggle to step into the club of rich, developed economies. At that point, China could rival the US economically and militarily. Why would Biden's defence and intelligence advisers choose that?

Both sides also view every aspect of China-US relations through the lens of national security. Beijing sees export controls on US technologies as a threat to China's future growth; Washington sees anything that can promote China's technological capacity as shooting itself in the foot. In a military sense, it currently does not have much to fear from China. According to official figures, US defence spending was almost three times higher than China's. But Xi has indicated that he wants to modernise China's military by 2035. By 2049, it should be a 'first-class' military force capable of 'fighting and winning wars'.

Wars will also look very different in the future. According to the US Department of Defence, China is betting heavily on the development of 'intelligent' warfare. These are military strategies based on disruptive technologies, such as artificial intelligence and cyber-attacks. The merger of civilian and military entities – Chinese technology companies collaborating with the defence industry – should make that happen. As far as the US is concerned, technology that can also be used for military purposes can no longer go towards China or any of its allies.

'The Pentagon has decided that semiconductors is the hill that they are willing to die on,' says James Mulvenon, an expert on Chinese cybersecurity, in The Economist. 'Semiconductors is the last industry in which the US is ahead, and it is the one on which everything else is built.' Between August and October 2022, the Biden administration launched a wave of initiatives aimed at preventing China from acquiring advanced technologies and building on the US lead: CHIPS act, restricting export licences for certain technologies, restricting the use of Chinese chips, and so on. Later, Biden issued further executive orders, such as investment restrictions in certain Chinese technology sectors.

The application of the rules poses a serious threat not only to China's longer-term chip ambitions, but also to other top Chinese companies, both in technology and in related sectors such as AI and electric cars (e.g. Alibaba, Baidu, ByteDance, BYD, Nio, Tencent, Xiaomi and XPeng). They see their ambitions for AI, big data, smart/self-driving cars and cloud computing seriously cut short by shrinking technological capabilities against rival US and Western companies. 'In our base case, decoupling will therefore accelerate to become the default operating mode of US investors and other close US allies over the next five-year period of Xi Jinping's third term,' predicts research firm TS Lombard.[85]

The Chinese response

An aggressive response from China would fail to materialise, everyone thought. 'There are many soft targets China could strike against – Tesla, Apple, Starbucks, American banks, to name a few,' writes TS Lombard.[86] 'However, we expect Beijing to spare firms operating in the mainland. A key emphasis in Xi's Political Report was "accelerating reform and opening".' China is still limping around four years behind American and Taiwanese companies on high-tech chips. Although it is a global leader in other technologies, such as batteries, losing that top technology is China's Achilles' heel.

But in the first half of 2023, China brought in a spate of new rules, ranging from a list of 'untrustworthy entities' over an export control law to tightening data and cybersecurity rules. America's salvos in the trade war are being answered. In early February 2023, Lockheed Martin and Raytheon Missiles & Defence were the first to land on the blacklist. US chipmaker Micron is no longer allowed to supply chips for critical infrastructure. At the same time, Beijing is doing everything it can to become self-sufficient even faster, in terms of technology, through state-led innovation and selecting winners within sectors. Smaller Chinese companies in the chip sector, for example, receive cheap loans, subsidies and a guaranteed outlet: the public sector.

There is also the 'nuclear' option: Chinese dominance in the supply chain of rare metals and critical minerals. A first missile was launched in mid-2023 with the imposition of export restrictions on gallium and germanium. The restriction followed a day after Dutch company ASML announced it would no longer export its most advanced chip machines to China. China produces 98% of global raw gallium, a necessary ingredient for advanced military technology. Gallium nitride underpins a new generation of high-performance semiconductors.

The threat of being cut off from China's supply chain for raw materials led to the US IRA in 2022. That law provides at least $369 billion in tax credits and subsidies over the next decade in an attempt to set up a full US supply chain for chip and green technology production. The huge mountain of money should attract domestic and foreign producers, and it is succeeding nicely. Investment in these sectors doubled compared to 2021.[87] The US Treasury Secretary also launched a friend-shoring proposal in April 2022. The aim is to outsource and share the production of components and raw materials within a group of countries with common values. The US, in common with most other countries and regions, cannot dig up and refine all the necessary raw materials itself. The concept does raise some pressing questions. After all, who are your friends? And will your current friends still be friendly tomorrow?

The cards are being shuffled

World power shifts from the United States to...

'Reports of my death have been greatly exaggerated.'

———

MARK TWAIN

If one theme has received above-average attention over the past 20 years, or certainly since the end of the Global Financial Crisis of 2008–2009, it is the superior performance of US stock indices. Let us take the S&P500, and compare it with any European, Japanese or Chinese index, and the picture is clear...

Outperformance, S&P500

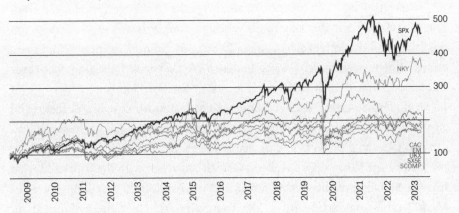

Throughout that period, we constantly hear people questioning whether US markets are too expensive, or speculation about the end of the US as a world power. About China, which is eager to take over the hegemony of the Americans. The often-drawn conclusion? The US stock market will lose many of its feathers if those doomsday scenarios materialise. The (relative) valuation of US equities would then take a hit.

This is oversimplification, and it is quite harmful. Much of America's better performance in recent years can be attributed to the composition of US indices compared to other stock markets. Nowhere in the world are there as many technology stocks in the indices in percentage terms as in the US today. Moreover, the vast majority of the world's tech giants, such as Apple, Google and Microsoft, call the nation of wide prairies and the Rocky Mountains home. If you want to bet on a structural underperformance of the US, you are not only betting on the loss of its status as world leader. You are also betting that all those companies will lose their dominance in technology. And that's quite something. Of course, there will be periods in the coming years when technology values lag behind more value-related companies (which are the more traditional, often slower-growing companies). Those will be the times when European stock markets will outperform their US counterparts. There will also be times when growth markets finally live up to their potential in terms of returns. In that case, US indices may do relatively less well for a few months, or even years. But betting against what is still the world's largest economy, with technological leadership still in place, is certainly a bridge too far.

Its position between two oceans also gives the US a huge advantage. Author Tim Marshall puts it this way in his excellent book *Prisoners of Geography*: suppose you won the lottery and you could buy any country in the world, as real estate. Which country would you choose? We all know the saying that three things are important in real estate: location, location, location. America's position is almost perfect. Its neighbours, Canada and Mexico, are peaceful and largely unproblematic. From the north come raw materials and in the south, you can run industrial projects at reasonable wages. But perhaps most valuable are the waters. The Mississippi River connects the corn belt with the Gulf of Mexico. It is the lifeblood of the United States and the intellectual breeding ground of Mark Twain's wonderful stories, like Tom Sayer and Huckleberry Finn, about riverboats and great rivers. In fact, the entire east is filled with waterways, which offers ample opportunity for transportation.

New Orleans, which was initially called New Orléans, was bought by the Americans from the French in 1803 along with the entire area of Louisiana (named after Louis XIV) for $15 million. Louisiana comprised the present-day states of Louisiana, Arkansas, Missouri, Iowa, Oklahoma, Kansas, Minnesota, Nebraska, North and South Dakota, Montana and some stretches of Wyoming, Colorado and New Mexico. It was larger than the area of Spain, Italy, France, the UK and Germany combined. A real bargain. Or, as the famous American historian Henry Adams once put it: 'Never in history did the United States get so much for so little.' The area of the country doubled and, in the process, the still-young nation gained complete control over the fertile Mississippi basin, the lifeblood of the United States.

Add to that the idea that the US has the strongest naval fleet in the world, and that there were so many warships after the victory in World War II that some had to be destroyed, and we are looking at a country that can invade anywhere from a military point of view, yet is superbly protected by its two coastlines.

The fact that the country also has some of the best agricultural land in the world and, especially after the development of shale oil and shale gas, has virtually all the important resources, is naturally a nice bonus.

But above all, it is and remains a story of location. Let us do the following thought experiment. Suppose the world map were to look as we know it today, but with the location of 300 million years ago, the Late Palaeozoic. It was the period when all the continents combined to form the supercontinent Pangea. It was also a time when, due to a large amount of CO_2 in the atmosphere, the earth was a lot warmer (sounds familiar), and so there was no ice to be seen. Unfortunately, it was also a period of mass extinctions. For our thought experiment, we imagine that all seas are navigable, and all countries have the resources they have today.

The question then becomes: is the US still so well positioned? Suddenly, you have a whole bunch of neighbours and are no longer protected by two oceans. Even the Mississippi no longer joins the ocean, which severely limits transport options. To say something positive, we can still note that at least there is access to water and trade. On such a large continent, everything looks a bit like Australia today. Or the interior of Africa, where a lot of countries are landlocked and need their neighbours for trade and transport. In that view, countries like Brazil, Argentina and Saudi Arabia would have a distinctly less favourable location. And China, like Australia, would be pretty much at the end of the world. Antarctica seems to fare pretty well, and this is probably even more true of Russia. The country has been striving all its history to have usable seaports and accessible sea routes all year round. That goal would have been reached in this scenario. Siberia, which is right on the ocean to transport raw materials, is certainly not to be overlooked either.

So what would such a world look like? The important trading centres would probably be on the coasts, where the vast majority of the world's population would also live. It is the same in our current world. The interior, like Australia, would be a lot emptier and mainly used for agriculture and resource extraction. Transport would probably be by rivers, but also by roads and trains. Maritime trade would perhaps be even more important and a strong fleet vital. Would we eventually move towards more or fewer countries and towards peace or a state of constant war? The closeness here is reminiscent of Europe from the 15th century onwards. A period of much conflict, wars, inventions, but still relative peace after many centuries. Is one connected land more difficult or easier to unite into larger wholes? There's certainly much to say about that.

If the world map today looked as it did 300 million years ago, there would be better contenders than the US to be the world power. Because no country could be fully protected from all the others, there would probably be no world power. But the map looks very different today. And in this age, the US remains extremely well positioned militarily with what, up until now, has been the strongest naval fleet as well as two oceans as a buffer. Add to this the fact that the country has tracts of the most fertile farmland in the world, brims with resources, capital and technology, and has a relatively young population compared to Europe and China. The 21st century could well be the century of the United States once again, even from an investment perspective. The challenges facing the country are enormous, but betting on its decline is not a good strategy.

What does China offer?

We often see the rise and fall of empires as a kind of relay race in which the baton of world leadership is passed from one civilisation to another. In reality, however, these are chaotic systems that unfold over very long periods, where luck and chance often play a major role, and where world powers and empires share power for the vast majority of the time. Periods during which the world is unipolar, i.e. where one world power is in control, are rather rare. Such periods are often characterised by relative peace and prosperity, at least for the world power and its allies. The two most obvious examples are the Roman Empire from, say, the first century BC to the first century AD (the period of the Pax Romana), and more recently the hegemony of the United States since World War II. It is therefore tempting to compare the two. The change from a unipolar to a bipolar or even multipolar world, with the US losing relative power and influence, is then contrasted with the fall of the Roman Empire. As we will argue in this chapter, this reasoning is too linear and simplistic. On the other hand, we cannot ignore the fact that China and the emerging countries make up an increasing proportion of the global economy. Leaving this ever-growing slice of the pie to one side, despite the undoubtedly increased risks, is obviously not a good idea either.

Markets often have good predictive value in 'foreseeing' which way things will go. In the fantastic book *War, Wealth and Wisdom*, Barton Biggs describes very well how markets immediately interpreted the battle of Midway, the most important naval battle between Japan and the US during World War II, as a turning point in the war, long before strategists and historians came to this understanding. The German stock market saw its peak in 1943, and the British market at that time was at what was subsequently a generational low. As the odds turned in the war, the British stock market began a strong bull market, while the German stock market slumped. Unlike the terrible war in Ukraine today, stock markets went up and down with the success or loss of battles. This is not illogical, because the fate of the free world was at stake then. Nonetheless, it remains a good idea to leave our library from time to time and take a look across the pond, for the rise and fall of empires are also waves, albeit very long-term ones. For instance, since ancient times, it has usually been the case that the leading power can borrow at the lowest interest rate because everyone is confident about their ability to service their debt. Thus, structurally higher (relative) interest rates are often a sign that a power shift may be in the making.

If we follow this reasoning, we could and should logically conclude that America is still the world power. Just look at how easily the enormous public debt gets financed, albeit often with the help of the Fed. But even if we look at the stock market performance of recent years, no country or index can keep up with US (mega) technology values. Still, from an investment perspective, it would be a strategic mistake to simply ignore Chinese markets.

Writing a horror story about the Chinese economy or investing in Chinese assets is not that difficult at the moment. Despite its huge economic growth and the historically unprecedented rate at which its population's standard of living has increased, the country is currently facing massive problems. If you pursue a one-child policy long enough, you should not be surprised that at some point, the population begins to decline. It actually peaked about 20 years ago. Recently, the Chinese government admitted as much. If you know that economic growth consists of population growth plus productivity, it is not hard to see that even if

China's productivity growth maintains or increases a little more, the economic growth rates of the past will no longer be achieved – not to mention the undercurrent of the property crisis that the country continues to face.

And just when China more than needs its export engine, it has entered a trade war with the United States, while many other Western countries are also re-examining their relationship with the world's second largest economy. But is it really a trade war? We might be better off talking about a technology war. In all likelihood, China will be the world's largest economy within a decade. The question is whether it will also become the most powerful. That depends more than ever on technological leadership. The speed of innovation and the technological and military leadership associated with it is nowhere more beautifully described than in Steven Johnson's book, *Where Good Ideas Come From*. In it, the author reaches for, among other things, the concept of 'adjacent possible'. With a rock-solid metaphor, he shows how 'the light of knowledge' spreads across the world and makes the world a better place.

Imagine a large table in an enclosed space, with a number of items on it. Smart people are sitting around the table. Scientists experiment with the parts until new ideas and new products emerge. Then the door to the next room opens, where the process starts all over again. In adjacent possible, the point is that a new product is only possible if all the parts for it are present. Da Vinci's flying harnesses could not be realised because there was no engine yet. Computers became possible only after the invention of the microchip. In other words, you can't skip any steps. Still, when the time is right for a new product or idea, it will be invented.

For most of the 20th century, the table with the most parts was in the US. But recently, there has also been a table in China, and no one knows how big it is. The country has big ambitions. And who is to say that a society so focused on control will not make faster progress in, for instance, AI? Or a country where ethical issues perhaps receive a little less attention will not be able to force breakthroughs faster in the field of genetic engineering?

Considering this, the US CHIPS Act and Chinese countermeasures to restrict exports of strategic rare earth elements can be better understood. The strategy behind both is to remove components from the opponent's innovation table and thus slow down its innovation process. In turn, the US Inflation Reduction Act can be seen as a way to become less dependent on strategic raw materials from abroad and start mining them closer to home. Or in other words, trying to get the parts China takes off the US table back onto it.

All this has very far-reaching investment implications. The main one is: as an investor who knows there are two tables, can you afford not to sit at one because you don't know where the fastest progress will be made? A second is that this will make life difficult for (technology) companies. I can perfectly imagine a world where the technology and standards for the two blocks will grow apart. But the dichotomy may as well drive progress, so continuing to invest in technology is natural. And so is sitting at the Chinese table, despite the risks obvious to all.

How about a possible (armed) conflict over Taiwan? This is indeed a risk. I am probably not the best person to comment on this. After all, I also did not believe until the last moment that Russia would invade Ukraine. Nevertheless, again, I believe that China will not be foolish enough to actually invade the island. The chances are that the US fleet would then immediately block the Strait of Malacca, cutting off the raw materials supply route. Without those raw materials, not least oil, China deindustrialises in about six months. The impact on the US and the global economy, apart from the terrible consequences of war and human suffering, would also be huge. A lot of world trade passes through the Strait of Malacca. Moreover, China is not only extremely important for world trade and the global economy, but the world's two largest economies are very much intertwined. As a result, in terms of impact on the economy, a conflict would be between five and ten times greater than that of the war in Ukraine. The impact on financial markets is easy to guess, so I sincerely hope I am right here.

Time for growth markets

*'We are so used to looking at America and China
that we sometimes dare to forget the rest of the world.'*

GEOPOLITICAL STRATEGIST LOUIS GAVE

We know by now that the centre of gravity of economic and political power is slowly but surely shifting over the long term. I am talking about very long-term trends. About 2,000 years ago, China accounted for 32% of the global economy. Later, the centre of power moved to Europe, then to America, and now we are moving back to a multipolar world, in which the emerging economies are claiming an increasing share of the pie. More than 20 years ago, emerging economies (if we include China) accounted for about 40% of the world economy. Today, that figure is heading towards 60%. And if we add another 20 years, we are at 70%. Then, at first glance, it also seems logical that the market capitalisation of emerging countries and the portfolio weighting should be 60%. Or should it?

The chart below shows the relative performance of the emerging markets versus the US S&P500 (if the chart is rising, the emerging markets are doing relatively better; if it is falling, they are doing relatively worse). The chart tells a distinctly different story, indicating once again that economic cycles and market cycles do not necessarily coincide, and investment decisions are never easy.

Emerging Market Equities vs S&P500   Source: Topdown Charts, Refinitiv Datastream

● MSCI EM vs S&P500 Relative Performance (USD)

The reason for the relatively weak performance since, say, the 2008 financial crisis, is not so much the weakness of stock markets and emerging-market currencies, but simply the result of the impressively strong performance of the US stock market. That remains the big gobbler in terms of total market value of listed companies. Nothing could keep up with US technology stocks in recent years, including Chinese technology stocks, which have repeatedly faced restrictions, both from its own government and from the US.

In the slightly longer term, we are probably looking at a serious investment opportunity. It is impossible to predict when this trend will reverse. But in terms of valuation, there is certainly something to be said for the emerging country complex – although 'emerging country complex' may no longer be the right way to talk about these countries. Some time ago, the biggest among them had been gathered under the acronym BRICS (Brazil, Russia, India, China and South Africa). That term has decreased in popularity over time. We need to start looking at emerging countries more and more individually and analyse them for their growth potential, which is very often linked to how the country is managed. In the slightly longer term, I certainly see a bright future for a country like India, or some countries in Southeast Asia and commodity countries. Beyond that, we can certainly add some African countries.

In contrast to deglobalisation in the West, trade between emerging countries is increasing. There are huge infrastructure projects supporting that process. For instance, major train lines have been developed between Russia and Iran. The same can be seen in aviation. Today, there are no direct flights between the global cities of Beijing and Dubai, but within a decade, this will be very different. With its Belt and Road investment programme, China is taking the lead in infrastructure projects. And Russia's raw materials are no longer going west, but east and south. So, just as it would be unwise to ignore China from an investment perspective, it is not smart to ignore the opportunities that can be found around the world. In this regard, I personally feel that countries such as India and Vietnam have all the tools to come out particularly strong in the coming years. Just make sure they are well diversified. Because these are investments with above-average risk. In the words of Forrest Gump, 'That is all that I have to say about that.'

Europe between
the two warring parties

'Is the definition of "friend" really the same in the US as it is here?' European politicians must have wondered after the introduction of the IRA. For example, the IRA
specifies that US citizens can receive up to $7,500 in tax credits on the purchase of
a new US-manufactured electric car. The components of those cars must come from
the US or from countries with which the US has a free trade agreement. The EU and
the US share the same values, but unfortunately no free trade agreement. The IRA
is a thorn in the side of Europe, which sees large investments from top European
companies heading to the US. 'IRA is your solution, but our problem,' French President Macron stated during a visit to Biden to discuss the matter. The EU has set up
a working group with the Americans to remove the most toxic stings from the IRA.

Strategic and philosophical-ethical importance of commodities

But Europe is as dependent on China as the US. By 2030, by its own calculations,
the EU will need 18 times more lithium, 15 times more cobalt and ten times more
rare earth elements. 'The war in Ukraine has exposed Europe's dependence for
numerous raw materials besides oil and gas,' explains Cind du Bois, professor of
geo-economic policy, in our monthly podcast *Stand van Zaken*.[88] 'That is why the
European Commission launched the European Critical Raw Materials Act. With it,
Europe wants to strengthen its self-sufficiency for raw materials that are essential
for the green and digital transition.' The strategy states that by 2030, no more than
65% of annual consumption of any strategic raw material should be sourced or processed from a single country outside the EU. That will be tough, argues a Western
intelligence official: 'It's taken 30 years to build up our dependency on China for
critical minerals and rare earth elements, and it will take the same amount of time
to unwind it.'[89] By 2030, 10% of annual consumption, 40% of annual processing
and 15% of annual recycling should also come from European extraction.
    Professor Holslag sees two other reasons besides strategic importance for
mining and reclamation within Europe. 'In the long run, it is very difficult to keep
up with high value-added activities – especially knowledge-intensive ones – if the

supply chain shifts to your competitors.' And that is what the Chinese are now ruthlessly playing out: first T-shirts, then steel, then electronics. 'And little by little, they are forcing that technology transfer.'

Second, he also sees a philosophical-ethical dilemma. 'As long as your society depends on those sectors for many of its needs, you yourself are actually responsible for making them more sustainable. It is easy to say that mining and refining lithium, nickel, or cobalt is polluting and better done in poor countries. But I think we should strive to make things better.' That does not necessarily mean that we should do all mining better in Europe. 'But we had better go and get cobalt ourselves in Congo and help develop sustainable mining there. Then we make sure the cobalt is brought to us in a sustainable supply chain and we tie a circular story to that. You're going to make serious productivity gains with that, especially when you factor in the environmental damage.'

Europe turns green

In terms of climate transition, the European Union is ambitious and solidly leads in comparison to the US. According to the International Energy Agency (IEA), it holds a quarter of the global production of electric cars and 20% in the supply chain. This far outperforms the 10% US share of electric cars and the 7% battery capacity. Today, Europe remains dependent on Chinese batteries, but according to S&P Global Market Intelligence, it is well on its way to becoming the world's second-largest battery producer by 2025. The European Battery Alliance was formed in 2017, following Brexit, Trump's election, and the lack of in-house battery expertise. By 2025, public and private investment in the entire supply chain should create a regional market of €250 billion a year.

It does not want to let its accumulated lead in green technology slip away. The response to the IRA and the other US initiatives came in early 2023 with the presentation of the Green Deal Industrial Plan. That plan builds on previously launched initiatives such as REPowerEU, NextGenerationEU, and the European Green Deal, but adds four key pillars: simplifying regulation, accelerating access to finance, boosting the skills of available labour (training technical profiles for renovation, heat pump and solar panel installers, and so on) and protecting and boosting trade.

And what about money? 'Even if no additional money is made available through the Green Deal Industrial Plan, the EU is not behind the US on financing. Quite the contrary,' argue our BNP Paribas colleagues at Markets 360.[90] 'Subsidies and tax incentives under the IRA amount to about 1.5% of US nominal GDP over a 10-year period*. All funds provided by the EU for the climate transition we estimate at €700 billion, or 5% of GDP. The bulk of that €700 billion we believe will be spent in the next five years.'

Yet European companies are screaming blue murder. Perception is important. 'Simplicity, I think, is one of the main characteristics of the IRA, and that is what counts with investors,' Josu Jon Imaz said in an interview with Reuters.[91] According to the CEO of energy giant Repsol, European initiatives are overly complex. Applying for grants in one's home state is an administrative nightmare that excludes the majority of SMEs.

That complexity also applies in granting licences. Opening mines is an eight- to 12-year process in Europe,[92] but so are wind or solar projects. If the Net Zero Industry Act is approved in its current form, that will be reduced to 18 months for projects under Europe's jurisdiction**. And, if no decision is made, it will assume tacit approval.

Will that convince European companies to stay here? Ultimately, their investment decisions do not depend solely on the size of subsidies. The chart shows the percentage of business federations that consider the listed topic a potential barrier to investing in the EU. The regulatory framework is being addressed, and the available workforce is being prepared and retrained. However, the first stumbling block for companies is the relatively high energy prices. Bewilderment at gas prices that were up to ten times higher than in the US in 2022 still reverberates. Previously, and from 2008 onwards, European companies paid 'only' twice as much for natural gas (due to the US shale gas boom). The transformation of the regional LNG market into a global one (see climate transition sidebar 'High European electricity

---

* Please note that Goldman Sachs sees the final amount of investment credit going up to three times, depending on how much the private sector uses it. There is no real government limit on it.

** The US is also grappling with this problem, with permits taking 4.3 years for transmission projects, 3.5 years for pipelines and 2.7 years for renewable energy projects (Progressive Policy Institute, 2022). Speeding up these procedures is more difficult. A recent proposal to change licensing procedures failed in Congress due to lack of support.

prices won't last forever') will ensure, in my opinion, that those price differences will gradually decrease in the coming years.

Which challenges are top-3 issues for investing in Europe? Source: BusinessEurope

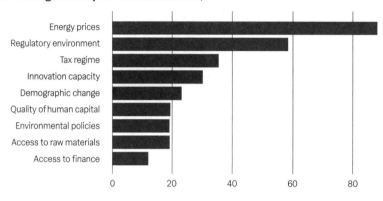

MULTIGLOBALISATION

KEY POINTS

✓ Globalisation shifted down a gear due to slower goods trade. This is 'slowbalisation', not deglobalisation.

✓ The decreased Chinese imports into the US is a sham. An extra stop between the two countries was simply added. Worse, the US is pushing emerging countries into China's arms.

✓ Companies are considering a 'China + 1' strategy, but supply chain diversification is very costly. There is little political appetite to exclude China from intermediate inputs.

✓ We are moving towards multiglobalisation. In the process, new emerging countries are taking their place in the supply chain, either as an additional intermediate station between China and the West or as a new supply channel. There are opportunities here for Southeast Asian and Latin American countries. India is also steaming ahead.

✓ The second facet of multiglobalisation is the digitalisation of the service industry. It creates livelihoods in emerging countries and reduces inequality.

Decoupling:
appearances can be deceptive

The European Green Deal Industrial Plan and the US IRA illustrate the renewed popularity of national and regional industrial plans. Their global resurgence accelerated from 2017, when Trump was wielding the bludgeon of trade tariffs. Other countries mainly used subsidies and export-related measures, often targeting specific companies and sectors. Technology and sectors linked to climate top that list.

But that does not mean globalisation is dead. It is resting, stunned by the sledgehammer blows of Trump and the pandemic. Recently, global trade rebounded towards the 2013–2017 trend, corresponding to an average annual growth in trade volume of 2.8%. This is lower than the 6% growth during the 2001–2008 period. From hyperglobalisation, we evolved to 'slowbalisation'.

World trade: slowbalisation, not deglobalisation
Source: Foreign Trade, CPB World Trade Monitor, SA, Index World, Total, Volume

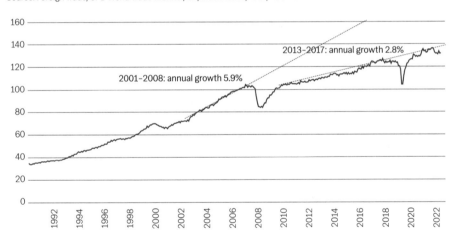

How did trade between the US and China evolve? The six-fold increase in US tariffs on two-thirds of Chinese imports pulled China's share of total US goods imports down 7 percentage points. Companies are adjusting their investment plans for the coming years as they realise that supply from China is becoming increasingly difficult. An annual survey of members of the US-China Business Council shows that a quarter of companies are moving part of the supply chain away from China. Chinese companies then again scaled back their investments in the US from $48 billion in 2016 to barely $3.1 billion in 2022.

Biden thus seems to have achieved his goal of reduced dependence on China, but appearances can be deceptive. '[American companies]… had specific requirements that we build factories outside of China, in countries such as Vietnam and Thailand, to continue co-operation with them,' Lu Yucong, chairman of one of China's largest solar water heater manufacturers, explained to the *Financial Times*.[93] And they did. But the supply of the intermediate products still comes from the cheapest and, above all, most efficient supplier: China.

So the apparent disconnect is false. 'Worse, from Mr Biden's perspective,' writes *The Economist*, 'his approach is also deepening the economic links between China and other exporting countries. In so doing, it perversely pits their interests against America's.'[94] For many poorer countries, Chinese investment and intermediate goods, and exports of finished goods to the US, are a source of jobs and prosperity. By refusing to conclude new trade agreements while China signed the Regional Comprehensive Economic Partnership (RCEP) in November 2020, the US is pushing those countries even further towards the enemy. With 15 Asia-Pacific countries and 30% of global GDP, the RCEP is the largest trading bloc ever. If the US wants to pry itself away from China for supplies of certain products, it will even have to ban raw materials and intermediate products incorporated into finished products. That is very drastic.

Companies have also invested significantly in China and do not like to see those investments go up in smoke. They speak of a 'China + 1' strategy. However, the costs associated with multisourcing are huge. Research by Antràs et al. in 2017 shows that only a very small percentage of US companies import the same product from different countries.[95] 'Current supply chain disruptions will prompt companies to rethink their previous strategies. But once they have calculated the extra costs, they will realise how expensive such bi- or multisourcing really is,' concludes the Harvard professor.

Exporting from China via a stopover seems to be the preferred option today. Until a valid alternative is found? China remains unique with its relatively low production costs combined with a highly advanced industrial base. 'It is going to be very hard to cut China out of supply chains and very expensive,' responds Rory Green of TS Lombard via email. 'Outside of a security sensitive areas, I suspect the political appetite to cut out China intermediate inputs is fairly limited.'

Multiglobalisation

China lost market share in the US but overcompensated by increasing market share in other countries. Growth countries are tightening ties with the giant, with 'the [Chinese] preference [being] for geographically close, low-cost producers with excellent trade ties,' according to Green. 'Vietnam, with its new EU FTA, topped the list. Companies in Guangdong and Zhejiang produce the high value-added items and final assembly takes place in Vietnam.' It makes things a bit more complex (and certainly not environmentally friendly). The result is strong growth in Chinese investment and Vietnamese exports. US imports from Vietnam have grown an average of 21% annually since the start of the trade war compared to 11% in the previous four years.

New growth countries in the global value chain

The foreign investment lost by China is being gained by other emerging countries. 'The current push toward more diversified supply chains presents great opportunities for countries and communities that have struggled to integrate into global value chains,' write IMF Managing Director Kristalina Georgieva and WTO director-general Ngozi Okonjo-Iweala in a joint article.[96] 'Bringing more of them into production networks – what we call "re-globalisation" – would be good for supply resilience, growth and development.' Vietnam, other ASEAN countries and Taiwan have already increased their share of US imports. Latin American countries are also entering the scene, with Mexico and its free trade agreement with the US in pole position (*see sidebar*).

> ### Who are the winners in this first stage of multiglobalisation?
>
> According to TS Lombard, the countries from the Association of the South Asian Nations are currently especially well positioned to challenge China on the cost side. Vietnam retains its competitiveness in textiles (*see chart*), but moved up the value chain towards electronics and other industrial products. Taiwan is uniquely positioned as a supplier of the most sophisticated chips, but is in the eye of the US-China trade storm, holding back new foreign in-

vestment. South Korea is strong in a wide range of electronic and electrical products, as well as cars. However, the US CHIPS Act will create difficulties in South Korean companies' highly developed Chinese supply chain. Mexico is on the same level as South Korea, benefiting from generous IRA subsidies as well as proximity to the US. However, US-Mexican relations may soon be under stress ahead of presidential elections in the two countries, with migrants and fentanyl both being incendiary issues.

What about Indonesia and India, sometimes called the new China? Both certainly have a cost advantage over China for producers looking for an alternative supply chain. Both also have the scale to attract a significant share of Chinese exports. So far, however, they have only been competitive in limited value-added products. Recently, Indonesia has benefited from South Korean interest with investments by Hyundai and LG, among others, in plants for electric cars and batteries. India is also succeeding in attracting high-tech companies and is developing its own computer industry. The main hurdle for investors in India is its poor infrastructure. In October 2023, I was on the ground exploring the huge potential of the Indian economy. You can read the report on my blog at www.bnpparibasfortis.com/nl/blogs/blog-chief-economist or via LinkedIn.

Global services without barriers

The deepening of globalisation encompasses not only a geographical but also a substantive aspect. 'Let's look for new wins,' argues economist Raghuram Rajan.[97] 'I'm very firmly a believer in the bicycle theory of reform. If you stop, you fall off. You need to keep going. What is the new area which we haven't reformed? Services.'

And that field has plenty of room for new opportunities. Services account for the largest share of GDP in industrialised countries. Moreover, many services do not require migration to offer them elsewhere. 'More of these services produced at a distance can do two things,' argues Rajan. 'One, it provides that livelihood at a distance, but it also reduces inequality. One of the biggest sources of inequalities is spread between high-quality services and manufacturing in industrial countries. If we liberalize services, it makes them more affordable for that worker that he can now find a doctor in finite time, and that doctor is affordable. That's a good thing for industrial country societies as well as for emerging markets. For the climate, it's very beneficial because many of these services are weightless, have low climate impact.' Therefore, according to Professor Rajan, we need to do away with all those existing qualification requirements for services.

Many barriers in the services industry will be removed by the digital revolution, which, according to Professor Richard Baldwin, will do away with transport costs. 'If it is possible to develop systems that allow surgeons to patch people up from a distance, then it should also be possible to develop systems that allow engineers in Stuttgart to make machines in Brazil. With the rapidly falling costs of telerobotics, it is only a matter of time before the limitations of the new technologies disappear.'

'Really good ICT also creates reasonable substitutes for face-to-face meetings,' he argues. 'This "virtual presence revolution" is based on very high-quality video and audio systems.' Combined with real-time machine translation, this is leading to a global talent wave in the services sector from emerging countries.

The doubling of 'other commercial services' – all services outside transport and travel – over the past three decades to 20% of total trade makes its future potential tangible. It is a mishmash ranging from payments to Spotify over outsourced call and ICT services to India, to Gazprom paying transit rights to Ukraine. According to Baldwin, intermediary services* in particular will fuel globalisation for four reasons:[98]

1   Natural barriers to trade in services are greater than those for goods, but they are mainly technological. No legislative or tax issues arise. 'Most barriers arise from domestic regulation. Much of this regulation, however, concerns "final" services, not "intermediate" services,' Baldwin explains. For example, there are rules about the quality requirements of an accountant, but he or she may employ anyone, including someone in a distant country, to enter digital invoices.

2   Digital technologies – telepresence, universal translation machines – are very quickly bringing down barriers to trade in intermediary services.

3   In emerging countries, the supply of people who can provide

---

* Intermediary services are services usually provided between two or more parties. These can be of a digital nature, such as routers, APIs that allow software applications to communicate with each other, and cloud services, but also services provided by people, such as financial, accounting, IT and other services.

intermediary services is much less of a limiting factor than for the goods sector. There is no need to build factories or tap into new sectors. These services are already offered in those countries.

λ The demand for these services is high within developed countries, as intermediary services are also crucial in the production of goods or in the primary sector. Administrative tasks and other services need to be provided there too.

The first two points indicate that barriers are much higher for services than for goods, but thanks to the digital revolution, these barriers can be brought down much faster. The last two points illustrate that there are no supply or demand constraints for intermediary services. 'The future of trade therefore lies in intermediary services,' Baldwin concludes. In 2022, global exports of digital services, such as consulting via videocalls, reached US$38 trillion, accounting for 54% of total services exports.[99]

the PRICE
of DEGLOBALISATION

KEY POINTS

✓ The Sino-US technology war is only in its early stages. Climate regulation raises new trade barriers. The risk of deglobalisation is real.

✓ Deglobalisation would undercut investment and climate finance towards emerging countries. This would result in a failure of the climate transition.

✓ The estimated total cost of deglobalisation fluctuates between 1% and 12% of GDP. The deeper the disaggregation, the higher the costs. Limiting the diffusion of knowledge and technology does the most damage.

✓ The beneficial effect of globalisation on inflation disappears in a world with more barriers.

✓ International coordination of migration, with climate refugee countries training the right 'profiles' for ageing host countries, would be a win-win.

✓ A fragmented international financial system increases complexity, risk, and hence costs. This depresses global growth and increases interest rates and, again, inflation.

Trade barriers rise

We are only in the early stages when it comes to the Sino-American technology war, believes Jon Harrison of TS Lombard.[100] 'Over the coming five years, we expect US-led tech bifurcation to expand to a majority of the Chinese hardware and software stack (including Chinese EVs). [...] Beijing's centralization this month of all scientific research (including tech innovation and patents) in the Party's hands will serve to bolster this trend, with the Communist Party on track to prioritize the very civil-military fusion that the US is keen to penalize with more export controls.'

There are also the subsidies: the US IRA, the European Green Deal Industrial Plan and the Chinese Five-Year Plan, among others. With non-trade barriers, Europe in particular is trying to reduce carbon emissions in the supply chain. In 2024, the new Corporate Sustainability Reporting Directive comes into force. Between 2024–2028, 50,000 companies will have to provide more and more details on their supply chain emissions. This increases the pressure on suppliers to comply with stricter requirements. There will be increasing trade restrictions between the European Union and emerging markets due to new regulations to combat deforestation (Deforestation-free Regulation*). And from 2026, there is the introduction of the first carbon border tax (see chapter on climate), which emerging markets label as 'one-sided' and 'discriminatory'. Costs for companies are rising, and so is inflation.

For some emerging countries, all these new rules are solid spanners in the works of multiglobalisation. 'Developing economies, unable to compete with subsidy packages of their own, may instead limit imports of clean energy technologies and impose export controls on raw materials, and especially on critical minerals, for the political and economic leverage they provide, in an effort to move up the value chain,' the IMF argues.[101] On the other hand, these climate 'sticks' are also causing emerging countries to adjust their climate ambitions for the better. For instance, Indonesia and India made progress in their plans to launch their own carbon markets. Brazil, a giant in renewable energy, recently rolled out plans to

---

* The Deforestation-free legislation aims to ensure that raw materials such as palm oil, soya, beef, coffee, cocoa, rubber, timber and related products imported into the EU do not contribute to deforestation. Controls are carried out through strict traceability requirements and enforced with fines for violators of up to 4% on annual EU business income.

produce green hydrogen and steel with an eye on the lucrative EU market. Emerging countries are aware of the huge potential for those who adapt.

Besides sticks, we also need carrots. Without additional deals with emerging and poor countries, such as the purchase and expansion of renewable energy and much more climate finance, the cracks in the global trade framework increase. Add the current geopolitical risks, and effective deglobalisation is not far off. The consequences would be enormous. All the beneficial effects I cited at the start of this chapter are reversed. Inflation would rise, and capital flows and foreign direct investment (FDIs) dry up. The necessary financing that developing countries need to achieve their climate transition would not happen. The climate transition would then fail.

'Many of today's most pressing global problems will not be solved without international trade,' argue Georgieva and Okonjo-Iweala.[102] 'We cannot overcome the climate crisis and get to net zero greenhouse gas emissions without trade. We need trade to get low-carbon technology and services to everywhere they are needed. Open and predictable trade lowers the cost of decarbonization by expanding market size, enabling scale economies, and learning by doing. To provide one example, the price of solar power has fallen by almost 90 % since 2010. Forty percent of this decline has come from scale economies made possible partly by trade and cross-border value chains, the WTO has estimated.'

Dissemination of knowledge
and technology declines

Trade is the way to gradually raise living standards. The spectacular income growth of countries like Bangladesh and Vietnam is a good example. Investment by foreign companies plays a very important role in this. Friend- and near-shoring risks limiting those investments. The flow of FDI towards Asian countries has contracted since 2019 and is only slowly recovering. Multiglobalisation leads to wins, while deglobalisation only leads to losses.

The most corrosive channel of deglobalisation, according to IMF chief Georgieva, is the more limited diffusion of knowledge and technology. Being open to trade stimulates innovation through increased competition, promotes technology adoption and knowledge transfer, and increases workers' skills. Technological fragmentation alone increases economic losses globally to as much as 5% of GDP, the IMF calculated.[103] That figure rises or falls depending on whether aligned countries restrict their trade entirely to the western (US) or southern (China) bloc to which they belong. If they take their place in the middle, they gain in some scenarios. Deepening deglobalisation would then lead to them becoming substitutes for the ex-trading partners: for example, India as China's alternative to the US and Germany. But usually most countries lose, and the losses increase with the degree of fragmentation.

Among the warring camps, the economic loss in all possible scenarios runs higher for China than for the US. In the extreme case where all OECD countries side with the US, the Chinese loss even runs as high as 8% of GDP just because of a technological split. In addition, the more open an economy is, such as that of Belgium, the greater the loss risk.

Flaring inflation

As fragmentation is a recent phenomenon, the number of studies quantifying its total cost is still limited. The IMF compares four, all of which point to considerable costs. The differences are significant and fluctuate between 1% and 12% of GDP, depending on the underlying assumptions and regions the studies take into account. Despite these differences, four main conclusions emerge in the literature:[104]

1   Costs increase as fragmentation cuts deeper. This is true for applying non-trade tariffs, such as export restrictions, or a carbon border tax on all sectors. It is also true when third parties are required to trade exclusively with one of the dominant trading blocs.
2   Limited knowledge dissemination due to technological decoupling significantly increases economic damage.
3   Growth and low-income countries are particularly affected.
4   When moving from one trade regime to another, the cost of supply chain adjustment can be significantly higher in the short term than in the long term.

Those adjustments in turn push inflation higher: in the short run due to temporary shortages and adjustment shocks, and in the longer run due to structurally higher costs because the most (cost) efficient supply chain is closed. The beneficial effect of globalisation on inflation disappears in a world with more barriers and regulation.

Necessary immigration declines

Immigration is also hit hard in a scenario of deglobalisation. Net immigration had already been falling over the past decade (including pre-Covid). Arguments for more immigration mainly emphasise the positive economic impact. It allows companies to expand and stimulates innovation, especially in the case of highly-skilled immigrants. There is also little evidence that immigration destroys jobs or depresses wages in developed countries. On the contrary, immigrants often do jobs that would otherwise go unfilled. Belgium's construction industry, for example, needs 20,000 extra workers to carry out all its construction and renovation plans.

Immigrants also tend to be younger than the average age in the host country. An ageing population is the Achilles' heel of industrialised countries. In Europe, immigration accounted for 80% of population growth between 2000 and 2018, while in North America it accounted for 32%. A declining population limits future growth potential and also challenges the financing of our social security model. In the US, the employment rate of immigrants is high and a large share of them are highly skilled. There, the net fiscal contribution of an immigrant who arrived in the last ten years averages $173,000 over their lifetime.

One would expect that in countries where fertility rates remain substantially below the replacement rate (the level at which the population stabilises, being 2.1 children per woman), people would strive to correct this via more immigration. This is not the case in Europe. Over the past 20 years, countries with the lowest fertility rates have had the lowest net immigration. In some of these countries, such as Hungary and Poland, governments have been elected that oppose migration. Therefore, the demographic problem will not be solved automatically. Politicians will need to take on an active role. Still, there is a ray of hope: in four of the five countries west of Ukraine (Hungary, Poland, Romania, Slovakia), the score did improve by 2022.

There are also benefits for the countries that are the source of migrants. While the emigration of highly educated people – the so-called brain drain – can have negative consequences, studies point to several positive channels, such as brain gain on the return of the emigrants, as well as remittances towards home countries. For countries such as The Gambia, El Salvador and Honduras, these amounts add up to a quarter of GDP annually.

Indeed, for a significant portion of the global population, emigration becomes the only chance of survival. '[But] if you fail on both mitigation and adaptation, what is left is migration,' explains Raghuram Rajan.[105] 'Canada, Greenland, Siberia, large empty places in the world, will become much more attractive to inhabit as we get global warming. Now, if we have uncoordinated migration as it has been so far, we are going to have a lot of pushback. Climate refugees will move to the richest welcoming country until that rich welcoming country becomes welcoming no more because it's overwhelmed by people coming there.'

But we know where the climate refugees will come from. 'And I want to argue that there's a demand in rich aging countries for people, but people of the "right kind," people who can come in and provide sort of contributions to the labor force, et cetera. Why not start that market now in preparation for the climate refugees that'll come 20 years, 30 years from now? Create a global market in people to serve the aging Germans, South Koreans, Chinese of the world, and start creating some self-interest to getting people from outside to keep your economy going,' Rajan says.

Moreover, those with the most negative attitude towards immigration today are precisely those who would gain the most from it: the elderly. 'The good news is that it appears that such negative attitudes are due more to generational differences than to a simple effect of "aging",' believes Professor Giovanni Peri of the Global Migration Center.[106] 'A relative lack of exposure to immigrants among the currently old generations in Europe and the United States may be the reason for such attitudes. In Europe, for instance, surveys suggest that millennials and Generation Z have more positive opinions of immigration than do older generations.' If they maintain that attitude and their relative importance in the vote count increases, the positive effects of immigration may yet be realised.

International financial system becomes more complex

Deglobalisation also puts the international financial system (IFS) at risk. The IFS ensures international stability and growth by sharing risks. If the system notices a problem – for instance, in case of a country's over-reliance on foreign capital – it makes adjustments. It prescribes the medicine to be taken and, in case of excessive debt, provides financial assistance in return. It brings the various creditors around the table. Therein lies an important task of international institutions, such as the World Bank or the IMF. They oversee global risks and intervene.

Ghent economics professor Koen Schoors is less worried about the demise of those international institutions:[107] 'If you really talk about deglobalisation, you have to give up on the IMF. I observe regionalisation rather than deglobalisation. And this is also reflected in the IFS. There is already a South American Development bank at the moment. There is also an African counterpart. And a European and Asian alternative. And the People's Bank of China also plays a similar role. So it is not like there are no facilities in terms of regions. I see plenty of opportunities to support regions.'

Thorough regionalisation does have implications for the international monetary system. It then becomes much more difficult to get all of a country's creditors on the same page, as is already the case today (see chapter on debt). The fewer links we have with each other, the less we talk to each other, and the harder it will be to defuse debt crises. This leads to more risk and greater fluctuations in the business cycle.

International payment systems are then also at risk. SWIFT, the messaging system for executing international payments, is under pressure today. Russia has been banned from it since the invasion of Ukraine, making payments to and from Russian companies via banks much more difficult. If current geopolitical tensions escalate, other countries might also want to become less dependent on international financial infrastructures and standards. Possibly because they are concerned about sanctions or because they want a partial denomination of trade and financial transactions in another currency, or for other considerations. Russia and Iran, previously barred from the SWIFT system, are said to be working on a crypto currency backed by gold. That stablecoin would then replace the dollar as an international payment currency. This creates new parallel systems that cannot communicate with each other, leading to higher transaction costs and other inefficiencies. I am happy to leave all insights on stablecoins and crypto to my friend Philippe.

A fragmented global payment system also leads to a more limited risk spread. The IMF has calculated that an increase in tensions, as has been seen between China and the US since 2016, pulls down banks' bilateral portfolio investments and exposures by 15%.[108] Investment funds are particularly sensitive to this. Their investments in countries with a different policy outlook plummet by a quarter over time. More limited risk diversification increases fund volatility. Add imposed financial restrictions, and the result is a rise in banks' funding costs. Less foreign interest and more volatility also brings higher interest rates on government bonds. This in turn reduces the value of portfolio bonds and the cost of funding. With the current high debt levels, higher interest rates are not something countries are looking forward to. All those impacts are much bigger for banks in emerging and developing countries.

In summary, a fragmented international financial system increases complexity, risk, and hence costs. That pushes global interest rates and inflation higher and depresses growth, with the main victims being the least developed countries – again. An evolution of the international financial system adapted to current realities (diversity of creditors) and needs (climate finance) is certainly desirable; a revolution absolutely is not.

Astropolitics: are UAPs the ultimate black swan?

*'In another moment down went Alice after it, never once considering
how in the world she was to get out again.'*

———

LEWIS CARROLL, *ALICE IN WONDERLAND*

Far away from the camera, according to tradition by a pleasant fire, Ronald Reagan began his first face-to-face conversation with Michael Gorbachev by asking: 'What would you do if the United States were suddenly attacked by beings from outer space? Would you help us?' Michael Gorbachev did not hesitate to reply: 'Of course.' To which Reagan replied, 'So would we.' This amazing moment, witnessed live only by a few interpreters, took place in a log cabin in Geneva on 19 November 1985. It only became known to the public when the then leader of the Soviet Union recounted it in New York in 2009.

The story caused a stir, and as so often for the wrong reasons. It was argued in some quarters that Ronald Reagan was already out of his mind. It is probably closer to the truth that the president wanted to break the ice and thus help lay the foundations for better relations between the two superpowers.

Still, the story has stuck in my mind for quite some time. What would it mean for humanity, the global economy and markets if we actually came into contact with aliens? This would undoubtedly be the biggest black swan event in human history. Black swans – sprung from the mind of author Nicholas Taleb – are events that come out of nowhere and suddenly change everything. Another characteristic is that afterwards, everyone is convinced they saw the event coming. In this case, that might be more difficult.

I debated for some time about whether to bring this up in the context of this book. It is my job to see the risks, as well as (investment) opportunities. But even if this risk turned out to be real, how do you protect against it? Right now, these are not things the investment community takes into account.

What convinced me to do it, apart from my innate curiosity, is the fact that one of my favourite podcasts on investing/trading and trend following, *Top Traders Unplugged* by hedge fund veteran Niels Kaastrup-Larsen, recently started discussing the topic 'Galactic Macro'. In addition to AI and technology, UAPs were also discussed extensively in the process. UAP stands for Unidentified Aerial Phenomenon. It partly replaces the term UFO (Unidentified Flying Object), which more automatically brings aliens to mind. The term UAP does not rule out the extra-terrestrial origin of the countless unexplained phenomena, but assumes that they could also be weather phenomena, advanced earth-made devices, things from the future or other dimensions, or projections of our future.

The people behind the podcast are just about the most rational and methodical specialists you can imagine. There are also growing voices in government circles, especially in the United States, that take this kind of phenomena extremely seriously. Space agency NASA recently created a team of 16 to investigate UAPs. In addition, the FBI, CIA and who knows how many lesser-known teams are investigating.

So perhaps this is worth a thought experiment after all. Let us assume that we are dealing with life forms from another planet or dimension. The mere fact that they can touch down here is enough to assume that their technology is vastly superior to ours. If observations are to be believed, this idea is confirmed by the way and speed at which they move.

The idea that they would observe us, possibly even without malicious ulterior motives, may not be so evil then. One analysis from Galactic Macro states that the number of UAP sightings rose dramatically when nuclear weapons were being experimented with, and again since the development of AI. Are these things somehow getting their attention?

One question I ask myself from a market perspective is what would happen the moment this unimaginable news hit our Bloomberg screens. Would the stock market crash? Or would we be so busy that no one would press the sell button? What would technology values still be worth if technologies potentially become available that catapult everything we know today back to the stone age? I would still dare to bet on a fall in the stock market, and especially the Nasdaq.

You might expect this to be an emergency, bigger than the Covid pandemic. Governments could then take on emergency powers and do what they thought necessary for the population. The political, economic and market system as we know today would freeze and possibly even cease to exist.

Communication would never have been more difficult, but also never more important. Therefore, you can believe that if there are agencies in the world that have evidence or more information, they will release it only very gradually to allow humanity to get used to the idea. If the aliens don't decide otherwise, the whole world would see images that leave nothing to the imagination. But would we believe them then? You can do a lot of fun and not so fun things with deep-fake today. Somehow, I feel that UAPs and AI are connected.

Even without the giant black swan of an encounter with aliens, the concept of astropolitics will gradually take hold in the coming years. Little by little, we will colonise space. That will bring with it enormous (investment) opportunities, technological developments and astropolitical issues. After all, who owns the Moon or Mars, or even the North Pole? And quite possibly, in a very distant future – in a galaxy far, far away – we will become a giant black swan for another civilisation, although there will probably be another name for that.

TEN
to REMEMBER

1   Globalisation depressed inflation and interest rates in recent decades, and significantly increased global prosperity. Globalisation is a wealth booster.

2   The recent slowdown in global goods trade is due to reshoring. Outsourcing the manufacturing process has reached its limit and companies want to reduce the complexity of the global value chain. The Covid pandemic and the war in Ukraine exposed the dangers.

3   Protests against globalisation are greatest in Anglo-Saxon countries. They were least successful in distributing the gains of globalisation fairly in a contest of low(er)-growth environment.

4   For Americans, China is the big bogeyman. It threatens the US in its hegemony and does not play the trade game fairly.

5   Technology is the hill on which the US is willing to die. Goal: nip China's rise in the bud before it can compete with the US technologically.

6   There is growing resentment from the European Union over China's unfair trade practices. The symbiosis of past decades - technology in exchange for a huge market - is in jeopardy now that China is also entering the European market with its own products.

7   China counters shielding US technology by denying the West minerals and metals necessary for the climate transition.

8   Europe spends more than the US to attract companies, but the mechanisms for accessing the funding are more complex.

9   From globalisation over slowbalisation, we move to multiglobalisation. New emerging countries are taking their place in the supply chain. Digital services are poised to accelerate and become the new growth pole of global trade.

10 The risk of deglobalisation remains. This would be catastrophic for growth, inflation, productivity, poverty reduction, financial stability and the climate transition.

TEN
to **INVEST** *in*

1. The day aliens land on Earth – a black swan event – the Nasdaq is likely to drop.
2. No country is better located geographically than the United States. Two oceans, peaceful neighbours and fertile land. They have the young population and technological know-how. The US is still worth investment.
3. Despite the huge challenges the country has on its plate, it would be unwise not to sit at the Chinese table from an investment perspective. They play by different rules there than in the US.
4. The same goes for low-cost growth markets. However, a proper spread is essential, as it's hit or miss.
5. Our reptilian brain says the US dollar is still the world reserve currency, even if US debt is rising.
6. It is not foolish to believe that the gold price could double in the next few years.
7. *If you like gold, you should love silver*. After all, silver takes it both ways: it is an industrial gem.
8. Bitcoin is many things, but not a currency. It is a technological marvel, to which many other innovations are attached.
9. Buy a piece of Van Gogh's long-term cash flow via a smart contract soon.
10. Bet on (e-)sports teams or a metaverse. These are areas that are still grossly underestimated.

4
DEBT

UK debt crisis, ten years on

15 July 2052, *The Global Times* – by Frits Van Steeland in Brussels

This week, central bankers looked back on the aftermath of the devastating UK debt crisis a decade ago. The crisis sent shock waves through the global economy and resulted in the UK's readmission to the European Union.

'The debt crisis that hit the UK revealed the vulnerabilities of our economic systems and the consequences of rampant debt accumulation,' Sir William Thompson, former governor of the Bank of England, said in his speech. 'We ignored the warning signs and the need for fiscal sustainability.'

Economically speaking, the UK has been slowly sinking into the North Sea since Brexit in January 2020. For 22 years, it tried to prop itself up with ever-increasing debt – peaking at 195% – but in 2042, financial markets gave the weakly governed UK the death knell. The UK government could no longer get rid of its sterling loans, even with interest rates close to 20%. Britain's central bank had lost all credibility.

European rescue

'It was our duty to help our British neighbours,' argued Giovanni Ricci, the then ECB president who convinced the European Union, after much hesitation, not to abandon the British to their fate. 'And no, it was not pure altruism. We saw the interest rate differential between the EU's strongest and weakest countries creeping upwards. An out-of-control UK debt crisis had also left big scars on the EU economy.'

With the support of a large and even enthusiastic majority of Britons, the island nation was gradually but decisively reintegrated into the EU over the following years. Afterwards, the ECB did have to sell a lot of euros for a long time to curb excessive appreciation. Today, the economic bloc is in a stronger position than ever. There are always problems with hard-nosed member states, but strict rules with maximum debt ratios combined with a common budget of almost 15% of European GDP has convinced bond market watchdogs that targeting Fortress Europe is a kamikaze manoeuvre. Today, the EU can easily borrow at 4%, even cheaper than the US. And China,

India, Indonesia and Saudi Arabia are also interested in EU bonds.

Financial repression

The United States also managed to avoid a financial crisis, notwithstanding a debt level comparable to that of the UK in the early 2030s. The country halved its debt by introducing ever tighter financial controls, artificially low interest rates and a 4% inflation target. The dollar's status as a world reserve currency offered a clear advantage over other countries. Today, that dollar feels the hot breath of the euro on its neck.

During her keynote address, Federal Reserve chair Janet Reynolds stressed the importance of proactive financial regulation. 'Over the past 20 years, we have taken steps to ensure the stability of our banking sector, control excessive risky behaviour, and maintain a healthy balance between inflation and growth. An ounce of prevention is worth a pound of cure,' she concluded. According to many economists, the Fed was simply reverting to a tried and tested historical recipe for deleveraging: financial repression. Savers footed the bill with a combination of low interest rates and high inflation. ●

DEVELOPED
COUNTRIES'
MOUNTAIN *of* DEBT

KEY POINTS

✔ Global debts are at their highest level ever. Government debts have often been higher, but only in wartime.

✔ The parallel between the post-Covid recovery and the Global Financial Crisis does not hold. The Covid pandemic left fewer scars, and notably less debt among companies and families.

✔ Public debts in particular rose in developed countries. On average, these are 110% of GDP with large differences between countries.

✔ Rising government debts have not been a problem in the past decades due to falling interest rates, but recently, those have been rising. Spending remains high due to an ageing population and the climate transition; revenue collection remains low due to lacklustre growth.

✔ If average nominal interest costs rise above nominal growth, governments have to run budget surpluses to stabilise debts and an interest rate snowball threatens. For the past decade or so, deficit reduction was sufficient.

✔ The OECD suggests a long-term interest rate of 2.7% for the eurozone and 3.3% for the US by 2030. This would effectively put interest rates slightly above nominal growth.

For many politicians, debt is diabolical. The fact that a government should manage its budget wisely and not spend money excessively is beyond dispute. But, as Barry Eichenberg and the co-authors of the book *In Defence Of Public Debt* note,[109] 'A government that did not borrow in order to provide essential services during a deadly pandemic – or to ensure the national defense during a security emergency, or to invest adequately in the productive infrastructure [...] – would be accused of dereliction, and rightly so. Such a government, to continue the analogy with a household, would be like parents who refused to borrow to obtain life-saving surgery for a child.'

The United States is not the only country in which debt levels have been rising steeply in recent years. This is true for all countries worldwide, and not just governments, but also the debts incurred by households, companies, and financial institutions. The global debt explosion since 2000 has been immense, and the Covid pandemic was the icing on the cake. By the end of 2022, global debt was edging towards its historic peak at \$297 trillion, four times higher than in 2000. As a percentage of GDP, we are talking about 333%. In the first quarter of 2021, debt peaked at 362%.

Highest debt in peacetime

Never has the total debt been higher than it is today, at least in peacetime. Government debts have been higher, but almost always in wartime. Such war debts are justified, economist Adam Smith believed. Back in the 18th century, he warned that it was too easy for governments to burden future generations with increasing debts, but made an exception when the survival of the state and the protection of its citizens was at stake. Historically, major wars and their financing have always left their mark.

Today, government debts have peaked globally in peacetime. Why does this debt accumulate? Even before the great world wars, countries used debt not only to strengthen their borders, but also to invest in infrastructure and collective facilities, such as sewers. In the next step, social services such as schools, libraries and hospitals were financed alongside railways and canals. During the five decades from 1880 to 1930, the welfare state was established. Social insurance and transfers reconciled the uncertainty of industrial urban life with the economic dynamism of market forces.

The expanded set of tasks, including fighting financial crises, translated into greater financing needs and rising taxes. The fact that the latter did not suffice and thus led to higher debts can, according to Eichengreen et al., be partly explained because 'the pressure to expand these programs was most intense in hard economic times – when unemployment was high, dislocations were extensive, and the government lacked revenues adequate to meet immediate demands.'[110] The cry for more social services and transfers was huge after the two world wars and during the Great Depression of the 1930s. The pressure was intense during the 1970s, when growth slowed and unemployment skyrocketed.

Why were the good times that followed hard times not used to pay off debts? Democratisation probably plays an important role here. In a democratic society, creditors are just one of many interest groups with a voice. The more groups with representation there are, the more each of those groups pushes for more government spending on their favourite programme. Today, the more fragmented political landscape in many countries, where large coalitions have to be formed to reach a majority, reinforces this issue.

Primary budget deficit/surplus UK Source: Bank of England:
A milennium of macroeconomic data for the UK, IMF, own calculations
Structurally high budget surpluses were an important weapon in debt reduction in the past

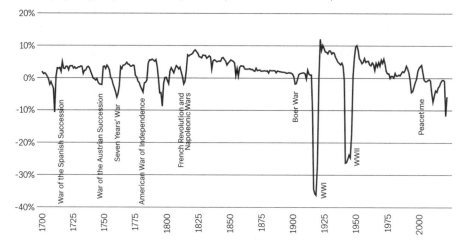

THE NEW WORLD ECONOMY

A second reason why governments have been less successful in posting long-term budget surpluses over the past half century – the last time the US posted a surplus (excluding interest charges) was in 2002 – is the blank cheque they got their hands on in the 1970s. With the abolition of the gold standard, where the dollar was backed by a quantity of gold (and therefore also the other currencies, which were pegged to the dollar), we moved to a fiat currency regime overnight, based on trust, in 1971. Money could now be created without the need for a gold supply. Deficits or surpluses no longer had immediate economic consequences.

Freed from their 'gold chain', budget deficits increased systematically. The social welfare state continued to expand without providing sufficient income in return. A democracy is a difficult context in which to achieve a balanced budget. The problem with taxing workers is that they vote. The challenge with higher corporate taxes is preventing corporate flight, especially in an era of accelerated globalisation. The result today is the highest peacetime debt burden for the bulk of developed countries.

Mounting debt

Total debt in developed countries – of non-financial and financial firms, households and governments – has risen from 269% of GDP since 1998 to peak at 426% of GDP in the first quarter of 2021. By the end of 2022, they stood at 386%. Public debt rose the most. During the Covid crisis, it shot from 110% of GDP to a peak of 132% (due to an implosion of GDP and an explosion of Covid outlays)... and back. Corporate debt also made a yo-yo move from 90% to 100% and back. The healing power of hefty inflation and a growth surge did their work. Yet some, not least economist Carmen Reinhart, are warning of a debt crisis in the making. Especially as it is also feared that the Covid pandemic may well leave a scar and weigh on economic growth potential, as happened in the Global Financial Crisis of 2007. But is this true?

Scarring occurs when aggregate weak demand in an economy undermines the future potential of aggregate supply. This has two consequences. After the kink downwards in the growth path – a temporary shock – there is no full catch-up and thus no connection to the pre-crisis path. This means a permanent loss of economic output. A second, more permanent shock is a slowdown in the growth path and thus a long-term decline in the growth trend. Both issues occurred not only after the Global Financial Crisis, but also in most of the recessions in 23 developed countries since 1966, according to a study by our colleague Arne Maes.[111]

Five scars can depress growth potential: increased bankruptcies, more unemployment, more zombie companies, less investment and higher debt. Bankruptcies, long-term unemployment and a drop in investment were largely avoided during the Covid pandemic, although investment still lagged behind. The number of zombie companies, enterprises that can barely repay their debts with what they earn, did increase.[112] These weigh on the economy's productivity growth due to their lack of investment.

The fifth scar is higher debt. After the Global Financial Crisis of 2008, the debt of households and financial institutions in particular undermined economic recovery in the US. Families were groaning under the weight of mortgage loans, many of which could not be repaid. This in turn weighed on financial institutions. They cleaned up their balance sheets and reduced credit. Households started saving, doubling their savings rate in the following years only to stabilise it. The result? The slowest economic recovery in recent economic history. In Europe, it was not households but governments that tightened the austerity reins, with a similar effect.

Today we see higher household and bank debt only in Canada and a few European countries. They came out of the crisis unscathed in 2008 and saved less afterwards. There is a risk of deleveraging there. In the other countries, only government and corporate debt rose this time. Rising corporate debt leaves fewer macroeconomic scars than periods when households are over-indebted. This makes the comparison between Covid-19 and the Global Financial Crisis misleading. There is no convincing negative relationship between rising corporate debt and subsequent macroeconomic performance in terms of the depth of the recession or the pace of recovery.[113] The recovery profile is similar to that following a 'normal' recession. In contrast, the profile following a household debt explosion shows a deeper decline in GDP per capita and a slower recovery.

And what about high government debt? Its level varies greatly from country to country. The chart shows gross public debt as a percentage of GDP, with Luxembourg and the Nordic countries as positive outliers. On the other hand, Southern European countries stand out in negative terms, as does Japan in particular.

Belgium is not yet the 'Greece of the North Sea'*, but with a gross public debt of 106% of GDP *and* a sky-high budget deficit, it seems to be working towards it.[114]

Public debt levels developed countries in % GDP, Q1 2023 Source: Global Debt Monitor

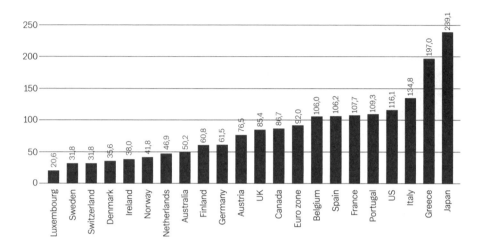

Are future expenses under control?

High government debts are not problematic, as long as the debt burden remains bearable and future spending remains under control. These are two key conditions, which could be highly questionable in the future. 'After a massive fiscal expansion during covid, governments will face additional pressures from climate change, defence spending, crumbling infrastructure, the emerging cold war with Russia/China, the new appetite for domestic industrial policy and a polarized electorate that finds it impossible to prioritize the needs of one group in society over another,' Dario Perkins of TS Lombard articulates the challenge.[115] 'Which, as we saw during the recent energy crisis, means everybody gets a bailout.'

---

*   In early 2010, when presenting a joint campaign of Belgian employers' organisations, then-FEB president Thomas Leysen stated that 'without measures for competitiveness, Belgium risks becoming the "Greece of the North Sea" in the coming years.'

With the immense challenges of climate change and ageing populations, keeping budgets under control in the longer term is a test for a great many advanced countries. The US is heading for a federal budget deficit averaging 5% over the next decade, according to the Congressional Budget Office (CBO). Net public debt then rises from 95% of GDP to 110% in 2032, 140% in 2042, and 185% by 2052. 'Of course, this won't happen,' believes Martin Barnes,[116] former chief economist at Bank Credit Analyst. 'because markets will force a change long before we get to that point.' When? 'Any attempt would be pure speculation,' Barnes commented in November 2022. 'I am quite confident it will not be in the next 12 months but would put a 75% probability it will be within the next five years. At that point, debt-servicing costs could be at new highs. This would make it a problem for the next administration. What has happened in the UK in terms of fiscal policy and market reactions is a good indicator of what the US ultimately will face.'

In Europe, the demographic profile is more challenging and energy dependence is greater. On top of that comes defence spending, which needs to go from the current 1.3% of GDP to 2%. The peace dividend Europe enjoyed after World War II is a thing of the past. 'This growing "peace dividend" created fiscal space for a steady reduction in debt and expansion of the NHS and the wider welfare state,' writes the UK Office for Budget Responsibility (OBR) in its *Long-Term Public Finance* report.[117] Some of that space is also falling away in other countries.

The impact of interest charges

Debts seem unbearably high. Fortunately, there have been low interest rates. The falling average interest rate on outstanding debt in the 19 eurozone countries fell from 7.8% to 1.6% in 2021. Expressing that as a percentage of GDP, government spending fell from 5.3% to 1.5%. Governments thus had to spend 3.8% of GDP less on interest expenses in 2021 than in 1996, despite a much higher debt.

Since 2021, interest rates have been rising and a tipping point has been reached. The reverse movement beckons. A percentage point less or more in market interest rates makes a big difference over time, according to a simulation by the OBR. In its baseline scenario, with an interest rate of 3.9%, UK government debt rises to 267% of GDP over 50 years. If that interest rate goes one percentage

Country	Implied interest on gross debt 2023 IMF	Average growth 2023–2028 nominal, IMF	R-G	Gross debt 2023, Ameco	Required primary balance to stabilise debt	Projected primary deficit/surplus 2024, IMF	Average primary deficit (-) / surplus (+) 2010–2019	Current ten-year interest rate juni 2023	R-G if implicit interest rate rises to current ten-year rate	Required primary deficit (-) / surplus (+) to stabilise debt at current interest rate
Belgium	1,74%	3,19%	-1,45%	105,95%	-1,49%	-3,53%	-0,13%	3,48%	0,29%	0,30%
Germany	1,30%	3,85%	-2,55%	67,16%	-1,65%	-1,04%	1,51%	2,83%	-1,02%	-0,66%
France	1,86%	3,26%	-1,39%	111,44%	-1,50%	-3,03%	-2,10%	3,38%	0,12%	0,13%
Italy	2,95%	3,10%	-0,16%	140,29%	-0,21%	0,83%	1,28%	4,76%	1,66%	2,26%
Netherlands	1,45%	4,12%	-2,67%	48,18%	-1,24%	-1,67%	-0,44%	3,17%	-0,95%	-0,44%
Portugal	2,07%	4,19%	-2,12%	112,36%	-2,29%	0,95%	-1,00%	3,59%	-0,59%	-0,64%
Spain	2,35%	3,92%	-1,57%	110,46%	-1,67%	-1,26%	-3,93%	3,91%	-0,01%	-0,01%
Japan	0,57%	2,15%	-1,58%	258,19%	-4,00%	-3,85%	-4,51%	0,41%	-1,74%	-4,40%
UK	4,46%	3,95%	0,51%	106,24%	0,53%	-2,54%	-3,15%	4,43%	0,48%	0,49%
US	3,52%	3,79%	-0,28%	122,23%	-0,33%	-4,07%	-4,04%	4,59%	0,80%	0,94%

Source IMF WEO April 2023, own calculations

point higher or lower from 2027–2028, the debt rises to 325% or the increase is limited to 220% of GDP.

Three parameters are important to keep debt under control: the average nominal or implicit interest rate payable on the fully outstanding amount of debt (R), the primary deficits (budget deficits excluding interest expenses) and the nominal growth realised (G). By subtracting two of these parameters – interest rates minus growth – we arrive at the crucial growth-adjusted interest rate. If it is positive and high, the debt ratio can rise very rapidly. If it is negative, then limited primary deficits remain possible without pushing the debt ratio higher.

How is this growth-adjusted interest rate doing today? In Italy, it is already positive. The average interest rate payable there is already higher than nominal growth for the next five years. To stabilise its debt, it needs to (and does) post a primary surplus. For the European countries included in the table, a primary deficit of 1.6% – on average – is sufficient for public debt stabilisation. But in the majority of countries – the coloured boxes – the current primary deficit is more negative. This includes the UK and certainly the US. An abnormally low budget deficit is not that 1.6%, however, if we look at the ten years preceding the pandemic. Belgium barely achieved a (primary) balanced budget (-0.13%) over that period. Germany and – surprisingly – Italy even posted solid surpluses. The aftermath of the Covid pandemic is clearly still working its way through public finances.

The problem is that those implicit interest rates will not stay that low. By June 2023, ten-year government bonds in many European countries were already trading one and a half percentage points above the current implicit rate. As more debt is refinanced, the implicit or average interest rates paid will inevitably rise towards current rates. What happens then? Then those average interest rates exceed nominal growth in many countries. Instead of reducing budget deficits, they must achieve structural surpluses. As the amount by which the implicit interest rate exceeds growth increases, the fiscal effort required in countries with high public debts gets exponentially larger. Without such savings, there is a risk of a snowball effect with rapidly rising public debts.

This situation occurred in Belgium in the early 1980s, when public debt hovered at 77% of GDP. But then things moved fast: the primary budget deficit doubled from 4 to 8% in 1981, while interest rates jumped from 9% to almost 14% between early 1980 and January 1982. The debt exploded first to 100% in 1982, then to 130% in 1987 to reach its peak in 1993 at 138%. The final stabilisation cost

Belgian citizens blood, sweat and tears. The huge 8% budget deficit was turned into a balanced budget as early as 1985 through index jumps that undercut income in real terms. Meanwhile, the snowball effect had public debt in its grip, as interest charges rose faster than revenues. The Dehaene government issued additional measures through the so-called Global Plan, using the prospect of joining the European Monetary Union as an excuse. The mission succeeded: the primary budget surplus peaked at 6% of GDP in 2000 and public debt fell to 110%. In the end, two decades of austerity were needed to curb out-of-control public debts.

How high do long-term interest rates go?

Do we risk going in that direction again? One key difference is the much lower nominal interest rate today. And if central bankers keep inflation (expectations) under control, those rates are likely to remain low in the future too. How low? For the eurozone, the OECD expects long-term interest rates of 2.7% by 2030, with a very slight rise thereafter to 3.2% by 2060. Germany is slightly below this, Italy slightly above. For Japan, the UK and the US, they assume 2.5%, 3.1% and 3.3% respectively. Most countries, except Japan, are slightly above that today. Getting inflation under control is going to be slightly harder than expected.

The OECD also forecasts nominal long-term growth rates. Combined with the forecast interest rates, that produces the all-important R-G snowball lever. And the conclusion there is tedious: for all countries included in our table, long-term interest rates exceed expected growth from 2040 onwards. The difference is limited: between 0.05 percentage points for Belgium and 0.4 to 0.5 percentage points for Spain and Italy. But the hitherto positive leverage is slowly coming to an end. Governments would do well to gradually put their budgets in order.

BNP Paribas 360° also pulled out the crystal ball to see what interest rates we can expect over time. In doing so, they look at the neutral equilibrium interest rate, or the R* (see Abbreviations and explanations). The problem with that R* is that it is a concept; it cannot be observed. It is determined, or estimated, based on several factors. Future potential growth (higher) and inflation (for nominal R*; also higher) are the most important ones. In addition, R* also reflects the balance between savings and investment in an economy over the medium and long term.

A savings surplus, for example, because an ageing population is saving extra towards retirement, weighs on real R* long-term interest rates. More savings also remain because of persistent inequality (rich people save more). In turn, the war in Ukraine triggered significant changes in European energy policy with potentially negative effects on potential growth. For instance, Germany needs to revise its industrial, export-driven growth model, which was based on cheap Russian gas and exports towards China. Fiscal policy is more flexible than in the past and investment demand higher with all the challenges governments face. The impact of climate change is mixed with climate catastrophes that depress growth versus huge investments boosting demand for money.

Factor	Pushes R* ...	Reason impact
Potential growth	Upwards	Slower labour market growth more than offset by productivity growth.
Inflation	Upwards	Structurally higher inflation pushes nominal R* upwards.
Demographics and inequality	Downwards	High demand for safe assets and inequality persists and pushes R* upwards.
Russia-Ukraine war	Downwards	Energy policy, like war, may have negative impact on potential growth.
Budget policy	Upwards	Budgetary spending has risen sharply and will remain relatively high.
Climate change	Neutral	Risk aversion and damage weigh on R*, but investment during transition pushes R* higher.

Source BNP Paribas Markets 360

Taking all those factors into account, BNP Paribas[118] mentions real R* at a range of -0.2% and +0.8% for the US and -0.5% and +0.5% for the eurozone. It remains low. Over the medium term, they note for the Eurozone inflation at 2.5% for the US and 2.2% higher than in the past. Adding up, we thus arrive at a nominal R* of 2.3–3.3% for the US and 1.7–2.3% for the eurozone. The average in both cases is slightly lower than the OECD expectations of 3.3% for the US and 2.7% for the eurozone. The R-G then turns from positive to stable to slightly negative. The feared negative leverage effect is avoided, and we see how minimal estimation differences in theoretical concepts such as the R* can quickly turn a half-empty glass into a half-full one.

Conclusion: on the basis of what we know today – and that is not much – the sovereign debts of developed countries seem narrowly manageable, perhaps 'manageable' for competent managers, in the coming decades.

EMERGING COUNTRIES' MOUNTAIN *of* DEBT

KEY POINTS

✓ Debt peaks, but a debt crisis has been avoided until now because emerging countries avoided the mistakes of the 1980s and 1990s. These included over-reliance on foreign creditors, too much short-term debt and high current account deficits. A local financial market also reduced foreign dependence.

✓ Still, emerging countries are vulnerable to rapidly rising interest rates and low growth. According to the IMF, that low growth will also persist in sub-Saharan Africa, Latin America and the Middle East over the next five years. Over the course of the last 40 years, they have barely managed to catch up with industrialised countries.

✓ The credit ratings of countries from these regions have fallen sharply since the Covid pandemic. Debt restructuring is complex due to China's large share of claims. Without a solution, a debt trap with sluggish growth and further rising debt ratios looms.

✓ Besides being the largest creditor, China is also a large debtor: its nominal debt has increased sevenfold since 2005. Today, its economy is also in a transition period from an investment-driven to a consumption-driven economy.

✓ Corporate debt, especially among real estate companies, is a big problem. China's real estate sector is at the beginning of a very difficult and multi-year restructuring process. History shows that debt-financed real estate booms end not with a whimper but with a bang.

Over time, exploding debt in developed countries becomes a problem. What debts are emerging countries dealing with? Total debt – corporate and household – rose from 227% in 2019 to peak at 254% of GDP in the first quarter of 2021. The credit ratings of quite a few emerging countries have already been downgraded, but for now, there is no emerging markets crisis. This is remarkable, as in the past, it was always the emerging countries that were the victims of the combination of what we have seen in recent years: rapidly rising interest rates, a rising dollar and a global growth slowdown. Emerging countries have learnt from the mistakes of the past.

These mistakes mostly involved over-reliance on foreign creditors and too much short-term debt. In the 1980s, Latin American countries in particular went head-to-head. Their debts increased tenfold between 1970 and 1980. In the early 1980s, the US central bank raised its interest rates dramatically to curb inflation and end years of stagflation. Real US interest rates rose from a low of −4% in mid-1980 to 9% three years later. The dollar doubled in value against the currencies of its trading partners and even more against those of emerging countries. This complicated the repayment of dollar bonds issued by those countries. They saw their local revenues plummet in dollar terms.

Does a rate increase spell trouble of low- and mid income countries? Source: BNP Paribas Fortis, BFFS project

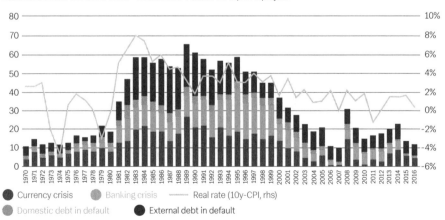

Mexico set the ball rolling in 1982, when its finance minister indicated that the country could no longer pay its debts. New loans through foreign investors in the international capital markets stopped. Refinancing of short-term loans became impossible and plunged the country into a crisis. Other countries, such as Brazil and Argentina, followed suit. Plunging currencies also fired up inflation, which peaked in the early 1990s. As a result of that perfect storm in low- to middle-income countries, the number of currency and banking crises and domestic and foreign defaults quadrupled.

Latin American countries also shared in the blows in the mid-1990s with – again – Mexico in the lead. Then it was the Asian countries' turn. The Asian miracle, the development model of countries such as Thailand and South Korea, which involved attracting short-term funding from foreign banks to invest in companies and sectors considered strategic, came to an end in 1997–98. But here again, a confluence of circumstances – real estate crash, again that strengthening dollar and weakness in the global chip market – meant that capital stopped coming in. Asian banks had to be bailed out. The cost amounted to 34% of GDP for Thailand and 35% for South Korea.

The plethora of crises strengthened the belief that sovereign debt and emerging markets were like oil and fire. Emerging countries were 'debt intolerant': they could only handle a limited amount of debt. According to Reinhart et al., a debt ratio of 35% is the limit beyond which debt becomes a problem for emerging countries.[119] For some countries, the limit is as low as 15%. The reason for this debt intolerance, according to the authors, lies in their history of defaults and inflation; their debt reputation.

Basic principles for prudent public debt management

However, according to Eichengreen, the tidal wave of defaults was not due to excessive debt levels.[120] While nominal debts went up, so did exports (which provided foreign exchange earnings) and growth. In fact, debt as a percentage of GDP fell in the first half of the 1990s. It was not due to some incompatibility between sovereign debt and emerging countries. The main reason was the failure of governments to adhere to some basic principles of prudent public debt management.

What are those basic principles? The first states that financing budget deficits with short-term debt is dangerous. Demand for debt securities can suddenly dry up, and then all that is left is for the country's own central bank to take on public debt with freshly printed money. However, that in turn leads to inflation and currency depreciation, which makes repaying loans in foreign currency – often dollars – even more difficult.

Foreign debt is dangerous anyway. Limiting those is the second principle. 'The sovereign's debt-servicing capacity will depend on its ability to generate foreign exchange receipts, which can fluctuate for reasons beyond its control,' they say. Foreign revenues can suddenly plummet for a variety of reasons. A commodity exporter may see its revenues plummet due to falling commodity prices. A competitiveness problem or trade conflict may depress exports.

If short-term foreign currency debts do arise, three rules apply to contain that danger. A first rule of thumb, the Guidotti-Greenspan rule, states that countries should hold enough foreign currency reserves to pay off all foreign debts falling due in the next 12 months, as well as all current account deficits. The latter is usually due to more imports than exports and means that more is paid abroad than comes in. Attracting foreign money in the form of portfolio investments or long-term investments by companies creates a balance (the foreign country does build up balances against the country in question). Providing a buffer of currency reserves prevents the sudden inability to pay for and thus import essential goods and services. With a foreign funding freeze – especially of volatile portfolio investments – it is also possible to continue to pay short-term debts. How do countries build up such foreign reserves? Just like households do: generate a bit more income than expenditure. In other words, more export than import.

A second, related rule is that governments should avoid volatile debt. Very short-term liabilities then risk having to be refinanced at a much higher interest rate when market conditions change. Third, it is best for governments to set up their own local market for long-term loans. Some countries do not yet enjoy the confidence to expect long-term loans from their own citizens. Others do not have pension and insurance funds. For those funds, investments in long-term loans in local currency are an ideal match for their equally long-term payouts. Building a liquid secondary market* with an effective mix of individual and institutional, local and foreign investors is a long-term process. Only after the crisis of the 1990s did emerging countries see the value of this.

A final important element is the role assigned to local banks. If little debt is traded in the local bond market due to lack of interest, borrowing becomes relatively expensive. This may make it seem tempting to legally require banks to hold local government securities. This is dangerous, as a problem with those government bonds then immediately translates into a banking problem. By providing less credit, economic growth falls, which in turn has an impact on public finances. This poses the risk of ending up in a doom loop. This diabolical downward spiral almost brought the eurozone to its knees in 2012. Fears of defaults in Portugal, Italy, Ireland and Spain led to a fall in their bond prices and pulled down the equity of local banks. Fears that governments would have to recapitalise those banks pushed bond valuations even lower. They eventually got out of this negative spiral thanks to ECB president Mario Draghi, who promised to 'do whatever it takes to keep the eurozone together'. That restored confidence. The EU reassured investors that it would cover member states' sovereign debts. This avoided a huge crisis that would probably also have resulted in the end of the eurozone, and the European Union.

Debts still under pressure

We were discussing the emerging countries, which drew lessons from the debacles of the 1980s and 1990s. In the following decades, these countries built up local financial markets to curb reliance on foreign currency loans. That share of government and corporate bonds had dropped to around 10% by 2021, although exposure to dollar loans in countries like Argentina, Turkey, Chile, Hungary and Mexico remains large. The share of government bonds held by foreigners was also scaled back: from almost all to less than half today. Finally, the average maturities of debts contracted have been significantly extended.

---

* The primary market refers to the market where new securities are issued to raise capital. Companies or the government can do this through a new issue of shares or bonds. Once issued, these securities can be traded in the secondary market.

The Guidotti-Greenspan rule was also considered. Current account deficits – more imports than exports – were turned into substantial surpluses with a peak of just under 5% in mid-2000 before slowly falling back. This built up a war chest of foreign currency reserves that could be used to pay off foreign debts if necessary. Those foreign currencies can also be sold, and the home currency bought when it is under pressure. From 2015–2018, current accounts dipped into negative digits again, but the Covid recession put an end to that. Imports plummeted while the lockdown in Western countries boosted demand for goods. This benefited factories (in emerging countries) and raw materials (mainly from emerging countries) to make those products. Current account deficits are no longer a problem.

Current account   Source: IMF, World Economic Outlook Database, April 2023

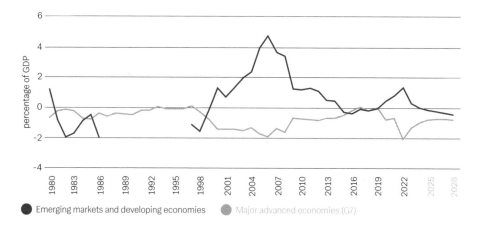

● Emerging markets and developing economies   ● Major advanced economies (G7)

Better debt management has prevented a major debt crisis in emerging countries. Still, the pressure is mounting due to the combination of historically high debt, low growth, as well as interest rates and the dollar, which are both rapidly rising. Total debt stands at 250% in the first quarter of 2023. Public debt stands at 65% of GDP (versus the safe limit of 35% set by Reinhart). Unlike in developed countries, where total debts have fallen by 40 percentage points since the peak, they remain very close to that in emerging countries.

Why can't we see a decline? The growth recovery after the Covid pandemic was weak, only marginally larger than that in developed countries. Since 2000, that positive growth differential for emerging countries has hovered around 3–4% on average. The war in Ukraine, supply problems and related inflation made things even more difficult for emerging countries. International sanctions make money shipments towards Central Asian banks, which are often connected to Russian financial institutions, impossible. Rising inflation erodes purchasing power worldwide, but food weighs much more heavily on average consumption in emerging countries. For example, in Belgium, food and non-alcoholic beverages account for 17.5% of the total consumption basket. In emerging countries, this varies between 20% (Brazil, South Africa) and 40% (Thailand, Egypt), and even more than 50% in India. When food inflation is high, social unrest is never far away. In his newsletter, renowned asset manager Jeremy Grantham reminds us of the chants in Tahir Square at the start of the Arab Spring: 'Bread, Freedom, Dignity'. To avoid unrest, a lot of low-income countries had to further boost public spending, especially in the face of lower-than-expected economic growth.

Lower growth weighs on the high debt ratio. Strong nominal growth facilitates debt sustainability and quickly reduces the debt ratio: the denominator – nominal GDP – then rises faster than the numerator – debt. But the pandemic hit emerging countries head-on due to their often large informal face-to-face economies and lack of sufficient means to protect themselves. GDP recovery is weak and fiscal deficits large. The debt ratio remains high. Despite all the lessons learned, emerging countries are vulnerable.

In the short term, there seems to be little change in this sluggish growth, at least for sub-Saharan Africa, Latin America and the Middle East. The IMF's projected cumulative growth over the period 2022–2028 is barely a fraction higher there than in the G7 countries (see table 'Cumulative growth'). The outlook for European, and especially Asian, emerging economies is much better. Looking at past growth rates, only those two regions are worthy of the name 'emerging countries'. In the 1960s and 1970s (not shown in table), all emerging countries grew at lightning speed. But those good times were followed by what William Easterly of New York University described as the lost decades of the 1980s and 1990s. During those two decades, average GDP growth per person in emerging and developing countries remained below that of the top seven economies (G7). It dipped in 1980–1983 and even below zero in 1991–1992. Strange, because it was during that period that the depth and functioning of financial markets improved, as did health, education and infrastructure. Easterly suggests that global factors such as the rise in interest rates, the increased debt ratio of emerging countries, the slowdown in growth in the industrial world and changes in technical skills sought were at the root of the stagnation.

Cumulative growth per capita, PPP, constant prices	1980–1990	1990–2000	2000–2010	2010–2019	2019–2022	2022–2028
Largest developed countries (G7)	28,2%	20,1%	7,7%	12,2%	2,3%	7,1%
Emerging countries	23,7%	18,0%	54,0%	33,1%	5,2%	18,5%
Emerging countries Asia	57,0%	68,0%	98,9%	65,0%	9,9%	28,5%
Emerging countries Europe	45,1%	-21,8%	54,1%	26,9%	9,0%	13,0%
Latin America and the Caribbean	-7,5%	15,0%	19,7%	3,4%	-1,1%	7,3%
Middle East and Central Asia	-19,6%	4,0%	24,5%	4,5%	3,4%	10,4%
Sub-Saharan Africa	-9,0%	-5,6%	32,0%	8,7%	-1,3%	9,2%

Source IMF, Raming World Economic Outlook (May 2023), own calculations.

The problematic countries are mainly found in three regions: Latin America, the Middle East considered together with Central Asia (including some former Soviet republics), and sub-Saharan Africa. With the exception of the 2000–2010 period, these regions have failed to narrow their gap with the world's richest countries. But not all emerging countries experienced bleak times. Asian emerging economies, with China in the lead, experienced a peak. In 2000, when China joined the World Trade Organisation, growth there shifted up another gear. However, in recent years changes have been happening in the global empire.

Is China (the saviour) in trouble?

Projected growth in many emerging and developing countries is weak. Are we heading for another lost decade? A debt crisis would significantly increase the chances of that. And China plays a doubly crucial role in it: as a creditor and as a debtor.

As a debtor, China has seen its nominal debts increase sevenfold since 2005. What was offered in return? In the expansion of the 2010s, China and its debt-doped growth engine played a key role. 'Every stop-go round of government stimulus provided a critical source of demand for the global industrial cycle,' writes research firm TS Lombard's Dario Perkins.[121] China's share of total outstanding global debt climbed from 3% in 2005 over 10% in 2013 to the current 21%. The share of its economy (in terms of purchasing power parity) since 2013 climbed from 15.4 to just under 19% by 2023.

China now wants to shift from a debt-fuelled, investment-driven economy to a consumption-driven economy. The engine of the global economy of the past two decades is going down a gear. Not only that, it is sputtering. China's debt challenge is on two fronts: sovereign debt and corporate debt. Central government debt is not a problem, at barely 21% of GDP. However, we must add local government debts. Our Chinese colleagues at BNP Paribas China estimate these between 76% and 88% of GDP, putting total public debt at 97% to 109% of GDP. Compared to some developed countries – which it almost is –, that is not excessive. Compared to emerging countries, it is sky-high.

Corporate debt totals a whopping 164% of GDP. Four-fifths of this is held by companies in which the government has a stake. If the Chinese corporate sector goes out of business, you take down one of the three global growth pillars (with the US and the eurozone being the other two). In recent years, real estate companies have been in trouble. These troubles started in 2020 when the Chinese government introduced 'three red lines' to stop extremely high debts. Real estate giant Evergrande's default on its US bonds followed in mid-2021.

The total value of Chinese real estate is estimated at $55 trillion, twice the value of the US real estate market, four times China's GDP. Property developers' renminbi revenue from property sales should be enough to repay dollar loans. But things get difficult when those revenues are no longer there and the Chinese currency underperforms against the dollar. In mid-2023, the Chinese currency approached its lowest level in 16 years against the dollar, and property giant Country Garden reported liquidity pressures and a monster first-half loss of €6.3 billion.

'The Chinese property sector is at the beginning of a very difficult, multiyear restructuring,' concluded real estate analyst Andrew Lawrence of Oculus Research Asia.[122] 'History shows that credit-fuelled real estate booms do not end in a whimper; rather, they end with a bang – and nearly always with a major banking crisis.

Can Beijing really manage the end of the largest property boom in history without ultimately triggering a financial crisis?' I hesitate.

Will China take part in a restructuring of low-wage countries' debts?

China is not only a major debtor. It is also a major creditor, and thus a key figure in any restructuring of the debts of problem countries. Under its 'Belt & Road' initiative, China lent to numerous developing countries. Net transfers towards developing countries were almost non-existent in the early 2000s but picked up from 2005 onwards.* Between 2010 and 2019, they fluctuated between US$8 billion and US$16 billion annually. As a creditor, China is currently bigger than the IMF or the World Bank. Almost half of the outstanding loans went to the African continent; just over a quarter towards Latin America. That money was used for infrastructure works (often led by Chinese firms), which today gives China a foothold in many developing countries, many of which have large resource reserves. But 60% of those countries now have payment difficulties.

The fewer parties involved, the more easily debts of troubled emerging countries can be restructured. Until 2000, negotiations mainly involved four parties around the table: the Paris Club, being an informal group of mainly creditors from rich countries, private investors (often banks), multilateral institutions (such as the World Bank, IMF...) and the country concerned. With China as a new major creditor *and* a much more diverse collection of private investors, those talks have become a lot more difficult. China prefers to solve payment problems bilaterally. No one knows the exact terms: strict confidentiality is the rule when obtaining a Chinese loan.

The most important thing in tackling their debt problems is 'reforming the international debt infrastructure', according to the IMF. Today, China is the largest

---

* Net transfers include new disbursements less capital and interest repayments.

official bilateral creditor in more than half of the 73 poorest countries benefiting from the Debt Service Suspension Initiative (DSSI), even if all 22 Paris Club creditor countries are counted as one group. Through the DSSI, those countries can request a temporary suspension of interest payments in case of liquidity problems But this only postpones the debt problem – it does not solve it.

There are several bottlenecks in the talks to achieve joint debt restructuring. China regards the World Bank as the political bank of the West. The idea that the West would be exempt in a restructuring and Chinese banks would not, is not an option. It doubts that private investors will bear their share of the burden, and it has almost always refused to reduce the face value of its claims, preferring other forms of relief. Debt extensions and inserting grace periods are negotiable. Instead of cancelling debt, the Chinese are pushing for in-kind payments (e.g. oil, agricultural products or a 99-year licence agreement to operate a strategic port, as with Sri Lanka).

Due to the lack of a standardised framework, debt restructurings drag on for a long time. Zambia, for example, entered what was almost its third year of discussions but still reached a deal with China and other creditors at the last minute in mid-2023. Elsewhere, stress continues to mount. Rating agencies highlighted that 2022 was the second worst year ever for rating downgrades of emerging-market countries. The number of countries with a CCC rating or lower has never been higher. Such ratings indicate that the countries concerned are very close to defaulting, if they have not already done so. They mainly concern the poorest countries, such as Pakistan, Kenya, Cameroon, Tanzania, and so on.

The lack of a solution is bogging those countries down in a debt trap. 'Liquidity is the first thing those countries need,' said Vera Songwe, under-secretary-general of the United Nations and executive secretary of the Economic Commission for Africa at a recent IMF seminar.[123] The 1980s and 1990s illustrate the dire consequences of such a debt trap, in which excessive debt undermined growth momentum. The affected countries can no longer support the economy when and where it is needed. The denominator of the debt ratio is squeezed, pushing the ratio further upwards. You need a quick fix, a quick restructuring to get out of this spiral. In the long run, a much wider contagion risk presents itself, according to Mohamed El-Erian, president of Queens' College in Cambridge in the same debate. 'If no restructuring emerges, you end up stumbling towards defaults. And since a lot of non-specialist private creditors are exposed to low-wage countries these days, you risk seeing problems suddenly crop up in unexpected places.'

So far, a tidal wave of defaults has been avoided, and the pandemic has slowly been brought under control. Still, there is no room for complacency. 'One reason is because we have flooded the system with liquidity,' El-Erian explains. 'But that in fact made the debt problem worse.' The top economist draws two relevant lessons from the Global Financial Crisis of 2008. The first is that IMF support for emerging countries then peaked in 2011, not 2008. The problems only surfaced after some time. 'And second [...] this is a golden opportunity to make sustainable and fair a lot of things – and the debt, the international debt architecture is a critical component of that.'

LESSONS LEARNED
from the PAST

KEY POINTS

✓ In the period from the 19th century to World War I, the debt ratio declined mainly due to budget surpluses.

✓ After World War I and the rise of the welfare state, there was a more proportional contribution of budget surpluses, along with low implicit interest rates versus higher nominal growth (R-G).

✓ During and after the Great Depression, debts were eliminated through defaults, re-structuring and, in some countries, hyperinflation.

✓ From 1945–1975, financial repression brought down skyrocketing debts. Government measures and legislation squeezed debts and the interest charges on them. Combined with a dose of inflation, real interest rates became negative. During that period, growth exploded due to productivity gains. R-G thus became even more negative.

Global debt is high, probably too high. An upward interest rate or downward economic shock could undermine confidence in its affordability. The fortunes of Liz Truss, the shortest-reigning prime minister in UK history, show that a tipping point is approaching. The expansionary fiscal policy she announced with substantial borrowing and tax cuts, combined with rising interest rates and an already high public debt, shocked bond traders. They sold UK government securities and interest rates promptly went higher. The UK was close to a financial crisis. Truss threw in the towel after barely 50 days. Successor Rishi Sunak restored confidence.

The so-called 'bond vigilantes', the guardians of debt sustainability, have been silent for decades. Have they now woken up for good? Or will we return to those ultra-low interest rates once inflation is back under control? I think not. The direction of real interest rates is a guessing game. But as we argue in this book, we see inflation averaging well above the central bankers' 2% target over the next decade with alternating peaks and troughs. More than being in an era of change, we end up in a different era altogether.

Debts do not have to be completely paid off. They do need to be brought to lower levels, where shocks will not lead to loss of confidence and debt crises. How? Different paths were taken in the past. There were defaults, followed by restructurings, and in a somewhat more distant past, significant fiscal surpluses. Another tried and tested recipe was to keep real interest rates negative by establishing an upper limit (as in Japan) with slightly higher inflation (which is difficult to increase in Japan). This is part of the financial repression recipe that we will discuss in more detail below. And as we mentioned earlier, higher nominal growth – through the boosting of productivity – relative to nominal interest rates also reduces, or at least stabilises, debt.

Ray Dalio, owner of Bridgewater, the world's largest hedge fund, adds money printing in his monumental study *Big Debt Crises*. In it, he examines the biggest debt crises of the past 100 years. In the case of money printing, a country's central bank buys government debt with freshly printed money to stimulate growth. If this is done to a limited extent, it can avoid a debt crisis. If this is overdone, hyperinflation beckons, as it did in 1921–1923 in the Weimar Republic.

Each of these methods has a different impact on the economy, according to Dalio. Some, like printing money, are inflationary and stimulate growth, while others depress debt (via savings and defaults) but also growth. 'Tools enough to spread the pain over time. The key to creating a "beautiful deleveraging" (a reduction in debt/income ratios accompanied by acceptable inflation and growth rates) lies in striking the right balance between them.' Climbing out of a debt crisis without too much pain is possible. The only condition is that debts are denominated in one's own currency. The emerging economies learned that lesson in the 1980s and 1990s.

Budget surpluses

So high debt and debt crises do not always have bad consequences. That was certainly not the case in the 19th century. The huge debts in Britain after the French Revolution and the Napoleonic wars, in the US after the Civil War, and in France after the Franco-Prussian War were each eliminated without severe crises. 'There was no involuntary restructuring or renegotiation of debts,' write the authors of *In Defense of Public Debt.* 'No measures were taken to artificially depress interest rates. Nor were debts inflated away.'

So how was debt reduction achieved? In 'the traditional way': by realising budget surpluses. The table divides the realised reduction in government debt into three components. The first is the cumulative realised primary budget surpluses (i.e. excluding interest charges). The second is the contribution of R-G. As seen earlier, an implicit interest rate below nominal growth reduces debt (under a balanced budget) and vice versa. The third term, stock flows, includes all other elements, such as capital gains on foreign debt or debt restructuring.

Before 1914, the entire decline – and more – came from budget surpluses. The UK recorded an average primary surplus of 1.6% for a century, which depressed debt by just under 300 percentage points. In the United States and France, we see a similar picture. 'The British, US and French government went to great lengths to repay their debts. This was partly a consequence of the enfranchisement and political influence of the creditor class and of the fact that most debt was held by relatively affluent, politically influential citizens.' A limited government was also in place then and public programmes, benefits and transfers were non-existent. Creditworthiness was also crucial to still be able to raise money in case of future wars. 'Finally, it reflected good luck – a limited number of major wars, crises, and other disturbances during the consolidation period.'

Breakdown of debt repayment/growth, pre-1914 vs. 1920–1930; 1928–32

	Period	Debt versus GDP ratio (in %)			Positive / negative (-) contribution to decline (in %-point)		
		Start	End	Decrease (%-point)	Primary balance sheet	Contribution R-G	Stock-flow adjustment*
United Kingdom	1822–1913	194,1	28,3	165,8	299,3	-158,5	25,0
United States	1867–1913	30,1	3,2	26,9	40,6	-12,5	-1,3
France	1896–1913	95,6	51,1	44,5	44,7	-0,8	0,7
Average	pre-1914	106,6	27,5	79,1	128,2	-57,3	8,1
Canada	1922–1928	75,6	53,2	22,4	19,7	8,2	-5,6
France	1921–1929	237,0	138,6	98,4	24,7	118,2	-44,5
Italy	1920–1926	159,7	89,4	70,3	0,1	44,3	26,0
United Kingdom	1923–1929	195,5	170,5	25,0	52,2	-25,6	-1,7
United States	1919–1929	33,3	16,3	17,0	18,8	-2,7	0,9
Average	1920–1930	140,2	93,6	46,6	23,1	28,5	-5,0
Developed econ..	1928–1933	61,4	83,7	-22,4	3,5	-26,9	1,0

Source Eichengreen et al., *In Defense of Public Debt*, own calculations

* Stock-flow adjustments refer to all factors other than the first two, such as capital gains and losses on foreign debt due to exchange rate changes, restructurings that write down the value of previously issued debt, and other extraordinary financial operations.

Strong growth

The stable political situation favoured debt reduction via budget surpluses. The aftermath of WWI turned that political balance on its head. The rise of the welfare state and democratisation created a completely different playing field for public debt. Instead of financing wars, the focus shifted to growth-enhancing infrastructure investment and paying for social transfers. From nil in the early 20th century, benefits rose to 5% of GDP in the late 1920s. Germany was the trendsetter in an attempt to 'deradicalise' the working class. In the 1930s, branded by the Great Depression, the US led the charge towards social security protection.

World War I left a lot of (European) countries with sky-high public debts. On average, debts in advanced economies rose from 20% of GDP in 1914 to 80% in 1920. The stable political coalitions of the 19th century had been exchanged for more volatile political alliances by the 1920s. The successful long-term austerity of pre-World War I did not compromise economic and financial stability. The periodic fiscal consolidation after the war did. Public debts fell due to an increase in private credit, exchanging public for private debt. In some countries, inflation was used as a tool to liquidate debts, which left a polarised society. Debt was still partly paid off, but it was now only partly via primary surpluses and half via realising a strong – and sometimes inflationised – growth (G).

Debts had fallen in the Roaring Twenties; during the depressed 1930s they returned. The reason was not budget deficits: most governments stuck to the doctrine of a balanced budget and were even able to realise small surpluses (*see last row, table above*). But those savings hit economic growth, which dipped below the average interest rate paid (or implied). R-G's contribution to debt reduction in the 1930s was negative: it increased debts by 27 percentage points. Striving for a balanced budget in times of recession is not a good idea. On the contrary, it stabilises neither output nor the debt ratio. Europe learned that lesson again after the 2008 crisis.

The debt legacy of World War I and the Great Depression was eventually eliminated, largely through defaults and restructurings. Those restructurings included forced conversions of domestic and foreign debt into new debt with typically lower interest rates, longer maturities and lower underlying value. The decade before, periods of hyperinflation in Hungary, Poland but especially in Germany – a consequence of money printing and the resulting currency crash – were already causing a large-scale liquidation of domestic debts.

Is there a role for financial repression in sustainable debt reduction?

The Great Depression of the 1930s, following the hyperinflation of 1923–1925, brought the Nazis to power in a dislocated Germany. World War II followed, again leaving developed countries with high debts. From 1945 to 1975, a prolonged and phenomenal debt consolidation followed. 'The UK's history offers a pertinent illustration,' Carmen Reinhart and Belen Sbrancia[124] argue in their study. 'Following the Napoleonic Wars, the UK's public debt was a staggering 260% of GDP; it took over 40 years to bring it down to about 100%. Following World War II, the UK's public debt ratio was reduced by a comparable amount in 20 years.' According to the two authors, this was only possible because of financial repression.

Financial repression refers to measures and legislation introduced by the government to keep public debts and the interest charges on them sustainable. This is often at the expense of returns for savers and investors. 'It includes direct loans to the government by domestic institutions (such as pension funds) that are 'trapped' in their countries due to the introduction of new laws, explicit or implicit limits on interest rates, restrictions on cross-border capital movements, and (usually) a closer connection between governments and banks [e.g. measures that encourage the holding of national government bonds]. The highly regulated financial markets of the Bretton Woods* system facilitated several restrictions and led to a sharp and rapid decline in the public debt ratio between the late 1940s and the 1970s.'

---

* During the post-war Bretton Woods system (1944–1971), most countries implemented some form of capital controls to control 'volatile' investment flows into and out of the country. The aim was to achieve reasonable currency stability for the participating countries relative to each other.

Breakdown of debt repayment post WWII (1945–1975*) in developed economies

Period	Debt versus GDP ratio (in %)			Contribution to decrease (%-point)		
	Start	End	Decrease (%-point)	Primary balance sheet	Contribution R-G	Stock-flow adaptation**
Average	95,5	22,4	73,1	22,6	82,6	-32,2

Source Eichengreen et al., *In Defense of Public Debt*

Low nominal interest rates limited interest costs. That was the goal, and the Treasury and central banks were working in lockstep. This was also no secret, for example when the US introduced non-negotiable bonds in March 1951. Short-term government bonds could suddenly no longer be rolled over into new short-term paper, but had to be mandatorily converted into 29-year non-marketable bonds. William McChesney Martin, then top Treasury official, said at its launch: 'Some people will think the 2.75% nonmarketable bond is a trick issue. We want to meet that head on. It is. It is an attempt to lock up as much as possible of this long-term issue.' The Treasury succeeded mainly because the bulk of the debt was held by domestic creditors and quoted in its own currency. Martin was appointed chairman of the US central bank a few months later. He would become the longest-serving chairman in history: from 1951 to 1970.

Low nominal interest rates are one half of the pincer of financial repression. The other is a hefty dose of inflation, resulting in negative real interest rates. This undercuts the real value of sovereign debt. 'Financial repression in combination with inflation played an important role in reducing debts. Inflation need not take market participants entirely by surprise and, in effect, it need not be very high (by historic standards),' Reinhart and Sbrancia explain in their paper. In the UK, as in Belgium, during the period 1945–1980, real interest rates were negative half the time. In those negative years, the average UK interest rate was −3.8%, in Belgium

---

* Episodes are defined based on a debt reduction of at least 10 percentage points of GDP during 1945–1975.
** The peak-to-bottom periods differ in some countries.

THE NEW WORLD ECONOMY

Average ex-post real rate on treasury bills: advanced economies and emerging markets (1945–2009)

Source: International Financial Statistics, IMF Fund; Carmen Reinhardt and M. Belen Sbrancia

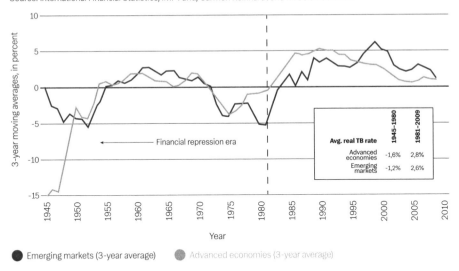

Avg. real TB rate	1945-1980	1981-2009
Advanced economies	-1,6%	2,8%
Emerging markets	-1,2%	2,6%

Emerging markets (3-year average)   Advanced economies (3-year average)

−4.2%. The financial world then turned upside down. Creditors lost money in real terms, but debtors – governments in this case – saw the real value of their debts eroded.

Particularly during the years immediately following World War II, inflation was high and real interest rates were very negative. Between 1945–1955, debt ratios in developed countries just about halved. Reinhart and Sbrancia calculated that, without financial repression and at a 'normal' real interest rate of 1% to 3%, those debt ratios would have increased by 20 to 30 percentage points in 1955 compared to 1945. The 1970s were very different from the previous decades. The 'gaps' in financial regulation were widening, fixed exchange rate arrangements under Bretton Woods were crumbling, and inflation reared its head again due to the global oil shock and excessively lax monetary policy in the US and elsewhere.

Financial repression played a large part in bringing down sky-high debts after World War II. But R-G's high contribution does not only reflect the positive effect of low (real) interest rates. The period was also marked by rapid economic growth due to a productivity explosion. In the US, new mass production methods had already led to a robust rise in productivity. The Great Depression and World War II delayed the rollout of electric motor and assembly lines to other developed countries.

Debt liquidation through financial repression, 1945-1955

	Public debt / GDP	
	1945	**1955**
Belgium	112,6	63,3
UK	215,6	138,2
US	116	66,2

Source Reinhart & Sbrancia (2011)

But a substantial catch-up followed. The formula was freely available. By copying new technologies and shifting investment from agriculture to industry, productivity shot up in Europe and Japan too. Debt again played a role, specifically in Germany. 'Foregiveness of debts owed to foreign governments allowed the new Federal Republic of Germany to increase social spending, ease its housing shortage, and assuage the anxieties of the displaced,' Eichengreen and co. explain. 'This helped Germany avoid the labor disruptions and divisive politics that had hindered investment and growth after World War I.'

The debt reduction (from 300 to 21%) enabled growth in Germany, and that German growth favoured European growth, given the dependence of European industry on German capital goods. Nominal growth ran towards 10% (6% real growth and 4% inflation) against a nominal interest rate of 3%. Moreover, policymakers in advanced countries successfully reconciled increased spending on education, healthcare and other social programmes with a balanced budget. Fiscal policy was growth-enhancing.

Was central bank intervention in post-war debt management an unqualified success? The differences in outcomes between the US and the UK offer important lessons for managing high sovereign debt, according to Ryutaro Kono and Hiroshi Shiraishi,[125] chief economist and senior economist at BNP Paribas Japan respectively. Strong economic recovery and high tax rates helped reduce debt levels in both countries for several decades after the war. But there were important differences in the extent to which they resorted to financial repression. The introduction of a maximum interest rate on Treasury bills and longer-term bonds in the US did not lead to a disruption of the economy or the financial system. The

Fed only abandoned that relatively quickly. In the UK, however, government debt was almost double that of the US after the end of the war. The authorities kept market interest rates low for much longer, despite relatively high inflation. This eventually culminated in the stagflation crisis of the 1970s. In 1976, the IMF had to come to the UK's rescue to break the negative spiral of currency depreciation and accelerating inflation. The danger of the 'success' of financial repression is the loss of fiscal discipline, our colleagues warn.

FINDING *a* SOLUTION
for our DEBTS

✔ Savings will be needed, as will increased government revenues. With the many challenges ahead, budget surpluses will not succeed, as was the case before and after the world wars.

✔ Financial repression, including negative real interest rates, is undoubtedly part of future deleveraging.

✔ Central bankers will again periodically buy bonds in the future – if necessary – to put additional pressure on interest rates. The purchased government bonds on their balance sheets will not be phased out any time soon.

✔ Cancelling those government bonds is dangerous and does not provide any benefit. Central banks would have to pay short-term fees for eternity.

✔ Real interest rates remain higher than in the past decade due to a higher term premium.

✔ Heavy savings are not necessary for debt sustainability, because the implicit nominal interest rate will generally not exceed nominal growth. Only when governments abandon all fiscal discipline will bond markets push interest rates sharply higher, risking getting highly indebted countries into trouble.

What lessons can we learn from the past to address the current high levels of public debt? Does a tight fiscal policy offer a solution? Or should we seek refuge in financial repression and the magic of a negative R-G?

Savings, but limited

Throughout history, savings have always helped eliminate debt. Politically coherent and consistent policies are an explicit prerequisite. 'Political polarisation and fragmentation lead to budget deficits,' say Eichengreen et al. 'It is therefore relevant to note that the share of extreme parties both from the left and the right in the legislatures of developed economies reached a low point in the 1960s and 1970s.'

Today, we see a fragmented political landscape in many countries. On top of that, economic growth and incomes have slowed down since the 1970s. The political will to put a brake on spending, especially social spending, is lacking. Every political group sees certain spending as indispensable. But where each group has just enough power to block tax increases for its constituency, it has too little power to impose new taxes on others. Electoral uncertainty adds to this. 'Politicians advocate more spending on their favourite programmes when they are in office, because later, they may be in a weaker position to push such spending through. And mounting debt today is someone else's problem tomorrow.' The result? The cycle of budget deficits, followed by budget surpluses from 1700 to the 1970s, has since changed to one of rising deficits during crises and slightly lower deficits during good years.

The challenges facing most countries, such as an ageing population, the climate transition and high inequality, will not make debt consolidation any easier in the coming years; at the same time, those challenges make it all the more necessary. After the world wars, this stabilisation took place partly through savings, but mainly through higher taxes. From the 1930s, progressive taxes were raised sharply to finance the war effort. During World War I, a wealth tax was introduced. The top income tax rates went to 80% or even 90% in recognition of the fact that extraordinary wartime gains were only possible thanks to the sacrifices made by the general public. The high tax rates remained in place until the 1970s and, combined with strong economic growth, supported the significant increase in tax revenues.

Top marginal tax rates (US)

Source: Saez & Zucman, *The Triumph of Injustice*; BNP Paribas Fortis

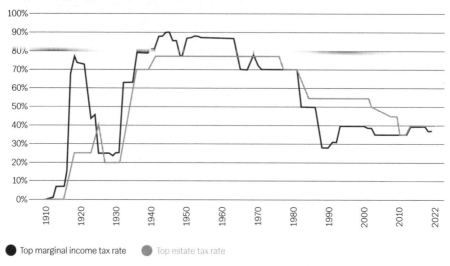

● Top marginal income tax rate ● Top estate tax rate

'There are some parallels in the recent UK and US debates about hiking corporate taxes and introducing new levies on the wealthy, who have once again prospered in a time of crisis,' our Japanese colleagues argue in their debt study. Technology and oil and gas companies saw their profits explode during pandemic lockdowns and the energy crisis caused by Russia's invasion of Ukraine. The wealthiest citizens, with large portfolios of stocks and bonds, benefited from central bankers' non-conventional measures during the decade before the advent of Covid-19. The sharp fall in interest rates pushed bond and stock prices sharply higher.

Will that observation translate into higher taxes for the winners of the crisis? The tide is turning, away from unbridled capitalism and liberalism. For instance, an agreement was recently reached on a global minimum corporate tax for multinationals. In Europe, the European Commission is working on a proposal to distribute the total corporate tax, collected fairly among the countries where the turnover was realised. Today, taxes from international companies mainly go to countries that charge the lowest rates. By the way, this also creates a distortion of competition against SMEs.

Other ways of raising revenue are also being sought. Since the Reagan-Thatcher revolution of the early 1980s, countries have been engaged in a 'race to the bottom' on corporate tax rates for fear of capital flight. These fell globally from an average of 40% in 1980 to 23% today, according to the US Tax Foundation. Figures from consultant KPMG, in turn, show that since 2008, corporate taxes have fallen by 5% overall against a 6% rise in personal income taxes. Brilliant for business owners, tough luck for workers. Inequality increases. The tax revenue base is being eroded, with an increasing share coming from personal income tax and VAT.

Moreover, lower corporate taxes have not led to increasing business investment, which would have boosted economic growth. 'Taxes on businesses and capital should arguably be ramped up in a world of worsening economic inequality,' our colleagues Kono and Shiraishi conclude. That is the direction the Inflation Reduction Act – a modified version of Biden's Build Back Better programme – is taking. New climate-friendly spending is funded by a 15% minimum corporate tax rate, tax loopholes for wealthier Americans are closed, and tax enforcement is tightened. Corporate profits total between 10–15% of GDP annually on average in the US and the European Union. An increase of 10 percentage points in corporate taxes produces additional income of 1% of GDP. Better still would be cuts to unnecessary government spending. In many countries, including Belgium, these run high.

Financial repression

Is financial repression making a comeback in developed countries? Jim Reid, strategist at Deutsche Bank, seems to think so. Real yields – the return on long-term government bonds minus inflation – have regularly dipped into negative numbers since the Global Financial Crisis and consistently dropped below zero since 2015 in Europe and 2019 in the US. With falling inflation and rising interest rates, real yields have been climbing since 2022. 'I'm also still convinced real yields on this measure stay negative for the rest of my career due to financial repression. If I'm wrong (maybe due to nominal yields rising more than I think and inflation falling faster) run for the hills given the global debt pile,' Reid wrote in his popular newsletter in April 2022. By mid-2023, US real yields were hovering between 1 and 2%. In Europe, many countries are also creeping above 0%. I wonder which hill Reid is currently running for.

The top strategist exposes the true danger of high government debt. Up until 2022, financial repression was the logical solution to the sky-high debt mountain.

But suddenly, central bankers started pulling out all the stops to bring down out-of-control inflation. It is crucial for central banks to act quickly and decisively before inflation becomes entrenched. The 'financial repression forever' scenario thus takes a big hit. Higher interest rates fortunately translate into higher debt only gradually. But real interest rates risk rising structurally even without central banks. The main reason? The upward pressure on the term premium, part of the real interest rate (*see table*).

Why term premium and real interest rates will climb structurally higher

What is the term premium? The ten-year nominal interest rate can be split into real interest rates and (expected) inflation. The real interest rate reflects current and all expected future short-term interest rates (the expected monetary path) and a term premium. That premium includes all the elements needed to compensate for term risk. What are the risks that during the period I hold the bond, structural growth changes, or inflation expectations, the supply of or demand for bonds, etc. will change? Those things would push real interest rates higher or lower, but are not reflected in the predetermined monetary path. They are, however, included in the term premium. The greater those uncertainties, the higher the term premium.

From 1982 to 1995, the term premium fell from 4.6% to 1%. From 1996 to 2014, it fluctuated between 1% and -1%, after which it went almost constantly into the red at -2%. 'The reduction in term premium, particularly post-2014, must have helped cement the low default world as it created incredibly favourable funding conditions for the vast majority of global debt entities,' writes Jim Reid.[126] Low inflation put additional pressure on nominal interest rates. Still, the reasons that depressed the risk premium risk going into reverse in the coming years.

- Evolution from a low to a high inflation regime. This pushes inflation higher (and nominal interest rates), but also the risk premium due to the change in inflation expectations.
- Recent geopolitical developments risk reducing trade flows. Less trade leads to higher inflation risk and risk premium. Less trade also means less currency reserves to be reinvested. This in turn reduces demand from governments for bonds in which to invest those reserves.

- Larger budget deficits boost potential growth, absorb savings surpluses through a larger supply of safe debt and raise inflation expectations. All three have an impact on the risk premium.
- Higher inflation (risks) and fiscal surpluses may prompt central bankers to halt their government bond-buying programmes.

The US futures premium has risen from -2% to 1% since its 2020 low.

Nominal interest (10 years) vs. term premium

Source: Saez & Zucman, *The Triumph of Injustice*; BNP Paribas Fortis

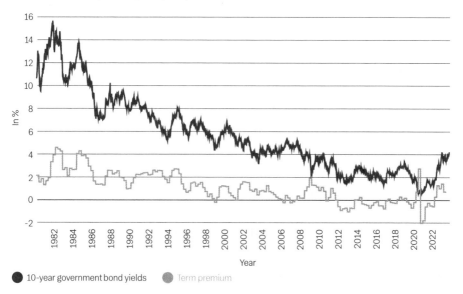

● 10-year government bond yields   ● Term premium

Quantitative easing

A devious way that central bankers keep debt sustainable is through bond buying or quantitative easing (QE). By doing so, they pull down interest rates (and term premium) further. It is actually a form of financial repression, but it 'deserves' a separate place. Bond buying not only lowers the interest rate burden for governments, but it was a necessary lifeline for many member states during the 2009–2012 eurozone crisis. Today, balance sheets filled with government bonds are being unwound via quantitative tightening (QT). Typically, central banks do this by not refinancing maturing bonds again.

US Government debt: total and held by Federal Reserve (in % GDP)
Source: Saez & Zucman, *The Triumph of Injustice*; BNP Paribas Fortis

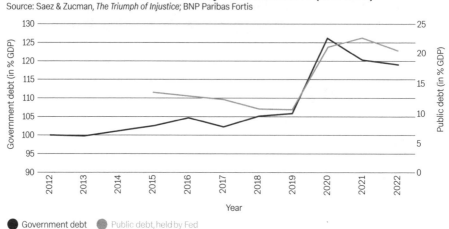

Government debt   Public debt, held by Fed

In 2017, Janet Yellen, then chair of the US central bank, reassured the market, still comparing the imminent process of QT to 'watching paint dry'. In 2018, QT took off. That year, Wall Street experienced its biggest downturn since the Global Financial Crisis. Long-term bond prices plummeted, and interest rates skyrocketed. The Fed, which had raised its interest rate from 0.25% to 2.5% since late 2015, halted its rate hikes at the end of 2018. In 2019, less than a year after QT started, that too was halted.

In 2023, anxiety regarding QT prevailed across markets once again. 'The Fed assumes that QT is a tightening, withdrawing liquidity from the market,' said Steve Blitz of TS Lombard. 'But that depends on what happens to the budget deficit, and therefore the Treasury's financing needs.' If the Fed does QT and does not refinance maturing government bonds on its balance sheet, then the market will have to refinance those bonds. 'If the fiscal deficit to be financed increases sharply on top of that, then there is indeed a tightening and real interest rates rise, as they did in the second half of 2018. However, if the fiscal deficit shrinks faster than what the Fed's QT asks markets to fund extra, then it is indeed "watching the paint dry"; Blitz said.

Nothing obliges a central bank to remove those purchased bonds from its balance sheet. The reason it does QT is to get money – reserves – back out of the system. A drop in balance sheet size signals to the outside world that the central bank is able and willing to keep inflation down. This tempers inflation expectations, which many believe underpin effective inflation. But central banks only exceptionally downsized their balance sheets in the past, Ferguson et al.[127] showed. A contraction of balance sheets came mainly from keeping nominal positions stable for long periods in the face of rising GDP. 'On the basis of the historical evidence, there are good reasons to expect the contraction of central bank balance sheets in our time to be slow and to take place relative to GDP rather than nominally,' the authors predicted in 2014. Indeed, after 2014, the total assets bought by the Federal Reserve barely shrank at all: from US$4.22 trillion to US$3.714 trillion by the end of 2019... before exploding again to nearly US$9 trillion by 2022.

Country	Gross debt (2022, Ameco)	Government debt held by a country's own national bank (in % GDP, end 2021)	Net public debt*
Belgium	107%	22,40%	85,07%
Germany	71%	20%	50,87%
France	113%	25%	87,58%
Italy	151%	37,60%	112,97%
Netherlands	55%	11%**	44,31%
Spain	116%	30%	86,38%
Japan	263%	130%	132,54%
US	126%	23%	102,57%

Source Macrobond, own calculations

* Represents total government debt minus the government debt on the balance sheet of a country's own national bank.
** The Netherlands: 2019 figure

It is not, therefore, completely unrealistic that government bonds will remain parked on central banks' balance sheets. In other words, the ECB, the Japanese central bank, the US central banks and all the others that have engaged in QE are simply refinancing government bonds that are maturing on their balance sheets. The funding requirement for the market would then fall dramatically. The impact on the debt ratio would be huge. Japanese government debt would then (in theory) be reduced by half to 130% of GDP. US gross public debt would be stranded just above 100% of GDP and in the eurozone, public debt would go from 95% to 71% of GDP. From that perspective, debt deleveraging has already well and truly begun.

However, this is not without risk, as Gert Peersman explained to us in an interview in August 2022. Peersman is a professor of economics at Ghent University and a research advisor at the European Central Bank and the BIS, among others. ECB interest rates were barely at 0.5% at the time. 'What does this quantitative easing actually mean? The central bank buys bonds in the market, and bank reserves are created in exchange. On those bank reserves, the central bank pays policy interest while collecting interest on the purchased bonds.' So what happens in QE is the exchange of long-term bonds for short-term deposits. This, contrary to what many claim, has nothing to do with monetary financing.

'As long as short-term interest rates remain low, there is no problem,' Peersman continues. 'But suppose short-term interest rates are raised to, say, 5%, then you have a problem.' The central bank – meaning the government – has exchanged government bonds with a maturity of, say, 10 years and an interest rate of 0 to 2% for bank reserves, on which it has to pay 5%. It has to pay a hefty difference – a very big risk, which persists as long as the bonds are on the central banks' balance sheets.

Meanwhile, European interest rates are heading towards 4% and US rates are at over 5%. Central banks are piling up losses today. According to Morgan Stanley, the ECB is going 40 billion into the red. The US central bank also faces a potential loss of hundreds of billions. Paying out profits to the government – up to 100 billion in the US – will be scrapped, which will place an additional burden on the budget. 'And as long as there is excess liquidity, there is little that can be done about it,' Peersman comments. Only fully deleveraging the balance sheet can avoid that. The National Bank of Belgium expects a cumulative loss of some 9 billion for the 2022–2027 period.

Those losses are also likely to lead to negative equity at central banks. In commercial banks, bankruptcy then beckons. Not so with central banks. As long as the central bank prints money, it can roll over the losses. But that, according to Peersman, undermines the credibility of the currency. On top of that, 'under the rules of the euro system, a prolonged period [of negative capital] should be avoided,' writes Klaas Knot, the chairman of the Nederlandsche Bank in a letter to the Dutch finance minister. 'Should the deficit be too large or expected profits too low, additional measures may be needed to restore a sound balance sheet. In extreme cases, a capital injection from the shareholder may be necessary.' In most countries, this is the state, and therefore the taxpayer. Public debts then deepen. The reputation of central bankers takes a hit.

Scrapping debts and other wild ideas

Alright, some argue, but why not just cancel those debts on the balance sheets? This goes a long way from permanently parking those bonds on central banks' balance sheets. A proposal to wipe out the debt on the ECB's balance sheet was launched in March 2021 by some 150 economists and politicians, including Thomas Piketty and Paul Magnette, president of Belgium's Parti Socialiste. And you can indeed do that. The government and the central bank both belong to the public sector. A consolidated balance sheet of the total public sector cancels the debts against each other. One act of removal from the central bank will suffice. This, according to proponents, frees up space to take on debt again. Countries' vulnerability in a subsequent crisis decreases because of the lower debt ratio.

Now for the counterarguments.[128] Advocates argue that cancelling debt should be accompanied by the absolute promise that this is a one-off. Because, as the money that backed those debts can no longer be taken out of the economy and has therefore increased the money supply, we risk heading towards the hyperinflation of the Weimar Republic in the 1920s. But nothing prevents the ECB from repeating the same trick in the next crisis and another round of bond purchases. If the ECB cancels those debts *de facto*, the bond market would immediately offset it in higher inflation and term premium. Interest rates would soar; reduced confidence in the euro would push the currency down. Foreign investors would see the storm coming and dump European member states' bonds. And suddenly, debt affordability would become an issue in many member states. Since the debacle in the UK, bond market watchdogs have been on the lookout!

'That cancellation of those debts is an illusion, by the way,' Peersman notes. The purchased bonds on the asset side of the central bank's balance sheet do disappear, but on the liability side, the bank reserves to be reimbursed remain. 'The result would be that the central bank would have to pay a short-term interest fee for eternity. So this would not provide any advantage.' Finally, scrapping implies interference in monetary policy. It threatens the independence of the ECB. It was partly because of the independence it acquired in the 1980s and 1990s that central bankers brought inflation to its knees. It would be a first step towards a modern monetary theory (MMT) that sees money as free.

As for MMT, we can keep it brief. Some saw it as the ultimate solution to the high debt burden and investment challenges we face. After all, money could be created out of nothing. However, since inflation has risen, love for MMT has cooled considerably. According to its own economic philosophy, when there is runaway inflation, governments have to tighten fiscal policy because supply in the economy can no longer keep up with demand. So spending has to be cut back. But no one in the MMT camp wants to proclaim the message that spending has to be cut. The dreamscape turns out to be an illusion.

MMT, the Magic Money Tree, will not break through in the short term: inflation has put a stop to it. But there is no appetite to return to the fiscal discipline of the 2010s. Governments are under pressure to pump even more money into their economies to deal with myriad future challenges, ranging from the climate transition to ageing populations to mitigating inequality. Biden has his Inflation Reduction Act, Europe its Green Deal. European budget rules were also recently relaxed to take into account the necessity of future investments.

Therein lies a great danger, says Peersman, referring to the R-G rule. Heavy cuts are not necessary, he says, as long as nominal growth remains above nominal interest rates. And in principle, it will remain so, despite the temporary rise in interest rates in 2022 and 2023. 'I expect R* to remain low due to long-term trends in the coming decades as well. Only a higher term premium could push interest rates higher.' So basically, Peersman does not expect any major problems. 'But,' he warns, 'if governments abandon all fiscal discipline, or start experimenting with things like MMT, sooner or later bond markets do stir, those term premiums go up sharply and some countries with high government debts do risk getting into trouble.'

Even for William De Vijlder, Group Chief Economist at BNP Paribas, temporarily higher primary deficits and public debts are inevitable. The price the country pays for this is smaller primary deficits in the future. So are debts sustainable in all circumstances? De Vijlder runs through the four possible scenarios:

1. Growth acceleration: long-term interest rates rise in parallel with the rise of short-term interest rates. On top of this, in some – less secure – eurozone countries, interest rate spreads (an additional interest rate payable) are rising compared to the benchmark country, Germany. Interest and debt payable (the numerator in the debt ratio) goes higher, but higher growth (denominator) neutralises this.

2. Contraction: the central bank cuts interest rates, and if interest rates cannot go lower, the central bank again resorts to quantitative easing. In this scenario, the interest rate burden falls with a lag following the likely temporary fall in GDP.

3. Supply shock, e.g. due to a spike in oil prices during an oil shortage: inflation goes temporarily higher, growth temporarily lower. But in principle, the central bank sees through this and interest rates barely rise. Higher inflation offsets lower real growth. Nominal growth, the important parameter in R-G, hardly changes and the same is true for interest rates.

4. Stagflation shock: in this case, a supply shock also occurs. Growth falls, but inflation remains high this time, as in the 1970s (and hopefully not like now). Such a shock is the most dangerous for debt sustainability, as it risks R rising above growth over time.

But even then, the issue is not irreversible. Central banks have greatly expanded their toolkit over the past decade. Today, quantitative easing is part of the programme, but if necessary, they will not hesitate to bring out those non-conventional measures again to push interest rates lower. 'You could argue that governments are moving a little closer to disaster,' De Vijlder concludes, 'but that does not mean that they will drown in it sooner or later as a result.'

Monopoly with debt

This is the chapter where I am going to add the least to Koen's diligent work. He has said most of what needed to be said but, in addition, there are no immediate major investment implications to be drawn from the debt issue. Except that if a sizeable debt mountain implodes, you had better not have invested in most asset classes. Still, I will give a few investment ideas at the end of this chapter that might be useful.

It might be a good idea to start with a definition. When someone, a person, a company or a government, is given money to do something, we call it credit. The counterpart of this credit is a debt that one has to repay. It is then important to know what you are incurring the debt for. If it is a productive activity that generates more cash flow than paying interest, there is no problem. Nor is there a problem if the intention is to acquire an asset, say a house, which hopefully holds its value and you can pay off with income from wages. If a government uses the credit to finance infrastructure works, such as roads or education – probably the best investment in the future – then it is certainly not a problem. If, on the other hand, the credit serves to consume immediately, without a future return, then repaying and recouping becomes a lot harder.

A big misconception about debt is seeing it in isolation. After all, for every debt, there is a debt holder. This is why the terms 'mountain of debt' and 'excess savings' are often used interchangeably. After all, what is it? Is there too much debts, or too many savings surpluses? The answer is both. On the one hand, there is a lot of debt, but on the other hand, there are the savings surpluses, the counterparties who are the creditors financing the debt.

So where is the problem? Let us start with the very simple situation encompassed in the game Monopoly, which everyone knows. At the beginning of the game, you need to acquire as many properties as possible. As the game progresses, cash becomes king, because if at some point you can no longer pay the rent of an opponent's property you land on, you have to sell your own properties or go bankrupt. In the game, everything is paid in cash and there are no debts or credit. There is a bank, but it is only there to enable transactions and provide money to the system, not to collect savings or provide loans. This also immediately means that if one player goes bankrupt, his property passes to the opponent, and he is out of the game. It is vital to see that this does not impact all the other players or the bank. There is a reason for the fact that somewhere in the rules of Monopoly, it says that the bank can never go bankrupt.

But let us suggest a more complex Monopoly game, which is already a little closer to reality. Perhaps this is an idea for the game maker to teach people the basics of an economic system. Suppose the bank can now extend credit and also hold player savings at interest. Suppose players can also take debts from each other. So a player can borrow to acquire a property and also borrow if he finds himself in a situation in which he cannot settle a rent at some point. Obviously, he will only get that loan if he himself still has sufficient assets (houses and properties). But as always, fate strikes, and a player finds himself in big trouble anyway. Eventually, his assets are liquidated: everything they are still worth goes to the creditors, being the bank or the other players. But if there is a deficit, it becomes a loss for the creditors.

Unlike the first simple situation, this has the effect of impacting other parties, say the rest of the economy. In this world, the bank may well go bankrupt if it takes too many losses because players cannot repay their debts. Players who are not directly party to the debts will also be impacted. Because when everyone sees that players are no longer repaying their debts, they become much more cautious about lending and try to start collecting their debts. Everyone becomes risk-averse, trying to hold onto as much cash as possible. Suddenly, the world on our game board is in a deep recession, from which no one escapes.

Let us go one step further. In the classic board game, there is no government, or rather, the bank performs some of the government's functions, such as paying out cash when a player passes go and collecting rather arbitrary taxes on real estate, among other things. But it is not a government that actively intervenes and implements policy. Let us also add this to the game. If the government sees that some of the players are in trouble, it can throw some money at them through benefits or subsidies. It can take the money for that from players it believes have too much. But let us immediately take another step towards reality. Usually, it is politically more difficult to tax than to hand out, with the result that the government too starts borrowing and accumulating public debt. To do so, it borrows from the players, the bank and abroad (somewhere virtual on another playing board). That government may now also run into trouble at some point if all counterparties lose confidence, and it has to pay ever higher interest and eventually cannot get credit from anyone.

An important difference now is whether the debts are in the currency of its own board or of the other boards (foreign countries). If the government can borrow in its own currency and create its own money, or if a lot of the debts are owned by the players around its own board (as in Japan), the debts can run very long and very high. In other cases, it can go fast. But there is no magic level of debt to gross national product at which a country goes bankrupt. Some countries have already gone bankrupt with a debt to gross national product ratio of 30%, while others are whistling along with a 250% debt ratio. It depends on when the counterparties decide to turn off the tap.

The main conclusion is that in the real world, it is not a story between two parties, as in the familiar version of Monopoly, but one in which shock waves go through the entire economy – including the foreign economy, if the story is big enough.

Financial history is littered with the wrecks of bankruptcies of individuals, companies and governments. The number of times Argentina has already gone bankrupt can no longer be counted on the fingers of one hand. Greece has been in default for, roughly speaking, more than half of its history. The first time was in the 5th century BC, when Pericles could not (or would not) repay his debts. Remarkably, financial markets are also quick to forget. Once the debts are cancelled – or in any way 'forgotten' – the country that is now 'debt-free' can soon raise money again. After which the whole process can start over again.

Of course, there is something to be said for cancelling debts at some point so that they do not run up too high, stifle the economy and possibly bring about a debt crisis, with all the dire consequences of recession or depression. Even as early as the Bible there is talk of a jubilee year every 50th year, when debts are cancelled and land is returned to its original owner.

Debt crises on a global scale are rather rare. Or rather, they are common in history, but there is often a long period of time in between, as the accumulation of debt until the bubble bursts can take a surprisingly long time. We can catalogue the 2008 crisis as a debt crisis, but rather a concentrated one and, despite its financial woes for those who lived through it, not yet of biblical proportions. The last really big crisis began just under 100 years ago with the crash of 1929, the subsequent Great Depression, and eventually World War II. Because of how long it sometimes takes, we cannot simply dig into our own memories, but must study history. Perhaps the best place to do so is still Carmen Reinhart and

Kenneth Rogoff's book *This Time Is Different*, which tells us the history of eight centuries of financial crises. The title is misleading, as it does not indicate that this time would really be different, but rather that every time people think it will be different when it is not.

Looking at the state of global debt today, the picture does not look very positive. Private and corporate balance sheets look good to very good. On the other hand, those of governments are a different story. Governments have made many transfers to the other parts of the economic fabric (read citizens and companies) in recent years. Or, in plain English: they have spent much more than they have received. This is a global phenomenon, with some countries evidently in better shape than others, although those in good or relatively good shape are clearly in the minority. The figures that most capture the imagination are those of the United States. Government debt there amounts to about 130% of gross domestic product, or roughly $32 trillion. Currently, interest on this amounts to about $1 trillion a year, which certainly does not help the policy space. And that is only the official debt. Because in addition, there are the so-called unpaid commitments the government has made – to pay for pensions and health insurance in the future, for instance – while the population is ageing rapidly, and huge efforts will also be needed to combat climate change.

With all these challenges in mind, what measures can a government take to bring the debt rate back within slightly safer margins? A first obvious option is austerity, by cutting spending and/or raising taxes. This has the drawback that if the government suddenly takes more money out of the system than it pumps in, there is a negative impact on the economy, which then often falls into recession. A second option is more drastic: debt defaults. As a country, you then make the front pages of the world press and have to face the anger of the rest of the world for a while. But as we have said, this is quickly forgotten. This is an option when it comes to the problems of a relatively small country. A US default would send such a tsunami through the ocean of the global economic and monetary system that it would dwarf the meteor that wiped out the dinosaurs. But 'fortunately', there is the third option. We may not call it printing money, but let's say the central bank uses its balance sheet to buy government paper ('quantitative easing'). Whether that paper is then actually destroyed or not is of secondary importance. The moment the debt becomes so large and/or there are too few other buyers, central banks, and especially US ones, can buy up their own debt almost without limit.

Going back to our Monopoly game in its more advanced form, in this situation you would see that the amount of money on the table is constantly increasing. As the number of streets, houses and hotels on the board does not increase, this means that the prices of all goods go up. We call this inflation. And so I end up with the only investment opportunity in this chapter, but it is one that can be important. People in debt benefit from rising inflation. People who have cash are heavily penalised. Let's follow the following thought experiment: imagine serious inflation. Add an extra two zeros to all the prices. Prices are multiplied by a hundred. This means that house prices go up times a hundred, as do department store prices and wages. And even more succinctly, stock prices also go up times a hundred, because these are pieces of companies. But which two things don't increase by a hundred? The debt you had, and the cash in your account.

The conclusion is clear. If governments try to bring down their debts by continuing to engage in quantitative easing and transfers, and if all this creates inflation, it is certainly not a bad idea, without exaggerating of course, to have some debt and not have too much cash. In that case, it is better to have real assets in your portfolio. Governments and central banks can do a lot. What they cannot do is de-value their own debt and not the other debts. It is all or nothing here. And finally, it is not important how much money is ultimately on the Monopoly board or how much is in circulation. What matters is who owns the land, houses and hotels...

TEN
to REMEMBER

1   Global debts of companies, households and governments are at their highest levels ever.

2   Government debts are at their highest level ever... in peacetime.

3   The key parameter of public debt sustainability is the ratio of average nominal interest charges on that debt to nominal growth. As long as growth exceeds interest costs, there is no problem.

4   Emerging countries have so far avoided a debt crisis because they avoided the mistakes of the past. But rapidly rising interest rates make slow-growth countries in sub-Saharan Africa, Latin America and the Middle East vulnerable.

5   China's real estate sector is at the beginning of years of restructuring. Usually, a debt-financed real estate boom ends not with a whimper but with a bang.

6   Debt has been eliminated in various ways in the past: fiscal surpluses, higher growth than interest paid (R-G), defaults, restructuring and hyperinflation.

7   After World War II until the 1970s, financial repression and R-G were the recipe for success. Financial repression combined low interest rates with some extra inflation. Thus, the debt mountain halved.

8   Again, financial repression is one of the ingredients of debt reduction.

9   Substantial savings are not necessary, because growth will usually be above the average interest rate paid. Only if governments abandon fiscal discipline are problems imminent.

10 Debt cancellation is an illusion, with perpetual consequences.

TEN
to INVEST *in*

1   If a credit is to be consumed immediately, the risk is a lot higher if it is a long-term investment or one that creates value.

2   Let's play a game of Monopoly and change the rules a bit. Players can borrow and if they fail, it impacts the other players. That is more in line with reality.

3   There is no magic debt level that predicts when a country will go bankrupt. It depends on when counterparties decide to turn off the tap.

4   After bankruptcy, the world quickly forgives and forgets. Greece has been bankrupt for almost half of its history.

5   Everyone always thinks 'this time will be different', but history keeps repeating itself, even when it comes to debt.

6   Governments worldwide are carrying the largest mountain of debt in history.

7   Reducing debt is unlikely to happen through savings or paying nothing back. Central banks are likely to 'inflate' the debt away.

8   Those in debt benefit from rising inflation. Those with cash suffer.

9   Holding real assets is certainly not a bad idea in an inflationary world.

10 In Monopoly, it is not important how much money is on the table, but who owns the land, houses and hotels.

5
AGEING

Reforms safeguard steady growth

Economic Times – 5 January 2053 | World Year in Review Economics and Strategy

The accelerated growth in many emerging countries, with Brazil in the lead, continued over the past year. Growth in industrialised countries varied between 1 to 1.5%. The stock markets more than held up, notwithstanding the recent rise in interest rates. Real estate had a harder time: the increase in interest rates came on top of the increasing supply of houses for sale.

The industrialised West continues its journey towards 'greyland' with lower growth rates. On the other hand, many emerging countries are benefiting from the demographic dividend of a growing labour force. The spectacular growth story of China from 1980 to 2000, the end of century event, was surpassed by Brazil, India, several African countries and Indonesia.

Brazil grows further

Indonesia is today ranked fourth in terms of purchasing power parity, and is only surpassed by the giants India, China and the United States. Brazil follows in fifth place. 'When elected ten years ago, I promised to boost our country's growth,' said Arthus Arjaujo Lula da Silva in a recent speech to his country. 'I kept my promise.' After his appointment, education received top priority. Development and investment in new sectors made the country less dependent on its natural resources. Economic mismanagement was uprooted.

This also true for some countries in Africa. The young elites, often raised or educated in Western countries, increasingly recognise that institutions are essential, though not necessarily as American-style democracies! Nigeria is the shining example, with an average growth of more than 5% over the last decade. In other African countries, however, the demographic dividend is turning into a nightmare.

Western growth holds steady

The economic growth of the OECD countries – the group of wealthy Western countries – foundered at 1.25%; Europe grew by a meagre 0.5%, pushed lower by the -2% recession in Italy. The economy has come to a standstill for months as a result of widespread protests against deep pension reforms. But slogans such as 'Deliver our money, hands off our pensions' don't help, especially because young people are also pushing for reforms. The average net wage stagnated for the twentieth year in a row.

Italy is following Belgium's path. Ten years ago, Belgium was compelled by high bond-market interest rates to institute radical reforms in the pension and health-care systems. Massive debt and sharply rising market interest rates brought the country to its knees. After months of violent protests in which different generations were pitted against each other, more tranquil times returned. Today the debt has been reduced to 120% of GDP with years of belt-tightening ahead.

The growth difference between European member states remains large. Some, such as the Scandinavian countries and the Netherlands, have fared better. In the 2030s they had the courage to impose the necessary radical reforms quickly and decisively. As in Japan, one fourth of the over-70s continues to work there today. This is still not the case for France and a fair number of Southern European countries, where even small economic shocks easily push the economy into the red.

Growth in the United States held up well at 1.4% – as it did for China. Silvering, the explosive increase in the number of people over 80, is also taking its toll here. 'I will not abuse the inexperience of my opponent,' joked the 92-year old Chelsea Clinton during her recent election debate with 82-year old Eric Trump. The strong growth performance of recent years was in the end sufficient for her to secure a second term in office.

Stock markets continue to fluctuate

With an overall return of 7%, growth hasn't harmed investors. An increase in the long-term interest rate – to 4.5% in the US and 3.8% in the eurozone – made the year end difficult. 'And Jack Montana, chairman of the US Federal Reserve, has clearly stated that the fight against inflation has not yet ended,' says Tim Jacqmain, economist at the Global Capital Bank. 'This must come below the 3% target.' The shrinking working population continues to put upward pressure on wage inflation.

In addition, the real estate market is groaning as a result of rising interest rates. Nominal prices fell slightly on average following a minimal increase last year. 'Inevitable,' says Joris Janssen, CEO of ImmoHouse, who has been warning of a huge crash for ten years. 'The decline of the baby boomer generation is only now really starting to weigh on the real estate market.' ●

DEMOGRAPHIC TRANSITION

✔ The world population is undergoing a major transition: it was stable until 1700, underwent a veritable explosion in the 20th century and stabilised at the end of the century.

✔ The global population is increasing and is expected to grow from 7.7 billion to 10.9 billion by 2100. By then, four out of five people will live in Asia or Africa. In Africa, the population is expected to almost quadruple.

✔ India has become, once more, the most populous nation in the world. The population in the United States will grow steadily. In Europe it will decrease, and in China and Japan, it will plummet.

✔ Worldwide, the number of children will slowly stabilise (child peak). The developing countries might profit from a demographic dividend, with the number of people in the labour force exploding. In developed countries, there is a significant increase in the elderly population.

✔ The number of dependents compared to the active working population is expected to increase by an average of one quarter over the coming decades. The retirement of baby boomers is a challenge for developed countries. Increasing the participation rate is the 'silver bullet'.

✔ According to my ageing index, the majority of Anglo-Saxon countries are the least vulnerable to the explosion in the cost of ageing. Japan, the UK and most Scandinavian countries show medium vulnerability. We find high vulnerability in Northern and Southern European countries. They combine a rapidly ageing population with already high taxes and significant debt. Italy and Belgium come out on the top of that list.

Demographics is destiny. In the short term, there is little you can do. You can regulate the birth rate by force, as in China. The country today finds that increasing the number of births again is a completely different job. In many Western countries, the fertility rate has also fallen below the replacement rate of 2.1 children per woman needed to maintain the population. In 2010, that figure was lower in 98 countries and territories. In 2021, that number of countries was 124, and will rise to 136 by 2030. In the very long term this will lead to extinction. Is this an extreme example? South Korea's exceptionally low fertility rate of 0.8 in 2022 suggests that the next generation is projected to be only about half as numerous as the previous generation. Since 2012, the UN has adjusted its forecast of a decline of one-fifth of the South Korean population to a halving to 24 million citizens.

Before looking at the economic consequences, let's first take a look at the scale of the ongoing transition. The median age rose globally from 21.5 years in 1970 to more than 30 years in 2019. A quarter of the world's population is younger than 14 years old, 8% is older than 65, and half falls into the 25–65 working age category. Since 1950, the population has tripled to 7.7 billion, and will increase to 10.9 billion by 2100. Overall, this guarantees an increase in consumption and growth. The challenge is to provide space, food and energy in a sustainable way.

The explosion of the world population is recent. From 10,000 BC to 1700 AD, 600 million of us walked the globe. High infant mortality compensated for a high fertility rate. As healthcare improved and mortality declined, events unfolded rapidly. During the 20th century, the world population quadrupled. The peak growth of 2.1% annually was reached in 1968. Growth has fallen back to half that peak today.

By the end of the century we will return to near-stabilisation. The great demographic transition of the past two centuries will then come to an end. We are reaching a new equilibrium, but it is different from the previous one. Previously, very high mortality kept population growth in check. In the new equilibrium, low fertility keeps population change stable.

Population growth versus decline

How can we be so sure that the very rapid population growth of recent decades will not resume? We are approaching the 'child peak': the moment when the number of children worldwide is no longer increasing. It is the harbinger of population stabilisation and an extraordinary moment in world history. Before 1700, infant mortality was extremely high. Only two children per woman reached adulthood, keeping the population size stable. The extended family with many children, which we often associate with the past – I personally come from a family of five – was a reality for only a few generations. Rising prosperity and falling child mortality are causing fertility rates to converge.[129] In the most developed countries, that figure rises from a very low 1.65 to 1.78; in the least developed countries it drops from 3.8 to 2.1. Two children was and will again be the norm.

Population growth (in millions)

		1950	2020	2100	1950–2100	2020–2100
Africa		227.5	1,360.7	3,924.4	1.625%	188%
Asia		1,379	4,664.3	4,674.2	239%	0%
	China	544	1,424.9	766.7	41%	-46%
	Japan	84.4	125.2	73.6	-13%	-41%
	India	357	1,396.4	1,529.9	329%	10%
North America		162	374	448	176%	20%
	US	148.3	335.9	394	166%	17%
Latin America		168.3	651.8	647.4	285%	-1%
Europe		549.7	746.2	586.5	7%	-21%
	Belgium	8.6	11.6	11.5	34%	0%
	France	41.8	64.5	60.9	45%	-6%
	Germany	71	83.3	68.9	-3%	-17%
	Italy	46.4	59.5	36.9	-21%	-38%
	Netherlands	10.01	17.4	16.6	64%	-5%
	Poland	24.78	38.4	23.1	-7%	-40%
	Spain	28.1	47.4	30.9	10%	-35%
United Kingdom		50.1	67.1	70.5	41%	5%

Source *Our World in Data*, United Nations, World Population Prospects (2022)

Future population growth will differ from region to region and will affect economic growth. The table shows an approximate quadrupling of the African population to 4.3 billion in 2100, thereby following the same trend as Asia did in the period 1950–2020. Asiatic population growth will continue for a few decades – in India and not in China and Japan – and will peak in 2050. Towards the end of the century, eight out of ten people will live in Asia or Africa. In the US, the population will increase by a third by 2100. In Europe it will shrink by 16%.

From pine tree to rectangle with point

The population pyramid reveals the strengths and challenges for the future. Having a relatively young population is advantageous. It offers the prospect of a demographic dividend: a period of strong growth in the labour force relative to the overall population. For the US and Europe, that period started from the second half of the 1960s. The baby boom generation, the large post-war generation born between 1945 and 1965, entered the labour market at that time. That great generation is now in full retirement.

How did the global population pyramid evolve over time? In the 1950s, the global pyramid resembled a pine tree with branches reaching the ground. The rapid narrowing of the pyramid just above the base testified to a high child mortality at that time. One in five children did not reach the age of five. Today that has been reduced to less than one in twenty. Over the past seventy years, the base has also broadened with an increase in the number of global births from 97 to 143 million today.

More children has been the story for the past seven decades. From now on we will move towards 'filling' the population above the base and moving towards a rectangle with a pointed hat. The number of children is stabilising and gradually decreasing. The number of people of working age and old age is exploding in African and Asian developing countries. Health is improving, meaning current and future generations will live longer than ever before.

In developed countries we are already moving to the next stage: an explosion of the elderly. In Japan, the elderly population has quintupled since 1950, with the number of people aged 65 and older now exceeding a quarter of the population. By comparison, that figure is barely 3.5% across all of Africa. Back then, a third of Japanese people were under 25 years old. Today, seven decades later, that is one in eight. This 'blessing' of ageing is to a lesser extent (for the US) or to a greater extent (for Europe) the benefit of most Western countries. That's also the case in Asia, where China is ageing at breakneck speed.

All this is reflected in the dependence ratio, which is crucial for economic growth and the sustainability of funding for social security. We distinguish three major age groups: children and young adolescents (-15 years), the working age population (15–64 years) and the elderly population (65 years and older). A large proportion of the population being of working age is essential for maintaining economic and social stability and progress. They have to care for the 'dependents' – the non-working younger people and the older population. The dependency ratio pits that group of dependents against the active population.

Working people versus dependents

In most countries, this age-related dependency ratio fluctuates around 50 to 60%. In many African countries it fluctuates around 70%, and in Niger and Mali it exceeds 100%. In these cases, it is the large number of children that pushes the dependency ratio higher. In the rich West, the elderly make up the majority of dependents. For a correct interpretation of the dependency ratio, you must know the ratio of the number of people over 65 versus those under 15 within that group of dependents, because this affects more than just the growth potential. The needs, behaviour and future plans of young and old population groups are very different. For politicians, this has important consequences for expenditure on education and childcare versus healthcare and pensions.

An additional problem with the dependency ratio is that far from all people of working age work. Those who do not must also be included with the dependents. People who are looking for work stay within the active population. This is how we ultimately arrive at the labour force dependency ratio (instead of the purely age-related dependency ratio).

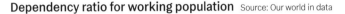
Dependency ratio for working population Source: Our world in data

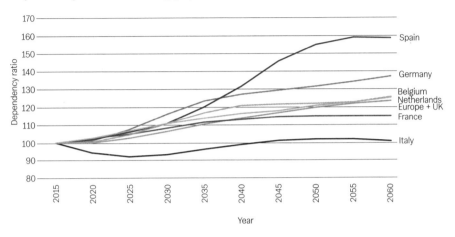

In Europe, the dependency ratio shows an unstoppable upward trend until 2060, according to the European Commission (EC) forecasts. The ratio increases, on average, from 100 in 2015, to 123. The world population will by then have to 'support' a quarter more people. These figures already take into account implemented reforms that can influence the behaviour of older workers and people who currently do not participate in the labour market. This would increase the effective retirement ages for men and women by just 0.9 and 1.3 years, respectively, by 2060.

Limited government pensions and higher school diploma make/made people work longer.

The rising participation rate of people over 65 has been going on for twenty years. The differences between countries, however, is huge. One explanation is the generosity of the pension system, which is substantial in Europe but meagre in the US. The result is a participation rate of roughly 6% on average for Europeans over 65, compared to almost 20% in the US. In Japan and Korea, a quarter and a third of them, respectively, continue to work.

Another determining factor is education. A study by the American think tank

Brookings shows that barely a quarter of men and less than a sixth of women without a secondary education diploma continue to work after the age of 65. The higher the education, the higher the participation rate. Two-thirds of men and just over half of women remain in the workforce after obtaining a post-graduate degree or doctorate.

In the UK, higher levels of education were the main reason why the participation rate among the over-16s has barely fallen over the past fifteen years, despite the rising proportion of over-65s. 'Over the period 2001–2021, the share of the 25–59 year age population with degree level education rose from 17% to 41%,' Michael Saunders, former member of the Bank of England's rate-setting committee, explained during his farewell speech.[130] 'As a result, the overall participation rate for this age group rose from 81.6% to 85.8%.' This increased participation rate compensated for the increasing group of over-65s within the 16-plus population, which would otherwise have led to a decline in the participation rate of the over-16s.

However, a further increase in that average education level is no longer on the cards, while the share of people over 65 continues to increase. As a result, the increase in the working population will halve from 0.8% annually over the past twenty years to 0.4% over the next decade. That will weigh heavily on potential UK growth... and that of other developed countries.

Once again, the differences between countries are enormous. Countries such as France and the Scandinavian countries (with the exception of Denmark) remain below the average increase in the dependency ratio for Europe. In Italy, the ratio is stabilising despite the strong increase in the number of pensioners. By 2070, pension reforms will keep men in the labour market for three years longer and women for almost four years. Linking the retirement age to increasing life expectancy is particularly effective, and almost a third of European countries have introduced the measure since 2000. In addition, Italy's low participation rate – the percentage of the working population that is working or looking for work – will also increase by 4.4 percentage points over the next fifty years, double that of the EU. A country with a plan! Now it's time implement it.

The participation rate of Belgium, which has the lowest rate in Europe except for three countries, will increase by just 1.1 percentage points, according to the European Commission's estimates. The average retirement age is also increasing at a glacial pace. No link with rising life expectancy for us! As a result, our dependency ratio will increase by a quarter, a fraction above the European average and as much as the Netherlands. A more than average increase in the ratio is mainly found in Eastern, Central and Southern Europe. Cyprus, Spain and Greece will see the ratio increase by half or more.

The increasing ageing bill

Such increases put a time bomb under the social security system, and not just in Europe. In 2003, the centre for Strategic and International Studies (CSIS) published an ageing vulnerability index based on four factors. The Anglo-Saxon countries (UK, US and Australia) appeared to have a low vulnerability in the final ranking; Canada, Sweden, Japan, Germany, the Netherlands and – just now – Belgium are a medium-sized one. Countries with high vulnerability were France, Italy and Spain.

We are two decades later: time for our own update (since the CSIS has not done it). I expanded the number of countries from twelve to eighteen. I also include five indicators instead of four. Conclusion: the Anglo-Saxon countries continue to score strongly, with only the UK losing some ground. The most vulnerable countries twenty years ago still appear to be the most vulnerable in the present, but are now joined by Germany, Portugal and Belgium.

The first parameter I take into account is the increasing financial pressure on future government finances. The IMF[131] expects that the total age-related government expenditure in the G20 – the group of the twenty most important economic countries – will increase by 6% of GDP by 2050 on top of the current (2015) 14% of GDP. Healthcare costs in particular are increasing, while the increase in pension benefits remains relatively limited. Countries with a sharply increasing bill are the US (health expenditure!) and Belgium (health expenditure and pensions).

The second and third parameters measure the fiscal room left for manoeuvring: how much more tax can still be levied and how much more debt can still be incurred? With tax revenues typically exceeding 50% of GDP, higher taxes are hardly an option for most European countries. In the Anglo-Saxon countries and Japan this is 40% or less. But for the latter, the net government debt is 161% of

GDP (gross is 260% of GDP*). But many other countries have also been saddled with huge government debts following the Covid pandemic, as explained in our chapter on debt.

The more people who continue to pay those taxes, the more sustainable the pensions remain. The increase in the degree of dependency is therefore the fourth parameter. As already mentioned, Southern European countries are taking a heavy blow here. Finally, there is the importance of government pensions in the total pension income. The greater the latter, the more politically sensitive it becomes to reduce it. In the Anglo-Saxon countries, social security is relatively cheap, with a well-developed private pension system. The government pension accounts for just over a third of a pensioner's total income. In Europe these percentages rise to 70 to 90%, and tinkering with pensions inevitably leads to protests.

In Europe, the lifetime benefits that the older generations receive are double compared to what they contributed (in premiums) during their active years. Reforms after the Global Financial Crisis of 2008 have reduced the benefits-to-contributions ratio to almost 1.5 for younger generations. This solved half of the problem. More recent reforms, however, have pushed the bill up again.

Additional measures are therefore needed in Europe to prevent our social security system (pension and health expenditure) from buckling under the pressure of ageing. Increasing labour participation is the silver bullet: it ensures more income and less pension expenditure. And why not: we live longer, and furthermore do so in better health. Researchers from the European Commission and the International Institute for Applied Systems Analysis[132] examined how the dependency rate based on the working-age population (see the 'Increase in dependency rate of the working-age population' graph) would evolve if all European countries were to achieve the Swedish participation rate of 82% by 2060. For the 28 EU countries (including then EU-member the UK) the dependency rate stabilises (as compared to 2015) instead of increasing by a quarter! Spain and Greece, whose indices rose to 158 and 164 respectively, now limit the increase to 122 and 102. The significant Greek leap forward illustrates the effectiveness of the measure for the current underperformers. France, with a participation rate of 72%, turned its index increase of 15% into a contraction of 15%. Belgium, with its paltry low participation rate of

* The difference between gross and net debt is roughly the share of the debt held by the government itself.

just over 70%, goes from an increase of a quarter to a decrease of 17%. Demography is not an economic *destiny*. It just warrants brave politicians.

Ageing vulnerability index (2023)
From least to most vulnerable

Low vulnerability

Australia
Canada
Denmark
Ireland
Sweden
United States

Average vulnerability

United Kingdom
Netherlands
Finland
Japan
Norway
Luxembourg

High vulnerability

Germany
France
Spain
Portugal
Belgium
Italy

Source own calculations based on data IMF, VN, OESO

The ageing trend

Interview with Thomas Malthus and David Ricardo: Not just an ordinary morning in Fleet Street

It is still early. I exit my Ibis London Blackfriars hotel and walk north in the direction of the Thames. I've had a love affair with London since I was twelve, and I now know almost every street, every stone and every story here. London has a great history. I have devoured Peter Ackroyd's *London: The Biography* and the novel *London* by Edward Rutherfurd many times. You may call it a minor quirk, but as I walk around London, I always try to imagine the city as it was in earlier times. And the 18th century, during the Enlightenment, is clearly my favourite period. I know that the Tate Modern and Shakespeare's Globe are to the right of me. At least, where the Globe now is, as the original, which was built near the Thames' Southbank in 1599, was destroyed by a fire in 1613. But I digress. Today I have an appointment with two special gentlemen. I therefore quicken my pace, cross Blackfriars Bridge, and walk a few hundred metres further ahead towards the Old Bell Tavern in Fleet Street. The building dates from the 17th century. It is claimed that Christopher Wren built it for his masons, who were working on St. Paul's Cathedral, just a stone's throw to the east of here. It's just another of those stories, but for once it could be right.

Despite the multicoloured stained glass windows that let in some blue and red light here and there, the pub is dark and radiates the atmosphere of a late 18th-century coffee shop.

Besides the innkeeper there are just a few customers. Most tables are unoccupied. There's a man at the bar who sits so firmly on his stool that he seems to belong to the decor. My eye then spots two gentlemen at a table in a dark corner. Their clothing is not of this time, but it suits the inn better than mine. There is an unoccupied chair and the man with the longest sideburns beckons me to sit down. They look like they could be brothers.

The gentlemen introduce themselves as 'Thomas Malthus and David Ricardo'. Even in this day and age, the man with the longest sideburns, Thomas Malthus, wouldn't look out of place in an Oxford lecture room. The other, David Ricardo, would attract attention in a modern market hall on account of his clothing. But everyone would gladly accept that, if his investment reputation and his knack for opportunities were only half of what it's reputed to be.

I signal the innkeeper to bring us three coffees. But Mr Ricardo stops me. 'We don't do this anymore...' I should have remembered it from Keynes. Since these kinds of conversations can end suddenly, I decide to get started right away. I turn to David Ricardo.

'One of the greatest traders of our time, a trend follower named Larry Hite, called you the first trend follower in history. He even named his book *The Rule* after your timeless principle: cut short your losses and let your profits run.'

'I've read that book, and if you look at it that way, it makes perfect sense. That Mr Hite has acquired from you the talent to make difficult things understandable. In contrast to my friend Thomas here, who can make even the simplest things seem difficult.'

'Look who's talking. I believe that if you read the later criticisms of your work, you'll find words such as "difficult" and "unreadable".'

'And "brilliant", I would add. Everyone learns, through some level of economic study, about comparative and absolute advantages and the major benefits of world trade. But I'm not quick enough.'

'Do you know what is possibly the most impressive passage in the book by your friend Larry? The story of the old religious man on Miami Beach. One day he hears that his neighbour had won millions on the lottery. He is so angry that he trudges across the beach and starts ranting at everyone. He exclaims: "God, I am so angry. I am a good husband, a good father, I go to church every Sunday. I have never won anything on the lottery." Suddenly it gets dark, as in church paintings, and a lightning bolt pierces the sky. A voice sounds from heaven: "Did you ever buy a ticket? To win, you must buy a ticket. If you don't play, you won't win..." We all had a laugh about that.'

'Just like when you placed a huge bet on the outcome of the Battle of Waterloo and bought large amounts of British government bonds at rock bottom prices. Wellington won and you made £1 million in one fell swoop and became one of the richest merchants of that time...'

'I remember well when the news arrived here in Fleet Street. The prices started to rise spectacularly. It was probably harder not to sell immediately and let the profits run.'

'I couldn't stomach it,' admits Thomas Malthus. 'My friend David had taken a nice position. But I repeatedly asked him to sell, which he did. I lost out on the whole rally. Story of my life, I think. But I have no regrets about it. I was always more of an academic than a trader.'

'How do you see the world? Let me start with you, Mr Malthus. Everyone agrees that your analysis of the Malthusian trap, which was named after you, was correct. The population did not increase after more than a thousand years because a large population always led to famine, as a result of which the population would decrease and the whole cycle would begin anew.'

'I have clearly underestimated the power of the progress that began with the Industrial Revolution. Living standards dramatically improved and I spent years observing with amazement the huge leaps forward made by medical science. And that is just the beginning...'

But he realises that he's told me too much and retracts his last words. I am trying to make sense of all this. There, where these gentlemen come from, do they know what lies ahead? All kinds of notions about 'time and space' come to mind. Is the future preordained? Or is there no past, present and future...?

But I know what else to ask. 'It's clear that the world population is reaching its peak, and we're unmistakably heading towards a period of ageing. Koen de Leus named one of his previous books, *Naar Grijsland* (*Towards Greyland*), after this era. Is a new version of the Malthusian Trap coming?'

'That was certainly not a bad book. But not as good as the biography that will be written in 2034, two hundred years after my death. There my ideas will be fully rehabilitated.'

'Wouldn't that then be good news for the world?'

'I find it a bit regrettable that David is always being portrayed as the optimist, and I as the pessimist. Perhaps that's only because he was more adept with money. But, to answer your question: much of that is within your control. If you all wish to become much older but want to stop working at sixty, then it's going to be a difficult ride. By the way, I like your term "seniorescence". A period where everything is possible, but nothing is obligatory. Quite nice.'

'Is this how you are now, enjoying "seniorescence"?', I want to ask. Anyway, even after a couple of hundred years, it's not easy to outsmart David Ricardo...

'Our academic has, as is frequently the case, a point. There appears to be some work to be done in the field of demography. But that also applies to globalisation. Less trade means less affluence. You can try to develop theories that dispute this. Good luck. But that is also within your control.'

'May I ask you both a personal question?'

'Quick then, because we can only keep this dimensional portal open for a very short time. You'll get there someday. Or perhaps you are already there. You spoke to Joseph Schumpeter recently, right? Or are you going to speak with him on this subject? Just a few more innovation clusters and you're there.'

'The two of you didn't agree during your lifetime. Yet you were friends. And apparently, you are still friends. Your first encounter was during a bitter fight in parliament over the Corn Laws, where you stood on opposite sides of the divide. What's your secret?'

Both gentlemen clearly did not expect this question. Malthus begins.

'In principle, it involves respect. You may differ in opinion, but if in the end everyone fights for what he believes in and a compromise is reached, or perhaps not, then everyone is the better for it.'

'Respect and keep talking,' adds Ricardo. 'That's of paramount importance. I have the feeling that there is very little room for conversation with you at the moment. The whole climate issue is a nice example of this. If you do not succeed in having a discussion in the tradition of the Enlightenment, then you have a serious problem.'

'Actually, when it comes down to it, it's a bit like you and Koen. When are you in agreement…?'

A barely visible smile shapes Malthus' mouth and Ricardo starts to laugh more audibly.

For a moment the blue light shines on Ricardo and the red light on Malthus and then both are gone. I step out onto Fleet Street and hear *The Gambler* by Kenny Rogers in my ear. *'You've got to know when to hold 'em, know when to fold 'em, know when to walk away, know when to run…'* And suddenly I am back in the 21st century. The more things change, the more they stay the same.

Seniorescence in a lifetime of at least one hundred years

'Live as if you were to die tomorrow.
Learn as if you would live eternally.'

————

MAHATMA GANDHI

When discussing demographics, the typical primary concern is how we are going to pay for it all.

But we could look at it differently. A person's life now lasts longer and we manage to stay healthy longer. A child born in the West today has more than a 50% chance of reaching 105. A child born in the previous century had less than 1% chance of reaching 100. Over the last two hundred years, life expectancy has increased by two years every decade. Someone who is sixty today has a greater than 50% chance of reaching 90.

The enormous extension of lifespan was initially driven by an explosive reduction in infant mortality. The next great catalyst was medical progress, with better control of diseases such as cancer and cardiovascular disorders. This catalyst will certainly strengthen in coming years. The next big thing is tackling the typical diseases of old age.

Finally there is the ambitious vision, such as that of people like David A. Sinclair, author of *Lifespan, Why We Age and Why We Don't Have To*, which posits that the ageing process is itself an illness that can be slowed down, stopped, and even reversed. The question then becomes: where is the limit? Could we, at some point, live to be 150 or 200 years old, or even older? There are the pessimists who argue that we have already come a long way and are almost at our limit. On the other hand, there are scientists such as Ray Kurzweil, who rely on new breakthroughs – first in biotechnology, then in nanotechnology and artificial intelligence – to constantly manage and restore the body at the molecular level, aiming to dramatically increase our life expectancy.

But do we want to live almost forever? What about the many generations that will come after us? Money no longer passes from one generation to the next. Long-term investment will become very, very long-term investment. The legal and economic cost of a person's life will become extremely high. And do you wish to spend an eternity and a day with the same partner? For me, the answer to the last question is definitely yes. For the rest, I am not so sure.

The truth, as always, will lie somewhere in between. Let us presume a life ex-pectancy of one hundred years. What follows will only magnify the anticipated consequences. The possibility of significant developments in the future serves as a compelling reason to adopt a healthier lifestyle. No one wants to miss out on a breakthrough that can add 50 healthy years to everyone's life.

Up to the industrial revolution, life was short, as seen from our perspective. You were born, started working soon after, then you died. Starting in the 20th century, life acquired a fixed form consisting of three phases: a first educational phase followed by a working phase, and finally a pension. And that's where the problem lies. It is becoming increasingly difficult to uphold the living standard of the working years during the ever longer pension period. This means: either work longer, or be content with less. It is this reasoning that fuels the perception of problems such as the ageing population and the affordability of pensions.

There is a risk that a longer life could be perceived as a curse. In the seminal book *The 100-Year Life* by Lynda Gratton and Andrew J. Scott, this idea is vividly illustrated through a French fable. The nymph Ondine, upon discovering her husband sleeping and snoring after committing adultery, places a curse upon him: as long as he remains awake, he will keep breathing and thus continue to live. However, if he should fall asleep, he will die. From that moment, Palemon has no rest because he is constantly in motion to avoid falling asleep. The pros-pect of extending our three-phase life can, in a way, evoke a sensation akin to Ondine's curse. We feel compelled to stay in constant motion, to keep working, regardless of how tired we may be.

But it doesn't have to be this way. And actually, it cannot be this way in the future. It would be quite difficult to retire at 65 if that pension period were to last 40 years or more. We will have to dispense in part with the traditional three phases and switch to a more flexible lifespan with possibly different working periods, pauses and transitions.

Given the speed with which technology today evolves and with which new jobs are created and old ones vanish, an education during the first 25 years will not build up enough knowledge for the subsequent 75 years. Knowledge that we will desperately need within 30 years is not even available today. Lifelong learning is the only solution. If someone today says: 'I am doing my master's,' then you know almost for sure that the person in question is 22 or 23 years old. The day that someone says this and you don't know if the person is twenty, forty, sixty or eighty years old, then we will have made a big step in the right direction.

A longer life is also boring if it is without meaning. We are creatures constantly in search of meaning. And what can give more meaning to a rich life than knowledge, passing on skills and ideas, initially to your children and loved ones, and in turn indirectly to everyone? The idea of mentorship and reverse mentorship is particularly compelling. For the physicist Richard Feynman, the man after whom the *Feynman Technique* is named, you only really learn something by explaining it and teaching it. In the new world, any young person or adolescent should have a mentor. Conversely, any mentor can learn about new technologies from his or her younger partner via reverse mentoring.

Initially, we should aim to fill the period of sixty to roughly eighty years, but preferably longer, in a productive and pleasant way. It should be a period during which we ride high on our happiness curve. We still work, maybe not full time, still have an income allowing us to maintain our living standard or even improve it, we can be there for our kin, and can make positive contributions to society.

Not so long ago, as people's lifespan lengthened, the term 'adolescence' was introduced – the period from about 16 to 21 years corresponding to the transition from youth to adulthood. In this phase, young people are focused on building reciprocal and intimate relationships. That appears to work so well that those people are now trying to extend the period of young adulthood by travelling, enjoying life, and especially by postponing the next phase (permanent jobs, a home, family responsibility) as much as possible. It is clear that this, in itself, already has a lot of influence on the job market, the real estate market, fertility rates, etc.

It is time to introduce such a period at the end of the traditional working life. I propose calling it 'seniorescence', in analogy with adolescence.

But this is just the first step on the way to where we wish to end up. It is time to rethink the old concept of a career. 'Career' comes from the Latin word *carrus*: wagon. Since the start of the 19th century, it began to be used its modern sense: the course of one's public and professional life. But that course is often linear and mono-disciplinary. Given the increasingly advanced levels of specialisation, this is not surprising. To be and remain good at something requires practice and time. But if we all wish to work longer and want to guard against our professional lives becoming too monotonous, difficult or irritating, a new concept is required.

Let us replace career with 'transiteer' – from *transitus*, that is, 'passage, transition' – to express the idea of repeated transitions from one career path to another, and to keep reinventing oneself. This will obviously require an adjustment and a change in many areas. We would have to be willing to start from scratch several times. And be prepared to take breaks and undergo periods of rejuvenation. This will blur the boundaries between the different age segments. We will then move towards a 'flat age society'.

A constant investment in skills for the future *is* the future, if that future keeps being extended. Investing in intangibles, in skills, will become more interesting and important economically as the payback period becomes longer.

Families will more often consist of four contemporaneous generations. If all members have a more flexible life cycle, fairly complex family structures may arise. For companies and human resource departments, this could become a major challenge. First and foremost, employees above fifty will have to be active instead of passive. And why should people who would like to keep working at 70 or 75 be compelled to retire? Employees will have to get used to the fact that a classic structure, in which older employees are traditionally higher in the hierarchy, will be turned upside down. And if governments are talking about pension reforms, they should finally make a real effort to encourage people to work longer. I can perfectly understand that people who have done heavy physical work for a long time become physically exhausted at some stage. But even then, there should be an opportunity to transfer knowledge to younger generations. There is a huge shortage of teachers and mentors. A broader connection ought to be made between people doing practical work and those working in education.

As we evolve towards a world where, I dearly hope, learning is a continual process in which skill set is stacked upon skill set, the gap will widen between those who embrace the new world and those who cling to an outmoded model. This will translate into greater differences in income and eventually greater inequality. This could again lead to conflicts, not necessarily between generations, but between lifelong students and the rest. For people who dislike learning in the broadest sense of the word, unpleasant times lie ahead.

From an investment perspective, it is more important than ever to keep your knowledge and skills up to date. Always invest enough in it: it is perhaps the most important investment advice you will find in this book.

IMPACT *on* GROWTH *and* PRODUCTIVITY

✓ In the coming decades, the developing countries could benefit from a demographic dividend and greater growth in productivity, potentially propelling them to the top of the world's largest economies by 2050. Among the top seven economies based on purchasing power parity, six are growth countries, with only the US in third place. The pandemic, however, has slowed this evolution.

✓ The prerequisite for this transformation is sound economic management and a good institutional framework, both of which are absent in some of the countries experiencing the largest population growth. Consequently, a growing cohort of young people will face an uncertain economic future.

✓ Productivity remains by far the most important factor for stabilising the living standard of pensioners and increasing that of the working population.

✓ A hump-shaped trend can be seen when displaying productivity versus the age of employees: it increases until about forty and then decreases towards the end of working life. The same trend applies to disruptive technologies. Ageing will reduce the total factor productivity (TFP) in the eurozone by almost a quarter, according to the EC.

✓ Besides TFP, there is also productivity from capital investments. In an ageing society, investments for the entire economy decrease, but per employee they increase. Automation must definitely compensate for the shortage of workers in Europe.

✓ According to the European Commission, total productivity growth would slowly evolve to 1.5% per year. That is also the long-term growth envisaged for Europe.

Emerging countries seize power

Real global economic growth averaged 3.8% from 2002 to 2019 (just before the advent of the Covid pandemic). In developed countries this was just half, while in emerging countries it was 5.6%. The latter's stunning performance was not unexpected. The rising labour force, combined with closing the technological gap compared to the West, pushed these countries to the top of the rankings. The excellent performance of China (9%) and India (7%) in particular pushed that average higher. Latin America, on the other hand, again recorded disappointing growth of only 2.5%. The South American superpower Brazil (2.4%) underwent a severe economic recession in 2014–2015 as a result of a political crisis and sharply lower commodity prices. But even in the first decade of 2000 it could not achieve its growth status. Corruption and economic mismanagement undermine growth potential. A rising labour force does not guarantee an explosion of growth.

What lies ahead until 2050? At the national level, the 'child peak' is followed by a period in which the country benefits from a 'demographic dividend'. The working population is increasing compared to the dependent young generation. This is happening today on a global scale. In 1950, for every child under the age of 15, there were 1.8 people aged 15–64; now there are 2.5, and by the end of the century there will be 3.4. Richer countries have benefited from the relative explosion of the economically active in recent decades. In the coming decades it will be the turn of the poorer countries.

According to consultancy company PwC, the world order could completely change in the coming decades.[133] In 1995, the economies of the E7 – Brazil, Russia, India, China, Indonesia, Mexico and Turkey – were half the size of the G7 countries[134] on a purchasing power parity basis.* In 2015 they were the same size, and by 2040 they could double in size. By 2050, six emerging countries will be in the top seven largest economies, with only the US in third place (*see table*). The Covid pandemic has probably delayed that evolution by a few years. And Russia

---

* When comparing economies, purchasing power parity is often used. This involves examining how many products and services can be purchased in both economies with the total realised income. Because the cost of products and services in developing countries is significantly lower than in developed countries, the economic size based on purchasing power parity can be the same in both groups in spite of the much larger economic GDP in developed countries.

has seriously mortgaged its economic future with its brutal invasion of Ukraine. Ending up in sixth place by 2050 has now almost certainly become unattainable, and I have removed it from the ranking.

**GDP ranking
(in purchasing power parity)
in 2016 and 2050**

	2016	2050
China	1	1
India	3	2
Russia	6	??
Brazil	7	5
Indonesia	8	4
Mexico	11	7
Turkey	14	11
Egypt	21	15
Nigeria	22	14
Pakistan	24	16
Philippines	28	19
Bangladesh	31	23
Vietnam	32	20

Source *The Long View*, PwC, February 2017

Europe steadily loses ground compared to the Asiatic giants India, China and Indonesia. The EU share in global GDP shrinks from about 15% to just 9%. The Indian share more than doubles to 15%. China will creep from 18% to 20%, while the US share will fall from 16% to 12% in 2050. India will then overtake the US as the world's second largest economy.

Virtually all emerging countries with a population explosion are improving in the rankings. Nigeria, Vietnam and Pakistan are making the biggest leap forward. The total population in Nigeria will exceed that of the US by 2050. The Pakistani population will increase by half to 338 million, while the Vietnamese population will increase from 97 to 110 million people. Strong population growth combined with a strong increase in productivity is an extremely powerful growth serum.

The shifts cited demonstrate the potential of a rapidly growing young population. But while demography may be destiny, demographic growth does not necessarily lead to economic growth. It assumes that the institutional and political framework is conducive to growth (*see box*). Unfortunately, the history of many developing countries shows that corrupt and incompetent governments often prevent economies from reaching their full potential. In the young, promising Nigeria, political and social unrest has ruined the growth potential in recent years. We previously mentioned Brazil's weak growth performance, but the same disillusionment was also the case for many South American countries. They face a 'strikingly unproductive workforce,' according to the Economist[135], as a result of poor education, corruption and a massive black economy.

Historic disappointments mean that a growing group of young people are likely to face a bleak economic future. In some cases, these young people are an excellent recruitment base for extremist groups. In that respect, it is an unfortunate – and dangerous – observation that there is particularly rapid population growth in some of the most troubled countries in the world.

Good institutions will help developing nations reap the benefits

What are the main drivers of long-term growth differences? Demography, investments, education, technological backwardness most certainly. 'But I would particularly emphasise the critical importance of the quality of institutions in long-term economic success or failure,' says Professor Michael G. Jacobides in an interview with PwC.[136]

'If we look at the rise of the West, for example, the development of economic and financial institutions like banking in Medici-era Florence, joint stock companies in the England and the Netherlands, and professional management of large companies in the US played a significant role in propelling economic growth from the 16th to the 20th centuries. This was supported by political systems that invested in public goods (including health and education as well as physical infrastructure) and provided legal systems that protected property rights and provided a conducive environment for long-term business investment.'

Economic development and the establishment of institutions can lead to either an upward spiral, where improvements lead to growth, or a downward spiral, where contraction leads to political profiteering and institutional decay. 'Look at Turkey: because of both politics and the weakening of institutions, the economy is stalling. Will it rebound, or will the Erdogan rule preside over an unstable period of Turkey missing out on the potential that the model predicts?' These words, spoken prophetically by the professor in a 2017 interview, seem especially relevant now as the Turkish economy grapples with a huge inflation surge.

In their bestseller *Why Nations Fail*, Daron Acemoglu and James Robinson convincingly demonstrate that the political and economic institutions created by humans are at the root of economic success, or the lack of it. Despite being a remarkably homogeneous nation, Korea presents a stark contrast. The people of North Korea are among the poorest in the world, while their counterparts in South Korea are among the richest. The South has built a society that fosters incentives, rewards innovation and enables widespread participation in economic opportunities. This incentive-based economic success has been sustained because the government is accountable to people. Sadly, the people of the North have endured decades of famine, political oppression and vastly different economic institutions, with no apparent end in sight.

According to Jacobides, institutional development will also determine whether India can match China's success. The old-fashioned bureaucracy that slowed growth rates in the past must be shaken off. China's future hinges on the enhancement of its politics and institutions. Can it transition from an economy driven by cheap labour and exports towards one that generates products and services with high added value? Only in this way can a richer middle class fuel much-needed domestic consumption and avoid the middle-income trap.

Productivity growth to ensure stability and prosperity

'We will all become Sweden!' If we examine the enormous potential of an increase in the participation rate to boost growth and reduce the cost of ageing, then people could still be happy to live in Belgium or Greece. An increase to the Swedish level of participation is unrealistically optimistic for most countries. In Belgium, the employment rate* increased by 4 percentage points to 71.9 percentage points from 2000 to today, mainly due to an increasing number of women in the labour market. The target for 2030 is 80%. We will not achieve that, nor in the decades that follow, no matter what rose-tinted glasses we put on.

Considering a realistic increase in the participation rate for the entire EU, the European Commission estimates a nearly 16% decline in the working population from 2019–2070.[137] That equates to an average annual decline of 0.2% in economic growth. In Belgium, the Netherlands and France, the decline is limited to an average of 0.1%. Meanwhile, in some central and east European countries, the yearly workforce will shrink by 0.5 to 1% as a result of emigration.

'The increase in output per employee holds the greatest potential for increased growth. A significant increase in labour productivity will be necessary if we want to stabilise the standards of living of pensioners and improve those of the working population,' said Alan Greenspan, the legendary former chairman of the US Federal Reserve.

Gert Peersman, professor of economics at the University of Ghent, fully agrees.[138] 'In Belgium we often talk of jobs, jobs, jobs and of our activity rate, which is indeed on the low side,' he says in an interview with business organisation Etion. 'But that problem does not weigh up against our lagging productivity. And this will, if possible, become even more critical in addressing our ageing population,' says the professor while referring to the growth projections of the Belgian Study Committee on ageing. 'The economic growth we need to cover the pensions bill must come from job growth (one-ninth), and from productivity growth (eight-ninths). Even if we were to get everyone to work tomorrow, we will still fall short of the necessary economic growth.' Growth, particularly growth per capita,** will only be possible through sufficiently rapid productivity growth.

Productivity growth involves investments in better machines and labour, and the way those two factors interact. When combined with the increase in the

---

*   This is the harmonised employment rate for 20–64-year-olds.
** Per capita growth is real growth divided by the total population. This also best shows the evolution of prosperity per head. Since the effective decline in the total population only follows years after the decline in the working population, per capita growth will show the negative impact more quickly.

number of workers, this results in growth. The increase in labour productivity in Belgium compared to the Scandinavian countries nicely illustrates the various components of productivity. 'Specifically for Belgium, the increase in labour productivity can be entirely attributed to a greater use of capital,' explains Peersman. 'What we achieved with more machines, other countries such as those in Scandinavia achieved this through better cooperation between labour and capital. That's what economists call 'total factor productivity' (TFP).[139] Historically, in Western countries, two-thirds of the increase in labour productivity has been accounted for by TFP. In Belgium, however, this proportion has remained constant over the past two decades, making our country an outlier. Peersman concludes that 'Belgium must, above all, work on enhancing its human capital to make it smarter and more competent in order to achieve even greater productivity.'

In general, it can be stated that an ageing environment is not really conducive to rising productivity. First of all, innovation and the dissemination of new technologies occurs more rapidly in a young society than in an old one. Secondly, a higher participation rate implies higher employment of both more low-skilled people and those aged 55 and older. Lastly, there is a potential decline in capital investments due to the decrease in the number of companies. A person who is 50 years old is less likely to start a business than one who is 25.

Oldtimers do not innovate

'Economies of scale also apply in knowledge creation,' said Norbert Walker, former chief economist at the Deutsche Bank investment bank. 'A growing population has a larger academic elite. Compared to a shrinking population, it can develop more new knowledge, through a more intensive exchange of ideas, among other things.' In addition, an older population also leads to a decrease in the number of innovations. 'Technical knowledge is produced by young workers: the majority of Nobel Prizes were awarded for scientific achievements before the age of 32.'

Research by economists Mary Kaltenberg and Adam Jaffe, and psychologist Margie Lachman,[140] points in that direction. First, they noted a peak in patent applications by researchers between the ages of late 30s and early 40s. But they also found that disruptive innovations – innovations that fundamentally change a scientific field and boost productivity the most – are most often developed by young inventors, as opposed to incremental innovations, which are small improvements made to a current product or service. The reason is that younger people exhibit what psychologists call 'fluid intelligence,' which refers to the ability to solve new problems and work on new ideas. Older people have 'crystallised intelligence', a store of accumulated knowledge of how everything works. There are no exact cut-offs, but most studies suggest that fluid intelligence peaks in early adulthood and begins to decline in our thirties. Both types of intelligence are useful, but when it comes to innovating to boost productivity, the liquid type has a strong upper hand.[141]

Older societies are also less entrepreneurial than younger ones. According to the results of the London Business School's Global Entrepreneurship Monitoring project, 'entrepreneurial' active adults are between 25 and 44 years old. That is problematic. The average age in the EU is expected to increase from 40–45 years in 2020 to 45–53 years in 2050. In Japan, the average age is projected to rise to 53 years, and in the US to 42.

Are the elderly also less productive in the workplace?[142] A more mature workforce will have more work experience on average, which is positive for productivity. On the other hand, the skills of the workforce also depend on the knowledge acquired before entering the labour market or in the early stages of an individual's career. This stock of 'new' skills will become obsolete as the average age of workers increases. This has negative consequences for innovation and productivity.

In addition, it is not always easy for older workers to adapt to job requirements that change over time. The increased flow of new information technologies is undoubtedly easier for the younger workforce to handle. The combination of these factors points to a hump-shaped trend when depicting productivity vs. age: increasing up to forty and declining towards the end of working life. This is in line with the declining productivity that we have observed in Western countries since 2000. The baby boomer generation slowly moved from their most productive years to declining productivity.

Based on demographic forecasts for the eurozone, the ageing of the working population would reduce TFP growth by about 0.2 percentage points annually between 2014 and 2035, according to IMF estimates.[143] With an estimated TFP of just under 1% over that period, this means that without ageing, the TFP would be a quarter higher.

Governments are powerless in the face of the ageing of the workforce. Many countries are trying to boost fertility rates – with limited success, however. But a high birth rate and a young population is not the only, and certainly not the decisive factor for productivity. Otherwise, the poorest countries in sub Saharan Africa would be the world's most dynamic region. The most evident way is to provide a good education. In developing countries such as China and Brazil, millions of children still do not receive a proper education. In some developed countries – such as Belgium – the PISA results are deteriorating every time they are measured. 'As the potential workforce shrinks, maximising the output of everyone in it will become essential, and could help offset the effects of an ageing population – at least as regards innovation,' writes *The Economist*.

Technology is a second way to mitigate the effects of demographic change. Telemedicine and robots help counteract the challenges posed by an ageing population. But the number of new ideas also decreases as a result of a decrease in the number of innovative thinkers. Perhaps this can be compensated for by the new ideas generated by artificial intelligence. Whether those new ideas can also be disruptive remains to be seen.

More, but limited, capital investment

Consider capital investment. The production per hour of a seamstress can be dramatically increased if she is provided with a sewing machine. This begins with innovation – the development of a sewing machine. Subsequently, it requires capital investment because the employer must provide a sewing machine for each seamstress. The greater the capital investment per employee, the higher the productivity. After the Global Financial Crisis, up until just before the Covid-19 outbreak, US capital investment growth remained at 0.5% per year. This is the lowest recorded in the entire historical dataset.

What are the prospects for future capital investments? The number of companies is decreasing due to an ageing population. The impact on investments in machinery and equipment, however, is less clear. Fewer workers require fewer machines and less equipment. But certain technologies, such as artificial intelligence, automation or robots, replace rather than complement human labour. And it will be necessary. In a scenario where, on top of investments in the current workforce, a portion of the decline in the labour force is also offset by automation, production per worker increases. The ratio between capital and labour rises.

A shortage of employees leads to automation... or lower growth

A simulation by the Flemish employers' organisation VOKA shows that employment increased by almost 500,000 during the period 2003–2019. The increase in 20 to 65-year-olds was limited to just over 200,000 during that period. Activation of the inactive population closed the gap.

To achieve potential growth over the next sixteen years, almost 600,000 additional workers are needed. However, the working population is expected to decrease by several tens of thousands over this period. A further increase in the participation rate could again close part of the gap. The rest can be attributed to automation. Rising wages (due to the shortage of workers) may also encourage companies to invest in increasingly affordable robots (see productivity chapter). If all this fails, many Flemish companies will have to outsource or refuse work. This leads to less growth and prosperity.

Professor Peersman notes that higher productivity, mainly derived from TFP rather than increased capital, remains preferable. 'Investment must be made in these machines, and that capital needs to be compensated. This leaves less room for higher wages. If productivity growth comes from TFP growth, you don't face that dilemma. Where productivity grows through more efficient, higher-quality, and more innovative processes, there is additional profit to be shared between labour and capital.'

The conclusion is that the impact of an ageing society on productivity is rather negative. Figures from the European Commission point to a long-term productivity growth of approximately 1.5%. The ageing population is eating away at a quarter of TFP, leaving it at 1%. Capital investments add 0.5% to this. 1.5% also corresponds to the long-term growth that the Commission envisages for Europe. 'Productivity isn't everything, but in the long run, it's *almost* everything,' said Nobel Prize winner Paul Krugman long ago. In an ageing society, productivity is really everything.

How does one invest in
a quickly changing demography?

The question of how, as an investor, you can respond to all these major demographic trends is not easy to answer. It is a very complex story. Moreover, there are several themes and ideas for which investment products are not immediately available. Nevertheless, I will try to go beyond the classic narrative of cruises, caravans, golf, healthcare and nursing homes that is traditionally presented. Although these are all valid ideas. We cannot ignore healthcare. But the substantial correction in some nursing home-related stocks indicates that even riding mega-waves is not always without risk.

With the births recorded today and those preceding today, you can make a fairly accurate prediction of the future. It becomes a bit more challenging when you start predicting births and deaths for the coming years. Maybe, or even probably, there will be fewer births. But on the other hand, people will probably live longer than we think. The prediction that later this century we will see a peak in the population of eleven billion, a little over 50% more than today, may be an overestimation. After that, we will begin to see a decline.

It is not difficult to see the challenges associated with this population growth. The pressure on the planet, resources and food supply will only increase. This means that commodities and agriculture should be part of any long-term investment portfolio – especially companies and stocks that offer solutions to handle existing resources more efficiently and in more environmentally friendly ways. The new Apple or Microsoft will be a battery technology company, or a company that succeeds in desalinating seawater energy-efficiently, or improves agricultural yields in an environmentally friendly way.

Changes always create winners and losers. With major changes, we are talking about big winners and big losers. We are at such a point today that fortunes can be made and lost. Progress is not a path that runs in a straight line from poverty to wealth. It is messy, confusing, and particularly threatening for those who handle it poorly.

The big winners and losers are found at country level to begin with. Developing countries, especially in Africa, with a still growing and particularly young population, will at some point benefit from a demographic dividend. For more mature countries, where the population is decreasing and (rapidly) ageing, it will be important to implement an immigration policy that has internal support and is both humane and economically responsible. Countries that manage to bring this extremely difficult balancing act to a successful conclusion have an advantage from an investment perspective. Examples include the United States, Canada, Australia, New Zealand and, to some extent, France. It is clear that outlooks for most other countries in Europe, as well as China due to its one-child policy, are less optimistic in this regard.

At the moment, longer life means being older for a longer time. In the new logic, longer life means being younger for longer. But at the end of the day, we all need help. And it's not enough to have enough money set aside. There must also be people to provide care. They must also live close enough, although some services in the future will be virtual and will also be rendered with the help of robotics (companies investing in this will have made very good long-term investments). If there is a shortage of relatively young people willing to care for the elderly, the price (wages) of this type of labour will rise, possibly pricing other jobs out of the market. One thing is certain: for nursing staff or staff in the medical sector, there will be almost near-complete job security in the coming years, though more will be needed than just an attractive salary to entice young people.

With pharmaceutical and biotech companies, we come to the big winners of the demographic revolution. We would need several books to describe the breakthroughs in the pipeline. According to scientists, we have almost completely unravelled human DNA. At the same time, there are declining costs for DNA research. The costs of a personal DNA test have dropped from 100 million dollars in 2001 to about 300 dollars in 2022. A challenge is to store all our DNA data, because it involves hundreds of terabytes. Moreover, we want to protect our DNA, and privacy also plays a prominent role. This shows how everything is connected. AI breakthroughs are facilitating developments in the biotech sector. But for that, as we already mentioned in the chapter on innovation, you once again need, for example, semiconductors and internet security.

It suffices to indicate here that the biotech sector is, in any case, one of the promising investment waves for the coming years. But beware: investing in this volatile sector is not without risks. Long-term charts show that the impressive upward trend is accompanied by strong fluctuations. Periods of several years in which prices multiply are interspersed with periods of stagnation and decline.

Nasdaq Biotech Index

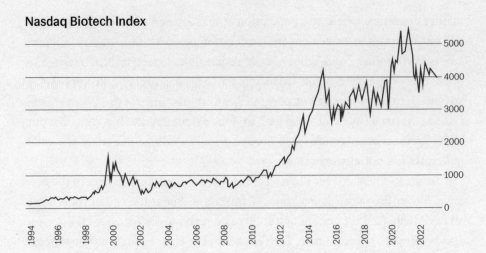

This is a great example of the elephant metaphor discussed at the beginning of this book. Is the money tap open or shut? Given that biotech companies, with a few exceptions, are not yet profitable and continue to burn cash in their quest for the ultimate new drug, an open money tap for this sector is even more crucial than it is for more mature sectors that generate actual cash flow.

When the cash tap is open, biotech companies often seize the opportunity to raise funds to weather the inevitable dry spells. However, they are not alone in this endeavour, as other companies are also trying to stock up on cash at the same time. This results in oversupply, inevitably leading to a lot of chaff among the wheat. During the last wave in 2022, more than 400 new biotech companies entered the scene. That was too much of a good thing. The sector must digest the oversupply before embarking on a new cycle.

Additionally, the risk associated with an individual biotech share is particularly significant. It truly is a 'winner takes all' sector. Companies that successfully manage to squeeze a new medication through all the various clinical test phases often witness their share price quadruple. A setback or even a delay in testing can quickly lead to a 30 to 50% drop in share prices. Bringing a new medication to market from scratch easily takes ten to fifteen years and costs an average of 2.5 billion dollars. The pharma sector, which naturally develops its own medications, 'uses' the biotech sector as a supply line. Sometimes, investments are made in promising projects. If these projects succeed, the pharma company often acquires the biotech company and then just plonks it into its pipeline. For the stockholders of the biotech company, this is the jackpot. Usually, the biotech company lacks the financial and marketing resources to successfully bring the drug to market. These are tasks that the pharma company excels in, so this approach significantly reduces risks.

To invest in the biotech sector, it is advisable to adopt the turtle eggs tactic. This means investing in many promising companies, knowing that many will disappoint, but the winners will compensate for the losers by a significant margin.

A caveat is in order. Governments foresee looming costs and will strive to keep healthcare affordable. As a result, new medications will enjoy less (or shorter) patent protection, and efforts will be made to control drug prices. This means that biotech companies and their investors may see lower returns from their new breakthroughs. Patent disputes will likely end up in court more frequently, and lawyers specialised in this area will have work for many years.

On the other hand, we may be on the eve of a massive switch to e-health and electronic care. Digitalisation, automation and robotisation will be deployed to assist the elderly. We will deploy robots to do the administration, building maintenance or meal preparation in residential care centre kitchens. Each resident in an elderly care centre may have their own personal robot. Companies that succeed in automating healthcare will offer excellent investment opportunities. In Japan – not coincidentally a country with a rapidly ageing population, and thus a place where robots are at home – robots are already being used to help patients in and out of bed and check if the bed is wet. Meanwhile, there are also publicly listed companies producing robots capable of performing medical procedures.

'Own the robots' remains a highly interesting investment theme. Imagine an extreme society where no one works and robots produce everything and perform all services. Sam Wilkin describes various ways to become very rich in his brilliant book *Wealth Secrets*. One way is to have others work for you. Robots are, of course, an inexhaustible source of labour. Who will then control production? Would that be compatible with a capitalistic, free-market system? Let us suppose that the answer is, more or less, yes. Then, investing in companies that make robots amounts to doing good business.

Another interesting demographic theme concerns the service economy. A decade ago, about 5% of Chinese adults lived alone. Today, that figure is 10%, and as the population becomes increasingly urbanised, it can rise to 20 or 30%. It is a trend observed in many mature and highly urbanised countries. Research indicates that single-person households spend, on average, much more on services and less on goods than multi-person households. They are less likely to buy a house or car and usually do not (yet) need children's items. Cash is spent on travel, luxury goods, outings to the restaurant or bar, for instance. These serve immediately as ideas by which one can respond to this trend. Especially if those trips are combined with an online platform. If the Chinese and, in their wake, many residents of Western countries increasingly frequent restaurants, this will also strongly support the wine industry and the prices of what we will refer to as fine wines. Therefore, when considering investments in such a scenario, one should not forget to combine the useful elements with the pleasant ones.

It is also abundantly clear that the experience economy belongs to the services sector. We want to live unique experiences, to record them, and share them on as many social media channels as possible – through selfies and photos. For people in their seniorescence, retro and melancholy is added to this mix with vintage video games and vinyl records. Other experiences include an expensive coffee in a prime location or dining at a table high up on some skyscraper. The most extreme experiences are currently provided by space trips and space tourism.

The experience economy, in turn, feeds the events industry, plus the media and entertainment world, prompting continuous innovation and reinvention in order to provide new and better emotional experiences. Finally, there is still investment in sport and vitamins (to remain healthy), remote health apps and education (both physical and online) as part of lifelong learning.

Even the real estate market cannot escape demographic trends. Drawing major conclusions is not easy because trends, like horses, pull in different directions, which means that as an analyst or strategist you risk being pulled in multiple directions (or hung, drawn and quartered in the worst case). All else being equal, a larger population means more demand for homes. A population that rises less rapidly, or even declines, results in less demand. Of course, there is no single real estate market; there are as many real estate markets as there are countries, regions, or even cities. The real estate market in Brussels differs from that in London or Singapore. Yet, they are all interconnected, as we experienced during the 2008 real estate crisis. When interest rates fall globally, prices are supported everywhere. Conversely, when interest rates rise sharply, the real estate market worldwide is pulled down as if by gravity.

As the age distribution of a population changes and more people move to cities, the average family size decreases (thereby leading to more one-person and two-person families), requiring more houses and especially apartments per capita. This usually concerns smaller residential units. This shift may reduce the demand for larger living units, especially in rural areas, which in turn has an impact on relative pricing.

Thus there still seems to be a bright future for real estate in the centre or close to the centre of large cities. The pandemic briefly disrupted this trend, because working from home and the desire for more space and larger homes outside the city became appealing again. However, one should not exaggerate these shifts. Despite an increasing part of our lives taking place in virtual worlds with digitalisation facilitating various online activities, the demand for leisure activities remains high. This draws both the young and elderly towards the city, where entertainment and facilities are abundant. If we can believe trend-watcher Herman Konings, and I do, cities are evolving into parks that also host residences and apartments. These resemble the ideal college town, an innovative and cultural hub where people of different ages can interact. Concepts such as kangaroo homes or cohousing, where unrelated individuals live together, will continue to gain popularity.

The 21st century will be characterised by a number of megacities of ten million people or more –places fostering the convergence of ideas and investments. At the same time, some of those cities will become more liveable again. The concept of ten-minute cities, where everything is within a ten-minute reach from your home, is gaining more and more attention. It might be a stretch to claim that we are returning to a city-state economic system and that national governments will fade away. Yet cities and their policies will play an increasingly prominent role in attracting people, professionals and investments. For example, the Great Lakes region around Chicago is showing promise as a new Silicon Valley.

As an investor, how does one respond to these trends? Is it still a good idea to buy real estate at these prices? The answer is simple: it is always a good idea to invest in real estate. Real estate is a tangible asset that, in the long term, shields you from the impact of rising interest rates and inflation. I often hear from clients who consider themselves over the top, exclaiming: 'I am too old.' That's nonsense. Debts incurred through the purchase of property are transferred to the next generation, along with the property itself, upon inheritance. At that time they also serve as protection against rising interest rates and inflation.

Investing in bricks and mortar is a secure investment. The value of money in twenty or thirty years depends on the interplay between interest rates and inflation. It is expected that governments will strive for a negative real interest rate (an interest rate below the inflation level) to keep the national debt and the interest on it affordable. This means that cash will continue to depreciate at a rapid pace. The same can be said for debt. Governments and central banks have many ways of exerting the leverage at their disposal. What they cannot do is depreciate their own debts and not those of individual customers. All debts depreciate. That is why, within reason and financial capacity, adding debts (preferably at a reasonable interest rate) to a portfolio is something that creates value. This does not change as one ages.

If the world has embarked on an inflationary course for the long term, it is then realistic to expect that rental income will increase more or less in line with inflation through indexation, while the monthly mortgage payments remain constant, at least in the case of a fixed interest rate.

It should be noted that many governments, from a redistribution perspective and to protect disadvantaged citizens, will (partially) slow down the increase in rents, as we recently saw in Germany, for example.

Those who, in spite of the above arguments, would rather not invest in physical real estate, can also invest in real estate without buying bricks and mortar. This can be done through real estate companies listed on the stock exchange. In Belgium we call these companies *beveks*, *sicavs* or *sires*. Anglo-Saxon countries usually refer to them (in the singular) as 'REIT' (Real Estate Investment Trust). These companies buy and rent real estate, in a specific branch or sometimes several branches (healthcare real estate, logistics real estate, etc.).

Real estate shares have a number of important advantages. To start with, you can invest with a much smaller sum than you can with 'physical' real estate. This not only allows you to make a nice spread, but you also get an investment that is much more liquid. In other words: you can monetise the investment, or part of it, more easily and quickly, with much less administrative hassle and costs. You will have fewer headaches anyway, because you have to worry less about payments by the tenant, vacancy or damage. But perhaps the biggest asset is the dividend yield. Many real estate shares pay 3% or more in dividends, which currently clearly trumps a traditional savings account. But because the dividend is compared with savings accounts or fixed-income interest investments, it is immediately clear that real estate shares, just like physical real estate, exhibit above average sensitivity to interest rate increases.

This has certainly affected the sector in recent years. As a result, the return gap between listed real estate and physical real estate has increased significantly. To an extent, that is logical because stock-market listed real estate is often seen as a share investment that can be relatively easily dispensed with in the event of market turmoil. One usually holds on to physical real estate for the long term. Nevertheless, despite that, the two are not be compared one-to-one (because listed real estate also incorporates logistics, healthcare real estate and retail real estate), we believe that the valuations have diverged too much. This may represent a great opportunity in listed real estate for the coming period.

Perhaps there are currently too many offices in places like New York and Brussels. But real estate is an ecosystem that constantly reinvents and transforms itself. Empty offices can be repurposed into co-working spaces, lofts or apartments. Places where the ideas from start-ups and freelancers can converge.

Another idea that capitalises on real estate opportunities linked to demographics is the expectation that so much will be built and especially renovated in the coming years, as to make Baron Haussmann jealous. We will need to separate more waste from rainwater and improve the insulation of our homes. Companies engaged in these activities stand to benefit. Furthermore, there will be significant demand for raw materials – especially copper.

Two figures: one reasonable, one nonsensical

Complex questions are often answered with a simple, evocative heuristic. For example, two important questions often arise concerning the financial well-being of pensioners or 'retirees' (a dreadful word, indeed).

The first pertains to how much money must be set aside in order to maintain their pre-retirement living standards. The rule of thumb suggests that you should have saved eight times your yearly salary by age 65. The human resources company Mercer conducted a similar exercise and calculated that approximately 85 times your net monthly salary should be set aside. Eight yearly salaries roughly corresponds to 96 monthly wages, which is in the region of 85. This calculation encompasses cash and various kinds of investment forms, but excludes the home, jewellery, cars and art. You may have anticipated this: whether or not this is enough depends, of course, on how long you live. Life expectancy continues to increase, bringing additional costs with it – especially in the medical field An added uncertainty here lies in how much of these costs will be covered by the government, given the ever-increasing deficits.

Another uncertainty is the expected return on savings while they are being used. The higher the return, the longer and more comfortably the savings will last. A second common question is which percentage of the portfolio should be invested in shares and fixed-income securities at a certain age. The rule of thumb suggests that the percentage invested in shares should equal one hundred minus your age. The reasoning behind this is that shares are the best investment in the long term, but are most volatile in the short term. Therefore, with fewer remaining years, there is a greater chance of a major setback and less time to recover from it. According to this logic, a 65-year-old should still have an average of 35% in shares and a robust 95-year-old should have 5%. At first glance, there is something to be said for the logic of investing more defensively as the years progress, but it doesn't align well with the idea of growing older with dignity. One should believe in the future at any age. Why shouldn't someone over 65 still invest in technology firms? Moreover, we currently live in a world of very negative real interest rates. In such a situation, shares are more necessary than ever to make the nest egg last longer. Moreover, the next generation will certainly not be unhappy inheriting a substantial portfolio. At any rate, what is more charming than grandparents investing in the future together with their grandchildren?

IMPACT ON INTEREST RATES AND INFLATION

KEY POINTS

✓ Various studies estimate that demographic changes have driven real interest rates down by 1.25 to 2%, mainly because of an increased supply of savings.

✓ This downward pressure on interest rates is expected to continue. The substantial savings accumulated by the middle-aged and elderly more than compensate for the modest reduction in savings by pensioners. This exerts further pressure on the interest rates.

✓ Demographic shifts in past decades have exacerbated global inflation through the relative increase in the number of workers compared to pensioners. Looking ahead, the labour market is expected to contract in countries with an ageing population, while consumption remains stable. This situation, characterised by the same demand but less production and consequently supply, points to higher inflation.

The availability of financing plays a crucial role in capital investments. Does an older society tend to save more than a younger one? Will the desired savings amount be greater or less than the desired investment amount? The necessary balance between the two can be achieved by adjusting the equilibrium interest rate or R*: if the appetite for investment, and therefore the demand for savings, increases, the interest rate (price of money) goes up. It's a fundamental matter of supply and demand.

Saving less

On the savings side, there is the life cycle hypothesis developed by Nobel laureates Franco Modigliani and Milton Friedman. The great baby boomer generation, which is now retiring, once again plays the leading role. According to the hypothesis, consumption throughout one's life remains more or less constant. This is confirmed in the real world. Young people often borrow money to sustain their consumption (including the purchase of a home). From about the age of 35, income gradually surpasses expenditures. We save from the age of 60 to 65. Once retired, income drops sharply. This compels us to 'dissave'. The retirement of the large generation of baby boomers should therefore result in a substantial reduction in accumulated savings, all other things being equal.

A study by the World Bank[144] confirms this savings behaviour in countries such as the US, UK and Germany. However, in Japan, Italy and Spain[145], the elderly seem to continue saving (for the time being). The unfolding of events remains uncertain, prompting us to break down the situation step by step. What happens with government spending on pensions and healthcare? In the final years of life, individual expenditures tend to peak as a result of rising healthcare costs. A substantial portion of these healthcare costs is covered by the public sector. This is a transfer from the young to the elderly that shows no sign of diminishing soon. In Japan, young people's stagnating income results from higher taxes intended to finance the rising health expenditure. A taste of what's to come for other ageing nations!

The 'silvering' – the rise in the number of individuals aged 80 and above – outpaces 'greying' (the rise in the number of those aged 65 and above), placing an additional burden on healthcare finances. In addition, the retirement age in many countries does not keep pace with the growth in life expectancy. This results in a lengthening of the period during which individuals enjoy their pensions relative to their working years. Some – those with more foresight – save more as a result, while others don't. The share of working life in the total lifespan has already shrunk significantly over the past half century, straining public finances. The finance burden on the younger generation, in the form of higher taxes, is expected to further increase, as they bear the responsibility of covering current and future debts. Are we heading towards diminishing pensions? The political influence of a steadily growing demographic of pensioners and almost-pensioners prevents radical change in pension and healthcare systems.

France: live longer, work less Source: own calculations

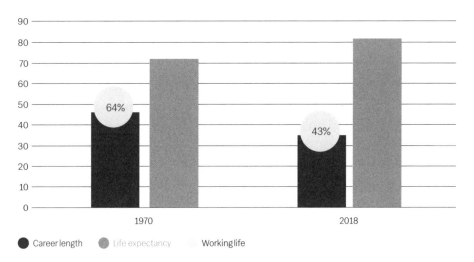

What is the net effect of saving? In 2018, Adrià Morron Salmeron of the Caixa-Bank[146] compiled all changes in the composition of the population pyramid for the US, Spain and Portugal. The result of this demographic shift, without considering other matters influencing savings behaviour, points to a decline in aggregated savings rates for the period 2018–2030 by approximately 1 percentage point. That is a one-fifth reduction compared to rates in 2017.

Effect on interest rates

The net balance between savings and investments influences the interest rate. How has this interest rate been influenced by the ageing population in recent decades? In the US and globally, an increase in savings combined with decreased investment – attributed to a slower increase in the labour force – led to a 1.25 to 2 percentage point reduction in short-term interest rates from the 1980s to 2015, according to studies by the US central bank[147, 148] and the Bank of England[149]. They also predict continued low interest rates for the future, mainly as a result of rising life expectancy. This will encourage households to save even more. In addition, the ageing of the population will lead to a greater relative proportion of older people with more saved capital. This means that a larger amount is saved for the entire economy.

The latter is also the reasoning of Gertjan Vlieghe, former member of the interest rate-setting committee of the Bank of England. In a speech[150] at the London School of Economics, he focused on the shift from the neutral R* as a result of the demographic transition. 'The crucial insight is that this demographic transition revolves around the desired asset position [savings stock] of the entire population rather than the savings flow of the elderly,' says Vlieghe.

So, the situation involves more than retiring baby boomers who, before retirement, accumulate substantial savings and thereafter spend them (the savings flow). That would make R* decrease at first, then increase again. More significantly, a growing segment of the population has a larger desired amount of savings to finance their retirement. 'People in the 50 age group hold many more assets than they did at age 40.' Assets peak around age 65 in the UK. Vlieghe demonstrates that the extra savings from the larger middle-aged group exceed the modest disbursements of pensioners. The group aged 60–90 is expected to experience the fastest growth in the coming four decades. How will the total assets held, or average assets per citizen, evolve in the future if the number of assets held per age profile stabilises at the current level?

'The ageing effect increased the asset ownership per citizen over the last thirty years (see graph). This process is far from over and, to all expectations, will not reverse. In fact we are only two thirds of the way into this demographic transition.' The effect on the equilibrium interest rate also partly depends on the extent to which people at a certain age anticipate increasing life expectancy and would therefore save even more. Vlieghe concludes: 'Either there will be more downward pressure on the equilibrium interest rate, or it will simply remain low. There is no upward pressure of a demographic nature, neither in the short term nor the long term.' This seems clear enough.*

Evolution of total wealth per capita taking into account age profile and current wealth Source: Gertjan Vlieghe, 'Running out of room'

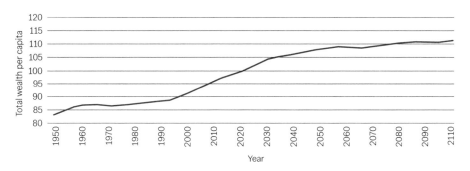

Effect on inflation

Demographic shifts have an impact on the real R*. Inflation becomes relevant when determining the long-term interest rate, and many factors influence inflation. Here we will limit ourselves to the demographic factors.

Demographic tendencies may have helped suppress inflation in the last decades. The overall ratio between the number of workers (taking into account labour force participation, unemployment, etc.) and the number of consumers – the so-called National Transfer Account support ratio – reached its lowest point in the 1970s. In the three decades that followed, the number of working individuals rose faster as more women went to work and the number of dependent children per household decreased. This rising ratio of employees to consumers corresponds to an increase in the ratio of production to consumption. Therefore, a rising support ratio is deflationary: it pushes prices lower.

---

* The total wealth in the world can be calculated by keeping the current wealth at a certain age constant and multiplying it by the most recent UN estimates of the yearly age profiles. To control for total population growth, the result is then divided by the total population.

Nevertheless, beginning in 2010 in the US and a few years later worldwide, the support ratio began to decline. The baby boomers are retiring, but keep spending. A decline in the number of workers in relation to consumption points towards inflation. The increasing share of health services among the elderly in this consumption also contributes to this. The costs of healthcare services, where efficiency gains are hard to realise, increase faster than the costs in goods producing sectors.

The increasing ageing costs will be passed on in higher taxes for employees, or the employees will choose to continue working for a longer period. These workers will not accept their fate helplessly this time. The tightness on the labour market gives them negotiating power, and they will use that to negotiate higher wages. At the same time, politicians will be under pressure from an older voter base to accommodate their caregivers. Wage inflation in these and other sectors ultimately leads to higher future overall inflation.

That is also the conclusion of a study by the BIS.[151] 'We find a link between a population's age structure and inflation, in line with the life cycle hypothesis,' the authors say. 'A larger share of young and old in the population is associated with higher inflation. Conversely, a larger share of working age people is associated with lower inflation. The finding is statistically significant.' The age structure and changes therein explain a large part of inflation trends in the long term, both at national and global levels. 'In the US, for example, it represents a 7 percentage point increase from the 1950s to the mid-1970s, and a similar decline since the 1980s.'

What lies ahead? 'Based on this historical relationship, it predicts rising inflation over the coming decades.' Over the past fifty years, the increasing share of people of working age has pushed down average inflation by 3 percentage points. In the next fifty years, the rise of the elderly will dominate, resulting in a 3% increase in average inflation. For rapidly ageing countries, such as Italy and Spain, this is slightly more. However, for all individual countries, there is an upward effect.

THE NEW WORLD ECONOMY

IMPACT *on the* STOCK MARKET *and* REAL ESTATE MARKET

✓ The asset meltdown hypothesis suggests that the recent inflow into pension funds will turn into an outflow as baby boomers retire. But for the time being, baby boomers are not dissaving.

✓ The hypothesis loses some of its power year after year. Fixed performance pension funds convert the amount saved upon retirement into an annual sum to be paid out to the pensioner. This automatic wave of dissaving increases with more pensioners. Nevertheless, such pension funds lose popularity every year.

✓ In recent decades, a winning investment strategy has been to identify the assets in which the early baby boomers invested their money and where they spent it, and then replicate those choices. This pattern is expected to continue in the future.

✓ Older people continue to live in their own homes longer than expected and often even invest in real estate to rent out. That limits supply and supports prices. Smaller households, and therefore more of them, also contribute to the demand.

✓ In about ten years, the housing market will be subject to the asset meltdown hypothesis due to the long lifespan of a home and the oversupply resulting from the decreasing number of baby boomers. Real house prices are expected to decrease.

✓ In the US, the crucial generation of 25 to 35-year-olds will grow faster than those over 80 in the coming years. Demand will therefore exceed supply. However, this does not apply to Europe.

✓ Rapid urbanisation in China in the coming decades is a positive factor for real estate. It temporarily dampens the downward pressure resulting from the high valuation and the rapidly ageing population.

Will Granny and Grandpa
crash the stock market?

In recent years there has been an inflow of money to pension funds and financial markets. The baby boomers are preparing for retirement *en masse*. But the inflow is changing into an outflow. By mid-2020, pension plans will need to sell assets to pay pension benefits to an increasing number of seniors. 'It is as if the waters of the Mississippi suddenly stopped flowing southwards and turned towards the north,' says a financial commentator. This results in a collapse, an asset meltdown of the financial markets.

Because the US controls more than half of the world's pension assets, the country plays a central role in the story. Many studies on this have been published and a nice overview – with frequently conflicting results – can be found in literature by Thenuwara et al.[152] Their conclusion: 'It is clear that the effects of population ageing on asset markets are more complex than predicted by the life cycle theory. The existing literature reveals that the changing age structure has an impact on asset markets that should not be neglected. An asset meltdown may never come to fruition, but it nevertheless remains plausible that ageing will have a significant negative impact on asset prices.'

The main reason for not predicting a crash is the fact that the elderly hardly dissave. Why not? Maybe they have friends who have grown older than 90 and as a result do not wish to use up their savings too fast. Maybe they are saving to cover the high bills of elderly healthcare. Or maybe they wish to bequeath a part of their savings to their children and grandchildren.

The percentage of assets invested in shares also does not collapse as one gets older. Yet this goes against the expected trend: as the investment horizon shortens, the preference should shift towards secure assets that aren't prone to a 25% drop from one week to the next. An American study[153] by John Ameriks and Stephen Zeldes based on a random sample of 16,000 accounts from a large pension fund found no evidence that ageing households are gradually allocating less to equities. And even if retiring baby boomers eventually reduce their stock ownership, this transition will be spread out over many years.

What about the pension funds? Some of the pension savings are invested in 'defined-benefit' corporate pension plans, which automatically 'dissave' – they automatically disburse funds (and this is mandatory in the US). In this system, the pensioner receives a fixed annuity upon retirement and the pension fund must liquidate part of the saved amount every year. However, the crucial question remains unanswered regarding other occupational pensions, specifically the 'defined-contribution' type,' notes James Poterba, professor at the Massachusetts Institute of Technology (MIT) and a long-time sceptic of the asset meltdown hypothesis. Will these pensions also be 'depleted'? 'With this type of pension, participants in the US are free to sell or not sell the assets upon retirement. Converting into an annual benefit has been the exception for these company pensions. The key question is whether beneficiaries will disburse funds following the philosophy of the life cycle hypothesis. If that does not occur, then the asset-meltdown scenario loses much of its significance.' Currently, that scenario is not unfolding.

Declining popularity of 'defined benefit' company pensions undermines asset meltdown hypothesis

To date, it appears that the majority of pensioners do not sell their 'defined-contribution' corporate pension plans. On top of this is the declining popularity of 'defined-benefit' corporate pension plans over the past two decades.

With a 'defined-benefit' plan the employee receives an annual fixed benefit until the beneficiary dies. Disbursement under these pension schemes amounts to automatic dissaving. Because of the guarantee of a certain fixed benefit, these company pensions are riskier for companies. In 2005, they totalled $2.251 trillion in the US. Together with the $3.739 trillion in fixed contribution pensions, this accounted for a third of the total US stock market capitalisation.

At the end of 2018, the combination still accounted for a third of the almost doubled total market capitalisation. However, fixed contribution pensions had doubled in value to $7.55 trillion, whereas 'defined-benefit' pension plans only increased by half to $3.4 trillion. The share of company pensions that are automatically dissaved is therefore systematically losing importance.*

---

* Note that the value of assets in individual retirement accounts (IRAs) is approximately the same as those in defined contribution company pensions. Under current law, pensioners must begin making withdrawals from tax-advantaged accounts when they turn 67. Such withdrawals may

Europe slightly more vulnerable than the US

Statutory pensions represent a much larger share of pensioners' total income in Europe. The second pillar of company pensions is – with the exception of the Netherlands, the United Kingdom and Switzerland – far less developed. Dissaving by company pensions is therefore much less of a threat, as assets are still relatively limited. On the other hand, and in most European countries, initiatives to further develop the second pension pillar could potentially support the financial markets. European politicians also have little choice, given the rising pension debt. There is a need for new legislation to prevent real pensions in the future from becoming smaller than they are today.

When company pensions are established, deposits exceed benefits in the first decades: all employees contribute, and only the elderly receive benefits over time. Company pensions usually achieve maturity about 40 years after their inception. This means that in most European countries, the second pension pillar will not reach full maturity until 2040–2045. After that, the benefits will exceed the deposits. In the period 2008–2020, according to the ECB, total assets for the eurozone grew sharply from 14% to 25% of its GDP. In most countries, assets remain below 20%. In the more mature Dutch market, where occupational pension payments account for 43% of total pension income, there was a near-doubling of assets to 210% of GDP.

The enormous overweight in the Netherlands is the Achilles heel in the story. Even if the build-up in other European countries continues, it can never compensate for the significant outflow from the mature Dutch – and British – company pensions. With savings of nearly 1.7 trillion euros (fully as 'defined-benefit'), the Netherlands accounts for two thirds of all company pensions in the eurozone. Outside the eurozone, the UK accounts for 2.7 trillion pounds (3.13 trillion euro), of which one third consists of 'defined-benefit' pensions.

In recent years, there has been a net inflow in the Netherlands. But that will change. In its *Ageing Report*, the European Commission requested long-term

depress share prices, but part of the money will be simply transferred to non-tax-advantaged retirement accounts to be reinvested in stocks.

projections from the member states on the expected evolution of pension funds over the period 2019–2070. Only ten countries provided this information, mainly smaller Central and Eastern European countries. But the Netherlands did provide this information, and its pension outflows will increase from 5% of GDP annually in 2019 to 6.5% in 2070. The deposits will evolve from 4 to 4.5% over the same period. The net outflow will therefore increase from 1% to 2% of GDP.

Today, the young European pension funds are not yet dissaving. This dissaving is the central pillar of the asset meltdown hypothesis. For pension funds, this seems inevitable in the near future. The UK is already in that dissaving phase, while the Netherlands is rapidly approaching it. This is also the conclusion of consultant Mercer in 2019. 'Across Europe, including the UK, 72% of "defined-benefit" pension plans expect to be cash flow negative over the next ten years.' More is then paid out to pensioners than the inflow of contributions.

It is challenging to determine the potential magnitude of the sales pressure. A rough calculation provides the following insight: for the major pension funds, notably in the UK and the Netherlands, almost 50% is invested in bonds, a third in shares (including funds) and the remainder mostly in cash. Based on a calculated total current estimated* pension amount of 2.981 trillion euros for 'defined goal' pensions, this translates to 990 billion euros. To put this into perspective, it should be compared to a market capitalisation of approximately 65,420 billion euros for the US, the UK and Europe combined. The 2018 net cash outflow of €14 billion – where benefits exceeded income in the UK and the Netherlands – will increase in the future. Even if that amount were to double to 28 billion euros (30 billion dollars), it would still represent a selling pressure of only 0.04% compared to the current market capitalisation of the three equity markets mentioned. This assumes that the disbursed amounts in the UK and the Netherlands go towards consumption and are not reinvested, and that the accumulated assets (210% of GDP in the case of the Netherlands) have not yielded an annual return that compensates for the net outflow. There are therefore many hypotheses with, in the

---

* Bond yields still fluctuated around 2019 levels in 2022. We assume that two-thirds of the shares are invested in Europe and the UK and one-third in the US. The European and British shares remained stable compared to 2019. American shares stood a third higher. A third of the $2.9 trillion in 'defined goal' pension assets (2019) will increase by 30%. We assumed that the rest of the amount would remain stable. This leaves us with $3.19 trillion in defined benefit pension assets for the UK and Netherlands compared to $2.9 trillion in 2019.

worst case, a slightly increased sales pressure. Based on this, anticipating an asset meltdown seems premature.

The baby boom python

'In past decades a winning strategy consisted in determining which assets the first baby boomers would invest in, and then do the same,' write the financial experts Sterling and Waite in their book *Boomernomics*. 'When they were investing in real estate in the 1970s and early 1980s, it was a good time for everyone to get into real estate. The switch to stocks in the 1980s was the signal for the rest to do the same.'

'And as they turn more to bonds as they get older, don't be surprised to see bonds outperform stocks for an unusually long period. One goes where the baby boomers go.' Prophetic words. And no, the excellent performance of bonds is certainly not just a result of a greater allocation towards more safe assets by baby boomers. But it won't have done any harm.

The baby boomers have an impact on interest rates, as well as on the demand for products and services. 'You shouldn't put all your money on the baby boomers,' cautioned John Rogers, the economist at the Bureau of Labour Statistics (BLS), who in the 2000s was tasked with overseeing the annual survey of consumer spending among Americans. 'But they are still the demographic pig wriggling through the python.' That pig will cause the population group consisting of people aged 65 to 80 and over to explode in the coming decades. In the US, the echo boomers, the children of the baby boomers, will push the 35–45 year old category even higher in the next ten years. In Europe, the population growth of all categories under the age of 55 is negative.

What is the spending pattern in each age category? Consumption expenditure statistics, including those from the BLS and the French INSEE (Institut national de la statistique et des études économiques), are excellent sources. These total expenditures follow a hump-shaped profile with a sharp increase between the ages of 25 and 45. The increase levels off and peaks between the ages of 45 and 55. A gradual decline then sets in until the age of 65 and drops more and more rapidly thereafter. The over-80s spend on average just over half that of 45–55-year-olds. In Europe, spending is falling faster than in the US after the peak in the 45–55

Eurozone: increase per age category, per decade Source: World Bank

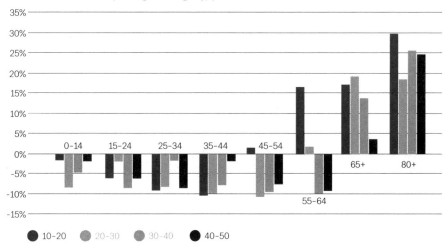

US: increase per age category, per decade Source: World Bank

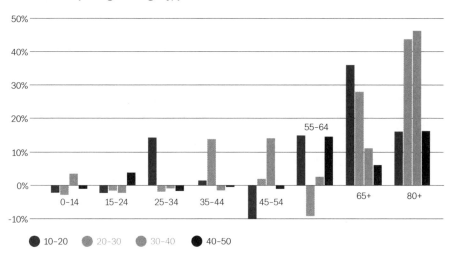

age category. In the US, most people don't retire until age 65 – or even later. In Europe, this retirement age only applies in theory and many people start enjoying their old age much earlier.

With a demographic profile of mainly more people over 65, the future spending pattern for the economy as a whole does not look great, does it? You need to be careful with that conclusion. The biggest mistake made in predicting the future spending patterns of baby boomers (or Gen X following them) is that it is based on what people from a previous generation did at a certain age. For the expenditure in ten years of current 45–55-year-olds, current over-65s are taken into account. But will the 45 to 55-year-olds of today behave the same way in 10 years as the current 65-year-olds? Baby boomers and the Gen Xers have – certainly in the US – grown up with Mastercard and Visa. Will they suddenly stop spending just because they have reached a certain age?

No, concludes researcher Marceline Bodier, who follows the evolution of spending within the same generation. This is equivalent to following one person's spending habits over their entire lifetime. In this way one can separate the age effect from the effect of belonging to a specific generation.

'The oldest generations undoubtedly did not start their lives with the same prospects for living standards as the most recent,' the INSEE economist writes in her study.[154] 'Their youth took place during one of the two World Wars or between the two, in other words, during times of scarcity, or times when the standard of living was much lower than in the second half of the 20th century. But afterward, even if the living standard of these families increased and even if the "consumer society" prompted them to consume more, they still clung to the habit of spending less than their offspring did at the same age.'

Although there were no world wars in the US, there is also a likely difference in spending patterns between the pre-war generations and the retiring baby boomers. We compared American expenditure statistics from 2004 and 2013. In 2004, 65-year-olds spent 12% less than 55-year-olds. For the 75 versus 65-year-olds, that difference was 23%. Ten years later, the difference between the 65 and 55-year-olds had fallen to 7%. 75-year-olds spent only 16% less. The retired baby boomers spend more for a longer time than the previous generation. But a 'settling of accounts' did follow as soon as they moved to the 80-plus category. There, spending plummeted by a third in the 2013 survey compared to 'just' a quarter in the 2014 survey.

The expenditure of baby boom seniors will be higher than that of the previous generation. But a reversal of the existing trend – lower consumption at a later age – will not follow. The sharp decline in expenditure among the over-80s, in combination with the rapid increase in that age cohort, puts additional pressure on total expenditure. The alert investor can best focus on products and services that ageing baby boomers prefer.

The New Seniors, or old wine in new bottles?

What do older families spend their money on? According to the INSEE study, expenditure increases for heating and lighting, household services and healthcare. Consumption of food is greatest in middle age; it decreases after 70. From the family expenditure reported by the BLS, we draw more or less the same conclusions. There are some other specific expenses that stabilise at a high level in both surveys from age 55 and later: insurance (life insurance, health insurance), care products and services (spending on hair salons), gardening, fresh fruit and vegetables, fish and wine.

The prospects are less favourable for clothing stores and vehicle sellers. Clothing and transport are regarded as work-related expenditures. In Belgium, there is also a requirement that the company car financed by the company must be returned at the end of an employee's career. Most seniors buy a car that costs significantly less when they are paying out of their own pockets.

Sectors of the future

Boomers like / need...	These providers benefit from that:
Financial advice	Asset managers, stock brokers, financial advisors
Adjustments to home interiors	DIY chains
Active relaxation	Gardening equipment, cruises, holiday-related items, luxury cars and mopeds, good hotels, casinos
Relaxation at home	Consumer electronics, pet and related shops, hobby shops
Eternal youth	Wellness, spas, vitamins and preparations, fitness-related products, cosmetic procedures, care products, fresh vegetables and fruit, fish, Weight Watchers products, wine, premium beers
Healthcare	Medicines for age-related diseases, orthopaedic industry, generic manufacturers, biotechnology sector

Boomers don't like...	This is painful for:
Clothing	Clothing stores, textile manufacturers
Reading material	Magazine and newspaper publishers
Unhealthy foods	Fast food, traditional beers

Real estate is very sensitive to an asset price meltdown scenario. However, the most important factor for the valuation of real estate remains location. In this respect, Flanders has numerous assets.

Source Koen De Leus, *Naar Grijsland*

389

What about relaxation? Seniors are less likely to jump on a bike for a small tour, but the electric version does appeal. More limited mobility at a certain age also provides less incentive to attend sporting events or theatre performances. But again, one has to be cautious in warning about gloomy days ahead for the leisure sector. INSEE[155] examined how expenditure on entertainment evolves *within the same generation*. That analysis points to peak leisure expenditure between the ages of 60–64 and 70–74. The amount spent by the 60 to 64-year-olds on leisure was 118% of what they spent when they were 40 to 44.

Real estate more vulnerable to meltdown hypothesis

What about real estate? The most controversial study of the demographic impact on the housing market was published in 1990. At the time, two renowned economists, David Weil and Gregory Mankiw, warned of an impending crash of American house prices. Mankiw, now a professor at Harvard University, was later appointed as chairman of the Council of Economic Advisers to president George W. Bush, a position he held from 2003 to 2005.

The two academics forecast a 50% drop in prices for the two coming decades. As baby boomers leave their prime home buying years, they predicted that demand for homes would drop sharply. It didn't take long before it became clear that the prediction was too pessimistic. Strong demand ensured steady price increases in most regions.

Part of the reason the two academics missed the mark was an overly pessimistic forecast of the increase in the number of families. 'In the mid-1990s, the US Census Bureau revised its projections upward,' according to BCA Research. 'It underestimated immigration.' The percentage of homeowners also increased sharply in the 1990s: from 64% to 69% in the period 1994–2004. There it stabilised until 2006, before tumbling to 63% in 2016 after the Global Financial Crisis.

Did the authors finally manage to drive their point home when the American real estate market crashed in 2007–2008, along with many European ones? No, because despite the collapse of the house of cards based on repackaged mortgages, the percentage of homeowners has in the meantime risen again to 65%. The value of homes as a percentage of total economic assets corrected from a peak of 39% to 37% in 2016 (latest available figure). But this is still 2 percentage points higher than when the authors made their forecast. In Belgium it increased from 39% to 47%, in France from 53% to 59%, and even in the Netherlands, which was hit hard during the eurozone crisis, it rose from 41% to 42%. In all industrialised countries the ratio is much higher than in the mid-1990s, and since the last available figure in 2016, house prices worldwide have skyrocketed by more than 20% in real terms.[156]

Falling mortgage rates have supported prices over the past thirty years. Smaller households pushed demand. From 2010 to 2018, the percentage of one-person families in the total number of families increased from 27% to 28% in the US and from 31% to 34% in Europe.

The elderly also do not dissave when it comes to homes. The BIS[157] conducted research into the evolution of house prices in various regions in South Korea, a rapidly ageing society. The study showed a positive link between the growing share of older people and house prices: the price increased in districts with many 65-plus-year-olds. Contrary to what the life cycle hypothesis assumes, the increased life expectancy of the elderly prompts extra investment in the housing market, for purchased as well as rented dwellings. Even when the elderly have an urgent need of money for medical expenses, they will sell their financial assets first. Housing is the last asset they are selling.

As members of the baby boomer generation die, it will undoubtedly have an effect on the housing market. Their homes will end up in the real estate market. Today, the baby boom generation is 57 to 77 years of age. The average life expectancy in the G7 fluctuates between 77 (US) and 84 (Japan) years. Whoever reaches 65 expects a life expectancy of 87 (including in the US). In a decade, the pressure on the real estate market will increase, unless this increase in available homes is compensated for by demand created through increased immigration. Immigration offers an elegant solution to many demographic and other challenges. The current trend towards more singles also increases the demand for housing. But even if the trend persists – in the face of the assured demise of the baby boomers – it will do so at a slower pace. By the way, half of all singles are renters. This is advantageous for smaller residential units, since their parents' larger homes are not sold as quickly.

The US has a lower life expectancy, but nevertheless it has some aces up its sleeve. The country is hitting a demographic sweet spot. The number of people in the crucial 25–35 age group will increase in the coming years. That is the age at which they are most likely to get married, start a family and buy a new home. This follows a decade when starting a family and construction were at an unusually low ebb because of the subprime crisis. 'The percentage of homeowners is still at a fairly low level,' said Peter Berezin, Chief Global Strategist at BCA Research during a client presentation in Brussels.[158] 'And less than 1% of homes are for sale. That is a historically low level.' This supports house prices in the short term, despite rising mortgage interest rates putting pressure on affordability.

Eurozone: demographic profile 2020

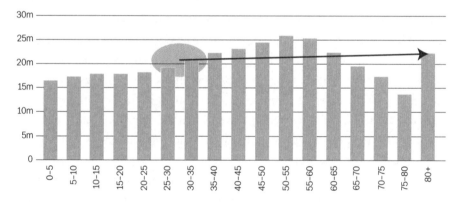

US: demographic profile 2020

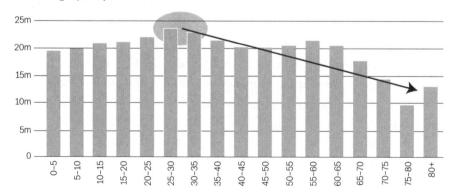

Unfortunately, we cannot discern the same potential in Europe. In Europe there are 19 million 25 to 29-year-olds and 21 million 30 to 35-year-olds compared to 22 million people over 80. The number of people reaching the age group of 30+ will not keep pace with the number of people reaching old age. Net demand for real estate will start to shrink.

In China, the peak of thirty-somethings was also reached quite some time ago. Yet house prices in the cities there continued to rise steadily until 2021*. The lifesaver is the growing degree of urbanisation. Citizens immigrating from rural areas to the city need apartments. The degree of urbanisation climbed from 50% to 64% between 2010 and today. The target by 2035 is 70%, according to a report by the National Academy for Economic Strategy. In Western countries, that is 80% on average. Does that prevent a correction? Not according to Berezin. 'In the short term, the money that the Chinese have saved up during their long lockdown will flow into real estate. That keeps it afloat. But in the medium term, there remains a significant surplus and over-valuation in the Chinese real estate market, and a correction will take place.'

In the US, the population will continue to grow in the future. Europe does not have that luxury. The likelihood of the asset price meltdown scenario is also much greater in the real estate market than in any other financial submarket. This is a result of specific characteristics of the housing market: namely the long lifespan of a home and the inelastic supply (supply cannot immediately adapt to demand). In spite of reduced demand, houses are not usually demolished due to oversupply. There is a surplus and prices fall.

The IMF[159] established as much in Japan. House prices fall faster in prefectures with a declining population (due to ageing or emigration). The fall in house prices in large cities, such as the broader area of the Tokyo, Osaka and Fukuoka regions, has remained limited. Cities will therefore probably withstand population decline better than rural areas.

Will prices fall in all other countries with ageing populations? In the short term that will depend on whether the market is under- or over-valued. After the

---

* The Chinese government-imposed lending restrictions on debt-laden real estate developers in 2020. Banks also had to scale back their exposure to the sector. The result was the bankruptcy of several large real estate developers, with Evergrande as the best known. The real estate crisis was more or less under control in 2023.

Covid pandemic, the valuation ratios pointed towards a reasonably high valuation for many industrialised countries. Increasing interest rates led to a correction, causing the over-valuations to decrease somewhat. In the medium and long term, however, the ageing wave will continue unabated. Once the population really starts to shrink, the pressure on real estate will rapidly increase, especially in Europe. Over the past half century, real house prices for 25 major industrialised countries have risen by 1.25% per year.[160] I do not expect this to continue in the coming half century.

The Lonely Century

'I wandered lonely as a cloud That floats on high o'er vales and hills,
When all at once I saw a crowd, A host of golden daffodils'

————

WILLIAM WORDSWORTH

Another important demographic trend is the growth in the number of single families in Western society. According to Datamonitor and Our World in Data, this concerns an average of a quarter of families, in some countries even 40%. In a city like Stockholm, three out of five residents live alone.

Single-person families can be roughly divided into three groups. First, there are young people who choose to live alone, for example students in student accommodation. Some of them continue living alone even after their student years. Second, there is the group of people who have ended their relationships, with or without children, who stay with one of the two ex-partners every other week. Finally, single widows and widowers are also considered single-person families if there are no more children living in the parental home.

Esteban Ortiz-Ospina, researcher at Our World in Data, wrote an interesting article about this trend. Historical data shows that the rise of single living began more than a century ago in early industrialised countries and accelerated around 1950. Figures show that people in richer countries live alone more often.

The national income per head of the population and the number of one-person homes are strongly correlated. There is a greater chance of people choosing to live alone in richer countries.

But loneliness is much more deeply rooted. Loneliness is observed not only in the various age groups, but also in all layers and social classes within our society. Even before the corona pandemic caused social recession, three in five American adults already reported feeling lonely. We see the same in Europe. There, two thirds of the population says that loneliness is a serious problem. In the United Kingdom, the problem became so acute that a 'Minister for Loneliness' was appointed in 2018; one in eight Britons claimed to have no friends. Three quarters of Britons don't know the names of their neighbours, while 60% report feeling lonely at work. We see similar results in many other countries worldwide.

According to a recent Japanese study, millions of young people between the ages of 15 and 39 isolate themselves without any form of social contact and feel lonely. The Japanese refer to these *hikikomori* as a lost generation. Many elderly Japanese look for radical solutions to escape their loneliness. The number of crimes committed by people above 65 has more than quadrupled in recent years. This usually involves relatively small matters, such as petty theft. The goal is to end up in jail, and thus obtain access to social contacts, to a community.

These are just some of the figures from the well-researched book *The Lonely Century* by Noreena Hertz. If you read these unsettling statistics and, like me, are at first surprised and then feel lucky, this hopefully means that you have a family and circle of friends to fall back on.

There is plenty of research clearly indicating that loneliness makes people not only mentally sick, but also physically sick. There are research reports indicating that loneliness is more harmful than insufficient exercise, alcoholism or obesity. One report even states that the impact on our health from loneliness is equivalent to smoking fifteen cigarettes a day.

For society, this trend once again means an explosion of healthcare costs and a huge decline in productivity. For innovation to occur, interactions are necessary. Less interaction equals less innovation. It can be that simple.

There is much discussion about the role that social media and our smartphones play in the whole story. A somewhat less radical approach than deliberately trying to end up in jail is to seek out an online community of like-minded people. The deep human need to belong drives entire groups of people towards extremism in all its various forms. On social media we follow role models with thousands of followers and friends, who look good and live a fantastically exciting (social) life. It is easy to become unhappy through comparison, and to feel lonely, especially if you don't get enough 'likes'. Moreover, this is not even taking into consideration the world of AI, where digital conclusions can quickly be drawn based on the data you leave behind in your online activities – conclusions you would rather not see.

Megatech companies know more and more about us, including how we feel, and AI can perfectly respond to that. If we are going through a grieving process, each of the steps can be accompanied by music and images specially chosen for us. If they are not only so deep into our heads but also into our hearts, then advertising for a product, service, person or party will be very effective, right?

But social media is only part of the story. The reasons for loneliness are numerous and diverse. There is massive immigration to 'anonymous' cities, radical change in working environment, and an even more radical change in how we live. We generally do less together and have less physical contact – however you may define it.

Now I am treading on thin ice. The way the pendulum swings from individualism to collectivism and back is generational – at least in part. Nowhere is this better described than in the book *The Fourth Turning* by William Strauss and Neil Howe. The ideas laid out there are very profound. You don't have to be in agreement with all their analyses, and I certainly do not agree with all their conclusions. But the book does what any good book should do: it provides insights and is a starting point for analysis and discussion. The idea is that every long life (the Romans call it a *saeculum*), which today extends to an ample eighty years, can be divided into 'turnings'. Every generation that comes to power sees life differently and organises the world differently. This is also and often one of the causes of generational conflict. That is because the generation that has previously been in leadership positions often does not particularly like the new direction. In this concept, which is reminiscent of Kondratieff waves, the succession of generations is particularly important. Within the whole list of characteristics there is always an individual or collectivist element. This would mean that today's world, with its focus on the individual and personal development, could shift back to the collective during a 'turning'. I often see this, perhaps because I expect to, in the younger generation. But I also notice it, and perhaps this is confirmation bias again, when I step into a bookstore. How many books are there about self-development, smart hacks, atomic habits and so on? They all address the individual: how I can become stronger, better, smarter or richer. For books about how we move forward as a group, the best place to go is the discounted books table, somewhere at the back of the store. These are usually not very recent works. It may be that the next generational switch will introduce a more collective society, a more collective capitalism and a slightly diminished lonely century. Then again, perhaps not...

Whatever the future may bring, it is clear today that a true loneliness economy is emerging. When 'economy' and 'emerging' occur in the same sentence, I automatically think of investment opportunities. Not because I want to make money from someone else feeling bad. But because part of my job is to spot trends and position our customers as ideally as possible on their surfboard so that they can ride that hopefully nice, long and not too fickle wave. Furthermore, some ideas from the loneliness economy might just be good.

On a Blue Monday I once thought about a café or café-restaurant with a 1980s theme. Including retro video-gaming consoles and vinyl records. This industry, by the way, is on the rise, which strengthens my belief in the idea. But perhaps this is more my own escape into the past than that of society in general.

If we take a more serious look at the loneliness economy, it is clear that social media companies will definitely grab a slice of the pie, especially if they are supported by AI in the future, keeping us company and telling us what we want to hear. Other ways of living and cohabitating, a kind of cohousing, also seem plausible – even if only to make living a little more affordable. From this perspective, it's no surprise that series such as *Friends* and *Melrose Place* have been so successful portraying young, and after a few seasons, slightly less young/ handsome people who share a close bond of friendship. Who wouldn't want to join in? And if you can't join in, you can at least watch.

Scott Rosenbaum, founder of RentAFriend, has tapped into a concept that originated in Japan. He provides a catalogue of 620,000 platonic flesh-and-blood friends who, for an hourly fee, will be your friend and go shopping with you, have a drink or just talk. The company has in the meantime grown to have branches in more than twelve countries. Customers are often lonely 30 to 40-year-old professionals. It is not difficult to predict that this role could be taken over by advanced, social robots in the future. It should come as no surprise that robotics remains one of our favourite long-term investment themes.

In addition, participating in social events such as concerts is on the rise. The event industry will experience golden times in the coming years. A logical addition to this is the virtual event and gaming world – the metaverse, so to speak. After the initial hype, the idea has currently been somewhat overshadowed by the even more powerful concept of AI. Nevertheless, the two are certainly compatible and mutually reinforcing. Give it time and we will all be spending more time in virtual worlds. And to power these, just like AI, you need huge numbers of semiconductors and lots of energy.

A related trend is that board games, such as Monopoly or Risk, are on the rise again. These can also have a virtual counterpart. It is easier to find fellow players online around the world than in a remote physical location at the wrong time and wrong day. But here too we naturally miss the pleasure of doing something with people who are physically in the same place. Technology can help us and will most likely be a good investment, but it is only part of the solution.

TEN
to REMEMBER

1   Global population growth will slow down and stabilise by the end of 2100. By then, eight out of ten people will live in Asia or Africa.

2   In the top six economies, based on purchase power parity, we see five developing countries in 2050.

3   The Anglo-Saxon countries rank highest in our financial ageing index related to vulnerability. Japan, the UK and most Scandinavian countries exhibit medium vulnerability. We find high vulnerability in Northern and Southern European countries, with Italy and Belgium at the top of that list.

4   Everyone knows that the 'silver bullet' for addressing rising pension and healthcare costs is working longer and increasing employment. But if you are a politician advocating this, how do you get re-elected?

5   While productivity may be the miracle cure, innovation is not one of the strengths of the greying population.

6   The ageing population will keep interest rates low: the larger savings held by the growing group of middle-aged and elderly people more than compensates for the modest dissaving of the pensioners.

7   Inflation will rise in the coming decades due to a faster increase in the number of consumers compared to the number of employees. It was the other way around in the past.

8   Grandparents don't pull the stock market down because they do not dissave.

9   The baby boomers were and remain the demographic pig that wriggles through the python. They determine which products and services are more or less consumed.

10 Real estate will face pressure as the baby boomers pass away in large numbers.

TEN
to INVEST *in*

1   You cannot win the lottery if you do not have a ticket. You have to play in order to win, says David Ricardo.

2   We are heading for a flat age society. We add 'seniorescence' to our glossary and replace the outdated concept of 'career' with 'transiteer'.

3   Given the speed with which technology evolves, a single education is not enough for building 75 years of knowledge. Lifelong learning is needed.

4   Investing more in yourself is the most sensible investment advice you will find in this book.

5   In addition to the 'classic' investment opportunities that the demographic revolution brings, such as biotech, cruise companies or caravan builders, there are many opportunities lurking in less obvious places.

6   Real estate remains, in any case, an interesting investment.

7   Considering yourself too old to buy real estate or stocks is nonsense. Moreover, a good stock portfolio is also a nice inheritance.

8   The shift from a production-based to a services-based society brings with it many opportunities. Wine is probably the most enjoyable.

9   The opportunities for Africa are immense. In the meantime, buy some African art.

10 If the statistics on loneliness surprise or even shock you, consider yourself fortunate, because you're in the right camp. Either way, there is a significant economy being built around loneliness.

✓ **In the short term** we see little change in innovation.
✓ **In the long term** we see a doubling of productivity because of innovation.
  ✓ Growth and the real interest rate increase.
  ✓ Productivity puts downward pressure on inflation.
  ✓ The nominal interest rate thus remains stable.

	Productivity	Realgrowth	Realint.rate	Inflation	Nominalint.rate
2024–2034	0	0	0	0	0
2035–2065	+	+	+	–	0

✓ **In the short term** new countries take part in globalisation.
  ✓ The impact on growth is slightly negative.
✓ **In the long term** the growth impact is positive due to the increase in digital services.
  ✓ This increases productivity and reduces inflation.
  ✓ A multipolar world increases risk premium and real interest rate.
  ✓ Nominal interest rates will rise in the short and long term.

	Productivity	Realgrowth	Realint.rate	Inflation	Nominalint.rate
2024–2034	–	0 / –	0	+	+
2035–2065	0 / +	0 / +	0 / +	0	+

✓ Productivity and real growth decrease
  ✓ The real interest rate decreases as a result of this and the higher amount saved.
  ✓ The higher inflation overcompensates for the lower real interest rate.

	Productivity	Realgrowth	Realint.rate	Inflation	Nominalint.rate
2024–2034	–	–	–	+	0 / +
2035–2065	–	–	–	+	0 / +

- ✓ **In the short term** climate-related investments increase.
    - ✓ Lower productivity due to stranded assets and less investment elsewhere.
    - ✓ Carbon tax is still low and does not weigh heavily on growth.
    - ✓ The real interest rate rises due to investments and high money demand.
    - ✓ Commodity shocks push inflation structurally higher.
    - ✓ The nominal interest rate increases.
- ✓ **In the long term** energy efficiency and productivity increase.
    - ✓ Higher carbon taxes weigh on demand and climate damage increases.
    - ✓ High money demand continues with ultimately neutral impact on real interest rates.
    - ✓ Inflation shocks are softening, but remain present due to climate disruption.
    - ✓ Nominal interest rates stabilise at a lower level than at the beginning of the transition.

	Productivity	Real growth	Real int. rate	Inflation	Nom. int. rate
2024–2034	–	0	0 / +	+	+
2035–2065	+	0	0	0 / +	0

- ✓ **In the short term** there is a flexible budget policy.
    - ✓ This increases real growth and interest rates (greater money demand).
- ✓ **In the long term** savings follow.
    - ✓ This depresses real growth and interest rates.

	Productivity	Real growth	Real int. rate	Inflation	Nom. int. rate
2024–2034	0	+	+	+	+
2035–2065	0	–	–	+	+

	Productivity	Real growth	Real int. rate	Inflation	Nom. int. rate
2024–2034	–	0 / –	0	+	+
2035–2065	+	+	0 / +	+	+

EPILOGUE

'Any sufficiently advanced technology is indistinguishable from magic.'

———

ARTHUR C. CLARKE

It is 17:00, 14 December 2044, and the voice of my personal assistant wakes me from my power nap.

'Time to get up. Your guests will arrive in two hours and we have a lot to do. We may need to make a few final adjustments, you need to get changed, and it looks like there's a lot of traffic.'

'Thank you, Maynard. But first I'm going to drink a cup of coffee in the dream room. Then we can review the presentation for our client.'

'Which environment did you have in mind?'

'Do the philosophy salon in Rue Saint-Roch.'

I enter the room and find myself in mid-18th-century Paris. I look out the window at the rain and the carriages rattling over the cobblestones. All my life I've been fascinated by how clusters of creativity have always formed throughout history around scientists, writers, philosophers, artists and – let's not forget – financiers and facilitators. These clusters push new ideas and inventions into the world. An example is the Velvet Underground, where people like Andy Warhol and David Bowie exchanged ideas. But my preference leans even more towards the philosophers of the Rue Saint-Roche, which is beautifully described in *A Wicked Company* by Philipp Blom.

While I drink my coffee, my thoughts go back to that rainy day when I left a meeting early in order to wander the streets of the City of Light and I discovered this place where philosophical history was written. Today in my dream room I smell how the scent of rain mixes with that of old books. The addition of scent has strongly improved the quality of dream experiences like this one. It has also done no harm to the Senso-reality share price. Maynard takes me out of my dream world.

'I do not think that many changes are required. The markets are presently stable. The NASDAQ is at 35,586 points, the commodity complex is still peaking, the prices of the currencies have hardly moved. And almost all trends for the themes and sectors we have identified are intact.'

'Almost all trends?'

'The Global South stock index is still above its fifty- and two-hundred-day average, but on a relative basis it is somewhat weaker compared to the rest of the world. A number of Latin American indices, in particular, are having a more difficult time. Commodity prices are under pressure and there is also an increase in political unrest. A number of African indices are breaking out again.'

The raw materials, especially the metals that were needed for the energy transition, have increased enormously in the last two decades. An increase that exceeds even my most optimistic predictions. And who said that the value of gold couldn't double?

'Okay, Maynard. Leave the graph of the Global South index, but add the graphs of the indices of Peru and Chile, as well as those of Nigeria and Kenya. And I would also like some headlines and some film material to dress up the case.'

'Which sources should I use: all of them or just the trusted sources?'

'As always, only the trusted sources. Maybe you can add a slide on the deep fake protection tracker, since that item keeps increasing.'

Since the emergence of AI, it is becoming more difficult to distinguish deep fake from reality. Twenty years ago, it was a no-brainer to include internet protection shares in your portfolio. But since then, a rampant arms race has grown between hackers, who were using ever-increasing computer power to create false images and information, and the programs that can detect this.

The best protection systems use even more computing power and are therefore extremely expensive. It is impossible to deploy all that computing power over the public internet. The deep fakers have virtually free rein there. This has created a number of closed and highly secured private virtual environments, for which you have to pay. Real private and protected data (*proprietary data*) are worth their bit weight in gold. Companies such as Bloomberg, Reuters, Visa, Uber and a number of banks and insurance companies are making a huge profit from this. As with every new technology, AI has brought forth unexpected winners.

This whole process started accelerating a decade ago when hackers succeeded in generating a realistic press release regarding the American jobs report. Everyone expected 310,000 jobs to be created. Instead, the hackers sent a message to the world reporting a loss of 450,000 jobs. Interest rates fell and the value of gold rose by 4 %. When the world realised a few minutes later that the story was false, the hackers had already hauled in their profits at the expense of many investors. The public internet companies came up with a measure that linked deepfake protection to a message going viral. The more people see it, the more automatic control there will be. That could only partly restore trust. At the moment, there is a block chain solution in development that can trace the origin of every data item to immediately see if and by whom changes were made.

'If I add those pages, you will have 46 slides. Koen already has 85. That's ambitious for a 1-hour presentation.'

'Just do it. We'll improvise.'

'Shall I send an update to Koen and Aladdin?'

'Yes, do so.'

I cast a glance at the street in Paris and don my suit and tie.

'I have ordered a self-driving vehicle. It will arrive in about five minutes. Shall I provide a bouquet of flowers for your wife when she comes home tonight? It's her birthday. Or shall I have it delivered to her at work?'

'Have it delivered in Brussels. And check if we can see another performance of the musical *Notre Dame* in Paris this weekend.'

'There are still enough seats. The best are in the fourth row. For how many people?'

'For two and also book a car, the train, and a hotel for Saturday and Sunday – the usual.'

We pick up Koen at his home; he fell off his bike again last weekend. Some things never change.

'How are you doing? I see that you have a fair number of slides.'

'You don't need slides to pass time,' answers a battered Koen. 'I have, by the way, added a section on the labour market. That reminds me to call someone to fix the bathroom leak. Aladdin, check if someone is available; things have to get moving.'

'Your plumber is fully booked for the coming four weeks,' answers Koen's personal assistant. 'But 'QuickandDirty' is still available. He has a rating of just over four stars. Shall I ask for a quote?'

'Skip it. One can't negotiate the price anyway. There is always more demand than supply and they can ask whatever they want,' grumbles Koen. 'Sometimes I hate it when I'm right. I wrote about it twenty years ago. It's not that easy to robotise specialised manual labour. *One fine day...*'

'Say, Philippe, shall we have a bottle of wine when we return? I have a beautiful Saint-Estèphe in the central wine collection that is just under twenty years old. It has to be drunk soon! If you want, I can have a drone ... *Shit!*'

We look at the dozens of red brake lights that announce a traffic jam.

'This increases the travel time approximately by 30 minutes and 43 seconds,' reports the ever-accurate Maynard.

'30 minutes and 46 seconds,' Aladdin corrects.

'Ok, ok, Aladdin. Stop the bickering. Better inform the taxi company that we are going into the air,' sighs a visibly pained Koen.

'Flying will raise the price by 100 euro and, because of the increased risk, both your insurance premiums will go up by 0.65 euro.'

'Nothing can be done about it. Go ahead.'

The taxi unfolds its wings and we're soon flying above the highway towards our destination. But we aren't alone. It is always amazing how air traffic control, when assisted by AI, can route everything properly.

Progress hasn't been linear in the last twenty years; it's never like that. There were shocks, black swans and regular market corrections. But in the end, the optimistic sorcerers emerged victorious and the false prophets were proven wrong. Earth can indeed support ten billion people. Though inequality remains, we have all clearly progressed.

'Hey Koen,' asks Philippe, 'do you remember twenty years ago when we wanted to look into the future with *The New World Economy*? Which of your bold predictions has surprised you the most?'

'I don't have to think long about that: that the impact of the technological revolution has not caused enormous social shocks. AI hasn't replaced us yet; it has made us better. We now have Maynard and Aladdin. They might possibly acquire real physical form and step out of their virtual environment. I already have an idea about Aladdin's ideal physical appearance, but I still have to coordinate that with Miriam. The productivity growth that this entire revolution has brought with it... That actually makes me euphoric. And you? You will probably mention those metal shocks and your strong conviction about the explosion of raw materials and gold.'

'The rise in raw materials is now coming to an end. Supply has finally managed to meet demand. But it has indeed been a ride. The exponential growth we'd been expecting turned out to be more exponential than we thought possible. And that ties in nicely with your productivity growth. But if you're feeling melancholy, let's put on some music.

Maynard, will you play *Piano Man* by Billy Joel, please?'

We approach Antwerp and see another traffic jam below. *Plus ça change*. One bright spot: the traffic jam is heading towards the Meir, where we will give our presentation. The light show of vehicles combined with the Christmas lights is breathtakingly beautiful. Everything can be made almost virtual, but that has not reduced the human need for contact and interaction, telling stories and having a drink. On the contrary...

'It's a pretty good crowd for a Saturday
And the manager gives me a smile
Cause he knows that it's me they're been comin' to see
To forget about life for a while...'

———

ABBREVIATIONS
and EXPLANATIONS

TFP = Total Factor Productivity   The increase in productivity – output divided by the number of hours worked – can be the result of increasing capital investments (more and better machines), better trained personnel and how efficiently all inputs are used. That efficiency is called 'total factor productivity' or TFP. An increase in output for a constant number of inputs (capital, labour, energy, materials, services) points to a more efficient and more productive use of the inputs. Research by the ECB in the 12 euro countries that adopted the euro in 1999 shows that the contribution of TFP growth between 1995 and 2019 was on average approximately 60% of labour productivity. Capital deepening, defined as the change in capital per hour worked, averaged about 40%. The contribution of capacity utilisation is limited, but plays an important role during specific periods. The picture is the same for the US.

BIS   Bank for International Settlements, the bank for central banks

CBO   Congressional Budget Office

OBR   Office for Budget Responsibility

Primary deficits   Budget deficits excluding interest costs

QE   Quantitative easing, the buying of financial assets – especially bonds – by central banks. In this way, they push down interest rates.

QT   Quantitative tightening – The financial assets on the central bankers' balance sheets are reduced, usually by not refinancing the bonds that reach maturity.

MMT   Modern Monetary Theory – Here the government pursues an expansionary fiscal policy by printing money to stimulate the economy. Inflation is the only limitation. That is a signal to withdraw money from the economy, for example through tax increases.

IEA   International Energy Agency

GHG   Greenhouse gases

Gt   Gigaton, a billion tons

Gross versus net government debt   There are different measures of debt. In addition to gross government debt, which includes all unmatured debt that the government has issued, there is net debt. Government assets – for example debt invested in a social security trust fund – are deducted from the gross government debt. Most economists consider this the most relevant measure of government debt. There is usually a limited difference between the two. However, in the US, gross government debt is 126% of GDP, but consolidated or net government debt is 'only' 99%.

EU ETS   The European Emissions Trading System

PIIE   Peterson Institute for International Economics

IPCC   Intergovernmental Panel for Climate Change

IRA   Inflation Reduction Act: a US investment program of $380 billion in subsidies and tax cuts for companies investing in the US. The goal is to develop a sustainable energy economy

WHO   World Trade Organisation

FDI   foreign direct investment

R*   Equilibrium interest rate or neutral interest rate: the interest rate at which the (investment) demand for and supply of (savings) money is in balance. It also refers to the interest rate that keeps GDP growth at its long-term potential under stable inflation. When the bank increases the interest rate to above R*, the economy slows down, and vice versa.

BLS   Bureau of Labour Statistics

CAT   Climate Action Tracker

AI   Artificial Intelligence

IA   Intangible Assets

IP   Intellectual Property

IFS   International Financial System

ENDNOTES

Innovation & productivity

1   N. Smith, 'Techno-optimism for 2023', *Noahpinion*, 12 December 2023.

2   T. Davidson, 'Report on Whether AI Could Drive Explosive Economic Growth', *Open Philanthropy*, 17 June 2021.

3   T. Besiroglu et al, 'Economic impacts of AI-augmented R&D', *Open Philanthropy*, 2 January 2023.

4   P. Krugman, *The Age of Diminished Expectations: US Economic Policy in the 1980s*, Cambridge, 1992.

5   W. J. Baumol & A. Blinder, *Economics: Principles and Policy*, Harcourt Brave Jovanovich, San Diego, 1993.

6   R. J. Gordon, *Is US Economic Growth Over? Faltering Innovation Confronts the Six Headwinds*, CEPR, September 2012.

7   K. De Leus, *The winner's economy: Challenges and opportunities of the digital revolution*, Tielt, 2017.

8   S. Cichon, 'Everything From This 1991 Radio Shack Ad You Can Now Do With Your Phone', *HUFFPOST*, 16 January 2014, https://www.huffpost.com/entry/radio-shack-ad_b_4612973.

9   'Average Time Spent Per Day With Digital Media In The US From 2011 To 2024', *Statista*, https://www.statista.com/statistics/262340/daily-time-spent-with-digital-media-according-to-us-consumsers/.

10 W. D. Nordhaus, 'Schumpeterian Profits in the American Economy: "Theory and Measurement 22"', *Nat'l Bureau of Econ. Rsch.*, Working Paper No. 10433, 2004.

11 H. Varian, 'Economic Value of Google', *Oreilly Static*, http://cdn.oreillystatic. com/en/assets/1/event/57/The%20Economic%20Impact%20of%20Google%20Presentation.pdf.

12 E. Brynjolfsson *et al*, 'GDP-B: Accounting for the Value of New and Free Goods in the Digital Economy 3–4', *Nat'l Bureau of Econ. Rsch.*, Working Paper No. 25695, 2019.

13 C. Syverson, 'Will History Repeat Itself? Comments on "Is The Information Technology Revolution Over?"', *International Productivity Monitor*, 2013.

14 M. Ridley, 'When Ideas Have Sex', *TEDglobal*, 2010.

15 M. L. Weitzman, 'Recombinant Growth', *Quarterly Journal of Economics*, 113(2), 1998, pp. 333–334.

16 M. L. Weitzman, 'Recombinant Growth', p. 331.

17 G. E. Moore, 'Cramming More Components onto Integrated Circuits', *Electronics*, 38(8), 19 April 1965.

18 A. Azhar, 'Exponential', New York, 2021.

19 'The Basics of Microchips', *ASML*, https://www.asml.com/en/technology/all-about-microchips/microchip-basics.

20 'Conversation with Jeffrey Immelt', Bank of America Corporation, https://www.merrilledge.com/Publish/Content/application/pdf/GWMOL/Transcript_Conversation-with-GEs-Jeffrey-Immelt.pdf, 13 November 2013.

21 B. Lauwers, '3D printing is still in its infancy', *Trends*, 22 December 2022.

22 A. Bergeaud *et al*, 'Productivity Trends In Advanced Countries Between 1890 And 2012', *Review Of Income And Wealth*, 62(3), September 2016.

23 'Global Economics Comment: Technology and the Productivity Rebound (Zhestkova)', Goldman Sachs, 19 November 2021.

24 K. De Leus, 'Survey of digitalisation points to clear acceleration', BNP Paribas Fortis, June 2022.

25 J. M. Barrero et al, 'Why Working from Home Will Stick', NBER Working Paper No. 28731, April 2021.

26 N. Smith, 'Distributed Service Sector Productivity', 15 January 2023.

27 K. De Leus, 'Survey readiness digital economy: Belgian "Factories of the Future" more positive than average companies', BNP Paribas Fortis, 10 October 2019.

28 'Economic Bulletin, Issue 7, 2021', ECB.

29 '2019 Annual Business Survey, Data Year 2018', National Science Foundation.

30 'The Green Swan: Central Banking And Financial Stability In The Age Of Climate Change', BIS, January 2020.

31 'Key Factors Behind Productivity Trends In EU Countries', ECB Strategy Review, European Central Bank, December 2021.

32 N. Roubini, *Megathreats*, New York, 2022.

Climate

33 L. Burrows, '1 In 5 Deaths Caused By Fossil Fuel Emissions', *The Harvard Gazette*, 9 February, 2021.

34 G. Fan, 'Net-Zero Energy Insecurity Paradox', TS Lombard, 21 April 2023.

35   M. McCormick et al, 'Lethargic Green Rollout Leaves Paris Targets "Close To Vanishing"',
      Financial Times, 27 September 2022.

36   R. Rajan, 'Climate Action and Continued Globalisation Joined at the Hip', IMF,
      (2022 Per Jacobsson Lecture).

37   E. Kirezi *et al*, 'Projections Of Global-Scale Extreme Sea Levels And Resulting Episodic
      Coastal Flooding Over the 21st Century', *Scientific Reports*, 10(11629), July 2020.

38   See 'AM Best – Special Report: Asbestos Losses Fueled by Rising Number of Lung Cancer
      Cases (2013)', www.ambest.com/ambv/bestnews/presscontent.aspx?altsrc=0&refnum=20451.

39   'The Economic Risk of Climate in the United States', *Risky Business*, 2014.

40   'Working On A Warmer Planet: The Impact Of Heat Stress On Labour Productivity And
      Decent Work', International Labour Office, 2019.

41   Pindyck, 2013, Stern, 2013.

42   M. Carney, 'Breaking The Tragedy Of The Horizon – Climate Change And Financial
      Stability', Speech Lloyd's of London, 29 September 2015.

43   K. De Leus & W. De Vijlder, 'Should we consume less or consume differently,' *Trends* online,
      4 November 2021.

44   K. Lenaerts et al, 'Can Climate Change Be Tackled Without Ditching Economic Growth?',
      Working Paper, 10, 16 September 2021.

45   L. Hook & H. Sanderson, 'How The Race For Renewable Energy Is Reshaping Global Politics',
      Financial Times, February 2021

46   'Carbon Pricing', *Bertelsmann Stiftung*, July 2021.

47   Ch. Gollier, *Le Climat après la Fin du Mois*, May 2019.

48   J. Albrecht & S. Hamels, 'The Financial Barrier For Renovation Investments Towards A
      Carbon Neutral Building Stock – An Assessment For The Flemish Region In Belgium',
      UGent, 2020.

49   A. Missirian. & W. Schlenker, 'Asylum Applications Respond to Temperature Fluctuations',
      Science, 358(6370), 2017, pp. 1610–1614.

50   M. Carney, *Values*, 2021.

51   'The Net-Zero Transition', McKinsey Global Institute, January 2022.

52   *'Framing stranded asset risks in an age of disruption'*, Material Economics, 2017.

53   'Sectoral Winner And Losers Form The Energy Transition', *Oxford Economics*, 1 March 2023.

54   'The Economics Of Climate Change: No Action Not An Option', Swiss Re Institute,
      April 2021.

55   L. Hook & H. Sanderson, 'How The Race For Renewable Energy Is Reshaping Global Politics',
     Financial Times, 4 February 2021.

56   'A New World: The Geopolitics of the Energy Transformation', IRENA, 2019.

57   'Long-Term EU Gas Volatility Will Increase', Bank Credit Analyst Research, 3 February, 2022.

58   'Climate Change And Monetary Policy In The Euro Area', ECB, September 2021.

59   J. Pisani-Ferry, 'Climate Policy is Macroeconomic Policy, and the Implications Will Be
     Significant', Peterson Institute for International Economics, August 2021.

60   S. Aramonte & A. Zabai, 'Sustainable Finance: Trends, Valuations And Exposures',
     BIS Quarterly Review, September 2021.

Multiglobalisation

61   E. Prasad et al., 'Financial Globalization and Productivity Growth', 5 January, 2009.

62   'World Development Report 2020: Trading for Development in the Age of Global Value
     Chains', Washington DC: World Bank, 2020, doi:10.1596/978–1–4648–1457–0.

63   X. Jaravel & E. Sager, 'What are the Price Effects of Trade? Evidence from the U.S. and
     Implications for Quantitative Trade Models', *Finance and Economics Discussion Series*
     2019–068, Washington: Board of Governors of the Federal Reserve System, 2019,
     https://doi.org/10.17016/FEDS.2019.068.

64   P. A. Samuelson, 'Where Ricardo and Mill Rebut and Confirm Arguments of Mainstream
     Economists Supporting Globalization', *Journal of Economic Perspectives*, 18(3), 2004,
     p. 135–146.

65   K. H. O'Rourke, 'How Great Trade Collapses: The Interwar Period & Great Recession
     Compared', working paper 23825, NBER, September 2017.

66   R. Baldwin, 'The Peak Globalisation Myth: Part 1', VoxEU, 31 August 2022.

67   R. Green, 'Decoupling and re-globalisation', TS Lombard, 31 March 2023.

68   R. Baldwin, 'The Peak globalization Myth: Part 2', VoxEU, 1 September 2022.

69   R. Foroohar, *Homecoming*, Penguin Random House, 2022

70   P. van Bergeijk, 'Deglobalisation 2.0: Trump and Brexit are Symptoms', 20 May 2019

71   V. Romei, 'UK's Goods Exports Lowest In G7 Following Brexit, Study Finds', *Financial Times*,
     13 April 2023.

72   E. Luce & H. Paulson: 'I Think It's Pretty Likely We Will See A Recession', *Financial Times*,
     15 April 2023

73 P. D. Fajgelbaum et al., 'The Return to Protectionism', *Quarterly Journal of Economics*, 135(1), 2022, p. 1–55.

74 G. Friedman, 'Free Trade and the G-20', GPF, 20 March 2017.

75 E. Luce, 'How To Think About Biden's First Two Years', *Financial Times*, 6 March 2023.

76 M. Wolf, 'Waging War On Trade Will Be Costly', *Financial Times*, 4 April 2023.

77 A. W. Wolff et al., 'Have Trade Agreements Been Bad for America?', Peterson Institute for International Economics, December 2022.

78 G. C. Hufbauer & Z. Lu, 'The Payoff to America from Globalization: A Fresh Look with a Focus on Costs to Workers', Peterson Institute for International Economics, May 2017.

79 A. Bounds, 'Global Trade Splits Worry WTO Head', *Financial Times*, 17 April 2023.

80 'PHOTOVOLTAICS REPORT', Fraunhofer Institute for Solar Energy Systems, ISE with support of PSE Projects GmbH, 21 February 2023.

81 N. Smith, 'Europe Is Not Ready To Be A "Third Superpower"', *Noahpinion*, 13 April 2023.

82 E. White & P. Nilsson, 'Can Volkswagen Win Back China?', *Financial Times*, 5 May 2023.

83 J.P. Helveston & M.R. Davidson, 'Quantifying The Cost Savings Of Global Solar Photovoltaic Supply Chains', *Nature*, 612, 2022, p. 83–87, https://doi.org/10.1038/s41586-022-05316-6.

84 Bank Credit Analyst Research, 'Will China let 100 Flowers Boom? Only Briefly', June 2022.

85 G. Fan & Rory Green, 'Tech War: Major Escalation, Heavy Casualties', TS Lombard, 21 October 2022.

86 G. Fan & Rory Green, 'Tech War: Major Escalation, Heavy Casualties', TS Lombard, 21 October 2022.

87 A. Chu & O. Roeder, 'US Manufacturing Commitments Double After Biden Subsidies Launched', *Financial Times*, 16 April 2023.

88 K. De Leus & Ph. Gijsels, 'De energietransitie en de race naar grondstoffen: hoe overleven we het geostrategische spel', *Stand van Zaken*, BNP Paribas Fortis, 6 February 2023.

89 G. Rachman, 'De-risking Trade With China Is A Risky Business', *Financial Times*, 29 May 2023.

90 D. Stoilova et al., 'EU Competitiveness Boost From Green Industrial Policy', Market 360 BNP Paribas, 30 March 2023.

91 R. Bousso & L. Hampton, 'U.S. clean energy "carrots" could put Europe behind in decarbonization race, execs say', Reuters, 9 March 2023.

92 C. Malström, 'Will The Scramble For Rare Earths Produce A Transatlantic Trade Accord?', PIIE, 6 April 2023.

93   P. Riordan, 'Chinese Company Moves Some Production Abroad To Escape Geopolitics', *Financial Times*, 17 April 2023.

94   'Joe Biden's China strategy is not working', *The Economist*, 10 August 2023

95   Antràs et al. (2017).

96   K. Georgieva & N. Okonjo-Iweala, 'World Trade Can Still Drive Prosperity', IMF Finance & Development, June 2023.

97   R. Rajan, 'Climate Action and Continued Globalization Joined at the Hip', Per Jacobsson Lecture, IMF podcast, 2022.

98   R. Baldwin, 'Globotics And Macroeconomics: Globalisation And Automation Of The Service Sector', paper presented at 2022 ECB Forum on Central Banking in Sintra, 2022.

99   K. Georgieva & N. Okonjo-Iweala, 'World Trade Can Still Drive Prosperity', IMF Finance & Development, June 2023.

100   J. Harrison et al., 'The Future Of Reglobalisation', TS Lombard, 31 March 2023.

101   N. Kaufman et al., 'Green Trade Tensions', IMF Finance & Development, June 2023.

102   K. Georgieva & N. Okonjo-Iweala, 'World Trade Can Still Drive Prosperity', IMF Finance & Development, June 2023.

103   D. A. Cerdeiro et al., 'Sizing Up the Effects of Technological Decoupling', IMF Working Paper, March 2021.

104   'Geoeconomic Fragmentation and the Future of Multilateralism', IMF, 2023.

105   R. Rajan, 'Climate Action And Continued Globalization Joined At The Hip', IMF podcast, 2022 (per Jacobsson Lecture).

106   G. Peri, 'Immigrant Swan Song', Finance & Development IMF, March 2020.

107   B. Van Heeschvelde, 'Keert de slinger terug?', Vision, BNP Paribas Fortis.

108   IMF, *Global Financial Stability Report*, April 2023.

Debt

109   B. Eichengreen et al., *In Defense Of Public Debt*, Oxford, 2021.

110   B. Eichengreen et al., *In Defense Of Public Debt*, Oxford, 2021.

111   BNP Paribas Fortis, 'Het Grote Herstel: verloopt het deze keer anders?', *Blog Chief Economist*, 8 June 2021.

112   B. Albuguerque & R. Iyer, 'The Rise of the Walking Dead: Zombie Firms Around the World', IMF Working Paper, June 2023.

113 Ò. Jordà et al., 'Zombies at Large? Corporate Debt Overhang and the Macroeconomy (December 2020)'. FRB of New York Staff Report No. 951, Available at SSRN: https://ssrn.com/abstract=3742973 or http://dx.doi.org/10.2139/ssrn.3742973.

114 See *Abbreviations and explanations*.

115 Dario Perkins, 'Revenge of the 3 D's', TS Lombard, March 2023.

116 M. Barnes, 'Soaring Government Debt: A Crisis In Waiting?', The Bank Credit Analyst, November 2022.

117 'Fiscal risks and sustainability', Office for Budget Responsibility, July 2022.

118 P. Hollingsworth *et al.*, 'Central Banks: Shooting for the r-starts', BNP Paribas Markets 360, 8 June 2022.

119 C. M. Reinhart et al., 'Debt Intolerance', NBER Working Paper No. 9908, August 2003.

120 B. Eichengreen et al., *In Defense Of Public Debt*, Oxford, 2021.

121 D. Perkins, 'Balance-Sheet hangover?', TS Lombard, February 2021.

122 A. Lawrence, 'The Late Late Show', TS Lombard, March 2022

123 'Averting A COVID-19 Debt Trap', IMF Seminarie, April 2021.

124 C. M. Reinhart, & M. B. Sbrancia, 'The Liquidation Of Government Debt', NBER, March 2011.

125 R. Kono & H. Shiraishi, 'Debt Sustainability – History: Post-War Lessons', BNP Paribas Markets 360, 30 July 2021.

126 J. Reid & K. Nagalingam, 'Default Study – 2022: The End Of The Ultra-Low Default World?', Deutsche Bank Research, 6 June 2022.

127 N. Ferguson et al., 'Central Banks Expansions And Contractions Across 12 Central Banks Since 1900', 2014.

128 K. De Leus, 'Overheidsschulden schrappen is onnodig en gevaarlijk', *De Tijd*, 12 March 2021.

Ageing

129 M. Myrskylä et al., 'Advances in development reverse fertility declines', *Nature* 460, 6 August 2009, p. 741–743, doi:10.1038/nature08230.

130 M. Saunders, Some reflections on Monetary Policy past, present and future, 18 July 2022, Bank of England.

131 H. Berger et al., 'Macroeconomics of aging and policy implications', IMF, 2019.

132 G. Maroisa et al., 'Population aging, migration, and productivity', PNAS, 7 April 2020.

133 PwC, 'The Long View', 2017. The authors recommend this 2017 PwC study over the more recent one from the OESO (2021) for inclusion of many fast-growing countries in the PwC study, such as Vietnam, Nigeria, Egypt, Pakistan and so on. These were not included in the OESO study.

134 US, UK, France, Germany, Japan, Canada and Italy.

135 'Why are Latin American workers so strikingly unproductive?', The Economist, 8 June 2023.

136 J. Hawksworth et al., 'The long view: how will the global economic order change by 2050?', PwC, February 2017.

137 'The 2021 Ageing Report Underlying Assumptions & Projection Methodologies institutional paper 142', European Commission, November 2020.

138 G. Peersman, 'Productiviteit, productiviteit, productiviteit', Etion, *Ondernemen*, March 2022.

139 Productivity growth definition: see legend.

140 M. Kaltenberg et al., 'The Age of Invention: Matching Inventor Ages to Patents Based on Web-scraped Sources', NBER Working Paper No. 28768, May 2021, JEL No. O31, O34.

141 'It's not just a fiscal fiasco: greying economies also innovate less', The Economist, 30 May 2023.

142 S. Aiyar et al., *The Impact of Workforce Aging on European Productivity*, IMF, 2016.

143 S. Aiyar et al., 'The impact of workforce aging on euro area productivity', IMF, 22 June 2016.

144 'From Red to Gray', World Bank, 2007.

145 'Microeconomic determinants of saving: a static analysis, box 1 in Spain: Consumption Outlook', BBVA Research, 2010

146 A. M. Salmeron, 'The demographic cycle of savings and interest rates', CaixaBank Research, 2018.

147 E. Gagnon et al., 'Understanding the New Normal: the Role of Demographics', Finance and Economics Discussion Series, Board of Governors of the Federal Reserve System, 2016.

148 C. Carvalho et al., 'Demographic Transition and Low US Interest Rates', Federal Reserve Bank of San Francisco Economic Letter, 2017.

149 N. Lisack et al., 'Demographic trends and real interest rate', Bank of England Staff Working Papers, 2017.

150 G. Vlieghe, 'Running out of room: revisiting the 3D perspective on low interest rates', 26 July 2021.

151 M. Juselius & E. Takáts, 'The enduring link between demography and inflation', BIS Working Papers No 722, May 2018.

152 W. Thenuwara et al., 'Demographics and Asset Markets: A Survey of the Literature', Theoretical Economics Letters, 7, 2017, p. 782–794, https://doi.org/10.4236/tel.2017.74057.

153 J. Ameriks & S P. Zeldes, 'How Do Household Portfolio Shares Vary with Age?', Working Paper, 2004.

154 M. Bodier, 'Economie et Statistique n° 324–325, les effets d'âge et de generation sur le niveau et la structure de la consommation', INSEE, 1999.

155 M. Bodier, 'Economie et Statistique n° 324–325, les effets d'âge et de generation sur le niveau et la structure de la consommation', INSEE, 1999.

156 Fourth quarter figures for 2022, Federal Reserve Bank of Dallas; see also: A. Mack & E. Martínez-García. 2011. 'A Cross-Country Quarterly Database of Real House Prices: A Methodological Note', Globalization and Monetary Policy Institute Working Paper No. 99, Federal Reserve Bank of Dallas.

157 J. Lee & H. Jung, 'Demographic shifts, macroprudential policies, and house prices', BIS Working Papers No 914, December 2020.

158 Lunch presentation by Peter Berezin, 'Macro Investors are about to make a huge mistake', Hotel Amigo Brussels, 15 June 2023.

159 Y. Hashimoto et al., 'Demographics and the Housing Market: Japan's Disappearing Cities', IMF Working Paper, September 2020.

160 Calculation based on 25 industrialised countries for which the Dallas Federal Reserve has real house prices since 1975. See: International House Price Database, https://www.dallasfed.org/research/international/houseprice.

www.lannoo.com

Register on our website and we will send you a regular newsletter with information about new books and interesting, exclusive offers.

Translation: Textcase
Design: Martijn Dentant, Armée de Verre Bookdesign

2nd edition, 2024

© Uitgeverij Lannoo nv, Tielt, 2023 and Koen De Leus, Philippe Gijsels

D/2024/45/203 – ISBN 9789401409018 – NUR 794

All rights reserved. No part of this publication may be reproduced, stored in an automated retrieval system and/or made public in any form or by any means, electronic, mechanical or otherwise, without the prior written permission of the publisher.